THE POWER OF SYMBOLS
AGAINST THE SYMBOLS OF POWER

THE PENNSYLVANIA STATE UNIVERSITY PRESS
University Park, Pennsylvania

JAN KUBIK

THE POWER OF SYMBOLS AGAINST THE SYMBOLS OF POWER

**THE RISE OF SOLIDARITY
AND THE FALL OF
STATE SOCIALISM IN POLAND**

Library of Congress Cataloging-in-Publication Data

Kubik, Jan, 1953–
  The power of symbols against the symbols of power : the rise of
Solidarity and the fall of state socialism in Poland / Jan Kubik.

    p.   cm.
  Includes bibliographical references and index.
  ISBN 0-271-01083-5 (alk. paper)—ISBN 0-271-01084-3
(pbk. : alk. paper)
    1. NSZZ "Solidarność" (Labor organization)—History.
  2. Socialism—Poland—History—20th century. 3. Poland—Politics
and government—1945– I. Title.
  HD8537.N783K83 1994
  322'.2'09438—dc20   93-9895
                                                                          CIP

Published by The Pennsylvania State University Press,
Barbara Building, Suite C, University Park, PA 16802-1003

To my Mother,
my Father (in memory),
my Wife,
Maciek, Janek, Adam,
and Mary Hannah

CONTENTS

PREFACE

The idea of this book occurred to me in early 1981. At that time I was working in the Department of Social Anthropology in the Institute of Sociology at Jagiellonian University in Kraków. My research interests were the sociology of art and aesthetics, but I was also studying political philosophy. The experience of Solidarity—the joyous experience of freedom—turned the hierarchy of my research interests upside down. A natural way for me to participate in the new movement was not only to join it but also to study its politics. Out of my new interest in politics and my old interests in culture, art, and aesthetics came the idea for my doctoral dissertation, "The Role of Symbols in the Legitimation of Power: Poland, 1976–81."

In 1982, I received a fellowship to study at Columbia University and was very lucky to be granted permission to leave Poland. After six years of graduate studies in the Department of Anthropology at Columbia and continuous research and writing, I finished the dissertation. That dissertation became the core of the present book. The many corrections, additions, and subtractions are the result of several revisions the manuscript underwent while I was looking for a publisher. In the meantime, Communism collapsed in Eastern Europe and the Soviet Union and the unexpectedly complicated process of transition began. My thoughts and observations on the relationship between the culture of Solidarity and the tenor of Polish politics in the early 1990s (particularly in the last chapter) were added when I updated the manuscript.

Since I have endeavored to write a scholarly book, I strove for objectivity. I wanted to describe a segment of reality as it presented itself to me in my own experience, documents, interviews, conversations, and pictures. I interpreted this reality using social scientific tools earlier tested on other cultures and in other circumstances. I was, however, acutely aware that no description and interpretation are ever free of the author's personal biases. Introspection allows me to detect two such biases. First, since the beginning of this project, I have been driven by a conviction that Solidarity was a powerful, complex, multidimensional phenomenon, whose meaning could not possibly be conveyed within a single categorization, such as "social movement" or "trade union." Second, during my research I internalized, almost as an article of faith, an anthropological generalization that cultural, particularly religious, identities are intricately intertwined with people's politics. Thus I should emphasize from the outset that the underlying and often subconscious objective of this work was to show that Solidarity was not only about people's political rights or a fairer distribution of goods but about people's identities. I tried to substantiate this conviction as best I could. In this context it is necessary to mention that I am a Lutheran, and only through studying was I able to grasp the vital, indispensable, though sometimes controversial, role of Roman Catholicism in my country's history and culture. Two chapters, particularly the one on John Paul II's visit to Poland in 1979, reflect this realization.

During the ten years I worked on this book many people came to my assistance with their advice and criticism. As grateful as I am to them all, only my wife, Martha, was indispensable. Without her nagging, biting "insider" criticism and—above all—her love, patience, and editorial skills I would be still working on the original dissertation, let alone this book.

My dissertation committee was the first and very demanding group of "outside" critics. It consisted of Alexander Alland, Jr., my advisor and unfailing supporter; Joan Vincent, the most stimulating teacher I have ever had; the late Robert Murphy, always provoking and challenging; and three scrupulous and demanding readers: Joseph Rothschild of Columbia, Andrew Arato of the New School for Social Research, and Stanisław Barańczak of Harvard. At Columbia, two more people took a lively and critical interest in my work, and I profited from their comments: the late Morton Fried and Barbara Price. I was also lucky to have an opportunity to work with the late Stefan Nowak, an unmatched guide during my studies on the systems of values of the Polish people.

Among my peers, three friends contributed to this book in many more ways than they realize: Michael Bernhard, with whom I shared the joys and trepidations of studying Polish oppositional politics of the late 1970s; Zdzisław Mach, with whom I shared countless conversations and who gave the most thorough criticism of the manuscript one can ask for; and Grzegorz Ekiert, who was always there to advise, quarrel, agree, disagree, and sustain.

I am very fortunate to have Penn State Press as my publisher. Sandy Thatcher was encouraging and supportive from the beginning of our cooperation; Peter Potter, through his detailed and pointed questions helped me sharpen many arguments; Andrew Lewis's editing was marvelous; and Cherene Holland's guidance through the editorial process was invaluable. I also benefited from the attentions of two groups of anonymous reviewers. In the process two of these reviewers ceased to be anonymous and I can thank them by name for their detailed and extremely helpful reviews: Jane Curry and David Kertzer. The photographs in the book were taken by Marek Stawowy and Witek Górka. Many thanks to both of them, my dear friends.

All those people, and many more, did their best to help me improve this work. The errors and imperfections are my own.

The writing was made possible by the Columbia University President Fellowships and a MacArthur Fellowship. The final rewriting would have been impossible without an American Council of Learned Societies Fellowship and a leave of absence, generously given to me by Rutgers University. Parts of the book have been published earlier under the titles: "Polish May Day Celebrations in the 1970s and in 1981. An Essay on the Symbolic Dimension of a Struggle for Political Legitimacy," *The Polish Review* 35(2): 99–116; "Who Done It? Workers or Intellectuals. A Controversy over Solidarity's Origin and Social Composition," forthcoming in *Theory and Society;* and "John Paul II's First Visit to Poland and the Collapse of the Official Marxist-Leninist Discourse," *Center for Research on Politics and Social Organization Working Paper Series,* Department of Sociology, Harvard University. Thank you for allowing me to include these materials in this book.

LIST OF ABBREVIATIONS

AWF	*Academia Wychowania Fizycznego* (The Sport Academy)
ChWLP	*Chrześcijańska Wspólnota Ludzi Pracy* (The Christian Association of Working People)
FSO	*Fabryka Samochodów Osobowych* (The Warsaw Car Factory)
GUKPPiW	*Główny Urząd Kontroli Prasy, Publikacji i Widowisk* (The Main Office for the Control of the Press, Publications, and Public Performances)
KKP	*Krajowa Komisja Porozumiewawcza* (National Coordinating Commission)
KOR	*Komitet Obrony Robotników* (The Workers' Defense Committee)
KPN	*Konfederacja Polski Niepodległej* (The Confederation of Independent Poland)
KPP	*Komunistyczna Partia Polski* (The Polish Communist Party)
KSN	*Komitet Samostanowienia Narodu* (The Committee for National Self-Determination)
KSS "KOR"	*Komitet Samoobrony Społecznej "KOR"* (The Social Self-Defense Committee "KOR")
KZ WZZ	*Komitet Założycielski Wolnych Związków Zawodowych* (The Initiating Committee of Free Trade Unions)
MKR	*Międzyzakładowy Komitet Robotniczy* (The Interfactory Workers' Committee)
MKS	*Międzyzakładowy Komitet Strajkowy* (The Interfactory Strike Committee)
MKZ	*Międzyzakładowy Komitet Założycielski* (The Interfactory Founding Committee)
NOWA	*Niezależna Oficyna Wydawnicza* (Independent Publishing House)
NZS	*Niezależne Zrzeszenie Studentów* (The Independent Students' Union)
OHP	*Ochotnicze Hufce Pracy* (Voluntary Work Brigades)
ORMO	*Ochotnicze Rezerwy Milicji Obywatelskiej* (The Voluntary Reserves of the Police)
PAP	*Polska Agencja Prasowa* (The Polish Press Agency)

PKP   *Polskie Koleje Państwowe*
           (Polish Railways)
PKS   *Państwowa Komunikacja Samochodowa*
           (The Polish Bus Company)
PPR   *Polska Partia Robotnicza*
           (The Polish Workers' Party)
PPS   *Polska Partia Socjalistyczna*
           (The Polish Socialist Party)
PSL   *Polskie Stronnictwo Ludowe*
           (The Polish Peasants' Party)
PZPR   *Polska Zjednoczona Partia Robotnicza*
           (The Polish United Workers' Party)
RMP   *Ruch Młodej Polski*
           (The Young Poland Movement)
RND   *Ruch Niezależnych Demokratów*
           (The Movement of Independent Democrats)
ROPCiO   *Ruch Obrony Praw Człowieka i Obywatela*
           (The Movement in Defense of Human and Civil Rights)
SB   *Służba Bezpieczeństwa*
           (The Security Service)
SDKPiL   *Socjaldemokracja Królestwa Polskiego i Litwy*
           (The Social Democracy of the Kingdon of Poland and
           Lithuania)
SKS   *Studencki Komitet Solidarności*
           (The Student Solidarity Committee)
SZSP   *Socjalistyczny Związek Studentów Polskich*
           (The Socialist Union of Polish Students)
TKK   *Tymczasowa Komisja Koordynacyjna*
           (The Provisional Coordinating Commission)
TKKŚ   *Towarzystwo Krzewienia Kultury Świeckiej*
           (The Society for the Promotion of Secular Culture)
TKN   *Towarzystwo Kursów Naukowych*
           (The Society for Scientific Courses)
WRON   *Wojskowa Rada Ocalenia Narodowego*
           (The Military Council for National Salvation)
ZBOWiD   *Związek Bojowników o Wolność i Demokrację*
           (The Association of Fighters for Freedom and Democ-
           racy)
ZCHN   *Zjednoczenie Chrześcijańsko-Narodowe*
           (The Christian-National Union)
ZLP   *Związek Literatów Polskich*
           (Union of Polish Writers)
ZNP   *Związek Nauczycielstwa Polskiego*
           (Polish Teachers Union)

Introduction

No one visiting Gdańsk during the memorable days of the August 1980 strike—which gave birth to Solidarity—could have failed to notice the unusual symbolic climate created by the striking workers. What was unfolding in the shipyard was not just another huge industrial walkout, but a gigantic pageant of images and symbolic performances.

The workers and their supporters adorned a gate of the shipyard with flowers and displayed pictures of the pope and the Virgin Mary. A wooden cross, erected on the spot where protesting shipyard workers were shot and killed in 1970, was also covered in flowers as well as religious and patriotic inscriptions. Slogans painted on the shipyard walls included the usual demands for higher wages and labor security, as well as demands for justice and liberty and declarations of devotion to Jesus and Mary. Ordinary strike proceedings—negotiations with Party-state representatives—were interspersed with the extraordinary, festive events such as Catholic masses, the singing of patriotic songs, and impromptu concerts during which professional actors, reciting famous lines of national poetry, shared the stage with workers reading their own newly created verses.

To understand the origins, meanings, and social functions of the Lenin Shipyard's uncommon decor one needs to reconstruct a complex cluster of social, economic, cultural, and political factors. In this book I am concerned with the last two: an elusive entity that may be called "the Solidarity culture" and its relationship with (political) power. I focus on the period 1976–81, but I describe and analyze earlier and later events when pertinent. In the concluding chapter I establish a relationship between certain aspects of the Solidarity culture and the character of Polish politics in the 1990s.

Basic Research Questions: The Scope of This Analysis

In 1944–45 the Soviet Red Army seized power in Poland on behalf of the *Polska Partia Robotnicza* (Polish Workers' Party, or PPR; after 1948 the *Polska Zjednoczona Partia Robotnicza,* Polish United Workers' Party, or PZPR). Well aware of the high costs of sustaining power by coercion, the leadership of the new Party-state moved immediately to establish a credible claim to legitimacy, despite the considerable difficulties they faced in this undertaking, having been installed by force from without.[1] This quest for legitimacy had to be conducted under a constraint inherent in the nature of the regime. *Any* regime must preserve its identity and adhere to its fundamental organizational principles if its survival in power is to have any meaning.[2] A *Communist* regime, therefore, cannot construct its legitimacy by invoking electoral democracy or political pluralism without doing itself in.[3]

---

1. According to Rothschild: "Both the authorities and the society benefit from ample legitimacy. The former, because they can then make difficult and controversial allocation decisions at lowest cost and with the widest margin of support; the latter, because it is then assured that its values will be sustained and possibly even augmented" (1979, 52).
2. The term *organizational principle* is used, for example, by Habermas and Arato. See Arato (1982).
3. Arato notes that "the constitution or reconstitution of civil society is manifestly incompatible with the organizational principle of the state socialist societies" (1982, 209). Mreła, in turn, observes that "it is also possible to identify a threshold of the system's

Limited by the usurpatory nature of their authority and the organizational principles of their regime, Polish Communists attempted to reshape the nation's culture and create legitimacy for their rule. They had three possible strategies to choose from: (1) imposing a totally new culture and the socialization of the populace to accept it, (2) partially remodeling the existing culture, or (3) accepting, or appearing to accept, the existing (political) culture of the country.[4] The first solution was rather unsuccessfully pursued by several Eastern European states in the early fifties and in some places (for example Czechoslovakia) even longer and proved too costly.[5] The third solution carries the seeds of the regime's collapse through an erosion of its identity and so was never truly followed. The second solution was therefore chosen (with varying degrees of success) by all Communist governments.

This strategy of (partially) remodeling the national culture to create a discourse that was "socialist in form and national in content" was carried out in the Polish People's Republic through the extensive use of public ceremonies and symbolic display by the Gierek regime (particularly in the late 1970s). The effectiveness of this strategy can be assessed by comparing the public discourses through which three major collective actors—the Party-state, the Roman Catholic Church, and the organized opposition—tried to achieve cultural hegemony and put forth claims and counterclaims to political legitimacy.[6] In other words, I set out to study (1) an aspect of the official culture in Poland of the 1970s—the public rituals, ceremonies, demonstrations, parades, emblems, costumes, sym-

---

identity crisis, the surpassing of which the authorities cannot allow. . . . The limit is marked by the communist party preserving political control over collective life." He quotes also a Party idealogue: "In our country, if it is to be socialist normality (even with temporary regression in some fields), only a Marxist-Leninist party may be the avantgarde" (Mrela 1986, 376).

4. In this I differ with Rigby, who assumes that "there are two ways in which an originally 'illegitimate' regime may acquire legitimacy, firstly by the regime itself increasingly conforming its actions to establish social beliefs and attitudes, and secondly by new beliefs and attitudes supportive of the regime's legitimacy taking root in the society" (1982, 17).

5. The extreme example of this strategy is, of course, the Chinese cultural revolution.

6. It is not easy to give a precise definition of the opposition (see the discussion in Friszke and Paczkowski 1991). In this work I follow Andrzej Friszke, who defines the opposition as "the deliberate and planned organizational or intellectual activity, based on a certain program, aimed at the overthrow of the system or its reform in the direction of the increased subjectivity of the society and the limitation of the Party's monopoly on power" (Friszke, in Friszke and Paczkowski 1991, 8). See also Rupnik (1979, 61), who defines opposition as the "articulate expression of disagreement with official policies by an organized body whether permanent or not, whether legal or not."

bols, and so on;[7] (2) how the political power of the Party-state was constructed, reconstructed, authorized, and legitimized within this culture; and (3) the emergence and major characteristics of counterhegemonic subcultures (or discourses) of the Catholic Church and the organized opposition, which, in turn, opened the way for counterhegemonic politics and the rise of Solidarity.

To many Poles, Polish social reality in the late 1970s was strongly polarized into private and public domains. The most influential conceptualization of this phenomenon was offered by Edmund Wnuk-Lipiński, who writes: "We could venture the general statement that the less democratic a given society the stronger the division into the private and the public sphere and the more acute the manifestations of dimorphism of values" (1982, 87).[8]

Yet this polarization existed more in the minds of the people than it did in everyday social practice. In order to see to their daily needs citizens had to interact frequently with the Party-state and its agencies. A complicated and usually informal network of mutual connections and dependencies developed and—in practice—blurred the distinction between "the society" and "the state." This was the reality of living within the "institutionalized lie"—as Vaclav Havel called it.[9]

In Polish social life there was, therefore, an incongruity between the (objective, practical) everyday *interpenetration* and the (subjective, sym-

---

7. All of these cultural forms may serve to construct both authority and legitimacy. The difference between authority and legitimacy can be conceptualized in terms of different kinds of cultural forms through which power is actualized. When the rulers invoke the ultimate values and symbols of a given group in constructing their public image, they are striving to establish legitimacy. To the extent that they use ordinary and mundane cultural forms, they are trying to produce or maintain their authority. There are several conceptualizations of how Communist regimes establish and sustain authority. See, for example, Liehm's "social contract" (1983), Staniszkis's "repressive tolerance" (1984), and Pakulski's "conditional tolerance" (1986). For an overview of this problem, see Ekiert (1988) and also Wright (1984, 145 n.9).

8. By "dimorphism of values" Wnuk-Lipiński means that people subscribe concurrently to (at least) two different systems of values (private and public, or "official socialist" and "Christian"). Another aspect of the schizophrenic dualism permeating Polish social life was described by Stefan Nowak, who summarizes twenty-five years of social research in Poland as follows: "The social structure of Polish society in the subjective vision of its members would . . . appear to be a 'federation' of primary groups united in a national community. . . . Our studies . . . revealed a kind of social vacuum between the level of primary groups and that of the nation" (1981, 51).

9. In the 1980s, Polish sociologists analyzed in depth "the people's cooperation with the system of paternalism" (Di Palma 1991, 64) and reconstructed the various strategies of adaptation and accommodation that had allowed the people to go on with their lives in an optimal fashion.

bolic/discursive) *polarization* of the Party-state and society (see Kennedy 1991, 168–71, and Rychard 1987b, 38–39). When, after 1976, some groups within the populace and the Catholic Church began developing public counterhegemonic discourses, this incongruity became more pronounced. During the period 1981–89 it came to dominate social life and had a significant impact both on the style of the confrontation between the Party-state and the opposition and on the nature of Polish post-Communist politics.

In this book I do not deal with the phenomenon of interpenetration (see Wedel 1986); I focus solely on the emergence, character, and social functions of the symbolic/discursive polarization between the Party-state and the populace, as it was reflected in *public* ceremonies, demonstrations, and spectacles.

I employ a simplified sociological model of Polish society; I do not analyze the differential impact of class, age, or gender on symbolic behavior. The reason for this simplification is not a lack of relevant sociological data (although such data are scarce). Rather, the reason lies in the semiological, not sociological, bent of my argument. In other words, I concentrate my analysis on cultural forms of opposition, not on the social composition of oppositional networks. Such a choice of emphasis is justified because gender, class, and age were not good predictors of participation in oppositional activities of the late 1970s. The oppositionists came from all walks of life, age groups, and socio-occupational categories and represented both sexes. The Solidarity revolution was carried out by a "cultural-political class" constituted *above* and *beyond* socioeconomic-occupational divisions.[10] I chose to examine the emergence of this "new" class. Socioeconomic class division in Polish society has been thoroughly examined elsewhere (see, for example, Słomczyński and Krauze 1986).

I set out to study not politics as a discrete realm of the social world, but the subtle and indirect ways power is realized within culture, often outside traditionally defined "politics." I share Michel Foucault's conviction that power permeates all of social life, that power is an aspect of all social interactions and, consequently, can be distilled from the cultural forms that frame such interactions.[11] The fundamental assumption of this study has been succinctly expressed by David Kertzer: "The medium of political exchange has always been symbolism; it is an exchange that not only redistributes political rewards, but that also builds our political under-

10. I discuss this phenomenon in Chapter 7.
11. See O'Brien (1989, 35). Foucault observes that "manifold relations of power which permeate, characterize and constitute the social body . . . cannot themselves be established, consolidated nor implemented without the production, accumulation, circulation and functioning of a discourse" (1980, 93).

standings. If symbols and rituals are used to build political reality, it is because, as humans, we can do it in no other way" (1988, 95). I am also guided by Abner Cohen's observation that "the less obviously political in form symbols are, the more efficacious politically they prove to be" (1979, 87).[12]

It is in Communist countries that these assertions can be most fully tested. The tendency of power to be omnipresent is there exacerbated by one of the principal strategies of Communist domination: a deliberate infusion of power into many apparently apolitical human relationships and cultural forms (such as through censorship or the imposition of uniform, "correct" artistic styles).

The Polish situation had its own peculiar features. In the 1970s the Polish opposition shared with other Eastern European oppositional movements a common disability—it could not express itself through open political channels (political parties, clubs, or trade unions). Yet the intensity of social activism in Poland, including underground political debates, clandestine publications, and independent ceremonies and demonstrations far surpassed anything created in other Eastern European countries. Having been unable to practice politics, Polish oppositionists often chose to express themselves through the "cultural" medium of symbolic public actions. A closer look at this independent culture (particularly at its demonstrations and ceremonies) should contribute to the understanding of the Polish "anomaly." This book is, thus, an attempt to answer Valerie Bunce's question: "How can we explain extraordinary forms of protest in Poland versus more 'everyday forms of resistance' (Scott 1985) in all those other states in the region which share so many structural parallels with Poland?" (Bunce n.d.). Two other questions guide my inquiries: "Why did Solidarity happen in Poland and not elsewhere in the Communist bloc?" and "Why did it manage to survive several years in the underground to emerge in 1989 as a formidable political force, initiating the collapse of Communism in Eastern Europe?"

I do not claim that the "Polish revolution" of the 1970s and 1980–81 is best understood from an anthropological perspective. I am merely trying to examine this "revolution" from yet another angle in order to complement several penetrating studies already published. For example, the political activities of the oppositional groups in the 1976–1981 period have been exhaustively described and analyzed by Jakub Karpiński (1982a, 1982b), Peter Raina (1978, 1985), Michael Bernhard (1993), Jan Lipski (1985), and David Ost (1990). These studies concentrate, however, on the internal workings of the oppositional movement. I want to portray the external,

---

12. Turner (1968) reaches a similar conclusion.

public dimension of the oppositional movement, that is, those activities which were visible to the "average" person on the street. The first period of Solidarity's legal existence (1980–81) has also been exhaustively studied from several viewpoints, including those of (1) historians (Holzer 1984; Goodwyn 1991), (2) a social critic and journalist (Ash 1983), (3) sociologists (Staniszkis 1984; Kennedy 1991), (4) a political scientist interested in the internal workings of the oppositional leadership or "intellectual elite" (Ost 1990), (5) political scientists and sociologists concentrating on a grassroots dimension of the movement's politics (Touraine et al. 1983; Laba 1991), and (6) a sociologist analyzing the "elitist" or "intellectual" dimension of the movement's culture (Goldfarb 1989). My study complements these works in that it is written by a cultural anthropologist concentrating on the "popular" or "mass" aspect of the oppositional movement's and Solidarity's culture.[13]

Theory, Key Concepts, and Methods

The bent of this study is more semiological than sociological. Formally, its intention is similar to that of the study of pilgrimage by Victor and Judith Turner. Since I am also moving "into a relatively unresearched realm of data" (that is, the symbolic dimension of the conflict between state and society in Poland of the 1970s), my inquiry "requires some preliminary mapping . . . to elicit the objective coordinates of cultural fields" (1978, xv) within which this conflict occurred. I have not set out to give a comprehensive description of all symbolic actions by all the actors or a coherent and exhaustive reconstruction of the social field in which these actions took place.

Legitimacy is a key concept in this study. According to several authors, the category of legitimacy is of no help or at least of "little relevance" in studying the political systems of the Communist world.[14] Such arguments are sometimes founded on an odd sort of logic: the lack of legitimacy in a political field (in this case in the Soviet bloc or parts thereof) proves the category superfluous. Similarly, I suppose, the absence of health among a hospital's patients would prove the category of health

13. It must, however, be emphasized that what I describe is the behavior of those small groups of Poles who were the most active, who organized and participated in "illegal" demonstrations and ceremonies. They can hardly be described as "masses"; however, their cultural productions (performances) were for the masses, certainly more so than Kundera's novels or Michnik's essays were.

14. See, for example, Ekiert (1988) and Wright (1984, 111).

useless. Since the Communists in Poland invested enormous amounts of time and money in putting forward their claims to legitimacy while independent groups of citizens and the Catholic Church were strongly preoccupied with the articulation and public presentation of counter-claims, good empirical reasons exist for studying legitimacy, at least in Poland. Such a confrontation of discourses may well be a Polish specific-ity but other Eastern European countries experienced similar, even if less spectacular, tensions between official and unofficial discourses.[15]

From the semiotic point of view, legitimacy, as a form of justification (Berger and Luckmann 1966, 110), constitutes an element of public dis-course. It can be defined as a state or a process of valorization in which a given action, institution, regime, or social order is "sacralized" or "digni-fied" by being related to a system of shared values contained in root paradigms and dominant symbols of a given group.[16] Legitimacy occurs when the "legitimized" elements are linked to the ultimate domain of "the culturally postulated and the socially unquestionable"—to use a very apt phrase of Sally Moore and Barbara Myerhoff (1977, 22). This most sacred domain may be religion.

From another point of view, actual legitimacy is created when a certain group of people accepts the claims of an individual or another group to hold power over them as just and binding. As Seymour Lipset puts it: "Legitimacy involves the capacity of the system to engender and main-tain the belief that the existing political institutions are the most appropri-ate ones for society" (1959, 19).

My approach and method rest on the assumption that if one detects a significant degree of congruence between the key (or at least politically relevant) values and principles held by both the rulers and the ruled, then there is (actual) legitimacy concerning some or all political institutions in that sociopolitical system. In order to assess the degree of such congru-

---

15. See, for example, Paul (1979) on Czechoslovakia.

16. Legitimation, according to Parsons, is "a value-reference at what is clearly a very high level of generality, and as such is applicable to any mode or type of action in the social system. . . . It also operates through many different kinds of mechanisms and modes of symbolization" (1958, 201). Gerth and Mills define legitimacy in a similar way: "Those in authority within institutions and social structures attempt to justify their rule by linking it, as if it were a necessary consequence, with moral symbols, sacred emblems, or legal formulae which are widely believed and deeply internalized. These central conceptions may refer to a god or gods, the 'votes of the majority,' the 'will of the people,' the 'aristocracy of talents or wealth,' to the 'divine right of kings' or to the allegedly extraordinary endow-ment of the person of the ruler himself" (1953, 277). Merquior, commenting on the works of Parsons, Kluckhon, Smelser, and Deutsch, agrees with their definition of legitimacy as "first and foremost, an effect produced by the linking of any given experience with symbols carrying authority due to their embodiment of core values of a given culture" (1979, 38).

ence one must compare the public discourses developed by the rulers and the ruled and try to determine to what degree the visions of (among other things) history, political community, national identity, and democracy contained in these discoursers are similar. The higher the degree of similarity the higher the degree of legitimacy.

The precise measurement of legitimacy seems to be impossible. It is, for example, very difficult to determine *how many* members of a group must acknowledge the rulers' claims to legitimacy as valid, before the rulers' power can be regarded as *actually* legitimitized.[17] Must the rulers' claims be accepted by more than 50 percent of the populace, or by some (or all) strategic groups, or by the power *apparat,* or perhaps by a combination of all three? In an attempt to overcome this difficulty Ferenc Fehér, Agnes Heller, and György Márkus offer the following:

> A social order is legitimated if at least one part of the population acknowledges it as exemplary and binding and the other part does not confront the existing social order with the image of an alternative one as equally exemplary. Thus the relative number of those legitimating a system may be irrelevant if the non-legitimating masses are merely dissatisfied. (1983, 137)

The commendable verifiability of this proposition seems to be too high a price for the dubious results it produces. In the light of this formulation, the American social order in, say, 1967, constantly challenged and confronted with alternative images, was less legitimate than the social order in Poland (unchallenged at that time). As several recent studies indicate, the lack of visible forms of protest and the apparent passivity of the populace can by no means be interpreted as an expression of support for, even less as granting legitimacy to, the ruling elite or regime.[18] Moreover, the silent majority of the population may "have an image of an alternative political order . . . which is acknowledged by them as exemplary," a necessary condition for the absence of legitimacy, without however being able to present this image publicly. Such a situation poses a serious methodological problem: it is difficult to grasp popular sentiments that are not publicly expressed. Surveys or opinion polls do not provide reliable answers either, since in the countries where people are afraid to express their views publicly they usually are not very likely to

17. I am not interested in studying the legitimacy of the rulers vis-à-vis their staffs and administrations. For interesting observations of this aspect of legitimacy in the Communist world, see Pakulski (1986), Rigby (1982), and Lewis (1984).

18. See, for example, Edelman (1971), Lukes (1974), Gaventa (1980), or Scott (1985).

reveal their true (or full) views to pollsters.[19] For this reason I do not use
in my analysis the results of attitudinal studies, although this type of
sociological research has been developed in Poland to a degree unknown
in other Communist or formerly Communist countries and produced
results that often, though not consistently, support some of my own
findings.[20]

I decided not to include the results of attitudinal studies for two more
reasons. First, the introduction of sociological surveys, with their specific
methodology and results, would destroy the thematic, theoretical, and
methodological unity of the book, whose primary concern is with the
interpretation of public symbolic behavior. Second, I realized that in order to
gauge the impact of symbols (or to be more precise: participation in ceremonies and rituals) on political behavior (such as involvement in clandestine political groups or voting preferences), one would have to be able to
isolate two groups of people: those who participated in such symbolic
actions and those who did not, and then compare their subsequent political
behavior. For a variety of reasons such information is unobtainable.[21]

A complete analysis of legitimacy must include an assessment of the key
dimensions of a political field, such as the power bases (that is, the *potential*
power) of the actors. But this study deals only with one aspect of the
power field: cultural forms and counterforms of power realization. So
instead of analyzing the power bases of the actors, I offer a short, simplified
picture of the situation. In countries ruled by Communists, the means of
production, the means of communication,[22] and the means of coercion are

19. The difficult issue of reticent cultures is discussed in Almond and Verba (1980). The
fear of revealing one's views in sociological surveys distorted the results of such surveys in
Poland, although the scope and strength of this distortion are not clear (Sułek 1989, 41).
Perhaps ethnographic participant observation is the best method to obtain reliable data on
such politically sensitive issues. The most convincing application of such a method is to be
found in Scott (1985).

20. The results of sociological surveys are thoroughly reported and analyzed by Mason
(1985). Antoni Sułek systematically analyzed a complex gamut of factors influencing the
reliability of the attitudinal surveys in Poland (see Sułek 1989).

21. Despite the shortage of evidence on this topic, many authors nevertheless assume (or
theorize) that "by repetitively employing a limited pool of powerful symbols, often associated with emotional fervor, rituals are an important molder of political beliefs" (Kertzer
1988, 95).

22. In Poland of the 1970s, the Church did not have access to TV or radio. In 1974 the
official press had 3005 periodicals, with a total circulation of 41 million, 10 million of which
were dailies. The Catholic press that was related to, though not always controlled by, the
Church hierarchy had 3 weeklies and 23 other periodicals with a total circulation of 300,000
(or, 1 copy for each 120 Catholics). The Catholic press that was not related to the hierarchy
(and usually followed the official line of the Party-state), had 1 daily and 5 weeklies with a
total circulation of 270,000 (see *Spotkania,* January 1978).

tightly controlled by a single political elite. Because of the scope and depth of this control, the rules of the political game in these countries are *qualitatively* different from those rules in the Western democracies. The Polish situation was, however, exceptional because of the predominantly private ownership of land by peasants and the institutional independence of the Catholic Church.[23] Yet the power potential of the state was always vastly superior to that of the other actors in the public domain. My study can be seen as an attempt to answer the question whether during the 1970s such an extensive power differential was translated into the acquisition and maintenance of legitimacy by the regime. Or, using Antonio Gramsci's terminology, whether the Party-state's political domination was turned into or replaced by cultural hegemony.[24]

This brings us to the second important concept of this study: cultural hegemony or, in brief, hegemony. This concept has recently appeared as an important analytical tool in several anthropological studies, including Sherry B. Ortner's book on Sherpa Buddhism (1989), Gerald M. Sider's work on the Newfoundland fisherfolk (1986), and David D. Laitin's analysis of the role of religious and ethnic factors in the Yoruba politics (1986). The concept of hegemony originates with Gramsci, but the locus classicus of its modern usage is to be found in Raymond Williams's *Marxism and Literature* (1977, 108–14). There is no room here to engage in a detailed exposition of this concept.[25] Suffice it to say that hegemony refers to that aspect of power relationships which is not produced or guaranteed by coercion but by the acceptance (even if fragmentary and not fully conscious) of the rulers's definitions of reality by the ruled. Such definitions are to be found not only in the more organized bodies of ideas propagated by the "rulers," such as "official" ideologies or scientific theories, but also (or first of all) in various forms of everyday consciousness, such as habits or customs, and, which is particularly important for this book, in public ceremonies and rituals staged by the rulers.

The concept of hegemony forces us to think about culture and power—which are often analyzed separately—as two closely intertwined

23. The situation as far as the means of production are concerned could be described as an *almost* total monopoly, for the majority of land in Poland was controlled by private farmers. They did, however, depend on the state in all aspects of the production process, for the state controlled all sources of supply of fertilizers and fodder, all banks, and all distribution and sales networks.

24. On the distinction between political domination and cultural hegemony, see, for example, Gramsci (1971, 55 n.5).

25. A penetrating composite picture of the analytical strengths and shortcomings of the concept of (cultural) hegemony can be constructed by reading Williams (1977, 108–14), Laitin (1986, particularly 102–8 and 180–83), Sider (1986, 119–22), Scott (1985), and Ortner (1989, 193–97).

and inseparable facets of all social interactions and social processes.[26]
Also, hegemony is not a stable attribute of sociopolitical systems; rather,
it is a process (Williams 1977, 112). Hegemony is always subject to
change since the official symbolic system propounded by the rulers is
always being contested (with varying intensity) by counterhegemonic
symbolic systems (discourses) embedded in both the everyday practices
of the ruled and the ceremonies and rituals they perform. Sometimes
counterhegemonic discourse breaks into public spaces with vigor and
high visibility, thereby openly and decisively challenging the monopoly
of the official, hegemonic discourse. As I demonstrate later in this book,
such was the situation in Poland of the late 1970s.

The concept of hegemony, however, shares with the concept of legitimacy a significant shortcoming: there is no way to measure with satisfac-
tory precision the "strength" of the hegemony achieved by the rulers
over the ruled. Both hegemony and counterhegemony, by definition,
reside in myriads of behaviors and cultural forms and, therefore, a hegemonic control of one level of social discourse (such as science or ideology) can be counterbalanced (or even annulled) by the lack of such control of other levels (everyday life or religion).

Much of counterhegemony seems to reside in the cultural forms of
everyday life (see Scott 1985),[27] a topic beyond the scope of this book.
What I will do is to portray qualitatively both the official and unofficial
public discourses (as they were developed in and through public ceremonies, rituals, and demonstrations in the 1970s and in 1980–81) to assess
(mostly in the last chapter) whether the official discourse became hegemonic; that is, whether the official discourse became a "natural" component of the nation's culture. I assess the "strength" of the official discourse
by comparing it with unofficial discourses, which are necessarily counterhegemonic, since they were produced "against" the official discourse.

An analysis of public ceremonies and rituals[28] should include a study of

26. This realization constitutes the theoretical core of many recent anthropological studies, including Arens and Karp (1989), Ortner (1989), and Sider (1986).

27. A comprehensive ethnography of everyday resistance against Communist rule in
Eastern Europe has not been written. Wedel's (1986) attempt is interesting on the descriptive, but not on the analytical or the theoretical level. Zinoviev's works on the Soviet Union
approach the ideal I have in mind. Some fiction writers, however, such as Milan Kundera,
Skvorecky, or Konwicki, have portrayed the feel of life as it was actually lived under
socialism with extraordinary depth and accuracy.

28. It is convenient to distinguish ceremony from ritual. I define ceremony as a mode of
interaction rather than as a mode of communication. Such a conceptualization allows a
more adequate interpretation of some of its characteristics, such as threefold evocative
power (on the individual plane ceremonies evoke thoughts, emotions, and volitions) and
transformative efficacy (on the sociocultural plane ceremonies transform the rules of the

the "rest" of the culture within which these cultural forms are produced. This "rest," however, is discontinuous and diversified, particularly in a large and complex society. Therefore, the study of ceremonial, including political ceremonial, calls for a concept more inclusive than "ritual" or "ceremony" yet not so broad as "culture." The term *discourse* seems to be a solution. In the most general sense a discourse or a discursive formation is a set of semiotic facts, that is, a set of human products that are to be interpreted (regardless of whether or not they were intended to communicate anything). Moreover, such a set is often organized according to articulable principle(s)[29] that govern the construction of a model of the "extra-discursive" world.[30] Such principles regulate, for example, the inclusion and exclusion of statements, an artistic style, or the choice of vocabulary or "basic units" (for example, in architecture). Discursive formations are therefore to be found not only among linguistic facts (oral or written) but among all human products that can be interpreted as a group of statements. It has been observed that within determinable spatial and temporal confines[31] discourses are often regulated by a single set of rules and display more or less definite (structural or stylistic) affinities.[32]

---

sociocultural game). In ceremonies people not only communicate, they congregate, and this togetherness often leads to an amplification of individual emotions (often to the point of ecstatic trance) and the suspension of rational faculties. Such an experience gives the participants a feeling that their lives have meaning and imparts to otherwise depersonalized social events a sense of emotional value. When a ceremony becomes formalized as a part of "tradition," it can be called a ritual. Ritual shares with custom or etiquette formality and repetitiveness; it differs from them in its extraordinary, aharmonic character.

29. Timothy Reiss writes that "the term discourse refers to the way in which material embodying sign processes is organized. Discourse can be . . . characterized as the visible and describable praxis of what is called 'thinking' " (1982, 9). Paul Q. Hirst notes that "discourse is conceived as forms of order and inclusion/exclusion of statements" (1985, 173).

30. Reiss puts it well: "If discourse speaks *of* phenomena (no matter what precise inflection one may wish to give to the word 'phenomena'), it orders them" (1982, 29).

31. Foucault calls such a spatially and temporarily delineated totality of cultural products *apparatus (dispositif)*, that is, "a thoroughly heterogenous ensemble consisting of discourses, institutions, architectural forms, regulatory decisions, laws, administrative measures, scientific statements, philosophical, moral and philanthropic propositions—in short, the said as much as the unsaid" (1980, 194).

32. Such affinities have been conceptualized in various ways, "Zeitgeist" being perhaps the most noble of all concepts applied here. Among the more concrete analyses of this kind, Panofsky's short essay (1951) on the analogy between Gothic architecture and scholasticism stands out. Other examples are Timothy J. Reiss's examination of the "aspects of the emergence and development, of consolidation and growth to dominance, of modern Western discourse" (1982, 9) and George L. Mosse's study of the development and basic premises of German nationalism from the Napoleonic Wars through the Third Reich (1975).

I do not know if the picture of "symbolic reality" I paint reflects the system of values of an "average" Pole. It does, however, seem to approximate the state of consciousness of some middle-level leaders, those people who pondered over their situations, were more or less active in the public (albeit unofficial) domain, and occupied key positions in emerging social networks. I am also well aware that the picture I paint is of necessity incomplete. My project is to construct a simplified model of a very dynamic situation. Under such circumstances, Edward Shils's warning that "what sociologists and social anthropologists call the cultural values or belief system of a society can be lived up to only partially, fragmentarily, intermittently and only in an approximate way" is particularly relevant.[33]

The period I have chosen to examine allows for a relatively precise comparison of the official and unofficial (counterhegemonic) discourses. In Poland during 1976–81 there were many public demonstrations, and they were documented relatively well. It is also a period that has been studied extensively.[34]

I learned to describe and analyze public symbolic behavior from many people, mainly from reading the works of Victor Turner, Clifford Geertz, Abner Cohen, Myron Aronoff, Maurice Bloch, and other anthropologists who concentrate their efforts on understanding the complex relationship between the symbolic and the political. In my analysis I focus on the verbal aspect of the ceremonies (such as the speeches) because in a literate society language carries the bulk of the message. However, the fact that the words were uttered in the ceremonial context enhanced the effect the messages they carried had on the audience, for as Robert Paine notes, the "drawing together of word and deed, in context, gives rhetoric its potency; the doing and the effect are inseparable" (1981, 19).

Focusing on symbols and discourses as a discrete analytical level allowed me to study their role in the legitimation of power without having to interview individuals about politically sensitive and personally embarrassing subjects, such as their support for the Communist regime or the nature of their religious beliefs. By concentrating on discourses, rituals, ceremonies, and symbols and by treating them as *autonomous* but *interde-*

Both these authors were able to discern, articulate, and document general premises ("the spirit of modernism" or "modern German nationalism") that organize several discrete discursive formations.

33. Shils (1970, 37). A similar warning permeates Robert Murphy's book (1970). It was Rigby who applied it to Eastern European studies (1982, 17).

34. See, for example, Barańczak (1983), Bernhard (1993), Goldfarb (1989), Goodwyn (1991), Holzer (1984), Karpiński (1982a, 1982b), Laba (1991), Lipski (1985), Ost (1990), Raina (1978, 1985), Staniszkis (1984), and Touraine et al. (1983).

pendent[35] with other social phenomena, not as derivatives of or mere vehicles for economic and political phenomena, I try to answer Lowell Dittmer's call for a more sophisticated symbolic analysis in the field of political culture. I share his conviction that "Although it is certainly useful—where feasible—to measure the relative assimilation of culture by questioning a sample of individuals, political culture should be conceptualized as an emergent variable, whose properties transcend the sum of its members' belief- and value-systems" (1977, 555).

My data come from six sources: (1) the accounts of public ceremonies, ritual, demonstrations, anniversaries, and so on published in official (that is, state-owned) and unofficial (that is, illegally published) periodicals; (2) interviews with participants in such events; (3) my direct experience (for example, I was present at the unveiling of the Gdańsk Monument in 1980); (4) examination of pictorial documentation made available to me by several professional photographers; (5) books published in Poland on the subject of official ceremonial (for example, Pełka 1980); and (6) studies by Polish sociologists, such as Stefan Nowak and his associates (on the system of values of the Polish people), Ireneusz Krzemiński and his associates (on the subjective dimension of the Solidarity's revolution from the perspective of symbolic interactionism), and the collective studies "Poles 1980" and "Poles 1981." I believe that I have some insight into the events of this period that I owe directly to having lived in Poland during this time as a member of Polish society. Yet working in the United States gave me the distance I needed to study many aspects of Polish reality I had not been aware of while living there. With some modifications, my anthropological imagination was shaped by a process M. N. Srinivas described as being "'thrice born,' once in [one's] own society of actual nascent, a second time by coming to terms with another culture, and a third time by returning to [one's] own society and applying the anthropological perspective to it." With this third birth, "We find that the familiar has become exoticized; we see it with new eyes. The commonplace has become marvelous."[36]

In the gathering and analysis of these materials I relied on three basic techniques: content analysis, interviews, and participant observation. Additionally, I analyzed three symbolic events in greater detail as case studies. They are John Paul II's first visit to Poland, the public spectacle in

35. As Sider puts it: "This paradox of the concept of culture—that it can be either primarily independent or primarily derivative—haunts both nonmarxist and marxist analyses alike. Clifford Geertz [1964] has stated that culture is 'independent but interdependent' with social organization" (1986, 6). (I cite Geertz [1964] as Geertz [1973]; see bibliography.)

36. The latter quotation is from Victor Turner. For the sources of both quotations, see Manning (1983, 8).

Kraków called *The Song of Wawel,* and the 1980 unveiling of the Gdańsk Monument, commemorating the workers shot in 1970. I was a participant in all three. In the case of *The Song of Wawel,* produced by Kraków's student theater *STU,* I spent a few years (1977–81) working as the theater's sociologist, acquiring thereby a close insight into the workings of this institution.[37]

37. My studies focused on the fluctuations of the public perception of the theater and their causes. See Kubik and Mach (1982a, 1982b).

1 Workers' Protests of June 1976 and Their Economic and Political Context

The strikes of June 1976 constitute a turning point in Polish history. The workers' protests, the intellectuals' actions undertaken in their defense against the regime's persecutions, and the subsequent emergence of the open, organized opposition triggered a chain of events that led to the collapse of Communism thirteen years later. There was a direct connection between the dramatic rearrangement of the political scene and the reversal of the economic trend: after a period of growth and increasing prosperity during the first half of the 1970s, the country's economy progressively deteriorated during the second half. It was against such a political-economic background that the "symbolic war" between the Party-state, the Catholic Church, and the organized opposition was fought. Eventually, this war became one of the key factors bringing about the collapse of Communist rule.

On Friday 25 June 1976, workers of at least 130 factories throughout Poland went on strike or took to the streets in demonstrations against unexpected steep price increases of basic foodstuffs announced a day earlier by Prime Minister Piotr Jaroszewicz at a session of the Sejm.[1] By 8:00 P.M. that very evening Jaroszewicz went on national radio and television and announced that the price reform, as it was euphemistically presented in the media, had been withdrawn. Soon afterward, in a unanimous (Bernhard 1993) response, the workers ended their protest actions. The next day, however, the police and security forces began a campaign of reprisals, including beating, arresting, firing on, and imprisoning (on the basis of summary proceedings of the Sentencing Courts for Misdemeanors) thousands of workers, especially in the cities of Radom and Ursus near Warsaw where protest actions had been especially violent.[2]

In their reports of what had happened on June 25 the authorities did not refer to the workers' actions as "strikes" or "workers' protests," because within the official reality of the Polish People's Republic there was no place for such phenomena. The rules governing the official discourse permitted only two ways of dealing with such actions: they had to be censored out of the system[3] or interpreted as deviant actions performed by systemic outcasts.[4] This latter interpretation entered the official discourse on Sunday, June 27. The former technique was used by Prime Minister Jaroszewicz in his Friday evening speech recalling the price increases. He did not mention any protests and informed the Poles that "consultations" had taken place "in the majority of enterprises all over the country" and the government had received "a very high number of concrete recommendations." On the basis of these recommendations—he said—the government had decided to withdraw the price increases, and this decision constituted "one more confirmation of the democratic rules which guide the actions of the government and the Party."[5]

1. Detailed descriptions of these events can be found in Karpiński (1982a), Błażyński (1979), and Bernhard (1993).

2. For a description of the reprisals, see Błażyński (1979, 261–63), Bernhard (1993), Raina (1978, 252–302), and Lipski (1985, 41–42).

3. The word "strike" entered the official discourse only in the last days of the August 1980 strikes, which at that time engulfed the whole country.

4. Alfred Meyer observes that such a tendency to "brand as criminal or subversive those who reveal compromising facts" about the system is a general characteristic of all Soviet-type states (Meyer 1972, 58).

5. *Trybuna Ludu* 27 June 1976. The same issue contains on the front page a commentary by a leading Party journalist Ryszard Wojna, who concluded that "a discussion about the common good of the Motherland, the nation, and the state can be carried on only while people work. This is a categorical imperative. This is a fundamental criterion of the proper attitudes pertaining to the most important issues." It is the only reference in the official media, though not a very clear one, that work was, in fact, interrupted.

Monday (June 28) official newspapers brought detailed reports of "spontaneous" rallies that had taken place in several major cities on June 27, with participation officially estimated at 50,000 to 200,000 people at each rally. The purpose of these carefully organized meetings was to show the people's "spontaneous" approval of the Party's policies. The most-often-used slogans read: "We guarantee that we will contribute with our work to the development of our Motherland," "We are for the further consistent realization of the program of the Seventh Congress [of the PZPR]," and "We will not allow hooligan elements to destroy our accomplishments." As *Trybuna Ludu* described it: "In mass rallies, the Polish working class expressed full support for the policies of the Party and its first secretary, for the government and its prime minister."[6]

The biggest rally was organized in Warsaw at the Stadium of the Tenth Anniversary. Radio Warsaw contended that about 120,000 people participated in this event. This number is exaggerated since the seating capacity of the stadium is 80,000, and a West German television camera revealed large empty sections carefully avoided by the Polish TV crews (Błażyński 1979, 262). The actual number of the participants is difficult to establish.

In the early afternoon, before being taken to the stadium, "the representatives of all generations of the inhabitants of the capital, the veterans of revolutionary struggles, the workers of the factories and agricultural enterprises of the Warsaw district, and people of science, culture, and art" were gathered at various "monuments of revolutionary struggle and patriotic deeds." According to *Trybuna Ludu,* "These monuments are the symbols, conventional signs, which contain the idea of what we struggled for, of what had become a basis of socialist Poland. The inhabitants of Warsaw here lay down their flowers."[7]

The real composition of the demonstrators is not easy to determine. The Party-state was always ready to mobilize huge numbers of people from the police, the *Służba Bezpieczeństwa* (Security Service, or SB), the *Ochotnicze Rezerwy Milicji Obywatelskiej* (Voluntary Reserves of the Police, or ORMO), the *Ochotnicze Hufce Pracy* (Voluntary Work Brigades, or OHP), and the Party itself. There were also other organizations, such as the *Związek Bojowników o Wolność i Demokrację* (Association of the Fighters for Freedom and Democracy, or ZBOWiD), an organization of war veterans who seemed to have joined mostly for financial reasons (such as higher pensions and extra social benefits), which could easily mobilize thousands of its members even on very short notice. A German

6. Ibid., 28 June 1976.
7. Ibid., 29 June 1976.

TV crew noticed that the crowd at the stadium consisted of "a selected audience, all those present having been equipped with special recognition tags" (Błażyński 1979, 262).

The spontaneity of the participation in the rallies of Sunday June 27 was, according to all independent observers, manufactured. The symbolic content of the demonstrations and their organization was carefully orchestrated by the authorities. All the slogans were prepared by the Party. Some of them read: "Full approval of the working people for the policies of the party and the state," "The line of the Party—the line of the nation,"[8] and "The leaders of the PZPR and the government can always count on the working people."

The main rally at the Stadium of the Tenth Anniversary began at 4:00 P.M. Later the official press reported that it had been attended by "the thousands of Party and nonparty people."[9] Workers from various factories reported on the fulfillment of plans for the first half of 1976. For example, Zenon Woś, a worker from the *Fabryka Samochodów Osobowych* (Warsaw Car Factory, or FSO) declared that working people understand that their obligation as citizens is to work hard.[10] Stanisław Ryszard Dobrowolski, a member of the Party and a poet, often referred to as "the bard of Warsaw" reminded everyone "that the blossoming beauty of the capital—the city in which he has lived for almost seventy years—has benefited in the last years from the rapid development of People's Poland" and added that "it was and is both a material and a spiritual blossom."[11] In the same speech he described demonstrating workers as "vandals" and "hooligans." As subsequent sociological research proved, the workers have never forgotten the insults he hurled at them (Bakuniak 1983, 289).

On 2 July 1976 a huge official rally took place in Katowice where Edward Gierek, the first secretary of the Central Committee of the PZPR, had ruled as the local Party boss until 1970. Gierek and Jaroszewicz were present at this "huge manifestation of the working class of Katowice province," organized under the slogan "Let us forge our love for the Motherland into a Deed." Gierek's speech was frequently interrupted by "spontaneous" ovation and chants. The audience bellowed:

8. Note that two of these slogans lack verbs. It is a characteristic of Communist newspeak, to be analyzed in the following chapter.

9. *Trybuna Ludu,* 29 June 1976. In the official discourse people were often divided into two categories: Party and nonparty. The official media often announced that some governmental or party initiative is supported by both Party and nonparty people to indicate unanimous support. I assume that the hidden message here was that a Party initiative is truly good if it is also supported by nonparty people.

10. Ibid., 29 June 1976.

11. Ibid.

"The Party—Gierek," Gierek answered: "Poland—Poland," and the audience concluded: "The Party—Poland. The Party—Gierek."[12] By the power of this peculiar syllogism, Gierek was equated with the Party and Poland. Communists often used such rhetorical maneuvers to express one of the most fundamental axioms of their doctrine, according to which such entities, or their interests, as "the nation," "the people," "the working class," and "the Party" were almost identical. In one of his speeches, Leonid Brezhnev observed that any attempt to "counterpoise the Party to the people would be like . . . trying to separate, say, the heart from the whole of the body" (Berki 1982, 164). The organizers of the Katowice rally went a step further, including in the equation the name of the first secretary, displaying a rather unabashed proclivity for a new cult of personality. In a speech closing the rally, Zdzisław Grudzień resorted to this "Communist principle of identity" once again, exclaiming: "Long live our beloved Motherland[13]—Mother: Polish Peoples' Republic! In honor of our People's Motherland, in honor of our wonderful nation, our Marxist-Leninist party—threefold hurrah!"[14] As one may suspect, many people joined in with the Party cheerleaders chanting "hurrah" to honor their Motherland. Needless to say, by doing so they inadvertently honored also the "People's" Motherland and the Communist party. The authorities were quick to interpret the whole event as an expression of spontaneous support for their policies.

The Party had also an elaborated repertoire of symbolic punishments. At the end of an official rally in Radom, where a few days earlier the demonstrating workers had set the PZPR headquarters on fire, Tadeusz Karwicki, the local first secretary, informed the participants that they would not be allowed to pass the official resolution condemning "the troublemakers" and expressing their unconditional support for First Secretary Gierek and Prime Minister Jaroszewicz. "This town so far does not have a proper mandate to do so" (Karpiński 1982b, 179), announced Karwicki, implying that the town should first engage in some act of repentance.

Another frequently used device of the official discourse, which served to turn the elements of the extradiscursive reality into their negation, was employed by the Warsaw Party secretary Józef Kępa in his speech analyzing the June events. Kępa, describing the striking and demonstrating

---

12. Ibid., 3–4 July 1976.

13. The Polish word *ojczyzna* (one's native country) is a derivative of *ojciec* (father). Thus "fatherland" would seem to be the best English equivalent of this word. But *ojczyzna* is a feminine noun, and Poles tend to think about their native land as *she*. Grudzień's identification of the *ojczyzna* with *matka* (mother) sounds natural in Polish. For the same reason I translate in my work *Ojczyzna* as "Motherland."

14. *Trybuna Ludu*, 3–4 July 1976.

workers, observed that "in every lively and developing society there can be found shaky, passive, indecisive, and opportunistic individuals."[15]

The Economic and Political Context of the Events of June 1976

Any interpretation of the scope and intensity of the symbolic repair of the damage done to the Party's image by the protesting workers should include an analysis of the major economic, political, and cultural developments initiated by Gierek's ascent to power in 1970.

At 8:00 P.M. on Saturday 12 December 1970, Polish Radio and TV informed a shocked audience about "changes in the retail prices of a wide range of products." The prices of forty-six categories of goods rose, in some cases by as much as 69 percent, drastically reducing the purchasing power of the populace (especially its urban segment).[16] On Monday December 14, the workers of the Lenin Shipyard in Gdańsk (employing sixteen thousand people) went on strike, initiating a wave of protests that soon engulfed at least one hundred enterprises in seven provinces.[17] In Gdańsk, Gdynia, and Szczecin the army opened fire on the workers. There were fatalities on both sides.[18] On Saturday 19 December 1970, Władysław Gomułka was forced to resign and Gierek replaced him as the first secretary of the Central Committee of the PZPR.

Gierek's Innovations in the Economy and Politics

The Economy. The ruling principle of Gomułka's economic strategy was self-sufficiency if not austerity. When, in 1961, his regime started a second

---

15. Ibid., 24–25 July 1976.

16. For more detailed information on the December 1970 price increases and the reaction to them, see *Trybuna Ludu,* 13 December 1970; Wacowska (1971, 13–15); Karpiński (1982a, 157); Błażyński (1979, 7); Korybutowicz (1983, 43–44); and Laba (1986, 1991).

17. This is the estimate made by Mieczysław F. Rakowski, a high-ranking Party official (Korybutowicz 1983, 76).

18. The exact number of the dead was never determined. An official communiqué from 18 January 1971 reported that nine people were killed in Gdańsk, eighteen in Gdynia, sixteen in Szczecin, and one in Elbląg. This official version was never accepted by the public. Unofficial estimates range from several dozen to several hundred deaths (according to a special commission of Solidarity whose meeting I attended on 15 December 1980; see also Korybutowicz 1983, 112).

industrialization drive (the first wave of rapid "extensive" industrialization swept Poland in the early 1950s), domestic accumulation (forced savings) became virtually the sole source of investment capital (Fallenbuchl 1982, 4). This strategy contributed to the stagnation felt by the populace in the form of a very slow improvement of the living standard.[19]

By contrast, Gierek's "new development strategy," designed to modernize the entire economy and improve the supply of food and consumer goods, was based on the principle of large-scale import of capital and technology from the West. The growth rate of the Polish economy (domestic net material production) grew from 6 percent per year in 1961–70 to 10 percent per year in 1971–75[20] (Fallenbuchl 1982, 6; Brus 1983, 29). A very high investment rate during these years[21] was achieved primarily through the massive import of Western technology bought mostly on credit. This high rate of accumulation was, however, not accompanied by restraints on consumption; in fact, both accumulation and consumption were on the increase. An observer of the Polish economy stated:

> The usual contradiction between raising investment and consumption at the same time was, as it were, suspended. By borrowing abroad on a really grand scale the government was actually calling on Poland's future resources to meet the present consumption and, above all, investment needs. The reallocation of resources was thus not from consumption to investment, but, through the use of foreign trade, from the future to the present. (Gomułka 1979, 13)

But these "future resources" were never created. Gierek's economic reform never permeated the basic premises of the system, such as the dominance of politics over economy or the centralized decision-making process.[22] As a team of independent economists observed: "The essence of the economic philosophy of the 1970s constituted a naive belief that the efficiency of the economy can be guaranteed without a basic remodel-

19. The index of real wages illustrates well the rate of improvement of the living standard. Here are the comparative figures for 1960 and 1970 for Poland and her neighbors (the level for 1960 = 100); Poland 119; Rumania, 146; Bulgaria, 143; East Germany, 137; USSR, 134; Hungary, 129; Czechoslovakia, 127 (Brus 1983, 29).

20. It was to fall to 1.4 percent in 1976–80.

21. The average annual growth of investment ("accumulation") in 1961–70 was 7.4 percent; in 1971–75, 19.0 percent; and in 1976–80 it fell to *negative* 11.6 percent (Fallenbuchl 1982, 6).

22. A short-lived partial reform involving some decentralization in the economic decision-making process had already been curtailed in 1973 (Fallenbuchl 1982, 5; Brus 1983, 33–34).

ing of the rules of the system" (Bojarski et al. 1981).[23] The investment program was based on arbitrary ideological and political deliberations, not on economic calculus.[24] For example, the reform was to lead to the harmonious and comprehensive development of the whole economy, but at the same time certain projects (such as the Gdańsk Northern Port and the gigantic Katowice Steelworks) were given priority in terms of both supplies of materials and wage policies.[25]

The influx of Western technologies and hard-currency credits improved the performance of the economy only temporarily; it was—as in the 1950s—an "extensive development." Low capital and labor productivity, resulting from the mismanagement endemic to command economies, and unstable agricultural policies,[26] accompanied by rapidly growing nominal personal incomes, led to serious market imbalances, felt already in 1975–76, that assumed disastrous proportions in the late 1970s.

The standard of living rose significantly in the early 1970s, although the growing purchasing power of the populace (money incomes in 1971–76 increased by 111 percent) was only partially matched by the increasing production of food and consumer goods (the supply of meat and meat products, for example, increased in the same period by 66 percent) (Gomułka 1979, 17). After workers' protests in 1970 the government froze the prices of basic foodstuffs and consumer goods, but in 1974–75 the prices of certain fruit and vegetable products, restaurant meals, bus

23. The same group concluded that in the long run Gierek's economic policies were more disastrous than anything done by his predecessors.

24. For an exhaustive analysis of the economic decision-making process in the 1970s, see Kuczyński (1987); for a short informative account, see Brus (1983). Growing chaos in the Polish economy of the 1970s—stressed by Brus—is well illustrated by the "open plan concept" invented "to cover huge numbers of ad hoc decisions, frequently of crucial significance, made in a great hurry with barely any technical possibilities for proper scrutiny and coordination" (Brus 1983, 38–39).

25. The Katowice Steelworks, "which, together with supplementary projects, swallowed up 175 billion zlotys [over $5 billion at the official rate of exchange], was started, in 1972, without having been included in the original version of the [five-year] plan" (Brus 1983, 38).

26. In 1970–73, because of such policy measures as the legal regulation of property rights to agricultural land, a sharp increase in the prices paid by the state for agricultural produce (especially meat products), abolition of compulsory deliveries (from 1972), elimination of the steep progressiveness of land taxes, easier access to credits for purchasing agricultural machinery, better supply of consumer goods to the country, improved social security provisions for peasants and farmers, and, additionally, excellent weather conditions, the growth of agricultural production was "impressive" (Brus 1983, 35). But the first symptoms of the instability of governmental policies had already appeared by 1975. The so-called State Land Fund (which sold and distributed land to individual farmers) sold two-thirds of its land in 1973, but only 5.5 percent in 1975 (Brus 1983, 36).

and train tickets, cigarettes, alcoholic beverages, metal products (including kitchen utensils), and some services (Karpiński 1982b, 93) were raised. Because of these surprise increases real incomes of the population grew slower than nominal incomes.

Politics and administration. During his reign, Gierek and his regime modified the Polish Constitution, changed the territorial-administrative organization of the state, sanctioned the dominance of the Party *nomenklatura* over the state functionaries (appointed or elected), partially reformed education, and liquidated the remnants of pluralism in the youth movement. Given these changes, the image of Gierek as a pragmatic and benevolent ruler, ready to compromise with the populace, is inaccurate.[27]

The modifications of the Polish Constitution figured highly in the Gierek regime's agenda since 1971. In documents prepared in August 1975 for the Seventh Congress of the PZPR, there was the following clause: "The Constitution should affirm the historical fact that the Polish People's Republic is a socialist state in which power belongs to the working people of the cities and villages, and in which the PZPR is the leading force" (Karpiński 1982a, 184). This formulation was the cause of several protests. The best known were the "explanatory note" from the Polish Episcopate dated March 1976 and a statement signed by fifty-nine intellectuals (later known as "the letter of the fifty-nine"). The bishops strongly objected to granting the PZPR the status of "the leading force" in the country, fearing that the ideology of "the leading force," Marxism-Leninism, could be thereby constitutionally established as the official worldview in this predominantly Catholic country.[28] The signatories of the letter of the fifty-nine "emphasized the need to guarantee the freedom of conscience, religion, work, speech, information, and science, not only in the constitution but also in the laws based on the constitution" (Karpiński 1982a, 185). They observed:

> Guarantees of these basic freedoms cannot be reconciled with the official recognition of the leading role of one party in the state system of power, which is now being proposed. Such a constitutional statement would confer on a political party the role of an organ of state power, which would be neither responsible to nor controlled by society. Under such circumstances, the Diet cannot be regarded as the highest organ of power, the government is not

27. For another negative assessment of Gierek's policies, see Pańków (1982, 41–42).
28. The full text of the bishops' statement can be found in Raina (1978, 224–28).

the highest executive branch, and the courts are not independent. (Karpiński 1982b, 144)[29]

These protests were not reported by the Polish media. The populace learned of them from foreign broadcasts, such as Voice of America or Radio Free Europe, and from foreign and Polish émigré newspapers.

On 23 January 1976 the Extraordinary Diet Commission prepared the final version of the constitutional changes. The next day these changes were made public. According to one of these amendments (referred to as "minor" by the Party leadership), the Polish People's Republic, formally described in the constitution as a "state of people's democracy," was now to become a "socialist state." As Jakub Karpiński observed, the actual meaning of such a transformation was not clear, since the same amendment asserted that PZPR was the "guiding political force of society in the building of socialism" (Karpiński 1982b, 149). Thus Poland was already regarded as "a socialist country," and yet socialism was still being built. Another amendment contained the declaration that the Polish People's Republic in its policies "strengthens friendship and cooperation with the Union of Socialist Soviet Republics and other socialist states" (Karpiński 1982b, 148). The third proposed amendment stated that "citizens' rights are inseparably linked with the honest and conscientious fulfillment of duties to the Motherland" (Karpiński 1982b, 148).

After another wave of protests, including letters from intellectuals, artists, lawyers, and students and a critical sermon by the primate of Poland, Stefan Cardinal Wyszyński,[30] on 10 February 1976 the Diet adopted the final version of the modified constitution. The article linking citizens' rights with their responsibilities was replaced with a milder formulation stating that "the citizens of the Polish People's Republic should honestly fulfill their duties toward the Motherland and contribute to its development" (Article 57.3). The articles concerning the PZPR and friendship with the USSR and other socialist countries were adopted in their form recommended by the Diet Commission.

Since 1950 the administrative structure of the Polish People's Republic had consisted of three tiers: provinces (*województwa*), districts (*powiaty*), and the smallest units such as villages and settlements (called *gromady*). Power at each level rested with nominally elective *people's councils*[31]

---

29. More extensive excerpts from the letter of the fifty-nine are published in Raina (1978).

30. For a more detailed description of these protests, see Karpiński (1982a, 186–88) and Raina (1978, 214–28).

31. The Polish name of this institution *rada narodowa,* which should be rendered in English as "national council," is a direct translation of Russian *narodnyj sovjet,* which means "people's council." Therefore, the Polish equivalent of this term should be *rada ludowa*

whose *presidia* fulfilled the functions of executive branches of local government. The changes, initiated in 1972 and completed by 1975, came in three steps. First, 4,313 *gromady* were abolished and replaced with 2,381 larger units called *gminy*. Second, the facade of elective local government was torn down, and all executive power was vested in individual appointed officers. Third, 314 districts were eliminated, and the number of provinces was raised from 17 to 49.[32] The judiciary system was reformed accordingly. People's councils were no longer administrative organs; "they became simply organs of self-government whose functions were vaguely defined as 'directing,' 'affecting,' 'inspiring,' and 'controlling' " (Karpiński 1982a, 169).

The new administrative organs were vertically subordinated to the national government, which, in turn, was officially controlled by the Party. This was achieved in October 1972 when the Politburo adopted a detailed directive regulating appointments to all levels of the state administration. From then on, state functionaries were openly appointed by the appropriate organs of the PZPR apparatus. For example, the Politburo was empowered to appoint the marshal (Speaker) and vice-marshals of the Diet, the president, vice-presidents, members of the State Council, and the prime minister.

In order to complete the Party's comprehensive control over the entire system of government, on the recommendation of the First National Conference of the PZPR (22–23 October 1973), local Party secretaries became the chairmen of people's councils at respective levels of the government hierarchy.

As many observers noted, these sweeping reforms had three objectives.[33] Gierek wanted to improve the efficiency of the government, increase centralism, and subordinate the government itself to the Party. The first objective—if it had indeed been seriously considered—soon proved to be unattainable, since the centralization of government killed the remnants of local initiative and subjected "peripheries" to the arbitrary and often miscalculated decisions of the "core" more than ever before.[34] This led to the further decline of governmental efficiency.

(people's council) not *rada narodowa* (national council). This careless translation from Russian obscures, perhaps inadvertently, the character of this institution, which, according to its proper name, should have been an elective organ of local government.

32. For a detailed description of these changes, see Błażyński (1979, 128–32) and Karpiński (1982b, 98–102).

33. See, for example, Karpiński (1982a, 170) and Błażyński (1979, 128–32).

34. This process is well documented in Hann (1985, 79–99). He observes that after the *powiaty* (districts) had been eliminated, the new *województwo* (province) center was felt to be

In 1971 the Ministry of Public and Higher Education was divided into the Ministry of Public Education and Upbringing and the Ministry of Science, Higher Education, and Technology. Such a move suggested "a serious preoccupation with education on the part of the authorities. The name of the first-mentioned new ministry indicated that the state did not intend to leave the task of upbringing solely to the family and the Church" (Karpiński 1982a, 168). A special commission of twenty-four experts on education, led by a prominent sociologist loyal to the authorities, Jan Szczepański, prepared a report that recommended the introduction of a uniform ten-year curriculum in all elementary schools. Critics of this educational reform feared that such a curriculum would become an instrument of political indoctrination, but these objections were not reported by the official media. Interestingly enough, Szczepański admitted that some members of the Party apparatus had indeed seen the school system as an indoctrination tool.[35]

The implementation of the reform was delayed, however, by a serious shortage of qualified and ideologically reliable teachers,[36] an underdeveloped material infrastructure,[37] an insufficient number of new textbooks, and, last but not least, the protests of the Church, independent experts, intellectuals, and parents.

Despite all of these problems, propagation of the official ideology became an important element in the curriculum of the ten-year elementary school, which was ratified by the Diet in 1973 and elaborated on during the following years. Historical material, for example, was selected to illustrate exclusively the Marxist point of view on historical development. From this perspective, the Polish People's Republic was portrayed as the culmination of the long history of class struggles won by the

---

"no more accessible than the old" and "citizens now felt more exposed to the vagaries of the state machine than before. The *powiat* had permitted more feedback within the administrative system than was possible within the new streamlined version" (Hann 1985, 82).

35. *Literatura,* 27 September 1973.

36. Teachers were leaving their profession at a rate of about 15,000 a year in 1975. By the end of 1976 "more than 160,000 teachers, almost half of the total teacher force, still failed to produce academic diplomas which were required within the school reform." (*Słowo Powszechne,* 8 July 1976; quoted in Błażyński 1979, 134). Moreover, most of the teachers were Catholics. For example, 85 percent of the teachers interviewed in 1973 declared themselves to be believers. Only 5 percent admitted to being atheists (Błażyński 1979, 134).

37. The reform postulated the creation of so-called comprehensive community schools located in larger villages. Small and often understaffed and poorly equipped rural schools were to be eliminated. In practice, the state was not able to find enough suitable buildings for such schools and was not able to organize a viable and safe transportation system for students.

progressive forces of the Polish nation organized in various leftist and radical parties. The PZPR was presented as the only rightful heir to this tradition.

Gierek's regime "corrected" more than the school curriculum. Polish youth organizations were also reformed. In 1973 three such organizations active in the academic community were unified, despite widespread student protests. In the same year the word "socialist" was added to the names of all youth organizations still lacking this label.[38] Finally, in April 1976 the Union of Socialist Youth, the Socialist Union of Rural Youth, and the Socialist Union of Military Youth were merged to form the Union of Socialist Polish Youth.

Gierek's innovations were designed to centralize the state and increase the power of the Party within it. Jakub Karpiński categorized Gierek's rule as *enlightened autocracy*. It indeed seems plausible to assume that the authorities, at least in the initial stages of their reign, intended to improve the standard of living of the population and to close the economic gap between Poland and the industrial countries of Western Europe. Such a maneuver, if it had been successful, could perhaps have prevented a recurrence of the social unrest that had brought Gierek to power in the first place.

---

38. The Union of Rural Youth was renamed the Socialist Union of the Rural Youth, the Circles of Military Youth became the Socialist Union of Military Youth, and the Union of Polish Students became the Socialist Union of Polish Students. These three organizations together with the Union of Socialist Youth and the Union of Polish Scouts were then organized into the Federation of the Socialist Unions of Polish Youth.

2 The Official Public Discourse of the Gierek Era (1971–1980)

On **Sunday 20 December 1970,** one day after he took power, Gierek began his speech to the nation with the words: "Comrades and Citizens! Compatriots!" He proclaimed that the present problems "concern everyone in the nation, both those inside and outside the party, both religious believers and non-believers, and there is a place for every citizen to resolve these problems!" (Karpiński 1982a, 163). The speech was interpreted as a promise of a new *social contract* granting the populace, regardless of their worldview and party affiliation, wider participation in running the country. The terms of address also heralded Gierek's later inclusion of patriotic and nationalistic elements in his and his regime's public image.

The newspapers and radio and TV broadcasts were flooded with accounts of enthusiastic support for the new first secretary and his regime coming from all over the country. But not everyone was satisfied with the pace of political change, and already by January 1971 there were people who expressed disillusionment with the lack of significant improvements in the policies of the rulers.[1] On 19 January 1971 Szczecin's Party newspaper, *Głos Szczeciński,* reported that the employees of the pipe-works department of the Warski Shipyard in Szczecin had declared they would exceed the quotas of the production plan, that they had committed themselves to additional work on Sunday, January 24, and that they had decorated the shop with a slogan reading, "With extra production we support the new Party leadership." This information was false. The workers had never been consulted on this "spontaneous" initiative. Enraged by this discredited and allegedly abandoned propagandistic technique, the shipyard workers in Szczecin went back on strike and demanded that Gierek and the new prime minister Piotr Jaroszewicz come down and talk to them.[2]

On Sunday, January 24, Gierek and Jaroszewicz came to the Warski Shipyard. After a nine-hour meeting the workers declared that the strike was over. Gierek had not promised the workers much, and yet he had left them with the impression that he was a competent and dedicated leader.[3] From Szczecin, Gierek and Jaroszewicz went to Gdańsk, where the workers had been on strike almost continuously since December 1970. After informing the striking workers there that the country was in trouble and all people should start working together to improve the situation, the first secretary said, "You can be assured that we are all made from the same clay and that we do not have any other objective besides the one we have declared here. If you help us, I think we all will be able to achieve this common objective. Well then, will you help?" (Korybutowicz 1983, 134).

"Pomożemy" (We will help)—spontaneously declared the workers. "We will help" became one of the key words in the repertoire of the post-

---

1. Strikes and stoppages continued in January and February of 1971 in the Lenin Shipyard in Gdańsk and the Warski Shipyard in Szczecin as well as elsewhere. The following opinion is representative of the workers' mood there: "Many of us firmly believed that things had changed and were improving after all that has happened during December. But there is really no change. We complain about further deceptions being perpetrated by the leadership" (quoted in Błażyński 1979, 43).

2. The full list of their demands is available in English in Karpiński (1982a, 164–65).

3. The Szczecin meeting was recorded, and later the tapes were smuggled out of Poland. They were subsequently transcribed and published in *The Szczecin Revolt and Its Significance* (Wacowska 1971), which is unique because it is an uncensored and unpolished record of a meeting of a high-ranking Communist official with a group of citizens. On the 1970 strikes, see Laba (1991) and Goodwyn (1991).

1970 official propaganda in Poland.[4] The regime would use this slogan at critical moments to remind the citizens that they (through their representatives) had declared their commitment to help and thus—as it was interpreted in the media—to support the regime. It was never officially mentioned that on 14 February, when Jaroszewicz met in Łódź with the striking workers (mostly women) and asked them "Will you help?" the answer was no.[5]

The January and February 1971 meetings proved that Gierek was a very skillful producer of his own image and, consequently, of his authority as well. He came across as a young, vigorous, well dressed, modest,[6] and authoritative yet straightforward[7] and informal[8] leader. This image was a positive contrast to Gomułka, who was old, senile, badly dressed, emotional, also authoritative but inaccessible.

Using his initial personal acceptance by many Poles, Gierek managed to build up confidence in his regime, which was further enhanced in 1971–75 by a rapidly growing standard of living.[9] The regime was perceived as effective (or at least as more effective than its predecessors) and therefore achieved some degree of authority. Winning personal acceptance, however, was not Gierek's only objective; from the very beginning of his rule he strove to construct legitimacy for his regime and, by extension, the entire political order. To achieve this goal, Gierek presented himself as a patriot[10] who not only cared about the proper realiza-

4. In 1979 Lech Wałęsa recalled this moment in his speech during an unofficial rally commemorating the 1970 demonstrations and the massacre: "I am one of those who formulated and bear responsibility for the slogan 'We will help.' . . . Today I am in the same situation as all of us who have gathered here. We do not have the monument which Gierek promised us in the shipyard. We must hide and force our way in order to be allowed to honor our colleagues who fell here." (*Robotnik,* 20 December 1979; translated in Lipski 1985, 356).

5. It is interesting that the December 1970 price increases were recalled only after this Łódź strike, on 15 February 1971.

6. Gierek was the first head of the party who requested not to have his portrait displayed either in Party and government offices or in schools.

7. Gierek often referred to his working-class background. For example, he told the strikers: "I am a worker as you are. I worked eighteen years in a mine, down below and— you know—I do not need to be instructed about the problems of the working class" (Wacowska 1971, 32).

8. During the meeting with Szczecin shipyard workers Gierek publicly addressed the other officials present, such as Prime Minister Jaroszewicz or Minister of Internal Affairs Szlachcic, by their first names. This was the first known incident in which a public official addressed his peers in such an informal manner in the history of Communist Poland (Wacowska 1971, 32, 138).

9. According to an official survey (Sufin 1981; reported in Mason 1985, 44) in the first half of the 1970s, people assessed the regime's economic peformance favorably.

10. Whereas Gierek was perceived as a genuine patriot and also a man of the Western European mold (he spent his youth in France and Belgium), who was expected to imple-

tion of socialist ideals but also kept foremost in mind the common good of the whole country and its citizens. In his speeches and discussions with the workers he presented himself as an advocate of economic moderniza-tion, used the words "Poland" and "Poles" frequently, and discoursed on national dignity. The patriotic motif, already present in Gierek's first public address (to the "Compatriots") was later developed to become one of the dominant elements in the official propaganda of the 1970s. Kazimierz Dziewanowski observed that "in his programmatic speech of February 8, 1971, Gierek used the words 'Communism' or 'Communis-tic' only three times; the term 'patriotism' was used twelve times, 'Moth-erland' thirteen, and 'nation' twenty times" (1977, 282).

The first example of this theme of rejuvenated patriotism was Gierek's idea to restore the Royal Castle in Warsaw. On 20 January 1971 Gierek received a group of intellectuals and declared the willingness of his re-gime to rebuild the Castle (destroyed during World War II), which had been regarded by the previous regimes as a symbol of bourgeois Poland (Korybutowicz 1983, 108). Soon, however, the word "Royal" was dropped in most contexts from the official name of the Castle, which became "the Warsaw Castle." Patriotism was acceptable, but only in its socialist version, unpolluted by "royal" or "bourgeois" reminiscences.[11]

Paradoxically, the emphasis on national themes in the official discourse was accompanied by intensified propagation of the internationalistic and orthodox Communist motifs. Already during the Szczecin meeting with the workers Gierek assured the audience that the friendship between the Polish People's Republic and the Soviet Union must not and should not be challenged.[12] Propagation of internationalism as one of the principles of the PZPR had become conspicuous since 1974 when red flags were permanently installed on Party buildings and appeared in the vignettes of Party periodicals (Karpiński 1982a, 170).

There are three aspects of the official public discourse of Gierek's era

---

ment in Poland at least some elements of Western political culture, Jaroszewicz (the prime minister) was seen as a crude, uncultivated Soviet puppet.

11. In 1978, during the celebrations of the sixtieth anniversary of Polish independence in 1918, the following appeared in an editorial in *Trybuna Ludu:* "The history of these sixty years is the history of constant enrichment of the content of the notion of patriotism." In his programmatic speech at the Seventh Congress of the PZPR, the First Secretary Edward Gierek observed that 'Socialism includes intense [*gorące*] love for the Motherland' " (*Trybuna Ludu,* 11 June 1978).

12. During the strikes in 1970, the anonymous song 'A Szczecin Ballad" circulated among the strikers. The song explained that one of reasons of the Szczecin revolt was the fact that "the Pole remembers his struggle [during World War II] for freedom, not for the Soviet shackles" (Wacowska 1971, 214).

that seem to be particularly relevant to a study of legitimacy and authority. They are the introduction of new socialist customs and rites of passage, the official language, and the symbols, ceremonies, and rituals of the official public domain.

New Socialist Customs and Rites of Passage

Massive state ceremonies and rituals can be better understood if we analyze them not only in terms of the relevant economic and political processes but also in the context of the cultural forms of everyday life, such as customs and etiquette, or rites of passage accompanying (or defining) unusual events of the life cycles of individuals.

Totalitarian systems always strive to construct a "new man," to recast the consciousness of the "old man" through new customs, ceremonies, and rituals.[13] The Communist regime in Poland proved no exception in this respect, though it never was as systematic, thorough, or successful as the Nazis had been in Germany or the Soviets had been in Russia. Nevertheless, according to the official point of view, as the result of the emergence of the Marxist-Leninist theory of the social development, the whole realm of customs "acquired new methodological and theoretical foundations":

> The realm of customs first played an instrumental role in the process of class struggle for a change of existing social relationships. By contrast, in the conditions of the socialist states their fundamental role is the realization of the higher human needs through affirmation of human existence and full realization of human potential [upodmiotowienie], which they [customs] also endow with the humanistic sense of existence. (Pełka 1980, 26)

In the 1950s and throughout most of the 1960s, the Bierut and Gomułka regimes set out to restructure the existing cultural forms of social life in Poland, but they concentrated their efforts on the expansion of the official public domain and its major rituals, such as the parades on May Day and on the anniversaries of the October Revolution. The ceremonials of the private and religious domains were censored out of existence in the offi-

13. This process is systematically described in Lane (1981) and Lasswell (1949) for the Soviet Union and in Mosse (1975) for Germany.

cial media, but because they were supported by the family and the Church, their basic structure and content remained intact.

The Party-state launched a more systematic program to remodel national customs in 1964–65. These efforts were concentrated on the rites of passage (Pełka 1980, 76). The *Towarzystwo Krzewienia Kultury Świeckiej* (Society for the Promotion of Secular Culture, or TKKŚ, founded in 1969) replaced the *Towarzystwo Szkoły Świeckiej* (the Society for the Secular School operating since 1957), to promote secular, that is, socialist or Communist customs and ceremonies.[14] According to Władysław Bieńkowski:

> The founders [of the Society for the Secular School] . . . were almost exclusively the employees of the security forces and the party apparatus dismissed during the October turnabout. . . . The Society became gradually the second, "party [controlled]" ministry of education, supported by local party committees against the educational authorities and using this support to organize various acts of [antireligious] diversion.[15]

Gierek's regime increased the pace of centrally administered desacralization, claiming that it was only giving organized form to already existing processes of spontaneous desacralization of social life in Poland.[16] According to Leonard Pełka, an observer expressing the official view of the Party, "the last decade [the 1970s] brought a dynamic increase of the social demand for more expressive and richer forms of ritualization of the public and private life. The fact of the revelation of such a demand became in turn

14. The Society for the Secular School was created "to promote the rules of socialist secular upbringing and education. The main aim of the society is propagation of the rules of socialist pedagogy, especially concerning moral education" (*Wielka Encyklopedia Powszechna*, 11:607). In 1969 it was united with the Society of Atheists and Free Thinkers. The new organization was called the Society for the Promotion of Secular Culture. "It is an ideological and educational organization, whose aim is to actively participate in the shaping and developing of the socialist secular culture in Poland; in the promotion of secular morality, customs and the rational worldview based on the achievements of science." The society was to be based on the cooperation of believers and nonbelievers (*Mała Encyklopedia Powszechna*, 1077).

15. Bieńkowski was the minister of education during this period. Later, disillusioned with the official policies, he became one of the most outspoken critics of the Communist regime. The fragment quoted comes from his *Socjologia Klęski* (A sociology of defeat, 1971). I am quoting here from Michnik (1977, 49).

16. Following Daniel Bell I propose to distinguish two processes: *secularization* and *desacralization*. Secularization refers to an institutional process whereby the secular and the religious (including political organizations, domains of influence, power, even art) move further and further apart. Desacralization refers to the decreasing role of the religious worldview(s) in the modern culture. Weber called this process *disenchantment*.

the essential impulse to develop actions in the domain of working out the socialist model of national customs" (Pełka 1980, 71).[17] Whether or not this observation is correct, it can be viewed as an indication of the Party's readiness to step up its campaign to reshape Polish culture according to "the socialist model of national customs." Pełka criticized the authorities, especially those in Bierut's and Gomułka's regimes, for not fully taking into account "the instrumental role of secular customs in the realization of the program of the building of the developed socialist society." According to Pełka, this failure was the result of a mistaken view that secular customs and rituals are ludic and recreational, whereas they should be seen as "specific symbols of public and private life which carry certain weight as vehicles of [a certain] worldview and constitute a form of expression of a certain social message" (Pełka 1980, 72).

Family customs and ceremonies. These are the customs and ceremonies that accompany births, weddings, birthdays, namedays, wedding anniversaries, and celebrations of important events in the lives of family members, such as graduations, work promotions, achievements of scholarly titles, and the bestowal of public recognition (for example, in the form of medals or orders).

Writing about the 1970s, Pełka observed that the rich and varied customs and ceremonies related to family life contained "numerous traditional, even religious, elements" (1980, 77). He seems to be aware, therefore, that his categorization of these ceremonies as "socialist" is problematic. In the Polish People's Republic, including the time of Gierek's regime, the private domain became the major source of an individual's identification and the most vigorous area of social life.[18] Accordingly, family customs and ceremonies retained, if not strengthened, their private character (especially in urban areas); and although in many families they became desacralized, they did not acquire any features that could be referred to as "socialist." I participated in countless family celebrations, including several weddings within the families of Party officials, and never observed any significant transposition of customary forms of behavior from the official public

17. Official views were usually expressed in what I call the *language of propaganda*. This language (found also in popular publications, including the one I am quoting here), was characteristic of all official enunciations and although it becomes in literal translation even more convoluted than in the original I decided to provide the reader with some (approximate) instances of this linguistic formation.

18. See Nowak (1981, 51) and Wedel (1986). In Poland (and, as much as I can determine, in other totalitarian or authoritarian states) this normative and practical separation of the private domain was more pronounced than in the Western democracies, where many of the premises, norms, and customs of the official public domain are also valid in the private domain.

domain to the private one. It was, for example, unthinkable to sing "The International" at a family ceremony, whereas the singing of religious hymns, although infrequent, was deemed proper. The clearly delineated private domain, reflected (as it always does) certain premises, norms, and customs of the official and unofficial public domains; but they were predominantly religious and patriotic in provenance, not socialist.

Official rites of passage. This group includes such public state-organized rites of passage as the ritual of name-giving, the ritual of the first personal identity card,[19] the secular (or as it is called—civil) wedding, the farewell ceremony for new conscripts and the welcome ceremony for those discharged from the army, the twenty-fifth and the fiftieth wedding anniversaries, and the secular funeral.

This group of customs and rituals became in the 1970s a battlefield between the state and the Catholic Church. On 20 February 1976, the Third Plenum of the Central Committee of the PZPR accepted the resolution concerning "the necessity of increasing the significance of various events of family and private life."[20] Eight days later the Council of Ministers issued an executive directive concerning ceremonial forms that should accompany changes in the civil status of citizens. In order to expedite the implementation of these regulations, clerks employed by the Office of Civil Status were discretely urged to try to organize as many secular ceremonies as possible. Depending on how many such ceremonies were organized outside of regular working hours, a clerk could earn a bonus of up to 600 zloty a month, between 20 and 30 percent of his or her monthly salary (Gancarz 1979).

The state strove to create a system of public rituals to correspond to, if not replace, the religious ceremonies. The *ceremony of name-giving* was the secular counterpart of baptism; the *institution of honorary guardians*,[21] of godparents; the *personal identity card ritual,* of confirmation. Even penance was recreated in the Party ceremonial, taking the form of *individual conver-*

19. Every citizen of Poland, on reaching the age of eighteen, received a personal identity card (passport), which contained a picture and a record of one's place and date of birth, height, color of eyes, place of residence, history of employment, and (in the case of males) a history of military service.

20. In Gierek's words, "We need to popularize such customary forms of behavior which are based on the social values of socialism. This refers to human interactions in working collectives, in family life, in the living place, in leisure and rest" (*Nowe Drogi,* March 1976, 17).

21. Lane reports that in the Soviet Union such "secular godparents" were variously called Honorary Parents, Name Parents (*Nazvannye roditeli*), or *Krestnye roditeli,* which Lane renders as Godparents. This last name was acceptable to the authorities, I suppose, since it means literally (as in Polish) "Baptismal Parents," and thus does not contain reference to God (1981, 69).

sations and *public self-criticisms.* Tellingly, a concerted campaign, variously called *laicyzacja* (secularization) or *ateizacja* (atheization—this term was used by the Episcopate[22]), was coordinated by the Ministry of Internal Affairs—another proof of the high significance the desacralization campaign had for the authorities, who announced that "we should strive to achieve a situation in which at least every third child is named in an Office of Civil Status and one funeral in ten is secular" (Gancarz 1979). The state treated these new customs very seriously; censors were instructed not to allow publication of any materials "making fun of the secular ceremonies of name-giving, weddings, etc., and propagandistic efforts concerned with their popularization" (*Czarna Księga Cenzury PRL* 1977, 1:110).

The secular ceremony of name-giving was first introduced in the late 1960s in Opole and Wrocław. These events took place in the finest hall of the Office of Civil Status. It consisted of three parts: the introduction, the solemn declaration (largo), and the farewell.[23] During the introduction all present were seated, and the master of ceremonies cited the welcoming oration reminding everybody that "in the life of each family and those closest to it there are events of particular significance which, according to age-old custom, should be observed in a particularly festive manner" (Ciołek, Olędzki, and Zadrożyńska 1976, 213). The birth of a child was pronounced to be such an event. Then everyone was supposed to rise. The master of ceremonies put the national emblem (the White Eagle) on his chest and asked the parents to repeat the following formula: "We solemnly declare that our child born on . . . is given the name(s). . . . At the same time we pledge that we will exercise our parental authority in such a way as it is necessary for the good of our child and for the good of our Motherland, the Polish People's Republic" (Ciołek, Olędzki, and Zadrożyńska 1976, 213). Then the honorary guardians were asked to accept the duty of taking care of the child and giving him or her moral support "when such a need arises."

According to statistics quoted by Pełka (1980, 178) the name-giving ceremony became more common, slowly at first, but much more quickly in the early 1970s.[24] Still, with the exception of secular marriages (required by the law), secular ceremonies and rituals never became uni-

22. The Polish Episcopate distinguished between *laicyzacja,* a spontaneous process roughly equivalent to Bell's category of desacralization, and *ateizacja,* a planned and directed process of secularization and desacralization.

23. A fictionalized yet very accurate account of a similar ceremony in Czechoslovakia can be found in Milan Kundera's novel, *The Joke* (1983, 142–49).

24. Pełka gives the following figures for the Białystok district: 7,451 secular namegivings in 1969; 9,662 in 1970; 12,951 in 1971; 14,028 in 1972; and 21,609 in 1973 (1980, 178).

formly popular; according to another observer less than 2 percent of all citizens participated in them (Gancarz 1979).[25]

The establishment of new ceremonies and rituals by administrative fiat is always very difficult; it is particularly challenging in the case of funerals.[26] Like their colleagues in the Soviet Union, Polish specialists on secular rituals began working on the establishment of a secular funeral rite for ordinary citizens relatively late.[27] The initial attempts to create such a rite began in Wrocław, where in 1967 the first master of the funeral ceremony started his work (Ciołek, Olędzki, and Zadrożyńska 1976, 244). A script for such a rite was published in 1971 in *Argumenty,* a weekly published by the TKKŚ, and served as a model for secular funerals around the country.[28]

The secular funeral was modeled on its religious counterpart. The priest was replaced by the master of the funeral ceremony, who was responsible for the entire rite and made the farewell speech, which was usually prepared with the help of the deceased's family. Maciej Ciołek, Jacek Olędzki, and Anna Zadrożyńska observe that secular funerals lacked both the solemnity and the philosophical or ideological integrity of the religious rite. In the Christian funeral the basic equality of all people in the face of God is confirmed; there is only one scenario, which is more or less conspicuous depending on a family's finances, but which remains uniform in structure and meaning. By contrast, in the 1970s in Poland there were several types of the secular funeral. The degree of ceremonial elaboration was proportional to one's merit as defined by the Party-state. Such an arrangement obviously contradicted the otherwise often pronounced "socialist" ideological principle of the basic equality of all citizens.

A few final observations. In a situation of free competition between various philosophical, religious, and political creeds, the choice of a secu-

25. In Poland only secular marriage was considered legally binding by the state. Most couples, therefore, had two weddings, a secular wedding in the Office of Civil Status and a religious one in a church. The Catholic Church also controls firmly the rites of passage in some of the countries where desacralization seems to be more advanced than in Poland. In early 1970s in Albora, a predominantly Communist district of Bologna, Italy, "almost all communists [had] their children baptized," the overwhelming majority of weddings were religious, and only about 15 percent of all Communist funerals were carried out without a priest's participation (Kertzer 1980, 135–43).

26. Christel Lane quotes a Soviet expert who admits that "conducting a socialist funeral rite is considered to be a very difficult task" (1981, 82).

27. In the Soviet Union the first efforts to create such rites were undertaken in the mid sixties and early seventies (Lane 1981, 82).

28. A slightly shortened version of this script is reprinted in Ciołek, Olędzki, and Zadrożyńska (1976, 301–7).

lar ceremony over a religious one indicates an allegiance to, or at least partial sympathy for, a secular worldview and a non- or areligious (be it Communist, socialist, liberal, or any other) political orientation or oganization. As David Kertzer's (1980) study on Albora, Italy, shows, such choices can be difficult and are not always consistently followed through. A person will often participate in both Communist and Catholic rituals because of the social and psychological pressures characteristic of either unstable transitory periods or closely knit communities with a high degree of social conformism. This is genuine confusion: a result of spontaneous social processes. In Poland after the 1970s, where such purely social mechanisms of confusion also appeared, participation in secular state-organized rites of passage cannot be interpreted simplistically as an indicator of the acceptance of the official ideology and politics. Undoubtedly, there were genuine Communists (or socialists) who participated in such ceremonies precisely because they wanted to express publicly their political and ideological allegiance. These were people who often belonged to or sympathized with the Communist party before World War II. I knew a few of them. My neighbor was one such person. A firm believer in Communism, she would never consider attending a Church ceremony, and during such family rites as weddings, baptisms, or funerals she participated only in civil rites and never joined the rest of the family in Church.

Most of the people who took part in secular rituals of the life cycle organized by the state did so for one or more of the following four reasons: (1) because it was legally required (as in the case of marriage), (2) because they were not religious (though they might have also been indifferent to the official ideology), (3) because they wanted to please their superiors in order to achieve some objective (for example, a promotion) unrelated to the manifest meaning of the ceremony, or (4) because they simply enjoyed participation in unusual, often colorful, events, regardless of their ideological underpinnings.[29]

Christopher Binns argues that it is precisely this last motivation which accounts for a high degree of participation in secular rituals in the Soviet Union (1980, 176). He claims, furthermore, that the main features of the new ceremonial system developed in the Soviet Union in the late 1950s and the 1960s were "centrifugal rather than centripetal; that is, whatever the regime's intentions of extending its ideological control into family life and leisure, the actual conduct of these ceremonies has given expression to, and thereby encouraged, pluralism, individualism and consumerism,

29. Even highly formalized and tightly controlled mass demonstrations in Cuba "permit joyful occurrences" (Aguirre 1984, 561).

which undermine a centralist ideology" (1980, 183). I do not believe this interpretation is complete with regard to the Soviet Union, nor that it applies to Poland. People have needs that I believe are more basic than the need to express individualism or consumerism,[30] namely, the need to endow the surrounding world with meaning and the need to play and enjoy the company of others. If a people are allowed neither to follow their "traditional" ways nor to choose their own means of expressing their needs, they will inevitably saturate the cultural forms available to them with their own emotions, meanings, and values. Such seems to have been the case of pre-Gorbachev Soviet Russia. In Poland, however, the state did not replace the Church ceremonial with its own, and people did not need to saturate state ceremonies, rituals, and holidays with their own meanings. They continued to observe their "own" ceremonies, including religious rituals. As a result the state ceremonial was "emptier" and less popular than in Soviet Russia. Subsequently, its ability to serve as a legitimizing device for the Communist regime was lower in Poland than in Russia.

The Language of Propaganda

Of all social and humanistic disciplines, linguistics has produced the most systematic and detailed body of knowledge about human behavior, probably because language is easier to analyze formally than other aspects of culture are. Studies done on the official language in Poland are a case in point. At least five small volumes and several articles analyzing various aspects of the Polish version of Communist Newspeak have already been published.[31] They not only provide a rich and well-documented picture of the official language but also serve as a heuristic model for the analysis of other types of the official discourse, such as ceremonies and rituals.

The major difference between political propaganda in Communist countries and in Western democracies is not to be found in the political languages used by these systems but in the state monopoly of the means of communication and strict preventive state censorship in the East and its lack in the West. In the 1970s in Poland every printed text (including bus tickets) had to be approved by the *Główny Urząd Kontroli Prasy,*

30. Needs are shaped during the process of socialization in a given culture; their biological substratum, though not insignificant, is rarely decisive in this process.

31. Głowiński (1979, 1991), Karpiński (1984), *Nowo-mowa* (1985), and Wierzbicki (1986).

Publikacji i Widowisk (Main Office for the Control of the Press, Publications, and Public Performances, or GUKPPiW).[32]

This major institutional difference notwithstanding, the language of propaganda in Communist countries, including Poland, differs also from its Western counterpart in its *two-valued orientation* and its *arbitrariness*.[33]

Two-valued orientation.[34] Many elements of the language of propaganda, especially its basic political terms, are assigned unequivocal values, usually in terms of a positive/negative dichotomy. Since the audience in a non-democratic country is exposed only to one uniform discourse (guarded by state monopoly and preventive censorship), the probability of successfully establishing the official evaluations in the minds of the people is much higher than in democratic countries, where people are exposed to various (often contradictory) evaluations of the same phenomenon. Here are examples of such pairs from the Polish version of this discourse (including Gierek's era):

partyzant (partisan)—*bandyta* (bandit)

A member of an armed resistance deemed ideologically correct and friendly was a *partyzant*. A member of a hostile resistance was a *bandyta*.[35]

pomoc (help or assistance)—*agresja* (agression)

32. The rules lying behind the censors's decisions were revealed when Tomasz Strzyżewski, a censor from Kraków, defected to the West, taking with him extensive documentation illustrating the type of work he did. See *The Black Book of Polish Censorship* (Curry 1984). I cite the English version as Curry (1984) and the Polish original as *Czarna Księga Cenzury PRL* (1977).

33. Students of the official languages of Communist and fascist states do not agree on what to call them (Newspeak is a frequent option) or on their basic characteristics. I have chosen a rather neutral term: the language of propaganda, since its purely linguistic characteristics are present in the propagandistic discourses of many, not only undemocratic, states. My two categories include the most often mentioned characteristics of the language of propaganda.

34. The term *two-valued orientation* was coined by Alfred Korzybski (1933). It is well described in Hayakawa (1978, 210–25).

35. A comparison with the congressional hearings on the Iran-contra affair is illuminating. Referring to Nicaraguan anti-Sandinista resistance, Colonel North and most of the Republicans used the term *freedom fighters*. Most of the Democrats referred to the same people as *contras* (a term that carries more derogatory connotations). People watching the hearings, exposed to a discourse utilizing both terms, were able to judge for themselves which designation was more adequate. Such a possibility did not exist in the official media in Poland. The official discourse would contain only one term (undoubtedly some equivalent of contras, perhaps *bandyci*) to designate Nicaraguan armed opposition.

Armed intervention by a friendly nation (for example the Soviet invasion of Czechoslovakia in 1968 or of Afghanistan in 1979) was called *pomoc* (assistance, usually friendly). Armed intervention by a country of the opposite ideological camp (for example the U.S. intervention in Grenada) was called *agresja* (aggression).

bony—kartki

Both these terms mean "food coupons." The latter term was, however, rarely utilized in reference to the rationing system of the Polish People's Republic, because, I suppose, it had been used during the German occupation of 1939–45 (negative reality) and could not therefore be applied to the postwar situation (positive reality).

porozumienia (accords)—knowania (machinations)

The results of negotiations between entities officially regarded as friendly to the Polish People's Republic, or between the Polish People's Republic and a friendly entity, for example the Socialist Republic of Czechoslovakia, were called *porozumienia*. Similar negotiations between two unfriendly entities, or the results of any negotiations deemed unfavorable for the Polish People's Republic were usually referred to as *knowania*.

The Polish language of propaganda used three rhetorical strategies to make rejection of its embedded evaluations more difficult. First, the sender of the message (the Party or the government) employed phrases suggesting the existence of a prior agreement between himself and the receiver (the populace). Phrases such as "We all know," "It is obvious that," and "No one doubts that" are common examples. Second, some slogans were formulated in such a way that even if negated they still conveyed a message that was favorable for the sender. A very popular slogan: "A tie between the Party and the masses is the source of our success" can serve as an example. Negating this phrase ("A tie between the Party and the masses is *not* the source of our success") still confirms the basic message that "we" are or were a success. Third, some slogans were difficult to refute because they contained no verbs: for example, "The Nation with the Party," and "Katowice Steelworks the Steel Pillar of the People's Poland." Such a phrase negated, "The Nation *not* with the Party," does not make much sense. Moreover, such slogans, because they lacked verbs, created confusion, since it was not clear whether they were normative (The Nation *should* be with the Party) or descriptive (The Nation *is* with the Party). Consequently, the audience's ability to distinguish illusion from reality was blunted.

Arbitrariness of vocabulary and phraseology. The vocabulary of a language of propaganda is limited in comparison with that of a natural language[36] (Bednarczuk 1985). Unlike a natural language, a language of propaganda accompanies and indeed constitutes traditional authority.[37] To do this it must be selective in respect to words and phrases. Certain words are *taboo* and are never or rarely used, others appear with high frequency. The names of certain authors were unmentionable or could be mentioned only in selected, clearly defined contexts. For many years, for example, the name of Czesław Miłosz, a great poet and a Nobel Prize winner, could not be mentioned even in arcane literary journals. For generations, many streets in Polish towns were named after Catholic saints, thus such names as "Saint Andrzej Street," or "Saint Jan Street," were common. The word "saint" was dropped and now these streets were called instead "Jan Street" and "Andrzej Street."[38]

Another example of the arbitrariness of a language of propaganda, closely related to its double-valued orientation, is the creation of counterphrases, which are designed to neutralize phrases that undermine the vision of reality constructed by the authorities. In the 1970s, according to this rule, any mention of civil and human rights[39] was countered by the reference to "the right to live in peace," which was, according to the

36. The notion of the natural language is the necessary logical complement of the notion of the language of propaganda. Natural languages are spontaneously created, sustained, and modified by social groups without any *systematic* outside interference.

37. See Bloch (1974, 1985).

38. A spectacular example of a related linguistic "invention" comes from Gomułka's regime; and although it does not fall within the scope of this book, it illustrates well the way of thinking of many Party officials responsible for culture. Miners' Day is traditionally celebrated on December 4 under the patronage of Saint Barbara (this story was reported in an underground publication *Głos Łodzi* [The voice of Łódź], 2 December 1984). The popular name of the holiday is *Barburka,* a diminutive of "Barbara." In 1965, as Gomułka engaged in a fierce struggle with the Episcopate over their conciliatory letter to the German bishops, a group of linguists and historians related to the Central Committee of the PZPR invented a proto-Slavic prince Barbor to whom the tradition of Barburka (now spelled Barbórka) was allegedly traceable. In the Polish language there are two forms of the phoneme *u.* One is spelled *u,* another *ó. Ó* is an allophone of *o.* If indeed the name of the holiday had actually been traceable to Prince Barbor, its name should have been spelled Barbórka (not Barburka) and thus its relationship with Saint Barbara would have been proved unfounded. The press was advised to use the newly "discovered" proper spelling; and although not all journalists followed the recommendation, the newspapers began using both forms. The miners however never accepted this new linguistic convention; and when after August 1980 they gained a measure of freedom, figures of Saint Barbara returned to the mines and the name of the holiday returned to its traditional spelling.

39. This subject was often brought up by the oppositional groups and the Church, especially after the Helsinki Conference on Security and Cooperation and because of the constant reference to it by the Carter administration (1977–80).

official media, constantly defended by the Soviet bloc countries but not by Western democracies, especially the United States. Similarly, during the Solidarity period, the official media often counterbalanced texts containing the word *solidarność* (solidarity) by inserting the word *odpowiedzialność* (responsibility), suggesting thereby that members and supporters of Solidarity should behave in a more responsible way, that is, according to the rules laid down by the Party.

Languages of propaganda are also *ritualistic,* in the sense that certain words and phrases occur in them with high frequency in easily predictable contexts. Here are some examples. In Gierek's era the word "democracy" was rarely used without further qualification. Usually one could read about "socialist democracy," often described as real and full-fledged, as opposed to its inferior "Western" or "bourgeois" counterpart. Such an inferiority was often indicated by the use of "so-called." A visit by an official from another Communist country was rarely referred to as just a "visit"; usually it was a "friendly visit." The adjective *pokojowe* (peaceful) was followed with high frequency by the two words, *inicjatywy* (initiatives) or *współżycie* (coexistence).

The arbitrariness of such discourse was also evident in the manipulation of euphemisms and hyperboles (Głowiński 1979; Głowiński 1991, 15). Negative phenomena in Poland or other Soviet bloc countries were described in terms of euphemisms diminishing their significance, whereas the significance of positive phenomena was exaggerated by the frequent use of hyperboles. In reports from Western countries the reverse strategy was employed. Negative aspects of Western reality were inflated and positive aspects diminished. Thus, for example, serious crises in Poland were often referred to as "temporary troubles" and marginal successes were often of "historical significance." Western countries, in turn, did not suffer from "temporary troubles," but were instead in a state of constant crisis.

Periphrasis was another frequently used stylistic device of the language of propaganda.[40] As with other figures and tropes, the occurrence of certain periphrases in the official language of the Polish media was highly systematic and easily predictable. Thus in the 1970s, the PZPR was always "a leading chapter of the working class" or "a leading force of society building socialism."[41] Germans, resettled from the western parts of Poland after World War II, who voiced their discontent were always referred to as the *kręgi odwetowe* (revengeful circles).

---

40. Michał Głowiński, a highly respected Polish theoretician and historian of literature, holds that periphrasis is the basic figure of the Polish language of propaganda (1979, 1991).

41. This formulation was even included in the Constitution of the Polish People's Republic.

When for ideological or tactical reasons Party journalists or their superiors did not want to name people, actions, or processes, the language of propaganda offered a whole repertoire of periphrases. Among the most often used words were *pewni* (certain), *określone* (definite), and *wiadome* (known). The most popular phrases were: "certain people," "certain circles," or "certain problems." Interestingly, the first two phrases are pejorative—those "certain people or circles" were engaged in some activities, against the interests of the Polish people, as defined by the Party. In the third case "certain" can be replaced by "insignificant"; the phrase was used to describe our problems ("their" problems were usually "serious" or "constant"). "People," "circles," or "problems" in the above examples were not specified in order to prevent the audience from realizing that perhaps they were not as suspicious (bad) or insignificant as it was claimed by the media. What is more important, use of these phrases suggested the existence of a common ground between the sender and the receiver. The Party winked at its audience saying, "We do not need to specify what we are talking about; we *all* know it."

Modes of operation and functions of the language of propaganda. In the language of propaganda the communicative function tends to be subordinated to other functions to a degree not found in natural languages. It is a tool of the *monologue* of the authorities directed at the populace, and not an instrument of a *dialogue* between them. Its low information value, a product of its arbitrariness and ritualism, both results from and reinforces this monologic tendency. Thus it tends to be not a mode of communication but a tool for persuasion and manipulation.

Persuasion. There is no agreement among students of propaganda whether persuasion is its basic mode of operation. It differs, for example, from the languages of persuasion used in advertising. Those languages (or discourses—they employ a variety of nonverbal signs) are extremely flexible and constantly change in order to fulfill their major function: to sell something. The language of propaganda, in contrast, is rigid and whatever it sells it does not sell very well. If we assume that it is trying to sell legitimacy, it is possible to argue that it does so reasonably well during the initial stages of revolutionary mobilization, but very poorly under more stable circumstances.

There can be no doubt, however, that regardless of its effectiveness, the language of propaganda is often employed to persuade at least some segments of the audiences to which it is addressed; the Communist regimes use this function to persuade its supporters that everything is in order.

Manipulation. Whereas persuasion is a technique for constructing authority, manipulation is a direct exercise of power, since, by definition, the person being manipulated is not aware of this fact. Language, which furnishes people with the categories they use to build their models of reality, is the most powerful tool of manipulation. In *1984* George Orwell envisioned an extreme case of language manipulation, which, significantly, was possible not only because of the inherent features of Newspeak but also because of the totalitarian character of the society. It was a perfectly closed society with an absolute monopoly by the state over the means of communication. Such an ideal has never been realized, though Hitler's Germany and Stalin's Russia came very close.

In Gierek's Poland the manipulative function of the language of propaganda was not easily achieved because society was not perfectly atomized (family and friendship ties were strong); the Church continued a dialogue with the people in a different discourse; and the oppositional groups articulated their own vision of the world and were able to reach a constantly growing audience, especially after 1976.

Persuasion and manipulation can be defined as the basic modes of operation in a language of propaganda. Within these two basic modes several more specific functions can be pinpointed.

The language of propaganda as verbal noise. For many experts, one of the main purposes and actual functions of a language of propaganda is to clog society's channels of communication. As a special tool of manipulation, propaganda is nothing more than a verbal noise, a stream of words and phrases whose meaning is irrelevant but which prevent people from communicating and clearly articulating their own views, ideas, convictions, or beliefs. Thus even when a language of propaganda is not effective in realizing its other functions, it can still be highly efficient in obstructing social communication. One can even venture a sociological generalization: the higher the saturation of a society's channels of communication with the language of propaganda, the greater the probability of the emergence of apathy as a predominant social mood. Other forms of language are eliminated or contained—they appear in elite publications and are cultivated only in the private lives of citizens.

The language of propaganda as magic. Because the language of propaganda is unusually effective in creating an artificial reality or—as Walter Lipmann called it—a pseudoenvironment, it has often been called magical.[42] The verbal world is often seen as a more or less adequate *map* of the extensional world (Korzybski 1933; Hayakawa 1978, 25–28). The higher

---

42. For example, when in 1935, after murdering millions of people in the Ukrainian famine and Moscow purges, Stalin declared that "Zhit' stalo luchshe, zhit' stalo veselee" ("Life has become better, life has become more joyous"), he indeed engaged in an act of creation.

the degree of homology between such a map and its *territory,* the part of
the world to which it refers, the greater the individual's or group's chance
to succeed in the world. This fit is never perfect, high in some languages,
low in others. In the language of propaganda it is very low. In countries
where such language dominates public communication, people reporting
to the authorities often have no choice but to use it. As a result the
authorities themselves have trouble discovering the "real" situation. For
instance, the unexpected price increases in 1976, which triggered workers' protests, puzzled many observers, because Gierek came to power on
the wave of a similar public discontent in 1970. And yet he repeated a
mistake of his predecessor, defying the laws of rational decision making
in politics. Perhaps, this irrational decision resulted from the collapse of
communication based on the language (propagated by the authorities for
political and ideological reasons) that served to create rather than describe
reality. In such a language, the proper (or at least reasonably close) description and assessment of the situation as well as communication of the
results of an inquiry became impossible.

The language of propaganda as a social marker. Another important function of the language of propaganda is to establish the social boundaries of
the elite. It serves both as a *social marker* and as a *badge of loyalty*
(Bednarczuk 1985, 36), allowing the members of the elite to recognize
each other and notice aspirants. It is worth remembering, however, that
constant exposure to the language of propaganda often leads to the inter-
nalization of its rules and phraseology to such a degree that public officials are unable to use any other idiom even in private conversations or in
such contexts where it is clearly inappropriate.

Since in Poland the language of propaganda was not widely accepted as a
medium of communication outside the specific sectors of the official domain (such as, for example, Party meetings), I observed that the people
who used it in other contexts inadvertently displayed their social identity,
which, perhaps, they would have preferred to hide in order to avoid
ridicule or isolation. In 1982 I served as the secretary of a committee
interviewing potential students for a prominent Polish university. Martial
law was in full force. A prospective student answered brilliantly during the
oral part of his examination, and the committee was just about to let him
go when a representative of the Party stopped him and said: "Your answers
were really good, but would you mind interpreting for us the events you
described from a 'class' point of view?" After a brief moment of hesitation
the student replied: "And you must be representing the Communist party
on this committee." The others on the committee were unable to hide their
amusement, and a burst of laughter followed the departing student. A few
years earlier, no one would have dared to laugh aloud—the Party represen-

tative's question would have been treated as normal and routine. But despite the imposition of martial law, in the summer of 1982, the Communist party's ability to secure the obedience of citizens, at least at this university, was destroyed. Instead of confirming the Party representative's power, this routine question subjected him to ridicule.

Symbols of the Official Public Domain

A new political regime, to gain legitimacy, can either root itself in the domain of national symbols, that is, it can incorporate its image—its own symbols and emblems—into the existing symbolic discourse(s) of the society, or it can remodel the nation's traditional symbolic universe by destroying key symbols and substituting new ones.[43] The second solution, in its extreme version—destruction of the old symbols and the creation of the new—is costly and difficult, if not impossible. Symbols, the most subtle and powerful regulators of thought and action, cannot be imposed by force, law, or administrative fiat. They usually arise and evolve spontaneously. Signs and emblems newly imposed by the authorities or collectively constructed do not become symbols until they are spontaneously accepted by those for whom they are created.

Cognizant of this, the Communist regime in Poland relied mostly on the tactic of gradually remodeling the national symbolic domain. Those national symbols and values that did not obviously contradict the new Communist creed were retained. At the same time, by means of more or less overt manipulation, the regime tried to reshape this symbolic domain to incorporate its own symbols. The most graphic example of the reshaping of a national symbol was the removal of the White Eagle's crown from the national emblem. The crowned White Eagle had been the symbol of Poland for centuries.[44] "After the liberation in 1945"—according to the *Grand Popular Encyclopedia*—"the crown was removed in order to evoke the traditions of progressive and revolutionary Polish movements of the nineteenth and twentieth centuries."[45] Presumably, with the

---

43. As I pointed out in first chapter, it can also accept the existing culture of the nation, but such a solution must eventually lead to the erosion of the regime's identity and its subsequent loss of power.

44. The White Eagle as the emblem of rulers appeared on coins in the twelfth century. In 1222 it was used on the seal and the shield of Kazimierz, prince of Opole. The crowned eagle was used for the first time by Przemysł the Second during his coronation.

45. Such philosophical and ideological decisions of seemingly fundamental significance can prove to be purely tactical. In January 1982, Janusz Przymanowski, an army colonel,

crown's removal, the Eagle no longer stood for the class society of pre-war Poland, but for the classless society of the Polish People's Republic. Probably it was further assumed that the workers—who according to some Marxist doctrines do not possess homelands and are loosely, if at all, attached to national symbols—would welcome this crownless eagle as a symbol of their victory. Interestingly, however, on several occasions when workers rose in protest their banners incorporated the image of the White Eagle recrowned.[46]

The national colors, white-and-red, remained intact, although they had to compete for domination in the official decor with the red color of the state ideology.[47] In 1974 red flags became permanent fixtures on all party buildings. The national anthem, beginning with the words "Poland is not lost as long as we live," was also retained and more often heard than "The International."

Gierek's regime made sure, through a series of constitutional, legal, and political changes, that the status quo political order was reinforced. It also intensified the propagation of Communist ideology. At the same time, however, it strove to improve the Polish self-image and cultivate national pride. Warsaw Castle became perhaps the major symbol of the new socialist patriotism, carefully separated from older forms of patrio-tism (now called nationalism), which were not sufficiently infused with socialist overtones. The new reality, which supposedly was "socialist in content and national in form," was to be accepted, not discussed.[48]

"Socialist patriotism" was epitomized in the leading slogans of the Gierek era, "Polak potrafi" (The Pole can) and "Budujemy drugą Polskę" (We are building a Second Poland), which were repeated ad nauseam. The "Second Poland" motif was also symbolized by the Katowice Steel-works, which became the principal material emblem of the Gierek era of technocratic pragmatism.

In the countries of "real socialism," the construction of gigantic indus-trial enterprises was meant to accomplish two objectives. Pragmatically, such enterprises were the primary means of accelerated industrialization

---

writer, journalist, and the representative to the Sejm, proposed to restore the crown on the Eagle's head "in order to emphasize the sovereignty of socialist Poland."

46. By the decree of the Solidarity-controlled parliament the crown was restored on 1 January 1990.

47. White-and-red banners were used by Polish armies for the first time in the seven-teenth century. In 1831 the parliament officially designated them the national colors.

48. Discussions on national and international versions of socialism were usually unpub-lishable. For example, an article on Bolesław Limanowski, a leading Polish socialist at the turn of the twentieth century, who developed the idea of patriotic socialism, was barred from publication (*Czarna Księga Cenzury PRL* 1977, 2:16–17).

and urbanization; symbolically, they stood for the prowess of socialism and its superiority over capitalism.[49] The Katowice Steelworks were to be a monument of Polish economic achievement and technological progress (Gierek's economists often assured the nation that Poland has already entered the elite of the world's economic powers) and also as an ultimate emblem of the Polish-Soviet friendship. Leonid Brezhnev, first secretary of the CPSU, received the Katowice Steelworks's ID number one.[50] The purity of this symbol was, however, tarnished by the constant grumbling by some people that the construction of the wide-gauge (Soviet standard) railroad track, extending some 150 miles from the Soviet border to the steelworks, was dictated by military calculations, not by lofty friendship.[51]

The construction of this gigantic enterprise, whose economic justification was questioned by many independent economists, was the subject of countless newspaper articles and radio and TV shows.[52] In April 1976 the Department of the Press, Radio, and Television of the Central Committee sent the censors classified instructions regulating in great detail how the Katowice Steelworks was to be portrayed by the media:

> As the first stage of contruction approaches its final phase, the propagandistic action should be intensified. . . . The theme of the construction of the Katowice Steelworks, taken up so far only occasionally, must find its permanent place [in the media]. Formation of permanent sections or cyclical assignment of certain columns to this theme is desired. (*Czarna Księga Cenzury PRL* 1977, 1:233)

The Katowice Steelworks, the second gigantic endeavor in the postwar history of Polish metallurgy came to symbolize the "Second Poland"; the "First" had its own emblem: the Lenin Steelworks in Nowa Huta, which celebrated its twenty-fifth anniversary in 1974. The press was full of commemorative articles emphasizing that the Lenin Steelworks were "significant proof of the brotherly cooperation of Poland and the Soviet Union

49. Magnitogorsk, for example, a gigantic Soviet iron and steel plant founded in 1929, "instantly became the symbol of the revolutionary remaking of society that the October revolution had promised" (Kotkin 1991, xxi).

50. Brezhnev visited Poland in July 1974 to participate in the celebrations of the thirtieth anniversary of Polish People's Republic. During this visit he also received the title of *The Honorary Miner of the Polish People's Republic* and the Great Cross of *Virtuti Militari* Order, the highest Polish military decoration.

51. Such discontent was quite widespread despite the ban on mentioning this new railroad in the media (Curry 1984, 259).

52. Some titles (and reports) were almost poetic. See, for example, Stanisław Broszkiewicz's "Robota jak koncert" (Work is like a concert) (*Trybuna Robotnicza,* 10–11 August 1974).

and of a creative realization of the socialist integration."[53] It was never mentioned that Nowa Huta itself, which soon became a new district of Kraków, witnessed a solid measure of social conflicts and tensions.

Nowa Huta was intended as a workers' town built to counterbalance the ostensibly conservative and antisocialist population of Kraków.[54] No churches were planned for the city. During the anniversary celebrations, Gierek informed the audience that Nowa Huta was exemplary in its unconditional devotion to socialism. "We [the authorities] desire," said the first secretary, "that Nowa Huta develops fulfilling in the best possible way the needs of its dwellers."[55] A need to have a place of worship was not on Gierek's mind but its fulfillment was persistently pursued by the people. In 1977 Karol Cardinal Wojtyła, the archbishop of Kraków, conse-crated the church that because of constant harassment by the authorities had been under construction for twenty years. The opening ceremony, on 15 May 1977, despite pouring rain, was attended by tens of thousands of people. Cardinal Wojtyła told the enthusiastic audience that "the human being cannot be comprised only in terms of production and consumption. We do not belong to anybody. We belong to God." The parish priest, Gorzelany, declared that the church of *The Mother of God, the Queen of Poland* (as it was named), "was the monument of the Millennium of the baptism of Poland, the sign of Christian culture of today, . . . the symbol of Peter's ark which offers protection to every person."[56] In the 1980s this

53. These words are taken from the headline of the 17 June 1974 issue of the Katowice Party newspaper, *Trybuna Robotnicza*.

54. In 1946, the Communist authorities organized the referendum to determine whether Poland would have a unicameral or bicameral congress (Sejm); whether principles underly-ing nationalization of industry and agrarian reform should be incorporated into the Consti-tution; whether Poland's permanent frontier should remain on the Oder (Odra) and western Neisse (Nysa) rivers (Bliss 1961 [1948], 199). The Communists urged everybody to vote yes on all three questions, implying that such a vote meant expression of support for them. The results of the referendum were falsified, except for Kraków, where, as it turned out, 84 percent of the voters said no to the first question. The authorities interpreted this result as proof of conservatism of Kraków's population. The town was labeled "the bulwark of reaction," and the Communists began to act as if they themselves took this epithet seriously (see Kersten 1986, 219).

55. *Trybuna Robotnicza*, 17 June 1974.

56. *Tygodnik Powszechny*, 15 May 1977. A sociological study, conducted in Nowa Huta in 1971, revealed that every tenth person came from intelligentsia, every third from the peasantry, and every second from the working class. Sixty-five percent of the respondents declared themselves to be practicing Catholics, 60 percent attended Sunday masses, 41.9 percent confessed during the Easter season. Franciszek Adamski, the author of the study, concluded that despite the secularization of attitudes and moral behavior, Nowa Huta was one of the most religious urban centers in Poland, primarily because of the strongly peasant origin of the population (*Tygodnik Powszechny*, no. 20, 1977; Pomian-Srzednicki 1982, 146).

church became a focal point of several major demonstrations by the workers of Nowa Huta.[57]

Ceremonies and Rituals of the Official Public Domain

National holidays and feasts. There were three groups of holidays and feasts belonging to the established festal calendar: (1) holidays of national significance established to celebrate social roles and events of the private and familial domain of life, such as Women's Day (March 8), Mother's Day (May 26), Father's Day (June 23), Child's Day (June 1), and The Day of Remembrance of the Dead, better known as the Holiday of the Dead (November 1);[58] (2) social and cultural feasts of national scope, such as Days of Education, the Book, and the Press, feasts of Party newspapers (for example, *Trybuna Ludu*), Days of Soviet Films, Days of Hungarian Culture, and several song festivals; and (3) official state holidays (days off work), which included New Year's Day, May First (Labor Day), and July 22 (Holiday of the Rebirth of Poland).[59] This last group also included

57. The positive image of Gierek's Poland was also fostered by continual displays of Polish economic and athletic prowess. The Poznań Trade Fair and the success of the Polish national soccer team during the 1974 World Cup finals were thoroughly exploited by Gierek's propagandists (see Kubik 1989, 117–19). But as the official media were busy constructing this optimistic picture, the economy was just "moving rapidly toward a major crisis" (Fallenbuchl 1982, 7). In 1979, the annual growth of the "produced national income" (or domestic net material product—DNMP—the value of all goods produced and of some services connected directly to their production) was negative 2.3 percent. The depth of the crisis becomes obvious when we look at the figures from the previous years: 6.8 percent (1976), 5.0 percent (1977), and 3.0 percent (1978). The annual growth of the "allocated national income" (national net material product—NNMP—which differs from DNMP by the balance of exports and imports) was negative 3.4 percent. Compare the figures for previous years: 7.0 percent (1976), 2.7 percent (1977), and 0.7 percent (1978). These figures reflected a dramatic decline in the quality of life in Poland, felt, for instance, in the form of growing shortages of basic goods and more and more frequent blackouts (caused by energy shortages) (Fallenbuchl 1982, 6).

58. Traditionally this is a religious holiday celebrated as All Saints' Day. Secularization of the holiday was strongly favored by the authorities. The press was allowed to use only its secularized name (Holiday of the Dead), and by the late 1970s this form dominated the popular usage. This was an official national holiday declared as a day off from work.

59. Victory Day was declared as a day off from work in 1981. The full list of national holidays (days off work) includes also five religious holidays, namely, Easter Monday (movable), Corpus Christi (movable), All Saints' Day (The Day of the Dead, November 1), Christmas (December 25), and Christmas Holiday (December 26).

major state celebrations that were not days off from work, such as Victory Day (May 9), the Anniversary of the October Revolution (November 7), Lenin Days (April), the Month of National Remembrance (April), and the Party Action Day (movable).

Party Action Day was organized for the first time in 1972. It was a day off from work (usually a Saturday or Sunday) that was to be celebrated through voluntary labor donated to one's community or the country. Party members, organized in brigades of various sizes (from just a few to several hundred), were supposed to do jobs deemed necessary or important for their housing projects, places of work, or public spaces such as parks and playgrounds. The ideological and official sense of this work was seen as the participation in "the construction of the advanced socialist society" (Pełka 1980, 96). It was a tradition going back to the first *subbotnik* organized in the Soviet Union in 1919. Christel Lane observed in Leningrad in 1978 that people (especially white-collar workers) gladly engaged in various manual tasks completing some useful and otherwise neglected work for their communities (1981, 118). She concluded that in the late 1970s the *subbotnik* functioned both as a ritual and as a practical device encouraging people to donate their labor. As a ritual it was a celebration of Lenin's birthday and his support of voluntary work and a rite of status reversal in which those usually engaged in "mental labor" (and thus occupying higher levels of social stratification) could enact the "old communist myth that all labor is equal and there are no social differences between physical and mental laborers" (Lane 1981, 118).

A few Party Action Days from the 1970s, known to me either through observation or from reports, were different. Both the ritualistic and instrumental significance of the holiday was hardly preserved. First, the Party authorities did not seem to trust the voluntary enthusiasm of its members and often secured participation through threats or through promises of material rewards, or imposed participation on workers as a form of punishment for minor offenses. For example, in 1979, before May Day, workers in the Lenin Shipyard in Gdańsk were recruited to participate in the *Action Day for the Twenty-Fifth Anniversary*. If a worker was caught smoking in a locker room during his working hours, he was enlisted to work four hours during the Action Day. Some workers were offered fifty zlotys per hour (a high wage) for this allegedly voluntary work.[60] Often people were not allowed to take days off right before or after Sundays designated for action days. Second, tasks ascribed to such "voluntary brigades" were often senseless, and people complained that it

60. These facts were reported by Bogdan Borusewicz in *Robotnik Wybrzeża,* June 1979.

was a waste of their time.[61] The next day, however, they could read in the newspapers that the Action Day they had participated in was a great success and constituted yet another proof of society's support for the Party's program of "the construction of the developed socialist society." In the mid-seventies the rules governing the coverage of Party Action Days and other "public service projects" were changed. A censorship rule now demanded that "no photographs are permitted of the party and state leadership performing social volunteer tasks" (Curry 1984, 70). Perhaps, any association of the senseless activities of public action days with the leaders of the state and the Party was to be avoided.

Celebrations for the thirtieth (in 1974) and thirty-fifth anniversaries of the Polish People's Republic were intended to be gigantic symbolic displays of Gierek's undisputed success in building the "Second Poland." However, the two celebrations differed; their differences reflected the changing social and political climate of the country. In July 1974 the Polish People's Republic celebrated its thirtieth anniversary. Leonid Brezhnev came to Warsaw on July 19 and spent the next three days traveling around the country as the guest of honor. On July 18, Gierek went to Gdańsk to open the Northern Port, often referred to as "the port of the second Poland."[62] Warsaw celebrated the opening of two modern highways (*Łazien-kowska* and *Wisłostrada*) and the start of the clock on the Royal Castle tower. The celebrations culminated on July 22. The gigantic military parade, followed by the parade of eighty thousand young people brought on this occasion from all over the country, marched through Marszałkowska Street in front of the Palace of Culture in Warsaw. In the afternoon of the same day, tens of thousands of people participated in the Carnival of Youth, which culminated in the concert of several major Polish pop stars at the Stadium of the Tenth Anniversary. Two slogans decorating the Palace of Culture read "Long live and blossom peace and socialism" and "We salute the heroic Soviet nation—the builders of Communism."

The official tone of the celebrations was set by Edward Gierek in his Diet speech, "Socialism let Poland enter the current of historical progress." Gierek told his audience that "socialism released the creative forces of the nation" and allowed Poland "to return to her immemorial Piast territories on the Odra river and the Baltic Sea." In his vision, "the People's Poland [was] a legacy of the patriotic and progressive [Polish] tradition" and it "embodied the vital interests of the whole nation." In general, the celebrations of the thirtieth anniversary were dominated by a

61. See a critical article by Ireneusz Krzemiński in *Więź*, November 1975; reported in Curry (1984, 71).
62. See, for example, *Trybuna Ludu*, 18 July 1974.

mood of youthfulness, vigor, and pride in the achievements of postwar Poland. All the accomplishments of the previous thirty years were attributed to socialism and Poland's friendship with the Soviet Union.

In 1979, the Polish People's Republic celebrated its thirty-fifth anniversary. A gigantic rally attended by eighty thousand people was organized for this occasion at the Stadium of the Tenth Anniversary in Warsaw. The following are excerpts from its script:[63]

> To begin, all the people in the stadium warm up for an hour, practicing spontaneous group chants. Then thirty-five trumpeters play the trumpet call of the Federation of the Socialist Unions of the Polish Youth. "When the last note of the trumpet call is played the Guests of the Manifestation with the First Person [i.e., Gierek] enter the Honorary Tribune." Ovation. Guards of honor (300) march in parading [national] colors. The brass bands of the Polish Railways (PKP) and the Polish Bus Company (PKS) perform. Balloons fly up carrying the national flag. The Representative of the Federation makes a speech. The commentator begins the "Roll Call." Is the Polish Youth present?—The Youth: Present!—Is the Cavalier of the Order of the Builders of the Peoples' Republic of Poland, writer Jarosław Iwaszkiewicz,[64] present? Jarosław Iwaszkiewicz: Present! Mirosław Hermaszewski[65] marches majestically in from the tunnel, while the Orchestra of the Great Theater plays in his honor "The Welcome Symphony for the Cosmonauts" by Czesław Niemen.[66] General Klimuk[67] presents "his own Russian text." Colonel Hermaszewski throws in his "personal voice of solidarity with the manifestation participants" and declaims several appropriate slogans. The youth from forty-nine regions deliver reports to the First Person. . . . The leading pop singers

63. Stanisław Barańczak, an independent poet, essayist, and critic of the official mass culture, obtained a copy of this script and published it in an independent journal (*Biuletyn Informacyjny,* July–August 1979).

64. Jarosław Iwaszkiewicz, a highly respected writer, was at that time the president of the Polish Writers Union, a position demanding subservience to the authorities.

65. Mirosław Hermaszewski was the first Polish astronaut. His achievement was used as yet another symbol of the "Second Poland."

66. In the late 1960s Niemen was one of the most popular rock stars in Poland (and Eastern Europe). The title song from his hit album *Dziwny jest ten świat* (Strange world) was the first protest song recorded in Poland expressing the exasperation of youth involved in the generational conflict. Ten years later Niemen had become a member of the music establishment and was on very good terms with the authorities.

67. A Soviet astronaut in charge of the common mission with Hermaszewski.

(Maryla Rodowicz, Krzysztof Krawczyk, Urszula Sipińska,[68] Mieczysław Fogg,[69] and others) perform. Actors ("the precise list will be presented later") recite poems of great poets, such as Staff, Tuwim, Broniewski,[70] Henryk Gaworski and Marek Wawrzkiewicz.[71] One hundred and twenty small Fiats with huge letters on the roofs emerge from the tunnel. The commentator: "This small Fiat is also a symbol of the great leap forward." Airplanes fly over the stadium, discharging smoke in national colors, while the small Fiats are arranged so that the letters on their roofs constitute various slogans (MOTORIZATION, FERTILIZERS, THE CASTLE, etc.). The commentator in the name of the whole nation thanks "those who have led us all and are still leading" for everything, and intones cheers such as "Long live the Polish nation and its great leader Edward Gierek!" Parachutists jump from a helicopter. They discharge smoke in national colors which constitutes a roman number ten. Nine hundred students of the Sports Education Academy (AWF) create a pyramid. . . . Combined Army marching bands (1300 musicians) perform Chopin's Polonaise in A major (the commentator informs the audience that such a musical task is being undertaken for the first time in history). (*Biuletyn Informacyjny*, July–August 1979)

For many Poles the script reads like a parody of the official mass culture, yet it was realized almost without change. The ceremony was performed on July 20 and together with the changing of the guards in front of the Tomb of the Unknown Soldier on July 22 constituted the heart of the thirty-fifth anniversary celebrations.

A comparison of the two anniversaries is instructive. In 1974, the carefully constructed mood of the celebration was dominated by youthful enthusiasm and a strong emphasis on Poland's friendship with the Soviet Union. Brezhnev's presence epitomized the latter theme. The celebrations were to illustrate the accomplishments of the whole socialist period, but first of all they were meant to incite awe over the "economic miracle" produced by Gierek and his regime, while at the same time

68. A group of the most popular singers and pop stars of the late 1970s.

69. The most popular singer of the older generation.

70. Famous poets of the twentieth century. Broniewski was a self-proclaimed poet of the revolution honored by the authorities despite his several anti-Soviet poems, which were never officially published.

71. Relatively unknown poets. Putting them together with their three famous predecessors created a comical effect. The only conceivable reason for them to be so honored must have been their unconditional servility.

promising even more successes in the near future. In 1979, the general mood of the celebrations of the thirty-fifth anniversary was more patriotic and less internationalistic. The "enthusiasm" projected by both ceremonies resonated with different social moods: in 1974 there was a degree of genuine enthusiasm engendered by Gierek's program, but by 1979 this enthusiasm rang hollow and false. The heavy emphasis on success and patriotism was seen by many Poles to be a smoke screen for the country's drastically worsening economic situation.

May Day in the 1970s

From 1890 until World War II, the May Day demonstrations in Poland were organized by various political organizations and parties of the left. After 1945 the name *May Holiday* slowly replaced the older name *May Demonstration,* presumably to illustrate the doctrinal premise that a victorious proletariat does not need to demonstrate but only celebrate. Yet formally the demonstration continued to be the culmination of the celebrations, as the gigantic parade marched in front of viewing stands occupied by the rulers. Now, however, they were not spontaneously organized by various groups, but carefully orchestrated by a single group, the Central Committee of the PZPR.

In 1945, the main May Day celebrations, attended by about 200 thousand people, were organized among the ruins of Warsaw. The burnt balcony of the Great Theater served as the viewing stand. The mood was one of joyous celebration of the victory over fascist Germany and enthusiastic expression of the will to rebuild the devastated country. In 1949, after the Communists had eliminated all their opponents and consolidated their power, for the first time a military parade (later abandoned) became the focal point of the May Day celebrations. In 1950 May Day was declared a national holiday.[72] Since then, "May Day parades [were] becoming more colorful and joyous. They [were] also getting shorter, giving way to ludic and recreational forms of celebrating. Ceremonial meetings replace huge gatherings giving way to gala concerts and spectacles" (Pełka 1980, 91).

In 1971, after Gierek came to power, the tradition of the country's leaders marching in the first row of the May Day parade, which had disappeared in the 1950s, was reinstated. The rulers would kick off the event by marching at the head of the procession before moving to the

72. A Sejm decree of 26 April 1950.

viewing stand to watch the rest of the parade. According to a contemporary observer, it was "an act symbolizing the changes in our life after the
December events" (Ciołek, Olędzki, and Zadrożyńska 1976, 278). Other
new elements of May Day celebrations introduced in the 1970s were gala
concerts and meetings with the representatives of the authorities in which
people who had achieved the best results in their work were honored in
various ways.

Another prominent feature of May Day celebrations in the 1970s was
the stress on ludic and recreational elements, such as feasts, historical and
folkloristic spectacles, youth carnivals, theater and cabaret performances,
sport events, film screenings in the open air, book fairs, and art exhibitions.[73] An official journalist observed that the seventies witnessed the
rise of what he called the May tradition:

> May Day became a strong and permanent custom having a clear
> impact on private life; its spontaneity reaches deeper and deeper
> into individual behavior and personal plans. . . . The shape and
> content of this holiday is not only determined by general [i.e.,
> state organized] contributions but increasingly also by individual
> initiatives—miniature medals on jackets, little banners in chil-
> dren's hands, balloons, and colorful dresses made especially for
> the occasion.[74]

The ludic and recreational tenor has played an important role in May Day
celebrations since their institution in 1890, and the holiday was often
referred to as a secular proletarian rite of spring, "a time of renewal,
growth, hope and joy" (Hobsbawm 1983, 283–86). Nevertheless, as Eric
Hobsbawm observes, it has always retained a double, social and political,
quality: depending on the circumstances, May Day celebrations could
take on the character of a spring holiday or of a political demonstration.

In the 1970s in Poland the political character of the May Day celebrations was not neglected, although its ludic dimension was more pronounced. While people enjoyed recreational activities, the authorities
kept strengthening the propagandistic effect of the major element of the
celebrations: the May Day parade. Its imagery was to convey the principal message of the celebrations: the inevitable victory of the Communist

73. Rotenberg observed a similar relaxation in the 1975 May Day celebrations in Prague
(1983, 65).
74. K. Danek, in "Składniki obyczaju" (Elements of a custom), *Trybuna Ludu*, 29 April
1973.

(or socialist—these terms were used interchangeably) idea throughout the world. During a typical May Day in Poland of the seventies, people who chose not to leave town or shut down their radios and TV sets and decided to participate more or less actively in the celebrations were exposed to a powerful message. If they turned on their TV sets, on either one of the two channels they would see and hear a stream of reports about the proceedings of the May Day celebrations from Havana to Novosibirsk. Such coverage, extending through several time zones, guaranteed that from early morning (transmission from Moscow would start about 8:00 A.M.) until late afternoon one could electronically participate in May Day celebrations in one of the socialist countries. The highlights of the celebrations were also shown in the extended evening news. Reports from nonsocialist countries, insignificant in number and time, seemed to be constructed in such a way that eliminated or at least minimized the impression that May Day was also celebrated by a wide range of socialist parties and movements that were not controlled by Moscow. If one was bored with TV or radio coverage and decided to go for a walk, he or she would encounter a May Day celebration in his or her town or village. In short, festive or solemn, boring or exciting, colorful or dull, May Day celebration would be *everywhere*, constructed as a total media event.

Godfrey Lienhardt once suggested that the function of Dinka rituals is to ensure that "human symbolic action moves with the rhythm of the natural world around them, recreating that rhythm in moral terms and not merely attempting to coerce it into conformity with human desires" (Douglas 1966, 66). Perhaps it is not too farfetched an analogy to postulate that the ultimate function of the May Day celebrations, as they were presented by the state media in the Communist world, was to recreate the alleged rhythm of the empire in the personal experiences of its subjects, enhancing the feeling of the empire's omnipresence and longevity. Some official journalists came close to an explicit articulation of such a "hidden function" of the May Day celebrations. For example, the editors of *Gazeta Południowa,* a party daily in Kraków, wrote in the 1 May 1976 issue:

> Our victorious parade is marching through the streets all over the world. The red banner symbolizes the content of this march. On the First of May we think about the struggle of several generations of revolutionaries and solidarize with the progressive forces of the modern world, forces that still continue the struggle for justice, for equality, and for the right to live the life worthy of man. In

Lenin's homeland and in the countries of victorious socialism proletarian traditions are intertwined with the present. The May Day
parade is a manifestation of solidarity with our class brothers
throughout the world and, at the same time, it expresses our
respect for decent work, which begets everything that is beautiful
and valuable . . .

The authors of these words admitted that there are some countries where
"progressive forces" still struggle to realize socialist values of justice,
equality, and "the right to live the life worthy of man,"[75] but they emphasized that socialism has already been victorious in the Soviet bloc countries and continues its victorious march throughout the world.

Yet internationalism did not constitute the exclusive ideological focus
of the May Day ritual. As in other areas of the official discourse, it was
complemented by patriotic motifs. Ciołek, Olędzki, and Zadrożyńska
noted that "the May Holiday became an all-national holiday. *The red is
intertwined with the white-and-red*[76] [emphasis added], the interests of the
working class are inseparably linked with the interests of the whole
society."[77]

Each year had its special themes. For example, 1976 was the year of
constitutional changes. One of the most controversial amendments was
intended to link the rights of the citizens with their duties to the state.
Because of public protests the content of this amendment was modified.
In the Kraków May Day parade the employees of the local administration
displayed a huge banner reading "The unity of rights and duties the
principle of socialist democracy." In turn, the 1980 celebrations were
dominated by the slogans supporting the Eighth Congress of the PZPR
and Gierek's idea to organize a conference on peace and disarmament in
Warsaw.

75. After signing the Helsinki accords, the Soviet bloc countries found themselves in an
uncomfortable position of being exposed to constant criticism that they did not respect
basic human and civil rights (as defined in Helsinki). A notion of "the right to live the life
worthy of man" (that is, without a thread of unemployment) was introduced to counterbalance these charges and create an impression of peculiar symmetry between the West and the
East. The message read: "We have problems with some human rights, you have problems
with others."

76. Red is the color of internationalism, Communism, socialism, Marxism, and so on.
White-and-red are the Polish national colors.

77. Elsewhere they note: "The holiday was furthermore enriched by the additional
elements of patriotism, internationalism, brotherhood and friendship taken in a wide sense,
expressing respect for oneself and tolerance for the others. . . . It is a spectacular holiday
with unusual emotional power, nobilitating such an ordinary activity as work" (Ciołek,
Olędzki, and Zadrożyńska 1976, 281).

Anniversaries of the Great October Socialist Revolution

The anniversary of the October Revolution was never observed in Poland as elaborately as May Day was.[78] There were no street parades or mass demonstrations, although as a newspaper reported, "the celebrations of the October Revolution take place throughout the whole country. Meetings, concerts, and exhibitions are organized in dozens of towns, enterprises and institutions, colleges and schools. Representatives of the Soviet diplomatic missions and also Soviet specialists who work in our country building new objects participate in these celebrations."[79] In the 1970s the major national celebration was the gala concert in Warsaw, usually organized on the eve of the anniversary. For example, on 5 November 1976 the concert was attended by the highest authorities of the state and the Party led by Edward Babiuch and Wojciech Jaruzelski (both members of the Politburo and the government). The hall was decorated with red banners, an immense "1917," and a bust of Lenin. After playing the national anthems of Poland and the Soviet Union, artists recited revolutionary poetry and prose and played revolutionary music.

The Image of the Polish People's Republic Propagated by the Official Discourse

Four elements of public discourse during Gierek's reign constituted the regime's claims to political legitimacy. They were the visions of the ideal society, the political community, the regime, and the authorities.[80]

The ideal society. Dualism pervades not only the linguistic aspect of the official Communist discourse but also its fundamental philosophical premises. Gierek's regime, through its official enunciations, propounded a Manichaean vision of the world without any significant deviations or innovations from the canonical forms; the world was depicted as divided into two antithetical parts, the good socialist East and the evil capitalist West. It was assumed that as soon as a society passes over the threshold of socialist revolution it enters a path of growth and harmony. All imperfections result not from the (*a priori* perfect) nature of the project but from

78. In the Soviet Union these two holidays were equally important.

79. *Gazeta Południowa*, 5 November 1976.

80. The last three elements were proposed and theoretically analyzed within the classical functionalist paradigm as "basic political objects" by David Easton (1965).

human errors and some relics of the capitalistic past. The propaganda of the 1970s declared that those in power had returned to the right path leading to the realization of the ideal, after some years of mistakes. The "Second Poland" was to be built without further delay as long as the citizens let the leaders do their jobs.

This ideal society, soon to be realized, was to be harmoniously organized without any conflicts between its segments or between the whole and its parts (individuals), constantly developing and growing, securing the best possible conditions for the unlimited and universal development of individual people,[81] and secular. It was not clear when and how this ideal would be fully realized nor how long it would take. This confusion was perpetuated by numerous verbless slogans, such as "The Nation with the Party," which did not give any clue whether the declared state of affairs has already happened, was happening, will happen, or should happen. In such slogans the ideal seemed to be ambiguously coexistent with reality. The successes of Polish athletes and economic "miracles"[82] constituted proof that society was on the right track.

Polish People's Republic as an ideal political community. Since its creation in 1945, the Polish People's Republic, was portrayed in the official media and ceremonies as a political entity organized according to the rules of the scientific ideas of Marxism-Leninism and variably defined as *socialist* or *advanced-socialist-and-building-Communism*. It was presented as the only rightful heir to all progressive (that is, socialist or Communist) traditions ever developed by the Polish nation. This assertion was symbolized by removing the crown from the national emblem, the White Eagle.

Yet the image of Polish statehood constructed by Gierek's image-builders was not based only on "socialist" tradition. It also emphasized "nationalism," that is, the elements of the nation's heritage that concurred with the vision of the Polish state as an ethnically and culturally homogenous entity. The tradition of ethnic heterogeneity and cultural and political pluralism, which developed during the several hundred years of the Polish–Lithuanian Commonwealth, was far less emphasized.

Throughout its history the Polish state has expanded and contracted. During the first four hundred years of its existence (from 966 until approximately 1400), Poland, under the Piast dynasty had more or less the

81. "Socialist society is humanistic by its very nature. It creates natural conditions for the development of the man's creative skills, develops in him all moral values" (*Nowa Drogi,* May 1974).

82. Katowice Steelworks, the flagship of Gierek's economy, was by no means alone. Other priority projects, popularized as symbols of the "Second Poland," including Gdańsk's Northern Port, Bielsko-Biała's Small Fiat Factory, and even, in the late 1970s, a monumental project (never realized) of total regulation of the Vistula river.

same boundaries as after 1945. Beginning in the fifteenth century Polish expansion to the East resulted in a series of unions binding Poland and Lithuania in a commonwealth that lasted almost four hundred years. Throughout most of its history one of the major enemies of the Polish-Lithuanian Commonwealth was the ever-expanding Duchy of Moscow, which developed eventually into the Russian Empire. At the height of its power, under the Jagiellonian dynasty, the Commonwealth extended its borders to the Black Sea. A simplified picture, fossilized in the national tradition, presents the Piast state as an ethnically homogenous entity, which had to struggle mostly with its Western neighbor—Germany. By contrast, Jagiellonian Poland remains in the collective memory as a glorious multiethnic and multinational empire successfully containing the major enemy of Poland from the East—Russia.

Since the very beginning of it existence, the Polish People's Republic was "constructed" in the official discourse as an heir to the Piast rather than to the Jagiellonian tradition.[83] There were at least two reasons for this. First, in exchange for the eastern provinces that were annexed by the Soviet Union after World War II, Poland was given formerly eastern German territories, which soon became known as the Western Lands or the Recovered Lands. Despite the will of the majority of its population and over the protests of many non-Communist politicians, the country was relocated and returned to its "Piast borders."[84] Second, since Soviet Russia was proclaimed to be the greatest friend and benefactor of the new socialist republic, it was not feasible to revive the old Jagiellonian ideas about Polish domination in the East. Thus, construction of the image of an ethnically homogenous Poland was one of the priorities of the official propaganda and was guarded carefully by the censorship. One of the results of this policy was the almost total elimination of the Jews from official Polish history.[85]

83. Justifications of this idea were furnished by some official Marxist sociologists. One of them, Jerzy Wiatr, wrote, "The Piast epoch, in contrast to most of the Jagiellonian epoch . . . was . . . the period in which the main effort of the nation was directed toward the defense of the national existence against the German *Drang nach Osten*. Therefore the tradition of Chrobry [Bolesław the Brave], notching his sword on a Kiev's gate [an emblem of Polish military successes over Russia], is ideologically false. . . . The return to the tradition of the Piast Poland—it was the first great act of revision of the national historical consciousness" (1971, 133).

84. Any serious discussion in the official media of Polish objections to the decisions of the Great Powers concerning Poland or critical evaluation of the role of the pro-Soviet Polish politicians in the Potsdam conference was to be censored. See Curry (1984, 344–45).

85. For centuries Jews inhabited the Polish-Lithuanian Commonwealth in great numbers and later, in interwar (1918–39) Poland, constituted almost one sixth of the population. Their contribution to the Polish economy and their impact on Polish culture were enor-

The third major element of the officially propagated vision of the Polish political community—in addition to *socialist tradition* and *national homogeneity*—was *secularism*. Despite the fact that Christianity is one of the most powerful forces shaping Polish history, in the official rendering of this history religion played a minimal role.[86]

The Regime. The fundamental principle of socialist democracy, *democratic centralism,* epitomized the ambiguity of the official discourse. The principle, although logically contradictory, could be easily expressed in a speech or ceremony with some allegoric or symbolic image, these being discursive forms that thrive on ambiguities. It was, however, difficult to convey in spatially organized discourse: in concrete public manifestations of democratic centralism it was necessary to emphasize one of its components at the expense of the other. In the halls of Party conventions and congresses the hierarchical organization of space left no doubt that centralism, and not democracy, was the aspect of the principle to be taken more seriously.

Indeed, democracy was usually defined by the Communists as participation in the realization of a plan prepared by the central authorities (Strzelecki 1981a, 39–45; Strzelecki 1989, 79–95). This specific idea of democracy (resembling fascism and various forms of populism) was often symbolized in totalitarian (or semitotalitarian) regimes through gigantic spectacles involving thousands of people executing exercises with the precision of military drills. In such spectacles individual actors disappear in the mass, which is turned into flexible material for various configurations depicting official slogans and emblems. It is a perfect way to portray uniformity and conformism, the desired characteristics of an individual participating in the realization of the common good under the leadership of a Communist party.[87] Gierek's pageant masters used this device often, although mass spectacles staged in the 1970s were more colorful and relaxed than in Stalinist times.

The vision of the structure of authority. In as much as all political authorities tend to develop some "master fiction" or "cultural frame" to validate their claims to power and authority, they also tend to define a center of the political community, a center from which all power and authority

---

mous. Yet, in the version of national history propagated by the Communist regime they disappeared.

86. Curry observes: "Unlike Soviet policy, which has been to represent religion as one of the basic props of the system of repression preceding the Bolshevik revolution, Polish policy has been to remove references to religion and the Church that give them credit for playing a positive and progressive role in society prior to the Communist takeover" (1984, 321).

87. See Barańczak (1983, 17) and Gross (1974, 176–233), and also Aguirre (1984) on Cuba.

emanates.[88] In Communist systems such as the Polish People's Republic, in spite of the constitutional articles that place legislative power in the Sejm and executive power in the government, de facto power rests with the first secretary of the Central Committee of the PZPR and the Politburo.[89] The ceremonial system reflects and amplifies actual concentration of power; the first secretary and the highest Party officials always occupy central positions in parades and ceremonies. Such an emphasis on the de facto hierarchic nature of the official structure of power contradicts the often stressed de jure democratic and egalitarian character of the system. But, by using symbolic means this logical contradiction can be disguised or at least blurred. Before taking their positions on the viewing stand (hence displaying their dominant status), Gierek and other members of the Politburo and the highest state authorities, opened the May Day parade walking in the first row of the demonstration, thereby emphasizing egalitarianism. But this construction of ambiguity was not successful. The duration of the leaders' stay on the podium, an unequivocal sign of hierarchy, was much longer than the display of "egalitarianism" at the beginning of the ceremony and did not leave many people in doubt concerning the operating principle of the regime, that the leaders have total power.[90]

Gierek's pageant masters began the construction of his cult of personality right at the beginning of his rule. His youthful, energetic, well-dressed persona was omnipresent in the media. However, according to Jane Curry, an analysis of the censorship materials available now in the West reveals that Gierek's cult of personality was substantially toned down after 1974–75. She suggests that the entire propaganda of success was partially curtailed when serious economic problems could no longer be hidden from the populace. My reading of the available censorship instructions and other materials is different. Indeed, in 1974–75 those responsible for propaganda in Gierek's team increased considerably their control over the media's construction of Gierek's and his regime's public

88. Geertz's seminal essay on the symbolism of political centers (1977) inspired several authors. See, for example, Hunt (1984, 87–119).

89. The constitutional changes of the 1970s were intended, inter alia, to lend this situation an aura of legality. In official talks with foreign leaders it was always the first secretary, not the president of the State Council (the nominal head of the state) or the prime minister, who represented the Polish People's Republic.

90. In the Soviet ceremonial system such ambiguity was eliminated by the early 1950s. Initially spontaneous and "egalitarian" ceremonial was replaced by the end of Stalin's period (1953) with rituals characterized by "(1) regimentation and standardization; (2) dominance of nationalist and military themes and actions; (3) display of power and status differences" (Binns 1980, 171). Moreover, as Binns observed at the end of the 1970s, "most of Stalin's festivals still exist" (1980, 171).

images.[91] In some ways, the propagation of Gierek's cult of personality was indeed toned down: for example, only a small and carefully selected number of letters from Gierek to the citizens could be published, and all pictures of the leader had to come from a single source—the official press agency (the *Polska Agencja Prasowa,* or PAP). But the propagation of the optimistic image of a powerful and happy Motherland, led by the party and Its Leader, continued, using as its vehicle not a cult of personality but the economic symbolism of great projects such as the Katowice Steelworks and carnivalesque and robust images of various town tournaments,[92] song festivals, or interfactory competitions (all thoroughly covered by the most popular Saturday TV show—*Studio 2*). After 1976, as the official efforts to build Gierek's cult slowed down, the gap between reality and the image projected by the authorities drastically widened.

Palace of Culture: The Symbolic Center of the Polish People's Republic

The persona of the first secretary was the only clear symbol of ultimate power in Poland. Polish Communists never succeeded in producing a symbolic spatial center for the new sociopolitical reality that corresponded to the Kremlin and Lenin's Tomb in the Soviet Union, although it seems that the Palace of Culture, an enormous building towering over the capital, was erected to fulfill this role. Yet it was never accepted by the majority of Poles as the symbolic center of the new "socialist Poland." Popular feelings toward this structure (especially in the late 1970s) were perhaps best expressed by an independent writer Tadeusz Konwicki, who, in his 1979 underground best-seller *The Minor Apocalypse,* writes:

> Immersed in that cloud or those few consolidated clouds was the Palace of Culture, which once, in its youth, had been the Joseph Stalin Palace of Culture and Science. That enormous, spired building has inspired fear, hatred, and magical horror. A monument to

91. Information about and pictures of Gierek were available only from the official PAP (Polish Press Agency) materials. See Curry (1984, 67–80).

92. Town tournaments were arranged, nonspontaneous, "fakeloristic" media events. Barańczak observed that "in town tournaments the whole population of several little towns takes part. It is difficult, however, to talk about genuine cultural activism: the representatives of the masses are limited to 'bag' races and wood-chopping contests, whereas the 'artistic side' is taken care of by professional artists" (1983, 21).

arrogance, a statute to slavery, a stone layered cake of abomina-
tion. But now it is only a large unpended barracks, corroded by
fungus and mildew, an old chalet forgotten at some Central European crossroad. (Konwicki 1984, 4)

Basic Characteristics of the Official Discourse of the 1970s

The outward variety and artistic elaboration[93] of the official discourse
masked the growing ideological rigidity, administrative centralization,
and, most of all, the increasingly apparent economic decline. This conclusion finds an unexpected supporter in Paweł Bożyk, Gierek's chief
economic adviser, who commented on the strategy of dynamic development—as Gierek's economic policies were often described in the official
discourse—as follows:

> Until 1974 [this strategy] was obvious, from 1975 on it became an
> illusion. *The propaganda of success was simply a form of hiding reality*
> [emphasis added] . . . I think that the propaganda of success was
> intensified when the economy began to break down—the years
> 1975, 1976. The situation in the country was getting worse
> whereas the propaganda of success was intensified. (Hernandez-
> Paluch 1987, 149–51)

Yet, Gierek's propaganda was not only "a form of hiding reality," as his
chief economic adviser observed; it was also used to legitimize the regime's authority, for "the enfoldment of political life in general conceptions of how reality is put together did not disappear with dynastic
continuity and divine right" (Geertz 1977, 169).

But what is most important is the ambiguity of the social order
depicted in the official discourse. It was not a matter of the usually
noted ambiguity between theory (a rigid system of oppressive rules)
and practice (a flexible system of mutual accommodations between the
Party-state and the populace). It was an *internal* ambiguity of the official
discourse, which was based on two distinct syndromes of values: Communist and socialist.

---

93. In the late 1970s, in return for very high financial rewards, many good designers
engaged in mass production of posters, huge decorations for state holidays, and so on.

In his book *The Lyric Model of Socialism* (1989), Jan Strzelecki[94] reconstructed the system of values behind the official justifications for centralizing power in the Polish People's Republic. The power of the center (the omnicenter—as Strzelecki called it) was presented as self-explanatory for five reasons. The center was (1) the only *guardian of the Communist idea,* (2) the perfect and the most reliable *tool of its realization,* thus also (3) the most perfect and conscientious *custodian of the public good.* Moreover, since the center was able to identify in the most comprehensive (scientific) way all needs of the populace it automatically became (4) *the embodiment of ultimate (socialist) democracy.*[95] The claims to (5) *absolute power* by the personnel of the center were therefore only natural.[96] This justification of centralized power was developed in theoretical works, propagated through official ceremonies and rituals, and epitomized in the slogans produced on such occasions. It is such a system based on such a centralization of power that I call *Communist.*[97]

Socialism was propagated through the official media and ceremonies as the paramount ideology of the Polish state from 1945 through 1989. It was presented to the public as having all possible virtues one can ascribe to a perfect social system. Paradoxically, very similar views were articulated by the regime's most outspoken and influential critics: Leszek Kołakowski and Adam Michnik. Kołakowski listed among the features of the socialist society: sovereignty, democracy, pluralism, the rule of

94. Strzelecki, a sociologist and social critic, represented the antitotalitarian tradition of the Polish left. His *Lyric Model of Socialism* was completed in 1979–80, but was not published officially until 1989, after the collapse of "actually existing socialism" in Poland.

95. W. C. Afanasjev in his *Scientific Management of the Society* (1979) observes, for example, that "the policies of the party . . . are the policies that express the most deeply concealed ideas of the nation, its thoughts, interests, and dreams. From this results the necessity, the right, and the obligation to realize [the Party's] leadership" (quoted in Strzelecki 1989, 33).

96. Let me quote just one of several official statements collected by Strzelecki: "The center . . . due to its class foundation, the composition of [its] ideology, the rules of [its] structure and functioning is the only force objectively able to manage all domains of life of the socialist society. Only it can assure that the scientific program of the development of the socialist society is the foundation of the functioning of the whole political system and its constituent parts and that the whole mechanism of this system is built, developed, and works according to the fundamental interests of the working class and all working people" (J. Matejicek, "Partia komunistyczna i organizacje społeczne w społeczeństwie socjalistycznym" [The Communist party and social organizations in a socialist society], quoted in Strzelecki 1989, 45).

97. This definition of Communism is sometimes found in dictionaries. For example, in a dictionary edited by Wilczynski (1981) one can find seven different definitions of Communism, including the following: "a totalitarian system of government noted for the supremacy of the state over the individual, based on the mono-party system of all power exercised by the Communist party, as contrasted with Western parliamentary democracy."

law, liberalism (understood as respect for basic human rights), and finally "control of society over the means of production and the distribution of the national income and over the administrative and political apparatus, working as an organ of society, and not as a master for whom society is a handmaiden" (1971, 50).

Michnik defined the oppositional secular left, an orientation he represented and helped to form, in a very similar way: "This Left champions the ideas of freedom and tolerance, of individual sovereignty and the emancipation of labor, of a just distribution of income and the right of everyone to an equal start in life. It fights against national-chauvinism, obscurantism, xenophobia, lawlessness, and social injustice. The program of this Left is the program of antitotalitarian socialism" (Michnik 1993, 33).

The Communist/socialist ambiguity of the official discourse was achieved by constantly switching (through time and space) the emphasis between the elements in such pairs of principles as centralism and democracy, hierarchy and egalitarianism, internationalism and patriotism/ nationalism. I am not sure if this ambiguity was deliberately produced and sustained by the mass-media propagandists and pageant masters. It was certainly politically expedient and had at least three functions. First, it allowed the autocratic rulers to present themselves, especially at times of crisis, as champions of egalitarianism. When such a need arose, the "socialist" aspect of the symbolic system was temporarily stressed. Conversely, when the ruler needed to assert his power, the "Communist" principle of centralism was symbolically invoked. Such tactical symbolic operations were easy to realize since the symbolic system was ambiguous. Second, through sustaining the Communist/socialist ambiguity and thus through blurring the distinction between socialism and Communism, the authorities attempted (with some degree of success) to construct some aura of socialist legitimacy for their Communist practices. Third, the saturation of the public domain with the simplistic yet ambiguous discourse diminished the populace's ability to comprehend fully their situation and thus created the semblance of a legitimizing mechanism for the social and political status quo.[98]

The ambiguity of the official discourse was also perpetuated and amplified through aesthetic means. The more relaxed ceremonial of the 1970s

98. I call this a "semblance" to indicate that cultural ambiguity and indeterminacy cannot be properly classified as legitimizing devices. Yet due to the cognitive disorder and emotional anxiety they produced, they diminished the populace's ability to define their situation properly and therefore increased the probability of the populace's acceptance of the regime (system) or, at least, led to the prevalent mood of apathy, hopelessness, existential inchoateness, which in turn diminished the probability of organized actions against the regime.

was aesthetically more colorful and ideologically a bit more syncretic than in the preceding years.[99] Stanisław Barańczak observed that there was a tension between the persuasive and playful functions of mass culture in Poland of the 1970s (1983, 13). To be effective, persuasion had to be wrapped in some attractive, playful form so that it would be noticed, consumed, and eventually accepted. He concluded that

> the authorities [were] clearly aware that today [in the seventies] they [could not] shape the views of the society through repetition of direct orders and slogans, which cause nausea in an average recipient, but only indirectly: through smuggling directives, pressures, ideological schemes, and value systems wrapped as attractive products of mass culture, such as a rhythmic song, a colorful spectacle, or a sensational story. (1983, 12)

Yet the "repetition of direct orders and slogans, which cause nausea in an average recipient" did not stop. Some public events, such as openings of Party congresses, anniversaries of the October Revolution, May Day parades (especially their pictorial imagery), and the official language of the political domain were based on such repetition. The rules of the official discourse were always observed in the most sacred places of the Communist ritual, such as the halls of Party congresses and conventions, where the arrangement of space always followed a rigid hierarchical order draped exclusively with the red (with rare white-and-red accents). But in its everyday version the official decor was more relaxed, with white-and-red and a whole range of other colors as well.[100]

The ambiguity of the official discourse was further enhanced by a concurrent use of two rhetorical modes: manipulation and persuasion. The best example of the coexistence of these two modes is the May Day celebration. The general tenor of the Day's festivities (outside the parade) was relaxed, playful, and recreational and can indeed be seen as an exer-

99. Barańczak notes: "Since the antinomies [between the persuasive and playful functions of mass culture] could be neither bypassed nor avoided—the result was a hybrid-like character of all forms and functions of 'socialist mass culture.' There were red banners over discotheques and heroes of criminal novels, who instead of fighting crime made speeches about the superiority of socialism over capitalism. Playfulness came into conflict with persuasion and usually lost. There were more powerful forces and stronger interests behind the latter" (1983, 22).

100. The decor of postwar Poland evolved from the modest white-and-red, red, and multicolored first years, through the strictly red, white-and-red, and green Stalinist era (1949–56), and the rather subdued and gray, red, and white-and-red Gomułka years (1956–70), to the most colorful, with white-and-red accents and a clear red dominant in Gierek's decade.

cise in persuasion, especially in the first half of the 1970s. The parade itself, however, was an instance of manipulation. It was a total media event, whose rhetorical mode was hyperbole; it portrayed Communism/ socialism as the victorious force in the modern world. The manipulative strategy of the official media involved two techniques. The parade was an exercise in *magic:* it invoked a fictional, happy, triumphant world of Communism/socialism, to which Poland belonged as one of the chosen nations participating in the final realizaton of the utopia. Those viewing the parade from the podium were to be legitimized as leaders, for they had led the nation in this historical "march of progress." The parade functioned also as a multimedia equivalent of this feature of the language of propaganda, which I referred to as *verbal noise*. For days, the society's channels of communication were clogged with various verbal, pictorial, and ceremonial messages about the May Day parade and related events.

In conclusion, in the 1970s the propagation of the official ideology in all major domains of public discourse—that is, visual imagery, rhetoric, and ceremonial—was being constantly amplified. The workers' protests of 1976, revealing the illusory character of Gierek's economic reforms and leading to the emergence of organized political opposition, did not have any significant impact on the official discourse, which was built around the image of a happy "Second Poland" until the end of the decade. The rejection of Gierek's "master fiction" by large segments of the populace became possible only when the Church and the opposition developed their own counterhegemonic discourses and presented them publicly. By so doing they undermined the regime's monopoly on social communication and furnished the people with conceptual and symbolic tools to define the social reality afresh. As a result, the dismantling of the official hybrid of Communism/socialism began, and this allowed some oppositional groups to reclaim socialism, and eventually even link it with Catholicism, as in the case of the *Polska Partia Socjalistyczna* (Polish Socialist Party).[101] This newly resurrected party announced in its programmatic declaration of November 1987:

> Ninety-five years ago the Polish Socialist Party (PPS) was formed, organizing Poles in the struggle for independence and social justice. . . . Forty years ago, the Communists destroyed the democratic socialist movement. Many socialist activists died in Polish and Russian jails. . . . Today, on the anniversary of the Paris Con-

---

101. PPS, by far the strongest party of the Polish left, was de jure incorporated into the (pro-Moscow, Communist) Polish United Workers' Party and de facto destroyed in December 1948.

vention, we are restoring the PPS, being fully aware of the tradition we intend to carry on. We realize that the word "socialism," which has been co-opted by the Communists, is currently unpopular in Polish society.

Our program will be subject to modification over time and responding to the realities of our situation. We don't want to base it on an inflexible doctrine. We don't want to tie ourselves to any specific philosophy, although we admit that we feel more affinity with the social teachings of the Church, more specifically with those of John Paul II, than with Marxism.[102]

102. *Tygodnik Mazowsze,* 18 November 1987.

3   *The Song of Wawel*
An Example of the Didactic Pageant

The Main Office for the Control of the Press, Publications, and Public Performances was one of the institutional pillars of the Polish People's Republic. As its name indicates, its role was not limited to censoring the written word. Visual propaganda and public ceremonials were as thoroughly controlled as books and newspapers. This emphasis on scrutinizing visual arts as well as the ceremonial was well justified in the case of Poland, because *visualism* is, according to a prominent Polish art historian, Mieczysław Porębski, a basic feature of Polish culture. It satisfies a deep-seated need to present philosophical concepts, historical controversies, and political arguments in a tangible form (Porębski 1975). This need arose during the nineteenth century when Poland, partitioned by Russia, Prussia, and Austria, ceased to exist as a political entity. The nation survived the years of partition (1795–1918) as an ideal cultivated in images created by outstanding poets, writers, and painters.

The prominence of the arts for the stateless nation was highlighted when Jan Matejko, whose canvases had immortalized the major events of Polish history, was granted the scepter of the monarch of Polish art by admiring Poles. In his acceptance speech Matejko referred to the period of partition as an *interregnum,* a temporary disruption of the political continuity of Poland; a disruption serious enough, however, to cause worry over who should carry the scepter of Polish sovereignty. Kings and statesmen had disappeared; poets and artists had to assume their roles. The first part of the nineteenth century was dominated by romantic poetry praising the Poland that once was and deliberating over the reasons for its fall. In the second half of the century, the task of preserving the national heritage was taken over by both the historical novel, Henryk Sienkiewicz being its foremost practitioner, and pictorial art, best represented by the huge historical canvases of Jan Matejko and the allegorical drawings of Artur Grottger. Since then, Polish nationalism, in its various versions, has found its pivotal medium not only in the grand visions of poets and novelists, but also in pictorial imagery.[1] This is, perhaps, one of the reasons for its unusual vitality, for as Barthes once observed: "Pictures, to be sure, are more imperative than writing, they impose meaning at one stroke, without analyzing or diluting it" (1982, 95).

Therefore, the Communist regime, facing the task of reshaping the domain of national symbols and myths, concentrated its efforts not only on language but also on art (especially in 1949–56) and official ceremonial (especially after 1968), thereby modifying Lev Shestov's famous dictum that "Russkiy bolshevism vo pervikh tsarstvo slov" ("Russian bolshevism is first of all an empire of words").

Official state ceremonies were scripted and censored down to the most minute detail. The celebrations of the thirtieth anniversary of the Polish People's Republic in 1974, for instance, were so carefully orchestrated that no mention of spontaneous local initiatives was permitted in the national media. A censorship regulation also prescribed that "printing or reproduction of emblems, posters, pennants and the like, or information

---

1. Lampland observes that "although Anderson (1983) has focused on the novel and newspaper in his argument about the development of national consciousness, the "imagined community" of the Hungarian nation was to have its historical destiny forged and contested in poetic verse" (1986, 6). Even a casual glance at Poland allows one to see that the national consciousness may be formed through other media as well. For Poles, pictorial images (created mostly by Matejko) and Chopin's music have been equally or even more important than (romantic) poetry and the realistic novel as vehicles of the ultimate national identification.

on tourist events and competitions [are to be permitted only if] they are included in the Plan of Major Undertakings and Ceremonies Related to the Thirtieth Anniversary ratified by the respective party committee" (Curry 1984, 75).

Yet not all public spectacles of the 1970s were as carefully orchestrated or presented such a one-sided and uniformly optimistic picture of the Polish reality as the celebrations of the thirtieth or thirty-fifth anniversaries of the Polish People's Republic. In some instances, artists enjoyed a degree of freedom and created complex visions of the past that engaged the dilemmas facing the Polish nation. Therefore, I believe that a detailed examination of these productions is in order, because it is in and through them that the Party-state was able to influence cultural schemas, regulating—even if partially and imperfectly—citizens' thinking and behavior.[2] A gigantic spectacle entitled *The Song of Wawel,* staged in Kraków by the theater STU in the 1970s, is a perfect specimen for such a study.

In order to reconstruct the mechanism through which cultural schemas were (re)produced in *Song of Wawel* I will (a) present the theater that staged it, (b) describe its content, and (c) analyze its cultural and political meaning in detail, employing Victor Turner's interpretive technique.

Wawel, from which the spectacle took its name, is a magnificent castle sitting on a hill towering over a bend in the Vistula, a big, slow-moving river. Wide boulevards on the river banks create the perfect setting for some gigantic spectacle. Kraków, an old central European town, a former capital of Poland and still one of her cultural centers, furnishes a picturesque background for such a spectacle. Each element in this picture is full of historical significance for the Poles: Wawel Castle, which served as the royal residence until 1596, houses priceless historical and artistic collections, in its cathedral are the graves of kings and national heroes. The Vistula has always been considered the holy river of Poland. In short, it is—as Stanisław Wyspiański observed—a Polish acropolis, the symbolic center of Poland, the most sacred locus of national traditions, and a nostalgic reminder of past power and glory.

Throughout the centuries this symbolic density attracted numerous artists, who in turn, through their work contributed to its intensification. Some of them, such as Stanisław Wyspiański or Tadeusz Peiper, dreamt of using the magnificent vistas of Wawel Hill to stage a performance that would make use of the "natural" symbolic richness of the castle and its surroundings.[3]

2. I discuss cultural schemas on pages 131 and 228.
3. On Stanisław Wyspiański (1869–1907), the great painter and dramatist, see Miłosz (1983, 351–58). According to Miłosz, Wyspiański was inspired by Wagner's theater in

Their dream was realized in the 1970s by the Kraków theater STU. The first *Song of Wawel,* as the spectacle was called, was produced on 10 June 1972. By 1980, the last year of its production, it had been presented nine times.

Theater STU

The STU was a member of a group of nonprofessional student theaters that forcefully entered the public scene in Poland in 1970, the year Gierek came to power.[4] The final version of the script of *The Song of Wawel* was prepared by Krzysztof Jasiński, the leader and one of the founders of the group, and Edward Chudziński, the theater's literary advisor. Both of them were members of the PZPR and represented a revisionist current in Polish Marxism, often critical of the dogmatic versions of the doctrine propagated by the Party. The belief in the possibility of improving the system from within, shared by several leaders of the student theaters of the early 1970s, was best expressed by Bogusław Litwiniec, the director of *Kalambur,* who once said of his group that "ours was a dream of a more beautiful Marxism" (Goldfarb 1980, 88).[5] The realization of this dream was, however, carefully monitored by censors and Party secretaries responsible for culture. When the limits of "reasonable" criticism, as delineated by these officials, were trespassed, as in the case of the Theater of the Eighth Day, the Party, the patron of the arts, became the persecutor.[6] *The Song of Wawel* was not only monitored by the Party but also commissioned by it, and is there-

---

Bayreuth, which helped him to realize "that the theatrical spectacle should form a unity of word, color, music, and movement" (1983, 353). On Peiper, see Miłosz (1983, 400–401).

4. Polish student theater was studied by an American sociologist Jeffrey Goldfarb (see, for example, Goldfarb 1976, 1980). I studied public perception of Theater STU from 1978 through 1980. The results of my work were published in Polish (see Kubik and Mach 1982a, 1982b).

5. The role of Marxism as an ideology of the student theaters of the 1970s is discussed by Goldfarb (1980).

6. In 1976, the student theatrical movement polarized. Some theaters, including the STU, continued the line of moderate criticism and exploration of "philosophical" themes. Others, such as the Theater of the Eighth Day, produced a series of performances that reflected the mood of apathy, cynicism, disappointment, and anger felt by the growing segment of the population in the late 1970s in a remarkably accurate, penetrating, and creative way. The authorities harassed the members of the Theater of the Eighth Day and finally barred them from performing in Poland.

fore, a good example of the construction of official discourse through relatively sophisticated artistic means.[7]

In the early 1970s, within the relatively—in comparison with other Eastern European countries—unrestricted Polish cultural life, student theaters were most independent and provocative in their criticism of the official reality. It was during this period that the STU's philosophy and aesthetics were defined in *The Falling* and *Polish Dreambook,* two highly acclaimed productions. The former, based on a poem by Tadeusz Różewicz, one of the most renowned Polish contemporary poets, explored his pessimistic observation that in the past people "fell vertically, now we fall horizontally." Both Różewicz's poem and the STU's production diagnosed the late 1960s as a time of serious crisis, a time when old value systems collapsed and new ones were yet not created, thus undermining the moral stability of social life and making people "fall" both horizontally and vertically.[8] Such a diagnosis was by no means limited to Poland; the message of *The Falling*'s first version was universal. Only in the second version, produced in March 1971 after Gomułka's fall, during a brief period of a cultural "thaw," did *The Falling* attack in a straightforward manner various deficiencies of Polish social and political reality. *Polish Dreambook* was also produced in 1971.[9] An STU pamphlet described the play thus:

> *Polish Dreambook* brings to surface . . . myths and phobias, which have long existed in our tradition and national psychology. *Dreambook* is not attempting to mock, this would only lead to unintended fascination. Neither does *Dreambook* attempt to approve of these myths. In *Dreambook* we refer to our deeply rooted stereotype notions, ideas, and feelings, in order to force the audience into an intellectual reflection on their national fate. (Goldfarb 1976, 174)

The STU followed in the footsteps of Wyspiański's Konrad from *The Liberation,* trying to engage its audience in an act of self-analysis that

7. In a publication documenting *The Song of Wawel* one finds the following information: "*The Song of Wawel* was commissioned by the Organizing Committee of the feast of *Gazeta Krakowska* [at that time a local Party daily—J.K.], inspired by and with active participation of the comrades from the Kraków's Party organization, especially Jan Broniek and Franciszek Dąbrowski [Party secretaries responsible for culture—J.K.]" (Jasiński and Chudziński, eds. 1980, unpaginated).

8. In this production the STU used, among others, texts by Baudelaire, Ginsberg, Gorky, and Sartre and several fragments of official speeches by Polish Party officials.

9. For a condensed description of this spectacle, see Goldfarb (1976,173–4; and 1980, 92–95).

would allow them to locate and overcome once and for all the romantic myths and stereotypes entangling their minds. Yet, paradoxically, *Dreambook* was very romantic in its climate. A critic closely following the STU's artistic career, encapsulated the spectacle's ideology in the following statement: "Romanticism—yes, but Romanticism, so to speak—sober. Romanticism clearly thought out, Romanticism without fumes of mythology, without dreams about power, without daydreaming. Romanticism almost logical" (Nyczek 1982, 39).

Something was wrong with the Polish soul, and the STU had set out to heal it. New "logical romanticism" should replace the old romanticism, this intoxicating and amorphous body of ill-articulated ideas about the uniqueness of the Polish historical mission (Poland as a Christ of nations). Poles should finally sober up and straighten their thinking. Nyczek characterized the Polish consciousness portrayed in *Dreambook* as "contorted, complex, stretched between euphoria and despair, between deed and passivity, between the deep faith in the necessity of regaining independence and perfect ignorance of how to do that" (1982, 41). The pivotal element of *Dreambook*'s structure was, as in *The Song of Wawel*, the hypnotic trance-dance. It represented "a *Chochoł*-led spinning-wheel of not only individual virtues and shortcomings, but also [a spinning-wheel] of Polish shortsightedness and naivete" (Nyczek 1982, 41).[10]

When Chudziński and Jasiński began working on *The Song of Wawel*, they envisioned it as a simplified version of *Dreambook*.[11] These two productions belong, however, to different genres of theatrical art: *Polish Dreambook* is a condensed, highly dramatic and lyrical spectacle played in the small spaces of student clubs; *The Song of Wawel* is an epic with a clear historical narrative staged as a gigantic spectacle for a mass audience. The former wrestles with the dilemmas of the Polish psyche in an atemporal fashion, the latter offers a vision of Polish history as an arena for both the emergence and solution of these problems.

According to Chudziński, *The Song of Wawel* was to be a modern ritual whose function would be similar to past and present religious celebra-

---

10. In Poland, when winter comes, delicate trees and plants are covered with thick layers of straw. From a distance these straw covers resemble human figures and are called *chochoły*. The *Chochoł* is a symbolic figure in Wyspiański's most influential drama *The Wedding;* its significance is discussed later in this chapter.

11. Le Bon observes: "Ideas being only accessible to crowds after having assumed a very simple shape must often undergo the most thoroughgoing transformations to become popular" (1969, 56). Chudziński declares that in the case of *Polish Dreambook* and *The Song of Wawel,* "one can talk about a dialectical relationship of these two spectacles, conceiving of them as different though internally linked realizations of the same theme" (Chudziński 1982, 129).

tions. It was also a historical drama portraying "important national issues" (1982, 128–29). Yet it did not give a ready-made answer to the "Polish problem": *Chochoł*, a symbol of national inertia, was burned by the fire furnished by the workers—carriers of the new political order, but the crowd of historical and contemporary personages continued its dance. The authors seemed to believe that the institution of the new social and political order solved many problems but not all of them.[12] What was, however, this "Polish problem," which in *The Song of Wawel* is neither solved, nor even clearly defined? Was it just an intoxication with romantic myths and dreams and the lack of pragmatic thinking about the national situation, as diagnosed in *Dreambook?* An answer to this question lies in the vision of Poland's past and present, which, although not explicitly articulated, is discernible in the narrative of the spectacle. An analysis should reveal not only the main assumptions of this vision, but also the underlying politics of the choices made by the creators of *The Song of Wawel*.[13] Furthermore, it should also allow us to determine whether *The Song of Wawel* harmonized with the basic assumptions of the official discourse and if so what its political function was. Such a detailed analysis should be, however, preceded by a brief description of its content.

The Song of Wawel: The Script

The spectacle was envisioned as a modern version of the rites of Midsummer Night. It was to be staged on July 24, St. John's Eve. Actual presentations took place on various days close to this date, to coincide with weekends and the Feasts of *Gazeta Południowa* (earlier and later *Krakowska*), a Kraków party daily.

Form. The form and content of *The Song of Wawel* evolved considerably during the nine years of its existence. In 1972 it was a classic *son et lumière* spectacle, a collage of pictures without any recognizable story. Later the theater experimented with the technical side of the spectacle, searching for an appropriate formula to magnify the aesthetic splendors of the Wawel Hill. Finally, the technical aspect was perfected, and the

12. Miklaszewski, a critic closely collaborating with the STU, came up with a similar interpretation (Jasiński and Chudziński, eds. 1980).

13. In order to present a particular version of history lying behind *The Song of Wawel* and its political significance, I combine the historical analysis of its symbols with the reconstruction of what Turner calls the positional meaning of the symbol. *Positional meaning* is the function of the symbol's position within the larger context of other symbols.

dramatic scenery of the huge castle and the river was displayed through an elaborate game of light and bonfires.

Content. The content of the spectacle also evolved, and finally its standard (or canonical, as it was called) version emerged. It consisted of three parts: *The Heritage, The Liberation,* and *The Rite.* The script was written as a collage of several ready-made texts, although Wyspiański's *Liberation* and *The Wedding* constituted its ideological and thematic core. The story was related and commented upon by the Poet (Konrad), a hero of both Mickiewicz's *Forefather's Eve* and Wyspiański's *Liberation,*[14] who, thanks to his magical power, was able to call to life legendary and historical figures and to re-create past events.

The Heritage. Konrad (using lines from Wyspiański's *Legend*) brings to life characters from the founding myth of Kraków: old king Krakus and his daughter Wanda. The king is dying, and just as his subjects come to sing their farewell hymns, the castle is attacked by enemies (Germans in the most popular version of the legend: Wanda is often referred to as "Wanda who did not want a German"). They demand that Wanda go with them, since their prince is madly in love with her. But she would rather kill herself than suffer such an infamy (marriage to a German). *Rusałki* (female water creatures, similar to sirens) lure her to the water's edge with their song and ask her to join them. Wanda hurls herself into the water, drowns, and in so doing she ensures her people's independence.[15]

The next figure magically invoked by the Poet is Kazimierz the Great, the king who founded Jagiellonian University in 1364 and stabilized the Polish kingdom politically and economically. He is followed by Władysław Jagiełło, the victorious king who defeated the Teutonic Knights in the battle of Grunwald in 1410. The script presents Jagiełło as a symbol of Polish military power, especially the success of Polish armies in containing German expansion.

Zygmunt the Old and Zygmunt August are next. During their reign Poland reached her zenith. The Jagiellonian dynasty ruled over vast territories, and the country entered a period of prosperity. The arts and sciences flourished. Wawel was rebuilt and acquired its present shape with a prevalence of Renaissance elements. In *The Song of Wawel* Zygmunt Au-

14. The Poet was played by Jerzy Trela, an actor who had already portrayed Mickiewicz's Konrad in a critically acclaimed and very popular production by Konrad Swinarski, the best theatrical director of postwar Poland. Trela was widely identified as a personification of Konrad and by using him Jasiński enhanced considerably the dramatic strength of *The Song of Wawel.*

15. Jerzy Horzelski came up recently with an interesting interpretation of this myth linking it to known historical facts about proto-Slavic tribes inhabiting Kraków and its vicinity (see Horzelski 1987).

gust pronounces his momentous credo: "I am the king insomuch as I stand for the truth," a declaration of the rule of law.

Zygmunt August is followed by Jan Kochanowski (1530–84), perhaps the most eminent Slavic poet before the beginning of the nineteenth century.[16] Kochanowski recites his famous verses, often quoted in school textbooks, in which he warns the rulers (the nobility and the kings) to be just and care well for their subjects: "You who govern the Commonwealth, and human justice keep in your hands, . . . always remember that you hold God's place on the Earth, from which you should take care not of your own affairs, but of all the people."

Now the Poet calls Tadeusz Kościuszko, the most popular Polish national hero, who led a national uprising against the Russians in 1794. On 24 March 1794, in a ceremony held in Kraków's Market Square, Kościuszko proclaimed the *Act of Insurrection* and made a solemn vow to lead the nation to victory. This event survives in the collective memory as one of the brightest moments in Polish history, the last act of Polish heroism before Poland disappeared from the political map of Europe for over a century. Yet in the spectacle Kościuszko symbolizes first of all the spirit of social reform (realizing that in order to succeed he would need to mobilize the whole nation, he granted peasants personal freedom and reduced their labor dues). The Choir recites the words of a popular folk song in which peasants convince each other that it is in their interest to join the uprising. Kościuszko responds with the words of his vows: "This authority I was granted shall never be used to oppress anybody. It will be only used to restore our borders, regain national sovereignty, and reinforce freedom for all." The *Kosynierzy* (Kościuszko's peasant infantry armed with their scythes. The name comes from the word *kosa* = scythe) respond: "Long Live Kościuszko! Equality and Freedom! For Kraków and the Motherland!"

The next in this gallery of national heros is Edward Dembowski (1822–46), an aristocrat, but also a radical philosopher and revolutionary activist. As an exponent of a Polish variety of Left-Hegelianism he tried to combine the Hegelian cult of Reason with the glorification of the deep, raw emotionality of simple people. In his system, called "the philosophy of creativity," Dembowski stressed his belief that thought should be organically connected with action, which, in turn, should lead not only to national liberation, but also to a total emancipation of the peasants. Dembowski was the leader of the Kraków uprising against the Austrians in 1846 and was later killed. His legend lived among the peasants long

16. On Kochanowski, see Miłosz (1983, 60).

after his death (see Walicki 1982). In *The Song of Wawel,* a fragment of his speech announcing the abolition of all class privileges is recited.

Ludwik Waryński, the next figure, helped found the first Polish socialist party, the Proletariat, in 1882. This famous revolutionary belongs to the gallery of official forerunners and heros of the Polish People's Republic. His person is remembered in the words of a poet: "Unjustly divided, crop of earthy fields, aroused anger, called us under the red banner, stained with workers's blood."

The Liberation. This part is dominated by Konrad, a hero of both Mickiewicz's *Forefather's Eve* and Wyspiański's *Liberation.* Although the authors of the script incorporated in this part fragments from Wyspiański's *Legend II, Acropolis, The Wedding,* and also some verses of other authors, such as Jarosław Iwaszkiewicz or Adam Polewka, the dramatic structure and the central theme were taken from *Liberation* and *The Wedding.* Both dramas deal with the illusions and dreams that dominate the Polish ethos, hampering a sober and rational diagnosis of the difficult situation of the nation (when Wyspiański wrote these dramas Poland was still partitioned). At one point in Wyspiański's *Liberation* Konrad explicitly addresses this issue (the following words were not included in the script of *The Song of Wawel,* but they convey the basic message of its second part): "Away, poetry, you are a tyrant!—You who love ruins and praise dark mysteries, sing false paths and guide into labyrinths, you want to evoke moans not joy."

Wyspiański's *Liberation* is complex and multilayered; it does not yield to straightforward interpretation. Konrad tries to find a solution to the Polish problem in discussions with the Masks, which represent various attitudes and points of view on the question of how to liberate Poland. No clear solutions are offered; Konrad merely calls for abandoning romantic fascination with myths and illusions of the past glory. Both *The Wedding* and *Liberation* can be construed as gigantic psychoanalytic sessions in which Wyspiański tries to diagnose the state of the Polish mind and to locate and name the problems therein. His solutions, however, are not clear. A collage of scenes, constituting the second part of *The Song of Wawel,* conveys a very similar mood. Let me quote the script:[17]

> *Konrad:* I am coming to carry you to action.
> *Voices:* What do you demand?
> *Konrad:* My thought has rested on you. You are the strength!
> *Voice I:* What do you want?
> *Konrad:* Liberation!

17. The following fragment comes from Wyspiański's *Liberation.*

Voice I: From what?—Do you want to free the spirit—but can it be enslaved? Or something is wrong with your heart? Confess!
Konrad: I want to depict the nation.

There is a strong Freudian overtone in this sequence. As a patient overcomes his illness by locating its causes in some past experiences, a nation can be liberated by realizing the roots of its present situation. But there is more to Konrad's vision. He believes the nation cannot be liberated by the effort of one social class alone. So far, the national uprisings organized and carried out by the nobility had failed. Now, Konrad calls on all classes from different periods of Polish history to participate in the drama of national introspection and purification. In the actual performances actors and extras representing all these figures gathered under Wawel Hill. Konrad appeals for a "struggle of thoughts and words" and asks everybody who despairs over the tragic Polish situation to join in the gathering. "Whoever knows Polish speech. Come here—you will be revitalized by the grace of the word."

The crowd then begins to dance a polonaise. The dance reaches its culmination when yet another figure from a Wyspiański drama enters the scene: the *Chochoł*—The Straw Man. His entry freezes the dancers, who turn into mannequin-like "hollow men." The *Chochoł* is a key character in *The Wedding,* one of the most popular, yet complex, dramas in Polish repertoire. Since the play is a part of the standard curriculum in Poland, one can assume that most of the spectators were able to decode the basic message of the *Chochoł*'s appearance correctly. What is this message? Miłosz explains:

> Viewed as a whole, [*The Wedding*] offers a pitilessly exposed cross section of a Polish society that is touched by a strange paralysis of the will: a peasant's saying—"They do not will to will"—applies, above all to the intelligentsia. But peasants do not fare much better in the drama. If we have to delineate a plot in *The Wedding,* it consists in the growing expectation of some tremendous, extraordinary event, which remains unnamed (an uprising? miraculous recovery of the country's independence?). The phantom of an eighteenth-century wandering lyre player and minstrel, Wernyhora (a purely legendary figure), gives a peasant lad a golden horn at the sound of which the "spirit will be fortified; Fate will be accomplished." The lad is sent to signal from afar the coming of the big event. All those present are ordered to prepare themselves and to strain their ears toward the road from Cracow. Yet the lad returns empty-handed; he has forgotten about his mission and has

lost the golden horn. The big event never comes; instead, the play closes with a dreamlike dance of "hollow man" that symbolizes the inertia of Polish society." (1983, 356–57).

The *Chochoł* is yet another symbol of this inertia and lack of will power. At the end of *The Wedding,* when the dance resumes, the characters are still "frozen" mannequins who spin around to the tune of the *Chochoł's* violin. In *The Song of Wawel,* however, there is a different finale. Konrad breaks the spell, exclaiming, "Our game will be tragic, it will be a reproach and soliloquy. . . . Liberation will come to those who are able to liberate themselves by the power of their own will." The *Chochoł* is burnt. Chudziński interprets his own scenario: "Fire has here purifying power, it is a ritual fire" (Chudziński 1982, 128). In another version of *The Song of Wawel*[18] Jasiński and Chudziński depart from Wyspiański. Konrad recites some of Jasiek's lines. This time Jasiek, the lad who lost the golden horn in *The Wedding,* is not so absentminded. When he asks: "Strain your ears: can you hear horses coming from Kraków," some commotion can be heard from the side of Mogiła, a place where an artificial hill had been erected in memory of Wanda "who did not want a German." But by the 1970s Mogiła had become a part of Nowa Huta, a new town built near Kraków after World War II to house the hundreds of thousands of workers who work in the gigantic Lenin Steelworks. A cavalcade of workers on motorbikes enters the stage, escorting a huge crane carrying fire from the steelworks. The coming of the workers breaks the spell of the hypnotic trance-dance; the fire is used to burn the *Chochoł* and light candles in the wreaths, which will soon be placed on the water. Konrad recites the closing lines of the second part, Tuwim's prayer:

> Open Poland for us, as you open a clouded sky with a thunder. Let us clean the house of our fathers from ashes, sacred ruins, our sins and damned faults. Let it be poor but clean: our home from a graveyard erected. But above all—return to our words, slyly changed by manipulators, unity and truth. Let the law mean law, and justice—justice.

As the Poet recites these lines, the gigantic dance begins anew.

The Rite. The last part of *The Song of Wawel* was non-narrative. It was aimed at the senses rather than the intellect. The Poet and the Choir

18. Described by Miklaszewski and recorded as a script in Jasiński and Chudziński, eds. (1980).

praised the holy waters of the Vistula and the beauties of Kraków. Music, lights, and fireworks were used to create the "magic" mood of Midsummer Night. During certain years the spectacle ended with the ceremony of *Wianki* (The wreaths) in which hundreds of little wreaths with candles were placed on the water.

Interpretation

An interpretation of such a complex spectacle can never be comprehensive. It is almost impossible to determine how many layers of meanings the spectators might have decoded. Some may have grasped all the literary nuances and historical allusions; some may have treated *The Song of Wawel* above all as a festive and playful celebration of Midsummer Night, reflecting little on its complex meanings. I have never systematically interviewed the audience of the spectacle; it would be a difficult task for both financial and organizational reasons.[19] It is, however, necessary to reconstruct the multilayered meaning of the spectacle, for it created or reinforced—if only through subliminal mechanisms—stereotypes and perceptions of reality, though this didactic aspect might not have been fully realized by the creators and the spectators.

In the following analysis I employ some elements of Victor Turner's interpretive strategy, which consists in reconstructing three major layers of meaning in each ritual (or, for that matter, any cultural phenomenon): positional, exegetic, and operational. I will deal with the first two. "In the positional dimension, the observer finds in the relations between one symbol and other symbols an important source of its meaning" (Turner 1977, 190). In turn, "exegetic meaning . . . supplied by indigenous interpretation, given by those inside the ritual system" (Turner and Turner 1978, 247), consists of four types of elements: (a) nominal, (b) substantial, (c) artifactual, and (d) historical.

The Positional Dimension: The Temporal Context

In the 1970s, during May and June, Kraków's ceremonial calendar was particularly dense. State and Church ceremonies followed each other closely, creating a peculiar schizophrenic picture of the national symbolic space torn apart by two competing centers of power and authority. In this

19. According to Chudziński 150,000 people saw the spectacle between 1972 and 1980.

confrontation, a product of the coexistence of state and Church calendars, symbolic and political elements were closely intertwined.

The sequence of symbolic events began with the state May Day celebrations (described in the preceding chapter). It was followed by May Third, the holiday commemorating the so-called May Constitution, written in 1791, four years before the last partition of Poland. The Constitution functions in the collective memory as a symbol of the Polish traditions of democracy, tolerance, and social reform aimed at the strengthening of central authority, a move that was supposed to save Poland, but—according to many historians (including those servile to the Communist regime)—came too late to be an effective weapon against the overwhelming power of the partitioning armies. May Third was celebrated in prewar Poland as a state holiday, and this seems to be the main reason that the Communists dropped it from the Polish ceremonial calendar. In the late 1970s both the opposition and the Catholic Church considered May Third a holiday. The opposition observed that day as the anniversary of the May Constitution;[20] the Church celebrated it as the Feast of Our Lady, Queen of Poland. May 8th is the feast of Saint Stanisław, a patron of Poland and martyr.[21] It was celebrated by the Catholic Church and all Polish Catholics on the first Sunday following this date.

May 9 is Victory Day, a state holiday that in the late 1970s was celebrated by a whole range of events. In 1976, the soldiers of Kraków's garrison were joined by the young people from various official organizations in the Market Square. Together they went to lay flowers on all the graves of soldiers killed in World War II. In 1979, there was a rally of soldiers and youth in the Market Square on May 8. The ceremonial changing of the guards in Matejko Square, between the Tomb of the Unknown Soldier and the Grunwald Monument[22] was conducted on May 9. Flowers were laid on soldiers's graves and on all monuments commemorating the struggle of Polish and Soviet soldiers in World War II. The local authorities met with veterans; some sporting events and artistic shows were organized as well.

The second weekend in May belonged to Kraków's students. *Juvenalia* or the feast of youth was held from early Friday afternoon through late Sunday night. It was a joyous festival. Students dressed in costumes of

20. They are discussed in Chapter 6.

21. Stanisław of Szczepanowo, the bishop of Kraków who was slain by King Bolesław the Bold in circumstances vividly resembling the English story of Thomas Becket murdered by King Henry II. This event and its mythological significance are analyzed in Chapter 5.

22. The monument commemorates the victory of Polish armies and their allies over the Teutonic Knights at the battle of Grunwald, which took place on 14 July 1410.

their own invention filled the streets, playing music, "begging" for money, dancing, and drinking. The feast had a flair of a carnivalesque ritual of inversion, for it began with a ceremony in which the mayor of Kraków gave the symbolic keys of the city to the students' representatives, and ended with the ceremony in which the keys were returned and the city resumed its "normal" life. The event cannot be interpreted, however, as a full-fledged status reversion or a Gluckmanian ritual of rebellion, since the political overtones were absent. Even a mild political satire in the songs was rarely heard.

Then in June comes Corpus Christi.[23] In Poland, it is a religious celebration of such a significance that it is officially recognized as a holiday (a day off) by the state. The route taken by the procession in Kraków was a long-standing established tradition, leading from the Wawel Cathedral through Grodzka Street to the Market Square, the city's center. Beginning in 1945, however, the Communist authorities would no longer permit the procession to enter the Market Square and so its course was changed to include Franciszkańska Street and Straszewskiego Street. Only since 1979, the year of the pope's visit, was the procession allowed to return to its old route, culminating again in the Market Square. From 1945 until the fall of Communist Poland there was no mention of either the procession or any other aspect of the Corpus Christi celebrations in the official media. Yet the procession has always been among the most lively public events in Poland. The two processions I observed in Kraków in the 1970s involved tens of thousands of people. Along the processional course most of the houses were decorated with religious pictures, flowers, and decorative carpets hanging out of the open windows. The atmosphere was both solemn and joyous. Thousands of people stood on the sidewalks watching the procession as it passed. In contrast to the May Day parade, people were not grouped together in larger units such as districts or even parishes. They participated in the feast as individuals, not as members of some organized bodies. Participation was voluntary and there were no sanctions (beside moral) imposed on those who preferred not to participate.

The Corpus Christi procession moves through the four "stations" where it stops and the leading priest gives a sermon or a lecture. In the

23. Corpus Christi is a movable feast, its date always falls on a Thursday, eleven days after the Pentecost, which in turn is celebrated seven weeks after Easter Sunday. Corpus Christi was established as an official church feast in 1264 by Pope Urban IV in his bull *Transiturn de hoc mundo*. The procession became an integral part of the ritual in the fourteenth century and came to be regarded as an extension of the Corpus Christi mass.

second half of the 1970s Kraków's celebrations were led by Karol Cardinal Wojtyła, who invariably addressed in his speeches the most nagging social and political problems of the day.

The calendrical sequence leading up to *The Song of Wawel* is summarized in Table 1.

The Positional Meaning: The Spatial Context

The cultural meanings of *The Song of Wawel* can be further elaborated by an analysis of its place in the physical and symbolic space of Kraków. This spatial context of the spectacle is depicted in Figure 1 and summarized in Table 2.

The Market Square is the physical and social center of Kraków. Any public event taking place there has a high social visibility. Church ceremonies were barred (until 1979) from this space. Oppositional demonstrations were barred from all public spaces, including the Market Square, yet one of them was organized there in 1977; the circumstances of this will be discussed later. The Wawel Cathedral, one of the ultimate symbols of Polish nationhood, was used by the Church in its two major processions (Corpus Christi and Saint Stanisław); it also hosted the oppositional groups organizing masses to commemorate anniversaries bypassed by the state, such as May Third. Interestingly, the state never used Wawel as a site in which to hold its Communist/socialist ceremonies. Wawel was used in *The Song of Wawel* merely as a backdrop, not as a meeting place. Matejko Square, with its Tomb of the Unknown Soldier and the Grunwald Monument, served as a site for official ceremonies, such as May Day or Victory Day, but was also used by the opposition for its celebrations. In general, the symbolic spaces in which the state, the Church, and the opposition organized their ceremonies partially overlapped, although the boundary between the Church's domain (close to Wawel, without Market Square) and the state's domain (Market Square and Matejko Square) was carefully guarded by the state. The demonstrations staged by the opposition often used the sacred spaces of the Church's domain not only because these were the only available spaces relatively safe from the state's interference but also because the oppositional groups wanted to emphasize their affinity with the Church. Many oppositional demonstrations also "trespassed" on the state's territory (Matejko Square and Market Square in 1977) in an attempt to recover traditions and symbols annexed by the authorities (such as the Tomb of the Unknown Soldier).

Table 1. Calendrical sequence leading up to *The Song of Wawel*

Holiday	Main organizer	1976	1977	1978	1979	1980
May Day	State	May 1	May 1	May 1	May 1	May 1
May Constitution	Opposition/Church	May 3	May 3	May 3	May 3	May 3
St. Stanisław's Day*	Church	May 9	May 8	May 14	June 3 and 10	May 11
Victory Day	State	May 9	May 9	May 9	May 9	May 9
Juvenalia	State	May 14–16	May 13–15	May 12–14	May 11–13	May 16–18
Corpus Christi	Church	June 17	June 9	May 25	June 14	June 5
The Song of Wawel	State	June 19	June 19	June 17	June 16	June 21

*The official date of the Feast of Saint Stanisław is May 8, but actual celebrations take place on the first Sunday following this date. In 1979 the celebrations were moved to June 3 and 10. The significance of this fact is discussed in Chapter 5.

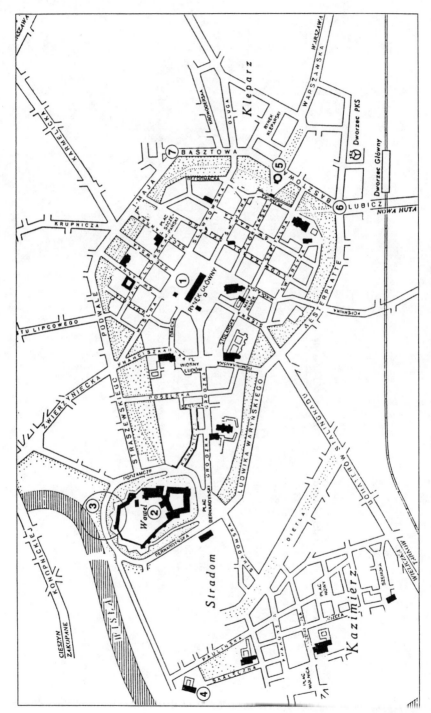

Fig. 1. Kraków: Spatial context of *The Song of Wawel* (Adapted from Saysee Tobiczyk 1966)

1. The Market Square
2. The Wawel Cathedral
3. Location of *The Song of Wawel*
4. The church of Saint Stanisław on Skałka
5. The location of the May Day Parade viewing stand (Matejko Square)

Routes of the Three Major Public Parades

A. Corpus Christi Procession: from the Wawel Cathedral (2) through Plac Bernardyński, Grodzka Street, Plac Wiosny Ludów, Franciszkańska Street, Straszewskiego Street, to Podzamcze at the bottom of the Wawel Cathedral (2).

B. Saint Stanisław Procession: from the church of Saint Stanisław (4) through Paulińska Street, Krakowska Street, Stradomska Street, Plac Bernardyński to the Wawel Cathedral (2).

C. May Day Parade: Basztowa Street, roughly from (6) to (7) with the viewing stand located at the Matejko Square (5). (Only a fragment of the route is indicated)

Table 2. Spatial context of *The Song of Wawel*

Holiday	Locations		
	State	Church	Opposition
May Day	Market Square, Matejko Square, Basztowa		
May Third Constitution		Churches, including Wawel Cathedral	Matejko Square, Wawel Cathedral
St. Stanisław Victory Day	Market Square, Matejko Square	Wawel-Skałka	
Juvenalia	The whole town, including Market Square		
Corpus Christi		Wawel-Wawel (1979, including Market Square)	
The Song of Wawel	Wawel Hill and the Vistula banks, not Wawel Cathedral		

The Positional Dimension: Summary of Findings

The Song of Wawel was not performed in a cultural vacuum. The temporal chain of official-secular, religious, and oppositional cultural performances and the spatial proximity of the arenas of these performances endowed it with a (potential[24]) significance unintended by its creators. The motifs of the national heritage omitted (religious myths) or deemphasized (the tradition of struggles for national independence) in the spectacle were kept in the collective memory by the religious feasts and oppositional demonstrations, increasingly visible after 1976. Hence, the propagation of the officially sanctioned vision of the national past constructed in *The Song of Wawel,* was counterbalanced by the actions performed in other symbolic contexts and referring to other visions of Polish history, albeit performed within the same physical space. In this way Kraków's audience was exposed over a period of two months to a cultural plurality that was hardly desired by the authorities.

The Exegetic Dimension: The Nominal Aspect

The name of the spectacle, *The Song of Wawel,* indicates its relationship to the "hottest" symbolic place in the cultural landscape of Poland. Since Wawel Hill, Wawel Castle, and Wawel Cathedral are perceived by the Poles as the most sacred monuments of national heritage, any spectacle near or making reference to them assumes, even if inadvertently, countless cultural and historical denotations and connotations of Polish national identity.

The Exegetic Dimension: Substantial and Artifactual Aspects

Substantial (that is, physical and biological) aspects of the spectacle's meaning proved to be unexpectedly significant. Unexpectedly, because we tend to assume that in modern complex cultures, sensual characteristics of cultural artifacts or acts are far less important than their cultural and historical meanings. *The Song of Wawel* was staged on the "magical" Midsummer Night, which endowed it with sensuality. This effect was enhanced by the integral role of fire and water in the spectacle, whose creators were fully aware of the powerful symbolism of the basic ele-

24. I qualify this statement because not all performances were always actualized and certainly not all of Kraków's inhabitants were aware of all of them all the time or in all their senses. This was a potential cultural field whose meanings were decoded selectively.

ments.[25] The water used in the spectacle was not just any water; it was the Vistula—the queen of Polish rivers, associated with countless myths, legends, and histories.[26]

Fire, another basic element used in the spectacle, also did not appear merely to evoke its archetypal or psychoanalytical connotations. It was fire with clear mythological and historical denotations, readily recognized by the spectators. It was the fire of the Midsummer Night festivities.[27] In the past, bunches of straw, tree branches, and huge straw puppets were burnt or drowned in the water (Gieysztor 1982, 210–12). A Russian ethnographer, Natalia N. Vieleckaya (see Gieysztor 1982, 212–14), has interpreted these facts as remnants of ancient rites involving human sacrifices, in which straw puppets replaced humans. In such rites people were sacrificed to ensure regularity of the vegetation cycle.

Differences in details notwithstanding, all these legends and folktales emphasize the unusual character of Midsummer Night. It is a liminal (transitional) phase of a rite of passage in the Van Gennepian sense. A period of early vegetation, long and full of anxieties, is being replaced by the last stage of growth leading directly toward harvest. All technological and magical skills have been applied and even if they have not succeeded, it is too late to change the course of events. Hence, demons, spirits, and nonpersonal forces, released in the spring rites (centered around Easter), are sent back (through burning or drowning) to the other world, so they cannot be used for evil by black magicians.

Popular folklore of today retains only the superficial meanings of the

25. Krzysztof Miklaszewski, associated with the STU, in his analysis of the spectacle quotes Gaston Bachelard, a French philosopher who explored the psychoanalytic significance of water and fire (Miklaszewski 1980).

26. Orgiastic baths are believed to have belonged to the celebrations in the past. In more recent times, swimming was allowed only after St. John the Baptist had "blessed the water" on his feast (Peszkowski n.d., 47).

27. Celebrations of the longest night in the year (Midsummer Night) belong to the old Slavic customs (recorded for the first time in the Polish territories in 1562, in Russia even earlier, in the thirteenth century (Gieysztor 1982, 206). As is the case of other Christian customs, the Church slowly incorporated the pagan rites of Midsummer Night into its own ritual calendar. The pagan sabbath (as it was often referred to in the Church sources) became the celebration of St. John the Baptist Eve. But the festivities retained its pagan, "magical" character until today. In Polish folklore fire is the focal element of the Midsummer Night rites (Gieysztor 1982, 212). It was to be ignited "in an old way," by rubbing two pieces of wood against each other (Bystroń 1947, 183). Such fire was new, therefore pure, suggesting that the idea of purification has always been strongly associated with the custom. People sang, danced, and jumped over the fire. There are reports from as late as 1861 that cattle were run through the fire, and sometimes local priests would take part in such events, saying appropriate prayers and sprinkling the cattle with holy water (Ciołek, Olędzki, and Zadrożyńska 1976, 96; Bystroń 1947, 183).

Midsummer Night rites. It is a joyous summer holiday, playful and recreational. Its deeper, agrarian dimension has been forgotten. The key attraction is placing wreaths on the water and setting bonfires on river banks. But people still like to believe that everything is possible on this unusual "magical" night.[28]

The Exegetic Dimension: The Historical Aspect (Motifs and "Traditions" Presented in The Song of Wawel)

In order to reconstruct the vision of the Polish past presented in *The Song of Wawel* I will identify all major historical motifs and "traditions" presented in the spectacle. Then, I will compare them with those elements of the potential reservoir of national traditions which were omitted. An analysis of the logic of such choices must reveal something about the politics of those who made them.

The personages presented in *The Song of Wawel* belong to the most popular figures in Polish mythology and history: each of them represents a set of values and functions as a multivocal symbol, lending itself to various, often competing, interpretations. From this potential repertoire of meanings, Jasiński and Chudziński, by asking their heroes to deliver short and clearly programmatic messages, opted for definite and easily identifiable interpretations. Kościuszko, for example, survives in the national memory first of all as the leader of an uprising against the Russians, as a hero of the struggle for national independence (Szacka 1981, 113). In *The Song of Wawel* this aspect of his historical persona was merely alluded to, whereas his other role—as a champion of peasant emancipation—was emphasized. Table 3 contains the results of an analysis, in which I try to identify the set of historical traditions[29] assigned in *The Song of Wawel* to each of the personages appearing in the second part of the spectacle, *The Heritage*.

The traditions of national culture, state building, and the struggle for social justice were represented by four historical personages each. The theme of cultural achievement (national culture) was, however, invoked

28. The most popular tradition related to Midsummer Night, still widely practiced in Poland, is a custom of "wreaths." Girls make little wreaths, often with a candle inside, and place them on the water. The course their wreaths take is believed to predict their future relationships with boys. Boys, in turn, wait downstream to catch the wreaths belonging to their sweethearts in order to assure a happy marriage (Peszkowski n.d., 47; Pełka 1980, 80). According to another, very popular folktale, flowerless ferns bloom on this night, and whoever sees a fern blossom will have all his or her wishes fulfilled.

29. I have employed a modified typology of national traditions developed by Szacka (1977, 1981).

Table 3. Historical traditions depicted in *The Song of Wawel*

National Culture	Military Power	State Building	The Struggle for Independence	The Struggle for Social Justice
		Krak	Wanda	
Kazimierz the Great	Jagiełło	Kazimierz the Great		
Zygmunt the Old		Zygmunt the Old		
Zygmunt August		Zygmunt August		
Kochanowski			Kościuszko	Kochanowski
				Kościuszko
				Dembowski
				Waryński

mostly indirectly rather than being independently developed.[30] Kochanowski, the most formidable historical representative of this theme, wrote on a wide range of significant social, cultural, and political issues of his day. Yet in the spectacle he was presented only as a guardian of social justice, warning against abuses of political power.

The tradition of peaceful state building was represented by one mythical prince and three historical kings. By the choosing these figures, the authors portrayed the development of Polish statehood as a cultural rather than as a political process. The latter (unrealized) option would have to include a presentation of the rivals of Poland. This was always a problematic task for a popular didactic spectacle, especially since one of the political antagonists in Polish history was (and is) Russia, an unlikely candidate for the role of an enemy in a country where the positive image of all things Russian was one of the axioms of the official public discourse. This careful avoidance of negative references to Russia is clear in the presentation of other traditions. The tradition of military power, represented by just one hero (Władysław Jagiełło), was invoked by reference to the Polish resistance against German expansion, a theme also symbolized by the mythical Wanda. Other nations and states with which Poland competed and fought throughout her history, especially Russia, were not mentioned. Kościuszko, the hero of an anti-Russian uprising, did not appear in this role in the spectacle. There was only a hint of the purpose of his struggle when he says, "This authority I was granted . . . will be only used to restore our borders, regain national sovereignty and reinforce freedom for all." It was not clarified who caused the loss of Polish sovereignty and under what circumstances: the issue of the partitions of Poland did not appear in the script.

The motif of national sovereignty and independence emerged in Szacka's 1977 study as an issue of primary historical interest among the students. And yet in *The Song of Wawel* this motif, represented only by Kościuszko and less directly by Wanda and Jagiełło, was emphasized far less than the theme of the struggle for social justice (which was not as popular among the same students), symbolized by the last four personages. Furthermore, the issue of social justice was clearly intertwined with the emergence of socialism. From the whole gallery of nineteenth-century heroes, most of whom fought in the uprisings against the partitioning

30. Some of the personages of *The Song of Wawel* figure in popular consciousness as symbols related to well-defined values. It seems plausible to assume that the audience identified these values and assigned them to the relevant personages, despite the meanings assigned to them in the verbal layer of the performance. At the risk of excessive subjectivity in my interpretation I nevertheless believe this to be true in the cases of Zygmunt the Old, Zygmunt August, and Kochanowski.

powers or often combined such struggle with social radicalism, the spectacle presented Dembowski and Waryński, both social revolutionaries rather than heroes of the struggle for national independence. In short, the independence tradition was not clearly articulated, whereas the tradition of social reforms and socialist movements of the nineteenth century—claimed by the regime as its direct heritage—was strongly emphasized.

There are two elements of Kraków's and Poland's national heritage whose absence in the script of *The Song of Wawel* is particularly conspicuous, which serves as a good indicator of the authors' vision of history.[31] The spectacle contained no reference to religion (especially the figure of Saint Stanisław) or to Marshal Józef Piłsudski.

The history of Kraków and Poland, as presented in *The Song of Wawel*, began in the pre-Christian foundation myths of Krak and Wanda and was narrated through a sequence of political and cultural events. The spectacle's narrative did not contain a single reference to Christianity, despite the abundance of religious motifs in Kraków's reservoir of myths and legends. One of them, the story of the conflict between King Bolesław the Bold and Bishop Stanisław of Szczepanowo constitutes one of the focal points not only of Kraków's folklore but also of the whole national heritage.

It would seem that Józef Piłsudski, the most prominent Polish political leader of the twentieth century, an architect of Polish independence in 1918, the victorious commander-in-chief of the Polish army in the war with the Soviet Union in 1920–21, and the undisputed leader of the Polish state until his death in 1935, would have been a logical choice for the parade of historical personages included in *The Song of Wawel*.[32] Piłsudski is privately revered in many Polish homes and became a symbolic focal point of many oppositional activities in the late 1970s. Yet he was a nonperson or, at best, a mythical villain of the official version of Polish history.[33] His absence in the official history was symptomatic of

31. The cultural and political significance of these omissions will become clear after I analyze the visions of history presented in the Church ceremonies and oppositional demonstrations.

32. Piłsudski's uniqueness is acknowledged even by highly critical Western historians. Seton-Watson writes, for example: "However much one may criticize the policy of the old Marshal, it is impossible to question his disinterested patriotism and his personal integrity" (1962, 163). These attributes of Piłsudski's character made him a figure of legendary proportions during his own life.

33. The silence in the official histories and the insults in the official propaganda were matched by the growing popularity of the Piłsudski myth among the youth. As Szacka's study showed, Piłsudski advanced in the years 1965–77 from eleventh to fifth in the ranking of national heroes. By contrast, in 1965 (the first year of Szacka's study) his popularity was in decline.

the treatment of the history of Poland between the wars, which the Party considered a "negative tradition" for the Polish People's Republic.[34] *The Song of Wawel* did not contain a single reference to Piłsudski.

Politics and Culture in *The Song of Wawel*

Regardless of whether the exclusion of any references to religion or Piłsudski in *The Song of Wawel* resulted from a desire to avoid censorship or from the ideological convictions of the creators, the production fostered a selective vision of the national past. Specifically, by omitting religious motifs and by belittling the theme of independence and sovereignty, the spectacle's creators contributed, perhaps inadvertently,[35] to the self-legitimizing efforts of the Party-state: the portrait of the Polish nation they presented was congenial with the official vision of Polish past and present propagated in May Day celebrations, official anniversaries, and all other forms of the official discourse. The new Poland depicted in this discourse was ethnically homogenous and secular, and constituted a successful culmination of all trends in Polish history that had been interpreted by the Communists as "progressive," that is, as facilitating their cause.

The *Song of Wawel* also addressed the major stereotype of Polish (post-nineteenth-century) mythology: the perennial national inertia and the lack of will. By discussing this issue in a highly allusive and metaphorical way, instead of unmasking the myth, the spectacle actually reinforced it. In *The Liberation,* the third part of *The Song of Wawel,* various national controversies were portrayed as ahistorical, archetypical vices of the Polish soul torn between the irresponsible impulses of romanticism and the calculating accommodationism of positivism. By placing the discussion in a mythical frame of reference, the spectacle bolstered the dominant tendency of official debates to avoid or ignore realistic and rational assessment of the political situation. Such an assessment would have had to

34. Jerzy Szacki, who coined the term "negative tradition," describes it as follows: "In no group do its members shape their attitudes in a vacuum; while developing their attitudes that take a stand toward the attitudes of other members of the group. If that amounts to a conflict of attitudes, then a positive tradition of Group A becomes a negative tradition of Group B, which opposes Group A. . . . Changes in negative traditions of the various groups are probably the most sensitive indicator of intergroup relations, and also of the status of a given group within larger group" (1974, 70).

35. My conversations with Jasiński and other members of the STU indicate that the theater never consciously intended to contribute to the self-legitimizing efforts of the regime.

include, for example, an (artistic) exploration of the impact Poland's limited sovereignty and her dependency upon the Soviet Union had on various domains of social and cultural life.[36] This, however, was a taboo theme in the official discourse of the Polish People's Republic and the only way to deal with such issues was through allusions and metaphors worked into small, exclusive artistic productions.

The Song of Wawel, as a cultural performance for a mass audience, was commissioned and scrutinized by Kraków's Provincial Committee of the Polish United Workers' Party. Despite the fact that it was less schematic and overtly ideological than other official mass-cultural performances and that it employed popular cultural themes (such as the Midsummer Night or national heroes), *The Song of Wawel* became a didactic pageant (Geertz 1977, 154). The "didactic effect," even if unintended by the creators, was inevitable because the spectacle confirmed and enhanced the official version of Polish history, thereby perpetuating the Party-state's cultural hegemony.

36. Such an exploration was undertaken, for example, by the Theater of the Eighth Day.

4 The Discourse of Polish Catholicism

The Polish Socialist Party declared in 1987 that it felt "more affinity with the social teachings of the Church . . . than with Marxism." But even as early as the late 1970s such a declaration would not have been out of the ordinary. All oppositional groups recognized Catholic Christianity as the highest moral authority and constructed their discourses on its foundation. It is therefore necessary to portray the Catholic discourse and elucidate its role in the construction of the oppositional counterhegemony.

Although the Catholic Church was an "automatic" adversary of the secular state, public clashes of their competing discourses were infrequent. When they occurred, however, the results were spectacular. In Nowe Tychy, for example, the authorities erected the May Day viewing stand directly in front of a chapel adorned with a one and a half meter high cross. On 23 April 1977 a group of workers from a nearby construction site brought over a crane, knocked down the cross, and broke it into three pieces. Soon, several thousand people gathered on the spot of the incident. The workers, who claimed that they were only carrying out orders, were chased away by a group of young people. The cross was restored with the accompaniment of prayers.[1]

In April 1978 I happened to be in Poznań. The annual May Day celebrations were coming, so the streets were richly decorated with red and white-and-red flags, posters, and stickers. Numerous banners carrying familiar slogans were already stretched above the streets. Thus I could read: "Long live the First of May," "Long live the Polish United Workers' Party—the vanguard of the working class," "Proletarians of all countries unite," and so on. Soon, in this sea of red my eye caught some blue accents. "Something about peace," said my well-conditioned subconscious; in the Communist color symbolism, blue is usually associated with peace. The blue banners contained some slogans, and again I knew to expect the word for "peace" in different languages.

I was shocked. The banners read "Mother of God be always with us" and "Welcome, Holy Mother of God—Our Queen." A closer look at the walls of the surrounding buildings revealed another surprise. Red banners and posters were placed on the walls or windows—*on their outer surfaces*. But *from the inside* of almost every window, the dark face of the Black Madonna of Częstochowa gazed out on the street. It would be very difficult to find a more explicit and dramatic exemplification of the schizophrenic dualism pervading public life in Poland, almost from the inception of state-socialism.

Religion in the Polish People's Republic: 1945–1961

In most modern societies the religious grounds of social order and political legitimacy have become problematic. Religion, the traditional producer, repository, and guardian of group values lost its monopoly: other subsystems of modern society, including the political domain itself, began to produce values that were potential legitimators of social and political order. The situation of religion had become especially precarious in the Communist countries, where the dominant Marxist ideology was

---

1. The story was related in the underground magazine *Głos* (Special Issue), May 1979.

presented as the ultimate cognitive, ethical, and social solution. Consequently, religion was declared obsolete. In a democracy, religion becomes a competitor in the market of values and ideas and thereby gradually loses its monopoly as a source of value standards for the society. By contrast, in those states founded on Marxist-Leninist principles, the ruling elites, supported by their "founding myth," declared as one of their objectives the total elimination of religion from the social life and worked actively to realize this end. Cardinal Wyszyński, the Polish primate in the years 1948–1981, illustrated this difference succinctly when he warned against confusing "the drama of unbelief" with "the machinery of official atheism" (Micewski 1984, 268). As if to confirm the primate's observation, Kazimierz Kąkol, director of the Office for Religious Affairs in Poland, announced in 1978:

> While allowing the Church to function, we will never go back on our principles. Even though, as a Minister I have to smile to gain [the Church's] confidence, as a Communist, I will fight it unceasingly both on an ideological and on a philosophical level. I feel ashamed when comrades from other countries ask me why so many Poles go to church, I feel ashamed when guests congratulate me on the spread of religion in Poland. . . . We will never permit the religious upbringing of children. If we cannot destroy the Church, we shall at least stop it from causing harm. (*Dissent in Poland* 1977, 148)

A mere glance at the postwar history of Church-state relations in Poland reveals that their coexistence was rarely what could be called peaceful competition; for most of the years from 1945 through 1990 it was a struggle. The elections of 1947, based on manipulation and accompanied by terror and the intimidation of political opponents by the Communists, eliminated all rivals from the political game, including the strongest political force in postwar Poland: the *Polskie Stronnictwo Ludowe* (Polish Peasants' Party, or PSL). At the same time, the Communists and their new Polish United Workers' Party began the confrontation with the most powerful institution in the country, the Roman Catholic Church. Many prerogatives of the Church were restricted or eliminated: most of its land[2] and hospitals were nationalized, its publications were subjected to state censorship, its radio broadcasts were discontinued, religious instruction at schools was suspended, and chaplains were removed from

2. Holdings of over fifty hectares (one hundred hectares in the Poznań area, Pomerania, and Silesia) were included in the nationalization.

hospitals, prisons, and the army.[3] On 23 January 1950 the Church was forced to relinquish control over the large charitable and welfare organization *Caritas,* thereby losing an important channel of interaction with society.

On 14 April 1950 the state and the Catholic Church signed an agreement, legalizing these forced concessions.[4] The agreement, perceived by some observers (Korboński and Wong 1984) as an act establishing a foundation for dual power in Poland and by others (Michnik 1977) as an act of despair on the side of the bishops who yielded to the growing governmental pressure, produced a short-lived truce. On 9 February 1953, in a move hardly explainable from the "dual power" viewpoint, the State Council decreed that the state was taking over one of the fundamental prerogatives of the Church, its right to make and revoke ecclesiastical appointments. The bishops who were gathered at the Plenary Session of the Episcopate held in Kraków on May 8–9 to commemorate the seven-hundredth anniversary of Saint Stanisław's canonization, responded with a strongly worded memorial.[5] Cardinal Wyszyński repeated the major theses of Kraków's memorial on June 4, in the sermon given in Warsaw during the Corpus Christi procession. He said there:

> Between the Eternal Minister Jesus Christ and His Disciples, there was no intermediary. There was no need whatsoever to pass the ministries through the hands of someone alien. . . . The Holy Church . . . firmly defends the Ministry of Christ . . . because the freedom of Christ's Ministry is the most visible sign of man's freedom of conscience. When the priesthood is free, God's children are guaranteed freedom of conscience. Thus it is difficult to speak of any freedom of conscience when a priest is no longer free, when he is transformed, against the will of the Church, into a bureaucrat. . . . It is impermissible to reach for the altar, impermissible to stand between Christ and His minister, impermissible

3. For a description and analysis of these policies see, for example, Michnik (1977), Dziewanowski (1977), Bingen (1984), Cviic (1983), Monticone (1986), Szajkowski (1983), and Pomian-Srzednicki (1982).

4. The text of the agreement is available in English in Stehle (1965, 306–10).

5. Micewski calls this memorial, signed by Primate Wyszyński, "historical." The memorial included, inter alia, the following passage: "If we are given the choice between personal sacrifice or turning the church administration into a tool of the secular authorities—we shall not waver. We shall follow the apostolic voice of our calling and priestly conscience, with inner peace and the consciousness that we have not given the last reason for our persecution, that suffering shall become a part of our share in the affairs of Christ and Christ's church. We cannot place what belongs to God on the altar of Caesar. *No possumus!* [We cannot]" (Micewski 1984, 116).

to violate the conscience of the priest. We teach that one must give to Caesar what is Caesar's and to God what is God's. And if Caesar sits down on the altar, we must say simply: *That is not allowed!* (Michnik 1993, 65–66; translation modified slightly)

On 25 September 1953, after a public sermon conveying a similarly uncompromising defense of the Church's independence, Wyszyński was arrested and interned for the next three years.[6]

The primate was released on 26 October 1956 by Władysław Gomułka who was reinstated as the first secretary of the PZPR. A short period of relative liberalization in 1955–57, which later came to be known as "the Polish October," saw not only a spur of spontaneous intellectual and cultural initiatives, political relaxation, and a measure of economic innovations but also a considerable improvement in the Church's situation.[7] Most of the restrictions of 1953 were repealed. The Church could again make its own appointments (subject, however, to the state's approval), religious instruction was reinstated at schools (as an elective subject), and the five bishops nominated by the Vatican were permitted to assume their duties in the Western Lands (the former German territories granted to Poland after World War II).[8] Gomułka, seen by many Poles as a symbol of reforms, de-Stalinization, and "the Polish road to socialism," sought the Church's support to further improve his public image and strengthen his considerable (at the moment) authority. In the fall of 1956 the first secretary and the primate enjoyed together the fame of national saviors, since many people believed that it was due to their principled moral stance and political skills that the Soviets had abandoned their plans to invade, allowing Poland to escape Hungary's fate.[9]

The period of the "October" thaw did not last long. In October 1957 the authorities closed down the weekly *Po Prostu,* the most influential independent magazine of opinion, edited by a group of intellectuals devoted to the program of the liberalization and democratization of Polish socialism. The relationship between the state and the Church also began to deteriorate. In order to facilitate the ideological struggle with the Church, the authorities established the Society for the Secular School in

6. By the end of the same year eight bishops and some nine hundred priests were in prison (*Dissent in Poland* 1977, 147).

7. For a detailed account of the 1955–57 period of liberalization, see Karpiński (1982a, 23–104).

8. The full text of the 1956 agreement is available in Stehle (1965, 309–10).

9. According to Micewski, "from the moment of his return [from the internment], Wyszyński was counseling calm to the literally hundreds of people he received, while shoring up their faith and eagerness to serve their Church and country" (1984, 163).

1957, which was staffed mostly by former employees of the security apparatus. In July 1961 religious instruction was eliminated from the schools.

The Black Madonna of Częstochowa: The Symbolic Center of Catholic Poland

> Jasna Góra is not only a place of pilgrimage for Poles from Poland and the rest of the world. Jasna Góra is the sanctuary of the nation. . . . Polish history, particularly of the last centuries, can be written in many different ways, there are many keys to its interpretation. Yet if we want to know how this history flows through Polish hearts, it is necessary to come here. It is necessary to put one's ear to this Place. It is necessary to hear an echo of the Nation's life in the Heart of Its Queen and Mother.

John Paul II spoke thus during his first return visit to Poland after his ascent to Peter's throne. Several years earlier, anthropologist Eric Wolf summarized his views on the role of the cult of Our Lady of Guadalupe in Mexico in a strikingly similar fashion. According to Wolf, Our Lady of Guadalupe provides Mexicans with a cultural idiom expressing all important social relationships. "It is, ultimately, a way of talking about Mexico: a collective representation of Mexican society" (Wolf 1958, 39). The Black Madonna of Częstochowa, even if not a collective representation of Polish society, is the most sacred symbol in the Polish ethos, the ubiquitous reminder of the Marian tenor of Polish Catholicism.

According to the legend recorded in the oldest surviving source from the first half of the fifteenth century, the icon, known as the Black Madonna, was painted by Saint Luke on a cyprus board taken from a table belonging to the Holy Family. Just when, where, and by whom the icon was painted and how it ended up in Częstochowa is not clear; there are several, more or less believable versions of the story.[10] It is, however, well documented that the Paulinian monastery on Jasna Góra (Bright Mountain) in Częstochowa was founded on 9 August 1382. P. Risinius, in his *Historia Pulchra* (1523), claims that the painting was given to the Paulinian monks on 31 August 1384. In 1430 the monastery was pillaged, and the Black Madonna suffered serious damage. The painting had to be

---

10. They are summarily presented in *Encyklopedia Katolicka,* 3:852–79. In my reconstruction of the icon's history, I used this source and Jacher-Tyszkowa (1982).

restored, and it is possible that the existing copy dates from ca. 1431. It is sometimes assumed that after the restoration, commissioned by King Władysław Jagiełło and executed by Italian masters, the image acquired a new quality. Its original, schematic flatness, characteristic of Eastern icons, was enriched by the roundness and softness of an Italian school. It is possible that the aesthetic uniqueness of the painting and its "soft magic," which attracts millions of believers to the Madonna's feet, results from this blend of artistic styles. As with everything related to the icon, this double aesthetic quality can be interpreted on a deeper symbolic level. Poles have, throughout the centuries, thought of their country as a place where the Western and Eastern civilizations and cultural currents merged. Perhaps this explains—at least partially—the enormous popularity of a painting that somehow epitomizes this stereotype of the dual nature of Polish culture.

An impressive body of written, pictorial, and even musical works inspired by the icon constitutes a discourse in which history and myth mesh imperceptibly. In 1655 the Swedish army broke a truce with Poland and virtually swept away the Polish army, forcing one province after another to render homage to Charles X Gustavus. Only a miracle could save Poland . . . and one did. Jasna Góra monastery unexpectedly resisted the enemy. After a forty-day siege, Polish soldiers carrying the Holy Icon with them into battle forced the Swedes to retreat for the first time during the war. After this victory, King Jan Kazimierz made a solemn vow. "In the name of the whole nation he proclaimed that the Blessed Virgin should henceforth be venerated as 'Queen of the Crown of Poland.' The Polish nation was never to be false to that promise. The cult of Our Lady remained its supreme consolation through epochs of the anguish which surpassed that of 1655" (Halecki 1956, 159).[11] Thus began a tradition: a long line of kings, noblemen, burghers, and peasants would acknowledge the spiritual presence and control of the Black Madonna over their lives through acts of unconditional submission to her divine authority. For the partitioning powers she was the "Main Revolutionary"; exiled rebels called her the Patroness of the Exiles. In the 1863 uprising against the Russians, one of the priests designed an emblem of a future independent Poland, an oval with the Black Madonna in the middle. The icon was crowned with the papal crowns three times: in 1717, 1910, and 1966 when the nation celebrated its millennium. Zygmunts

11. The conviction that Our Lady protects Poland and her inhabitants is actually even older. By the beginning of the sixteenth century Poles already believed that her divine intervention contributed to several military victories over the Turks, Tartars, and Russians (Kopeć 1983, 57).

Chapel on Wawel Hill, designed by Bartolomeo Berecci and later called by a German art historian "a gem of Renaissance style north of the Alps," was built to glorify Mary after several Polish military victories were attributed to her intervention (Kopeć 1983, 57). The title "Queen of the Nation," bestowed on Our Lady of Częstochowa already in the second half of the fourteenth century, reflects her position as the Patroness and Defender of Polish sovereignty, national identity, and culture.[12]

Cardinal Wyszyński, realizing the symbolic potential of the Marian myth for his campaign to renew Polish Catholicism, included in the program of the Great Novena the idea of a peregrination of a copy of the Holy Icon throughout the whole country. In a letter dated 27–28 June 1980, the Episcopate explained:

> The purpose of these visitations was to obtain the help of the Holy Mother in moral renewal of the Nation. This task was undertaken by the primate of Poland and the whole Episcopate before the millennium of our baptism. It was to be realized through the Jasna Góra Vows of the Nation and the Great Novena. The Holy Mother was to support personally the great undertaking of spiritual renewal of the whole society and our fidelity to the vowed oaths, which bind us forever. (*Krzyż Nowohucki,* no.2, 1980)

The Celebrations of the Great Novena of the Polish Nation and the Millennium

In May 1956, Cardinal Wyszyński, still interned, envisioned a long program of preparatory celebrations for the millennium of the Polish baptism and Polish statehood, which was to be celebrated in 1966.[13] The

12. There is an inevitable conflict between such particularism and the claims of Catholic Christianity to universalism (for more on this tension, see Morawska 1984, 32–33). The Polish Church set out to solve this problem not by curbing the excessively nationalized cult of the Holy Virgin, but by expanding it to encompass the Universal Church. It was the result of the campaign of the Polish bishops (especially Cardinal Wyszyński) that Paul VI proclaimed Mary as the Mother of the Church (*Mater Ecclesiae*) in November 1964. "No one doubted that the proclamation was a personal triumph for the Primate of Poland, the Episcopate, Jasna Góra, the propagators of the Marian cult, and the whole Polish Church" (Micewski 1984, 242). The Polish pope has continued the process of "universalization" of the Marian cult without, however, ever diminishing her place in Polish mythology.

13. Poles traditionally mark 966, the year when the Polish prince Mieszko the First was baptized, as the beginning of both Polish statehood and Polish Christianity.

program spread over nine years and was called the Great Novena of the Millennium: "Just as during a normal novena we ask God for some favor, so during the Great Novena, through nine years of prayer and profound moral works, the Polish nation was to renew itself spiritually and ask God, through Mary, for the victory of faith and freedom of the Church" (Micewski 1984, 157).

The Church prepared the nine-year long celebration, unprecedented in the history of modern Christianity, very carefully. Every year from 1957 through 1966, when the celebrations were to culminate, was devoted to one great theme corresponding to the general goal of the Novena, national and religious renewal. The following list of themes illustrates well the Church's major concerns:

1. Fidelity to God, the Cross, Christ's Gospel, and the Church.
2. Life in a state of sanctifying grace.
3. Defense of the life of spirit and flesh.
4. Holiness of the sacramental marriage.
5. Strength to the family through God.
6. Faith in Christ by the youth.
7. Justice and social love.
8. The struggle against national vices and the acquisition of Christian virtues.
9. The protection of the Mother of God, Queen of Poland.[14]

In Wyszyński's vision the nation was to take a solemn vow, dedicating itself to Mary. It was to be a renewal of the vows taken by King Jan Kazimierz in 1656.

A million pilgrims attended the opening mass of the Great Novena, held in Częstochowa on 26 August 1956. The text of solemn vows was read by Bishop Klepacz. Wyszyński, who was still interned in Komańcza, "stood before the picture of the Madonna of Częstochowa and recited the act of dedication at about the same time as Bishop Klepacz at Jasna Góra" (Micewski 1984, 158).[15] It was this spectacular ceremony that defined the cultural frame of the conflict between the Church and the state for decades to come.

On 11 April 1957, during the meeting of the Council of Bishops, the bishops decided to include a tour of all dioceses by a copy of the icon of

14. Various sources give different versions of these slogans (see, for example, Stehle 1965). I quote here (in my own translation) Wyszyński (1962, 7).
15. For the full text of the Jasna Góra Vows, see Appendix 1. My translation differs from Micewski's (1984, 158).

Black Madonna of Częstochowa in the program of the millennium celebrations. The authorities, aware of the enormous symbolic significance
of such a peregrination, accused the bishops of waging a "religious war"
(Micewski 1984, 170). This unusual war began on 26 August 1957 in the
Warsaw diocese and ended on 12 October 1980 in Częstochowa. The
Black Madonna was seen by virtually all Polish Catholics. After the
arrival in a given parish, the copy was sent to all the households that had
requested to host it and had received permission from a local priest. It
was therefore a special privilege, no doubt carefully distributed by the
clergy.[16] The painting usually stayed in each household for twenty-four
hours. These direct encounters with the Black Madonna strengthened
social integration on both local and national levels and rejuvenated the
religiosity of the Poles:[17] countless incidents of conversion were reported
from all over the country; there were massive returns to the sacramental
life (for example, in the Warmia diocese one million Holy Communions
were received).[18]

The Great Novena ended on Holy Saturday, 9 April 1966. The commemorative celebrations of the millenium began on April 14 in the
Gniezno Cathedral,[19] where forty thousand people participated in the
pontifical high mass. Paul VI had been invited by the Polish Episcopate,
but he was not given a visa by the Polish authorities. Therefore, the main
celebrations of the millenium of Polish Christianity on 3 May 1966 in
Częstochowa were led by Cardinal Wyszyński, whom the pope nomi-

16. According to Wierzbicki: "Hosting the picture was associated with substantial
expenditures (painting and white washing of the house and rooms, minor repairs and
general cleaning of the farmstead, etc.) and was considered to be an act of social recognition" (1980, 138).

17. Chris Hann, a British anthropologist witnessed a similar visit during a peregrination
organized on a diocesan level in the 1980s in "his" village. Here are some excerpts from his
account of this event: "During her stay in Wislok the Madonna spent twenty-four hours in
each house, before being carried aloft in a procession to the next. She was invariably
displayed in the best room in the house . . . there was no drinking of alcohol. Peasants and
non-peasant families nonetheless did turn out, in the early hours of the evening, at a time of
year when there was a great deal of work in the fields, and spend two or three hours singing
hymns and reciting all the prayers that they knew in front of the holy image. . . . This
image of the 'national virgin' was the most potent symbol for the individuals who gathered
before her, and the way in which she circulated helped to cement the social unity of the
parish" (Hann 1985, 112).

18. See *Encyklopedia Katolicka,* 3:878. In a sociological study on the religiosity in the
Katowice diocese, Woznica discovered that during the peregrination of the icon of Our
Lady of Częstochowa in the church year 1966–67, 471 couples who had lived for many
years without benefit of a church marriage were married in a Christian ceremony (*Czarna
Księga Cenzury PRL* 1977, 2:363).

19. Gniezno was the first capital of Poland.

nated to act as his legate. The primate dedicated the country "in servitude to Mary, the Mother of the Church, for the sake of church freedom in the country and the world. In a breve that he later directed to Wyszyński, Pope Paul called this act a 'second christening of Poland' " (Micewski 1984, 265–66). The icon of the Black Madonna was removed from the altar and was carried around the monastery in a procession. The portrait of Paul VI, surrounded by flowers, was placed on a chair prepared for him and it remained empty throughout the ceremonies.

During the celebrations the bishops dedicated the nation to the Holy Virgin, hoping to reinforce the nation's faith, which they believed was endangered by the Communist state. In the closing sermon of the May Third celebrations in Częstochowa, Wyszyński said:

> In the face of a totalitarian threat to the nation . . . in the face of an atheistic program supported by the PUWP, in the face of biological destruction [a reference to the government's liberal abortion policy—J.K.]—a great supernatural current is needed, so that the nation can consciously draw from the Church the divine strength that will fortify its religious and national life. Nowhere else is the union of Church and nation as strong as in Poland, which is in absolute danger. Our "temporal theology" demands that we dedicate ourselves into the hands of the Holy Mother, so that we may live up to our task. (Micewski 1984, 266–67)

This "temporal theology," in which the Polish nation was dedicated to the Holy Virgin, was mythical. Yet, at the same time, it was historical, for it began with the christening of Prince Mieszko and his court in 966 and included the May Third tradition,[20] an unequivocal reminder of sovereignty and independence.

The state chose to begin its celebrations of the millennium of Polish statehood on July 22, the anniversary of People's Poland, indicating thereby that the traditions it subscribed to and cultivated were altogether different. On July 21, a special ceremonial session of the Polish parliament (Sejm) was held. Gomułka in his speech, "The Destiny of the Polish Nation Is Forever Linked with Socialism," authoritatively defined the heritage of the Polish People's Republic. First he justified the choice of date:

20. May Third, the anniversary of the 1791 Constitution and the Feast of Our Lady, Queen of Poland, was celebrated in the prewar Poland, but was dropped from the official calendar by the Communists.

We chose the eve of the 22nd anniversary of the Manifesto of the Polish Committee of National Liberation,[21] July 21st, as the most fitting day for the Sejm session, precisely so as to lay emphasis on that inseparable link that joins Poland's present-day socialist reality with that which was the best, the most noble, creative and patriotic in her past. The past twenty-two years are not only the most recent part of the history of Poland, but, at the same time, crown the road traversed by the Polish nation through history towards freedom and progress.

Then, after declaring that "the traditions and historical achievements of the Polish working people are the closest to our [the PZPR's—J.K.] hearts," Gomułka defined his party's heritage as including "everything that was done in the past for Poland, for her development and for her benefit by other classes, estates and social strata—the monarchs and gentry, the town patricians and the clergy, men of science and culture." He noted, however, that

> we [the PZPR—J.K.] do not divide our national past into two parts that do not fit together: our part and the alien part. For us, history is not a lumber room of old things that we take out and dust at a given time when we need them. We feel that we are the heirs of the whole rich and complex historical heritage of the nation. (Gomułka 1966, 3)

Yet somehow, this "whole rich and complex historical heritage" did not include the culture of Polish Catholicism or the legacy of interwar Poland (1918–39).

The Communist state sought in its vision of history legitimization of its power. Edward Ochab, president of the Council of State, expressed this explicitly in his speech summarizing the state celebrations:

> The gaining of a more thorough knowledge of the ten centuries of the history of our nation has helped us better to realize the *greatness and correctness* [emphasis added] of the revolutionary transformations that have brought in their wake Poland in her present shape; it has helped us better to understand the need to develop socialist building here and to participate in the world struggle for peace and socialism. (Ochab 1967, 3)

21. A Moscow-sponsored group that formed the nucleus of the Communist government in Poland.

The Church and the state presented Poles with two different discourses constructed from different elements of the nation's past. The Church's celebrations of the millennium of Polish Christianity illustrated and reinforced a mythical frame of reference in which the deep sense of Polish history emerged as a consequence of the 966 baptism and subsequent fidelity to Christendom—symbolized by the Cross and the submission of the nation to the Holy Mother of God.[22] The state's celebrations of the millennium of Polish statehood exemplified the hegemonic official discourse, in which the Polish People's Republic was portrayed as the inevitable culmination of a historical process leading toward the realization of "freedom and progress." Ironically, the secular eschatology of the state was more complete: in the official vision, the nation's history had already entered its final stage—the period of building Communism/socialism. By contrast, in the Church's vision, the direction of the nation's history was determined by the (renewable) act of submission to the Cross and the Holy Virgin, but the time of consummation of the historical process—national redemption—was not specified.

The state and Church celebrations of the millennium continued until the end of the year, from time to time clashing with each other.[23] Already during the high mass opening the Church celebrations, held in Gniezno on 15 April 1966,

> the peace was shattered by the crash of artillery—Defense Minister Spychalski was receiving a salute in the nearby Freedom Square, where the authorities were beginning their own, competing celebrations of the one thousandth anniversary of the state. Gniezno established a pattern that would continue as the Millennium celebrations wound through the country: citizens broke through police cordons to stream away from the secular observances and toward the sacred ones. (Micewski 1984, 263–64).

22. In one of his sermons Cardinal Wyszyński said, "We will stand (under the Cross) for beneath it stands our Queen, the Queen of the world and the Queen of Poland, for beneath it human masses [have gathered]. . . . O Mother, we will not leave Calvary, for You are there, and since You stand there, the Cross and Calvary are for us simply power, victory, and joy. In the ages-long travel of the Nation this power has survived. Is it not an indication for us, who look for the strength for the next millennium, that we should rely only on such powers that survived and defeated time? We will remain, then, O Mother, faithful to the Church!" (Wyszyński 1962, 63).

23. In Kraków, for example, some students and Jesuit seminarians were arrested after incidents between police and demonstrators who accompanied the icon of the Black Madonna, which was leaving the town.

The police interrupted the Church celebrations in several places and harassed the people attending them.

> On the day when the icon was to come to Olsztyn, workers were kept at the factories until seven in the evening and students of the agricultural school were explicitly forbidden to take part in the festivities. In any case, the icon never arrived in Olsztyn: the police stopped it on the road and directed it to Frombork. After the celebrations in that town, the icon was to travel to Warsaw, but a few kilometers outside Frombork, motorized police stopped the motorcade in which the Primate and the icon were riding, seized the painting, and took it away, to what destination no one could guess. (Micewski 1984, 269)

As it turned out, the police took the icon to the Warsaw Cathedral in secret, thereby spoiling the planned welcome ceremonies in two parishes.

The icon was forcefully detained for three months in the Warsaw Cathedral, and then for six years (1966–71; see Kłoczowski, Müllerowa, and Skarbek 1986, 401) in a side chapel on Jasna Góra.[24] But the pilgrimage went on. The icon's empty frame, sometimes adorned with flowers, sometimes with a burning candle or a Bible inside, continued its tour and visited four southern and two eastern dioceses. The perils and power of religion in Communist Poland came to be symbolized by the vacant frame. According to the bishops, "The difficulties and harassment encountered [by the traveling icon] did not diminish the respect shown for the Mother of God. On the contrary, they inspired even greater love for the Divine Traveler. People, with broken hearts, looked at the empty frame, but gathered in ever growing numbers."[25]

The event that had a strong impact on the situation of the Catholic Church and religion in Poland was the Second Vatican Council (1962–65). In Poland after 1945, the Catholic Church was the most important value-generating institution. One of the reasons for the Church's strong influence was the fact that it responded creatively to the changed sociopolitical situation of postwar Poland by modifying its pastoral methods and accentuating new elements in its doctrine. Some of these changes were codified by the Second Vatican Council. Among the most important and relevant for the Polish situation were the introduction of the Polish ver-

24. In 1963, in Zielona Góra diocese "every parish priest who hosted the icon was fined, and one was imprisoned. Nevertheless, the clergy judged the visits to have a highly positive effect" (Micewski 1984, 217).

25. This is a quotation from "The Letter of the Episcopate on the Conclusion of the National Peregrination of the Jasna Góra Mother of God" (*Krzyż Nowohucki*, no. 2, 1980).

nacular in the services, which contributed to a more personal reception of the Church's message and undermined unreflective and ritualistic participation in the mass;[26] emphasis on the family as a basic unit of religious socialization, which elevated the significance of the family as a religious and social value; and intensification of pastoral work among the people, which led to more personalized ties between (especially younger) priests and the populace.

The Discourse of Polish Catholicism in the 1970s

In the 1970s, the Church's influence in society grew as people became increasingly receptive to its teachings. Growing numbers participated in pilgrimages, *Weeks of Christian Culture,* and festivals of religious songs, known as *Sacrosongs.*

The Paulinian Monastery in Częstochowa, which houses the Black Madonna, has become the symbolic center of Catholic Poland in a dialectical social process. The Black Madonna was famed for her miraculous powers and this attracted pilgrims; as the number of pilgrims who worshiped her increased the more famous she grew, and this, in turn, enhanced her socially constructed sacredness. The growth of the cult was not hampered even by the nineteenth-century partitions (Jabłoński 1984). During the Stalinist era, the number of pilgrimages diminished because of state-organized harassment, but by the 1960s it recovered its former vitality. In the 1970s an estimated 1.5 million people visited Jasna Góra shrine annually. According to a statistical yearbook (Adamczuk and Zdaniewicz 1991, 229), in 1974 it was 1.3 million and in 1977—2 million. In 1977, the number of pilgrimages made by foot was 101. The biggest was the *Warsaw Foot Pilgrimage,* a tradition going back to 1717, in which thirty-thousand pilgrims participated. This pilgrimage grew continuously in the 1970s. In 1968, seven to eight thousand pilgrims participated in it; in 1976, twenty thousand; in 1977, twenty-eight thousand; in 1978, thirty-five thousand; and in 1980, fifty thousand.[27] The pilgrimages had

26. This change was not unanimously accepted, and like other Catholic countries, Poland witnessed some grumbling and criticism. It seems that, at least initially, more conservative Catholics (for example, many peasants) felt that the gain in understanding was not worth the loss of "sacredness" emanating from unintelligible Latin formulas.

27. *Droga,* August 1978, and October 1978, 19; *Biuletyn Dolnośląski,* 16 September 1980. A statistical yearbook, edited by Adamczuk and Zdaniewicz (1991, 231), provides lower figures (for example: 9000 in 1970; 5000 in 1971; 16,000 in 1975; 20,000 in 1977; 36,000 in 1980), but the growing trend is equally clear.

their own rich cultural life, which was not limited to religious themes. In 1980, young people on a pilgrimage participated in discussions on various topics related to the actual political and social situation of the country. One of the masses ended with ten thousand students singing "Boże coś Polskę" (God, who saves Poland), with its "subversive" closing line "Lord, restore our free Motherland" instead of "Lord, bless our Motherland." A journalist from an underground paper observed: "For many participants in the pilgrimage it constituted true national recollections full of concentration and prayer."[28]

The first Week of Christian Culture was organized in 1974. It was an immediate success and soon became a major cultural event throughout Poland. There seem to have been three basic types of Weeks.[29] In large towns with a strong academic life and big parishes, such as Wrocław, the Weeks were diversified, including educational sessions and lectures on, for example, the social doctrine of the Church, the ethics of politics, or history; seminars addressing urgent social problems, such as family education or alcoholism; and artistic productions, such as film and theater shows or musical performances. The audience was comprised mostly of students and intelligentsia. Warsaw's Week, held in Saint Anna's church, was more religious and less educational. In the late 1970s, however, the cultural component of the Weeks expanded as more and more artists of national stature participated; the Weeks also became more educational as the audience demanded more information on the pope's teachings and the social doctrine of the Church. Again, students constituted the main body of the audience. In small towns, such as Przemyśl, Olsztyn, Koszalin, or Opole, the main topics of invited lectures included morality, family life, and the upbringing of children. The participating artists were local nonprofessional groups and individuals. The audience were the local people, often workers.

The Sacrosongs, the festivals of religious songs initiated in 1968, were carefully hidden from the public by state censors; even its name could not be mentioned in the media.[30] Nonetheless, more than ten thousand people attended the ninth Sacrosong, organized in Kalisz from 15–18 October 1977. Its slogan was the verse from the Bible (Luke 2:10), "Fear not: for I bring you good tidings of great joy." The festival propagated such values

28. *Biuletyn Dolnośląski,* 16 September 1980.

29. Most of my information on this subject comes from Józef Ruszar, one of the organizers of the Weeks (personal communication, Fall 1987). See allso Chrypiński (1984, 130).

30. On 17 September 1978 Cardinal Wojtyła opened the tenth Sacrosong, in this jubilee year taking place in Częstochowa. He observed that "it is embarrassing that despite the ten years of Sacrosong, even the name alone remains forbidden . . . in the Polish media, the Polish press, and the Polish radio" (*Biuletyn Informacyjny,* October–November 1978, 29).

as the freedom of faith, creativity, and the rights of the human person. The first prize was awarded to a song titled "Don't Be a Coward, Son." Four thousand people warmly applauded the actor Maciej Rayzacher who recited the UN Declaration of the Rights of Man. Perhaps the best measure of the real enthusiasm surrounding this event was the fact that the people of Kalisz offered about one thousand rooms to the participants free of charge.

The Model of Sociopolitical Reality Implied in the Catholic Discourse

Communists always strive to achieve a monopoly in the sociopolitical life of a country they control. Any independent institution is thereby inadvertently political because the mere fact of its existence challenges such a monopoly. In the Polish People's Republic "pastoral letters and sermons constituted the only free ideological thus, like it or not, also political, public life" (Kisielewski, in Michnik 1977, 4). The Polish Church after World War II was, however, explicitly as well as implicitly political. Through pastoral letters and other official statements that were read from the pulpits all over the country, the Episcopate propagated the Church's position on all important religious, social, and political issues. They had a tremendous significance in shaping public opinion; the bishops' support encouraged people to action, its lack killed many independent oppositional initiatives.

The specificity of Polish Catholicism results from the fact that the Polish Church acts as a creator, repository, and propagator of national, civic, and ethical values to a degree rarely found in other national churches.[31] On 27 January 1971, Poland was recovering from the massacre of the workers in Gdansk and the ensuing shake-up of the top Communist officials. The primate prepared the following statement, later approved as the official position of the Episcopate, on the December events:

> At this moment, our feelings lead us particularly in the direction of our Worker Brothers, who suffered greatly, undertaking a difficult task that has cost them so much. They had the courage to lay claim to the equitable rights guaranteed in all of law and nature—the right

31. This specificity of the Church in Poland has been conceptualized by Piwowarski as taking the form of four extrareligious functions: the integrative, the protective, the critical, and the humanizing.

to a just, fitting existence—because a worker deserves his pay. . . . There is an admirable proximity between the morality of God and social morality, between the Gospel and social morality, between the Gospel and the labor codex. We can even say that all the labor legislation, no matter what its authorship, that makes up great socioeconomic struggle of labor in the last century derives from the spirit of the Gospel. (Micewski 1984, 313)

These firm words of support for the protesting workers were, however, accompanied by a call for national unity and peace, and this tainted the statement with a degree of ambiguity. The primate said:

But—while we express our full respect and sympathy with our workers, conscious of our gratitude for their work and sacrifices, we see at the same time the whole state and the Country. We must well and accurately define the proportion of rights and obligations in the national community, which always arises from the good of the greatest numbers. (Micewski 1984, 313)

The primate's critics interpreted this fragment as an expression of premature support for the new Party leadership under Gierek, which did not bear direct responsibility for the tragic loss of human lives in December 1970, but had yet to prove its good intentions by promptly punishing those who were guilty. As it turned out, Gierek never lived up to the expectations he raised. The whole episode illustrates the difficult situation of the Church, which always tried, to the distaste of its critics, to balance its ultimate religious mission with its unavoidably political role as the advocate of the Polish people in confrontation with the authorities. However, criticism of the Church almost disappeared in the second half of the 1970s, as the Church developed a discourse that was increasingly opposed to the Communist system and the authorities.

On 9 September 1976 in a communiqué of the plenary conference of the Polish Episcopate, the bishops unequivocally protested against the persecution of the workers who participated in the June strikes and work stoppages.[32] Furthermore, both the primate and Archbishop Wojtyła expressed publicly their moral support for the persecuted workers, but they did not make any direct reference to those imprisoned and beaten. From

---

32. The bishops wrote: "The rights of the workers who took part in these protests should be restored, along with their social and professional status; the wrongs done to them should be rectified appropriately; and those who have already been sentenced should be amnestied" (Lipski 1985, 51). See also Micewski (1984, 367) and *Dissent in Poland* (1977, 155).

that point on the official letters and statements of the Episcopate grew more militant and often directly addressed the whole gamut of social and political problems. In these statements the Church propagated a model of society, the political community, and authority that challenged the views of the Communist state. For the sake of comparison I analyze the Church's discourse by using categories already employed in the analysis of its Communist counterpart.

The ideal society. In the 1970s, the Church intensified its involvement in social affairs. The bishops often criticized various practices of the Communist authorities which, they believed, had led to the erosion of the quality of social life in Poland. Certainly, for the Church the ideal society was religious, and most of the Church's efforts were concentrated on evangelization. But other-worldly concerns were accompanied by a this-worldly interest in the defense of basic human rights, which the bishops believed were grossly violated by the state. In his highly influential *Holy Cross Sermons*[33] Wyszyński deliberated, inter alia, on the nature of humanity. The individual—according to the primate—is first of all *homo Dei,* "of God," but afterward also *homo oeconomicus* and *homo politicus.* Yet, economic rights and responsibilities are not the most crucial in human life, and they should not be separated from "the meaning of humanity; the dignity of the human person. . . . The goal of man's work should above all be man" (Karpiński 1982a, 173). The primate emphasized that an individual must have the right

> to earn his living in a suitable way in his own community . . . in his own country . . . [and] each has the right to working conditions that do not sap his physical strength or leave him prematurely worn out. . . . Man has the right to engage in economic activity . . . to be paid according to the dictates of justice, and to have his family provided for . . . and from the nature of man flows the right to possess private property in such measure as to ensure the freedom and dignity of the human person. (Micewski 1984, 357)

In another sermon, delivered on 6 November 1976, Wyszyński presented a model of the national community, in which all these rights would be protected:

> As we work and toil, as we embark on all manner of labor, let us not forget one thing, that in carrying out the duties of the day, of

33. *The Holy Cross Sermons* were delivered by Wyszyński in the Holy Cross Church in Warsaw in January 1974 and again in 1975 and 1976.

the occupation, in godly fashion, we still desire and demand that our land be a land of Christ, a land of Mary. We are ready for many a drudgery, effort, privation, and even sacrifice but only at the price of breathing the spirit of freedom in our home. (*Dissent in Poland* 1977, 157)[34]

In the primate's vision, Poland was to be free and respectful of basic human rights; its religion was to be Roman Catholic. The Catholic discourse was ambiguous on this last issue: it often propagated ideological, political, and social pluralism but sometimes offered an image of Poland as an ethnically and religiously homogenous entity, in short, an image of Poland that mirrored the state's vision. This side to the Church's discourse always produced some uneasiness among those Poles who were not Roman Catholic, but were devoted to the ideal of independent and democratic Poland.

The ideal of political community. The Church also arrived at a coherent position on the political rights of the citizens. The biblical rule, according to which the Church should "render to Caesar the things that are Caesar's, and to God the things that are God's" (Matthew 22:21; Mark 12:17; Luke 20:25) was invoked to protect the Church's sovereignty in religious matters. "When Caesar sits down on the altar, we say shortly: You must not!"—declared the primate in 1955. The state was defined by the bishops as an instrumental entity; it was to serve its citizens. On 3 May 1977, the Church organized the ceremony of renewal of the Jasna Góra vows of 26 August 1956. The primate preached that

> the Nation has a duty to watch over its greatest treasure which is Man—the citizen. The state exists to ensure for its citizens the necessary conditions for subsistence and for life in freedom. . . . If as once [in 1656] the King stood up for the underprivileged and his Vows of Lwów declared the enfranchisement of the farming population, if later the Constitution of May 3rd was also to take up the cause of the underprivileged, then too the Vows of Jasna Góra of 20 years ago take their place in this tradition. Today we are, moreover, supported in our Christian demands by such international documents as the "Charter of Human and Civil Rights." (*Dissent in Poland* 1977, 163)

The Church incorporated into its sociopolitical discourse the tradition of May Third (rejected by the state) in order to present itself as a cham-

---

34. A similar motif was often developed in Karol Wojtyła's sermons. See, for example, Lipski (1985, 158).

pion of human rights, freedom, and genuine civil society. In one of his *Holy Cross Sermons,* Wyszyński made it clear that the Church was determined to defend and propagate democratic ideals. He said:

> The Polish bishops were distressed at the attempt to integrate all of Polish youth in one monopolistic organization, and they said no. Such attempts impoverish and lessen the possibilities of social sophistication among the youth, especially among the academic youth. This will without doubt harm the national culture, and even social and political life. Wisdom dictates that the organization of society should not be based on the general application of a narrow scheme but on the facilitation of free and unimpeded work of various strata and social groups, according to their reasonable and healthy preferences. The courageous defense of freedoms and of the right to unite or organize for one's aims is therefore absolutely necessary, as well as the freedom of the press, public opinion, publication, discussion, deliberation, and scientific research. These are the prerequisites for creating the wealth of cultural, social, national, and political life. (Karpiński 1982a, 173)[35]

Among the nonreligious values constituting the core of the Church's discourse, national identity was by far the most conspicuous. The Church retained its crucial role as a repository of national heritage. Józef Obrębski observed that in the nineteenth century:

> Peasants leaving their villlages on their way to Częstochowa . . . the most important holy place, did not enter a national system. They moved within another social sphere, one which was somehow connected with the national one, because of the holy place in both systems. [Their] experiences and transformations did not reflect an entry into the national system of values; [they] returned to their villages the same as they were before, members of the village community and not participants in the national community. They had moved within national physical territory, but not in the national social space. (1976, 51)

By the 1970s the situation was different. Pilgrimages to Częstochowa turned into gigantic demonstrations of Polishness. Whereas the official

---

35. After 1976, the tone of many official Church's statements was similar. See, for example, *Dissent in Poland* (1977, 149–64) and Lipski (1985, 158).

patriotic discourse lacked any clearly defined and popularly accepted center, the Church discourse had one. Jasna Góra, the house of the nation's Queen and Mother, the Black Madonna, has been the sacred center of Polish Catholicism, and the spiritual center of the country for the nobility and intelligentsia, at least since 1656; in the twentieth century it became the center of national identification for all Polish Catholics.

The constant presence of nationalistic motifs in the Catholic discourse strengthened the image of national identity in which religious and national dimensions were inseparable intertwined. Władysław Piwowarski, a sociologist and a priest, came to the following conclusion on the basis of his extensive studies:

> It is interesting that the dogmatic aspect of preaching was less important for the listeners than its existential aspect related to the existence of the nation. . . . Participation in religious practices contributed less to the deepening of the bonds with God, to the moral renewal of the members of the nation, or to the development of interactions on the religious level; it however contributed to the deepening of the social and national ties and identification with the Polish nation. (1983, 346)

Religious discourse of the Church encompassed Christian patriotism, a motif directly related to the politically relevant value of national identity. On 5 September 1972 the bishops announced the pastoral letter on Christian patriotism:

> The foundation and source of Christian patriotism can be found in the teachings of Jesus on loving thy neighbor and on the equality of all people before God and amongst one another. . . . True love for one's country entails profound respect for the values of other nations. . . . It eschews hatred, for hatred is a destructive force that leads to a diseased and degenerated version of patriotism. . . . There is another danger here as well, occurring chiefly among those individuals or nations who have lost . . . a sense of God as the supreme value and the basis of human conduct. . . . For when "there is no God," nation and fatherland come to be seen as absolute values. (Michnik 1993, 149–50)[36]

36. This letter can be also seen as an effort to overcome the negative aspects of the stereotype, *Pole = Catholic,* which often finds explicit expression in the chauvinistic attitudes and acts of Polish Catholics.

Patriotism, propagated by the bishops and understood as love for one's country filtered through the ideals of brotherly love for others, be it individuals or nations, seems to have been accepted by some segments of the society. Sociological studies proved that many Poles, including the younger generation, embraced the idea that one's responsibility to God should be realized through a complete fulfillment of one's duties to one's nation (Jerschina 1983, 36; Kennedy and Simon 1983, 128).

As can be seen from the above examples, the Church expressed its political ideals in the form of criticisms of the state's totalitarian tendencies, such as the lack of toleration of any form of legal political opposition or independent, spontaneous social activism. The state's ideal of democratic centralism was confronted with a vision of a democratic society; Christian patriotism counterbalanced the state's socialist patriotism. The tone of such critical statements was often conciliatory and diplomatic; the Church always tried to avoid a total confrontation with the state. But the overall position was usually clearly articulated and the criticism justified by reference to important religious, national, ethical, or civic values.[37]

The Language of the Church's Statements

Formally, the language of the Church's statements (including pastoral letters) displayed characteristics also found in the official language of propaganda. It included both the two-valued orientation and arbitrariness—the major characteristics of the language of propaganda. A careful observer of the Church's language noted that despite the constant evolution toward more flexible and modernized linguistic forms, pastoral letters were often plagued by rigid syntax and obsolete phraseology. The author analyzed a pastoral letter of 30 June 1977, "Why Did We Offer Poland to the Maternal Slavery of Mary—Mother of the Church?" The letter, which addresses the issue of freedom, was written in an authoritarian style; the main thesis of the letter was formulated as a hyperbole (a dominant trope of the language

37. The following quotation from a pastoral letter issued by the Episcopate on 17 September 1978 constitutes yet another example of such criticism: "We all know that the spirit of freedom is the proper climate for the full development of a person. Without freedom a person is stunned, and all progress dies. Not to allow people with a different social and political ideology to speak, as is the practice of the state, is unjust. State censorship has always been and remains a weapon of totalitarian systems. With the aid of censorship, the aim is not only to guide the mental life of society, public opinion, but even to paralyze the cultural and religious life of the whole people."

Table 4. Arbitrariness of Religious Language

	Episcopate's letter	Pope's letter
1. Archaisms	22—1.3% of all words	7—0.4%
2. Comparisons	13—0.8%	8—0.5%
3. Syllogisms	48—2.9%	35—2.2%

of propaganda): true freedom was defined as total surrender to the will of God, thus as a form of slavery.

Among the major features of the authoritarian style are the high frequency of (1) valuative expressions, (2) schematic expressions, (3) encouragements and orders, and (4) equivocal expressions, as well as (5) repetitions and clusters of synonyms. The high frequency of valuative and schematic expressions served to divide the world, as presented in the bishops' letter, into two antithetical halves: positive (ours) and negative (theirs). The high frequency of archaisms made the language of the Church highly arbitrary. *Spotkania*'s linguist compared the bishops' letter with one of the pope's letters in three respects: (1) the number of archaisms, (2) the number of comparisons (such as good-better-best), and (3) the number of syllogisms. The assumption was that the higher the number of such linguistic devices the more arbitrary the language.

Comparison of the two letters revealed significant though not drastic differences between them (see Table 4). The analysis confirmed a common opinion held by many Poles, that the pope's language was less rigid and much closer to everyday speech than was the language of many official Church statements. In the terminology coined by M. M. Bakhtin, the pope's language was *internally persuasive* to a much higher degree than the language of the Episcopate, which often resembled the *externally authoritative* language of the Communist state.[38]

In the 1970s, the institutional relationships between the Church and the state were partially normalized. Stylistically, their languages were similar, both were highly formalized, which might lead to a conclusion that in both cases we are dealing with instances of traditional authority.[39] But formal affinities between the languages of the Church and the state aside, the models of reality to which these two languages referred were diametrically different and had different social repercussions. On the philosophical and ideological levels the conflict intensified (especially after 1976) as

38. On internally persuasive and externally authoritative discourses, see Bakhtin (1981, 342–49).

39. The view that the formalization of language constitutes and sustains traditional authority is developed by Bloch (1974).

the Church's criticism of the state's model of sociopolitical reality and its implementation grew bolder. In the domain of public imagery and ceremonial the differences were equally pronounced. But before the pope's visit in 1979 public clashes of two opposing discourses were rather infrequent because of the careful maneuvering of both the state and the Church.

The Effectiveness of the Catholic Discourse

The relative effectiveness of competing discourses in shaping peoples' attitudes and actions is difficult to gauge, even when sociologists can ask any question they want (and in Poland of the 1970s they could not). This difficulty results not from the empirical inaccessibility of relevant data, but—as modern anthropology and sociology of culture suggest—from faulty theorizing. As Ann Swindler observes: "Culture influences action not by providing the ultimate values toward which action is oriented, but by shaping a repertoire or 'tool kit' of habits, skills and styles from which people construct 'strategies of action' " (1986, 273). These "tool kits" include "cultural schemas" that "recur throughout many cultural stories and rituals, that depict actors responding to the contradictions of their culture and dealing with them in appropriate, even 'heroic,' ways" (Ortner 1989, 14).

To test these ideas one can look at the impact of the "millennium confrontations" between the state and the Church on the populace. Almost everyone I spoke to believed that the Church, due to its uncompromising stand during the celebrations, strengthened its institutional position in the society and enhanced the faith of Polish Catholics. During the Great Novena and millennium celebrations "in every parish, believers personally promised Mary to live in grace, raise their children religiously, and keep their faith in God and the Church. Simple, accessible, at once personal and communal—embracing the whole country—these vows made a great moral and religious impact" (Micewski 1984, 171). Yet this optimistic picture was shattered by the results of empirical studies carried out by Piwowarski in 1967–70 in four villages. He asked, "What did you hear about the Great Novena of the Polish Nation (what was it all about, what was its meaning, how did you participate in it)? Two-thirds to three-quarters of his respondents had not even heard of it (Piwowarski 1971, 136). The results were unexpected and are not easily explainable: nine years of diligent instruction and numerous ceremonies had had shockingly little effect. One possible explanation is that rural population was indeed superficially religious, tied to the Church by bonds of cultural traditionalism and social conformism, often referred to as ritualism. The doctrinal dimension of the Church's teachings and activities had not reached them very effectively.

There is no comparable data pertaining to this issue on Poland's urban population. Yet it is plausible to assume that together with the more personal and "intellectualized" attitude toward religion characteristic of the urban population, there came a deeper understanding if not a wider reception, of the Great Novena's meaning. One must, however, be very careful in drawing any definite conclusions, for many intellectuals expressed serious reservations about the primate's program, perceiving it as a propagation of an unreflective and somewhat obsolete model of religiosity.

The results of the routine attitudinal survey do not allow for an assessment of how deeply millennium celebrations had affected the people's value systems. Still, one can speculate that the explosion of religious feelings in the late 1970s and early 1980s had its roots in the celebrations of the Great Novena and the millennium, which confirmed the definite Marian character of Polish religiosity and reinvigorated the faith of countless Catholics. More important, however, there can be little doubt that the Church, by presenting on a massive scale its vision of Polish patriotism, began developing a sociopolitical discourse that in the late 1970s became a significant alternative to the discourse of the Communist establishment. It meant that individuals developing "strategies of action" found in the Catholic discourse cultural schemas that were enacted as soon as an occasion presented itself. For instance, during the millennium celebrations and on many occasions during the existence of the Polish People's Republic, people singing the unofficial religious anthem of Poland, "Boże, coś Polskę" (God, who saves Poland), sang the version that originated during the time of partitions, with the line "Lord, restore our free Motherland," and not "Lord, bless our Motherland."[40] By doing so these Poles were redefining "socialist sovereignty" as "slavery" and opening the way to construe various forms of protest against the Party-state as a "struggle for freedom."

The most influential religious cultural schema, the myth of Saint Stanisław, was revived during John Paul II's visit to his native country in 1979. The next chapter deals with this event in great detail.

---

40. The first stanza of this religious hymn, composed in 1816, is as follows: "O God, who through the ages / Has girded Poland with power and fame / Whose shield hath kept Her in Thy care / From evils that would cause her harm / Before Thy altars, we bring our entreaty / Restore, O Lord, our free Motherland" (I quote here the translation given in Morawska 1984, 31).

5 John Paul II's First Visit to Poland as an Example of the Ceremonial Transformation of Society

On 16 October 1978 Karol Cardinal Wojtyła was elected pope and assumed the name John Paul II. One of the first questions Poles asked themselves after his inauguration was when he would be able to visit his native country. The historical and mythological justification for such a visit could not be better: on 8 May 1979, Catholic Poland was to celebrate the nine-hundredth anniversary of Saint Stanisław's martyrdom, Wojtyła's predecessor to the Kraków bishopric. John Paul II expressed his desire to lead the celebrations promptly after his election in a statement sent to Polish Catholics through the Episcopate's press office on 28 October 1978.[1]

The cult of Saint Stanisław has existed "for six and one half centuries,

1. For more details, see Weydenthal and Zamorski (1979, 24).

and has merged with the tradition of the nation to such an extent that it can no longer disappear" (Tadeusz Wojciechowski; in Buczek 1979, 34). The myth of Saint Stanisław conveys a paradigm *of* and *for* (to use a phrase from Geertz) thinking about the relationship between the state and the Church; it presents the latter as a necessary ecclesiastical counterbalance to the former's secular power.[2] Since such a message is hardly acceptable for the Communist officials, the government and the Episcopate entered a period of negotiations in which both the state and the Church tried to place the pope's visit in a cultural frame that would optimally suit their respective interests and reaffirm their rival visions of reality.

The Myth of Saint Stanisław

Stanisław Szczepanowski,[3] the bishop of Kraków, was killed by royal henchmen, acting on the orders of King Bolesław the Bold, on 11 April 1079. The motives and the external circumstances of this murder are not fully reconstructed and are still hotly debated by historians.[4] No contemporary accounts have survived, and the main sources of information are two chronicles, one by Gallus Anonimus ("the Anonymous Gaul," an unknown French monk who lived in Poland in the eleventh and twelfth centuries) written between 1113 and 1117, and one by Master Wincenty Kadłubek, the bishop of Kraków from 1208 to 1218. These chroniclers, however, present conflicting versions of the story. Gallus Anonimus depicts Stanisław as a *traditor*. According to the influential historian Tadeusz Wojciechowski (1904), this phrase must be interpreted as "traitor," that is, someone plotting with the external enemies of one's own country. This interpretation, however, was approved neither by other historians nor by the populace. Stanisław, canonized in 1253 by Pope Innocent IV, became a popularly accepted symbol of justified resistance against the excesses of royal or, for that matter, any secular power. This popular version of the legend has been, at least partially, supported by these

2. The myth of Saint Stanisław has its counterpart in the English legend of Thomas Becket, brilliantly analyzed from an anthropological perspective by Victor Turner (1974).

3. In addition to Mother of God, the Protectress of the Nation, there are two principal patron saints of Poland: Saint Wojciech and Saint Stanisław. Saint Stanisław, who was proclaimed as the patron of Poland on 8 September 1253, has the largest number of churches built in his name (219 in 1948). In comparison, there were 122 churches dedicated to Saint Wojciech and 51 to Saint Jadwiga (Ciupak 1965, 55).

4. It is not even entirely clear whether Stanisław's death should be considered a murder or a public execution.

historians[5] who demonstrated that the term *traditor* had at least two meanings in medieval Latin. It could mean both "traitor" and "rebel."
Stanisław, therefore, could be described by Gallus as a rebel, that is, an
illegal opponent of the legal authority, not a traitor.[6]

According to the most influential version of the events, initiated by
Kadłubek and firmly established as a root paradigm (cultural schema) in
Polish folklore, Stanisław was an innocent victim of the king's rage.[7]
According to Kadłubek, the bishop, a "learned, just, severe, and zealous
pastor," excommunicated the king after he had seriously maltreated his
knights and their wives. In later versions of the story, for example, in Jan
Długosz's fifteenth-century chronicle, Bolesław was even accused of com-
mitting repeated adultery with the wives of his knights (Buczek 1979,
22).[8] The king, outraged by the excommunication, according to Gallus
"sentenced the bishop to dismemberment of limbs" (Buczek 1979, 27;
Gurdziński 1986, 87) or, according to Kadłubek, "cast upon him [Stani-
sław] his sacrilegious hands" (Grudziński 1986, 89), that is, murdered the
bishop without a trial. An examination of Saint Stanisław's skull, com-

5. These historians include Sawicki (1958), one of the most outspoken critics of
Wojciechowski's hypothesis, and Grudziński (1986, 134–35).

6. For Gallus, a faithful royal chronicler, opposition to the king, morally justified or not,
had to be qualified as rebellion. According to *Vita Minor* (the oldest biography of the Saint,
written between 1230 and 1250 [Plezia and Plezia 1987, 105]) Stanisław died because he
dared to protest the king's unjust treatment of his subjects. He disapproved of the king's
behavior, who "ruled according to unjust laws and oppressed the poor" ("Boleslaus propter
iniquas leges et pauperum oppressiones") (Plezia and Plezia 1987, 114). Stanisław "abhorred
the execrable kind of exploitation consisting of the use of meadows and fields belonging to
the people; [practice] regarded by him (the king) and his entourage to be the law of the
land" (Stanisław "abhominabatur quoque execrabile genus rapinae, prata et annonas
hominium depascere, quod ipse [the king] et complices eius dicebant esse ius terrae com-
mune") (Plezia and Plezia 1987, 115). Yet, in popular opinion, represented by Stanisław,
such behavior was regarded as unjust (Belch 1965, 64–65).

7. Root paradigms (Victor Turner's phrase), key scenarios, or cultural schemas (Sherry
Ortner's terminology) can be defined as "preorganized schemas of action, symbolic pro-
grams for the staging and playing out of standard social interactions in a particular culture"
(Ortner 1989, 60).

8. According to an earlier version, in 1077 the king "embarked with his army on a long
expedition to Rus, in order to install one of his relatives on the throne in Kiev. While he
prolonged his stay for long months in this opulent city, obviously beyond any political
reason, indulging in the frivolities of life, a fresh rebellion broke out in Poland. Fearing for
their families and their property, some of his knights secretly left Bolesław and returned
home, whereupon the infuriated king ordered ruthless reprisals both on actual rebels and
[on] those knights who had deserted him. According to legend, he even went as far as to
punish women guilty of adultery by taking away their babies and giving them to dogs for
nursing, while the unfortunate females had to breast-feed the puppies, instead" (Celt 1979,
3); see also *Vita Minor*, in Plezia and Plezia 1987, 133–35).

missioned by Karol Wojtyła in 1963, revealed that he might have been hit from behind (Grudziński 1986, 111–12). This evidence was sometimes used to support the hypothesis that there was no trial and Stanisław was murdered. It is, however, not clear whether the king was the murderer or, if so, whether he acted alone.

Saint Stanisław's story was not promulgated by the official media and school textbooks in the Polish People's Republic. When it was mentioned, however, it was presented in a version drawn neither from the mythical renditions nor from the majority of historical works on the subject. In the official version advanced by the state authorities, Bolesław was portrayed as a king who "persistently pursued independence from ecclesiastical authority, disregarded the bishop, and treated him as an intruder when [the bishop] interfered with political affairs" (Ciupak 1965, 59). Edward Ciupak, an official sociologist of religion, interprets the outcome of the conflict and Stanisław's death as the defeat of the Church in its struggle with the state; the defeat "which was rehabilitated by the act of canonization" (1965, 59). This official rendition of the story neglects to mention that Bolesław sided with Pope Gregory VII against Emperor Henry IV, thus collaborating with the highest ecclesiastical authority during the controversy over the investitures and other conflicts between the pope and the emperor.[9] The king was presented by the authorities as a symbol of secularization—a trend defined as "progressive" in the mythology of the Communist state. In 1966, during the state-organized millennium celebrations, slogans declaring "Bolesław the Bold—hero and patriot" were displayed in several Polish towns (Piekarski 1987, 13).

Church hagiographies and countless folktales have presented a different image of Saint Stanisław. In these renditions of the story, the saint is

9. The conflict between the king and the bishop had an international dimension, related to the controversy over the investitures between Pope Gregory VII and the German Emperor Henry IV. The pope, in his edict of 1075, known later as *Dictatum Papae,* formulated the principle establishing the supremacy of spiritual (the pope's) authority over the temporal rule of kings and even the emperor. Soon, the principle was put into practice, Henry IV was excommunicated, and in 1076 he came to Canossa begging Gregory's forgiveness. During this controversy, according to yet another version of the story, Bolesław sided with the pope and as a valuable ally was crowned in 1076 with the papal blessing. This outraged Bolesław's brother Władysław Herman, who lost his place in the succession to Bolesław's son Mieszko. The German emperor and the Bohemian king Vratislav supported Władysław Herman in a conspiracy to restore him to the succession. Stanisław was reported to be a member, or even a leader, of this conspiracy. On learning of the plot, the king sentenced the bishop to death. The population, outraged by the severity of the punishment, rose to arms, and the ensuing rebellion forced Bolesław to flee to Hungary where he died as a monk after long years of repentance.

depicted as a martyr who fell victim to royal tyranny and brutality, the premier symbol of necessary ecclesiastical resistance and counterbalance to state power.[10] In Kraków, Saint Stanisław was paid homage to in the annual celebrations held on the Sunday following May 8. In 1978, the celebrations began in Szczepanowo, Stanisław's birthplace. Cardinal Wyszyński, who celebrated the mass, reiterated the basic meaning and the continuing relevance of the cultural root paradigm associated with the saint:

> The conflict between Bolesław and Stanisław revolved around the issues of justice and human rights. It proves that already nine hundred years ago the Church struggled for human rights and already nine hundred years ago there was in Poland a man of the Church who fought for human rights. The cult of Saint Stanisław is the symbol of the unity of our nation; this is not only a religious, but also a national symbol.[11]

Preparations for the Visit:
The Politics of Symbolic Manipulation

Mythical realities have indeed—as Marshall Sahlins (1981, 1985), Ortner (1989, 60–61), and others have recently reminded us—a tendency to force themselves back into history and influence its course as powerful metaphors, endowing historical situations with meaning and shaping human motivations. Following the logic of events dictated by the myth of Saint Stanisław, the Polish Episcopate began the preparations for the nine-hundredth anniversary of the saint's martyrdom. At this point nobody could know that the myth contained the seeds of developments that would change the course of Polish history in a most dramatic way.

John Paul II had already made it clear in October 1978 that he wanted to lead the celebrations. In December 1978 he sent a special Christmas letter to his former archdiocese in Kraków, in which he expressed, once again, his views on the significance of Saint Stanisław's myth in the Polish culture. He wrote that "we can see in Saint Stanisław an advocate

---

10. It is interesting that Wojciechowski, whose inquiries undermined or at least weakened the spell of the national legend, was well aware of this fact and diminished the significance of his own findings by claiming that his hypothesis did not foreclose the issue for which new evidence was still needed (Buczek 1979).

11. *Tygodnik Powszechny*, 21 May 1978.

of the most essential human rights, on which man's dignity, his morality, and his true freedom depend" (Weydenthal and Zamorski 1979, 26). The religious legend emerged as a powerful source of mythological legitimacy for the campaign against the abuses of human and civil rights in Poland. The authorities censored the pope's message before its publication in *Tygodnik Powszechny,* a highly respected Kraków Catholic weekly. The editor of the *Tygodnik Powszechny* refused to publish the censored version. After the incident achieved the proportions of a minor international scandal, the government backed down; the pope's message was published in its original form and read in all the churches belonging to the Kraków diocese.

Gierek and his advisors realized that the pope's homecoming during the celebrations of the nine-hundredth anniversary of Saint Stanisław's martyrdom in early May 1979 would be politically explosive. They tried to defuse the situation by postponing the visit. An influential clandestine paper *Robotnik* (1 April 1979) commented:

> The authorities of the Polish People's Republic were afraid of [the pope's] visit and of this date. They were afraid of the date because the cult of Saint Stanisław, the perserverant bishop murdered by King Bolesław the Bold, is identified with a dangerous word, *opposition.* They were afraid of the visit, because the pope's visit would elevate the significance of Church in Poland.

That the authorities feared the impact the pope's visit would have on the Poles was not just speculation by the oppositional writers. A clandestine periodical published excerpts from Party instructions for teachers dated March 1979.[12] It is worthwhile to quote these instructions at length, since they seem to illustrate very well the official mood in Poland at that time. According to the lecturer:

> The pope is our enemy, because he celebrated the mass for Pyjas.[13] Due to his uncommon skills and great sense of humor he is dangerous, because he charms everybody, especially journalists. Besides, he goes for cheap gestures in his relations with the crowd, for instance puts on a highlander's hat, shakes all hands, kisses children, etc. It is modeled on American presidential campaigns. . . .

12. "Jan Pawel II w Polsce. Wielka nadzieja" (John Paul in Poland: A great hope), *Biuletyn Informacyjny,* 30 April 1979.

13. Stanisław Pyjas, a member of the oppositional group, was found dead in a yard in Kraków. Police brutality is widely believed to have been the cause of his death. The mass said in his memory was followed by a political demonstration.

He is dangerous, because he will make Saint Stanisław the patron of the opposition to the authorities and a defender of human rights. Luckily we managed to maneuver him out of the date May 8. . . . The visit will cause some complications in our relations with the Soviet Union, because the pope will demand the, so-called, equal rights for the believers in the socialist countries. . . . His visit will cause some problems, because we will have to pacify 156 oppositional activists for its duration. . . . Because of the activation of the Church in Poland our activities designed to atheize the youth not only cannot diminish, but must intensely develop. We must strive at all costs to weaken the Church activities and undermine its authority in the society. In this respect all means are allowed and we cannot afford any sentiments.

In a publication dated 10 March 1979, called "[Our] Attitude toward the Holy Father," prepared for the PZPR secretaries in the Zielona Góra region, the authorities were equally straightforward:

The main purpose of this visit is an attempt to soften our system ideologically. It is not a visit that will be of help to us, but it is better that it takes place in this year. Therefore, it is necessary through additional actions to counterbalance this tension, which—as the visit approaches—will be stirred up by the clergy, activists, and various committees. And here comes the very important role of organized celebrations of the thirty-fifth anniversary of the Polish People's Republic and the fortieth anniversary of the German invasion of Poland. Our major task is to preserve our party in a good ideological shape.

The basic political message of the Saint Stanisław myth—that secular power should be counterbalanced by ecclesiastical authority—was unacceptable to the Communist regime. Thus the authorities' plan to maneuver the Church away from the eighth of May must be interpreted as an attempt to sever the symbolic link between John Paul II's visit and the myth. At the same time, by postponing the visit, the state tried to uproot the event from the long, cyclical time of the Catholic mythology and place it in the secular time of the People's Republic. Within this time, the pope's visit was interpreted as a gesture lending splendor to the celebrations of the thirty-fifth anniversary of this republic. Some official articles portrayed John Paul as one of the finest products of the Polish People's Republic (Głowiński 1981). Since the tradition to which this "socialist" Poland subscribed was "progressive," that is, secular, by the logic of this mind-boggling reasoning the head of the Catholic church appeared to be "produced" by a secular Communist state.[14]

The visit was perceived by the state as a conciliatory gesture as long as it was not associated with Saint Stanisław. A minister of religious denominations suggested in an interview with foreign newspapers that "any coincidence between the papal visit and the St. Stanisław celebrations would be most unfortunate as, in [the authorities'] view, St. Stanisław himself had become a 'symbol of division' between Church and state, rather than reconciliation" (Weydenthal and Zamorski 1979, 27).

The pope's own interpretation of Saint Stanisław's martyrdom stressed reconciliation, not division. In a pastoral letter dated 8 May 1979 he wrote: "Saint Stanisław has been regarded for centuries as an advocate of reconciliation with God of all his compatriots, both the rulers and the ruled."[15] John Paul II reminded that Bolesław the Bold "according to the tradition ended his life reconciled with God." In this symbolic struggle for the appropriate mythical framework of his visit, John Paul II had the last word. First, he firmly linked the visit to his Polish background and Saint Stanisław's cult. In the same pastoral letter the pope wrote:

> In this year in which the Church in Poland celebrates the nine-hundredth anniversary of the martyrdom and death of Saint Stanisław, Kraków's bishop, the bishop of Rome, Saint Peter's successor cannot be absent. Too significant is this Jubilee, too much related to the history of the Church and the Polish Nation, which for more than one thousand years of its history united with this Church in a particularly deep way. This voice [the pope's] cannot be missing, particularly at this moment, when to Saint Peter's capital, by the mysterious working of Divine Providence, the pope was called, who until recently had been Saint Stanisław's successor in the bishop's capital in Kraków.

Then he justified the date of his visit:

> This year *we decided* [emphasis added] to put off this main anniversary celebration of Saint Stanisław, not till the following Sunday, but till the Sunday of the Descent of the Holy Spirit and the Sunday of the Holy Trinity.

14. By contrast, the pope thought in terms of a totally different time scale, in which present-day Poland was embedded in the historical perspective of the millennium of Christian Polish statehood and in the mythical time of biblical references.

15. *Tygodnik Powszechny*, 20 May 1979.

The two Sundays mentioned by the pope were the second (June 3) and the last (June 10) days of his, already officially approved, visit to Poland. Unable to come to Poland to celebrate Saint Stanisław's death at the time prescribed by tradition, the pope adjusted the ceremonial calendar in a way not inconceivable in this tradition; Saint Stanisław's feast was always slightly postponed and customarily celebrated in Kraków on the first Sunday following the official Church date of May 8. The phrase "we decided" seems to indicate the pope's intention to avoid a confrontation.

The state's preparations for the pope's visit were pervaded by ambivalence. On the one hand, state agencies prepared elaborate communication facilities for the domestic and foreign press, all places to be visited by the pope underwent extensive renovation, and large numbers of security personnel were deployed throughout the country to maintain public order (Weydenthal and Zamorski 1979, 34). Municipal authorities in major gathering places, such as Warsaw, Kraków, or Częstochowa, prepared in advance huge parking spaces and the necessary facilities (such as buffets, WCs, medical help, and so on) to serve the visitors. On the other hand, however, the authorities issued regulations clearly designed to diminish the significance of the pope's visit in the official media coverage and to confuse the public. Strict censorship directives, regulating minute details of the coverage, were issued for the Polish journalists.[16] They included the following rules:

> (a) it is decreed that the centralized system of approval of all press materials related both directly and indirectly to the visit during its duration will be consistently complied with. This function will be carried on by teams of employees of the Department of Press, Radio, and Television of the Central Committee of the PZPR. . . .
> (b) the rule is established—that besides the exceptions described below[17]—PAP [Polish Press Agency] has the exclusive right to cover the pope's visit.[18]

16. These instructions, called "The Rules of Accreditation of Polish Journalists and Press Coverage of the Pope's Visit in Poland," were leaked to the independent press and published in *Kultura*, July–August 1979, and *Biuletyn Informacyjny*, July–August 1979.

17. The exceptions specified in detail which newspapers were allowed to carry their "own commentary" (only dailies controlled by the Party—*Życie Warszawy* and *Trybuna Ludu*) and allocated three versions of the "approved" news, prepared by the PAP (Polish Press Agency), to various other newspapers.

18. *Biuletyn Informacyjny*, July–August 1979, 38.

The program of the visit was announced only a few days before its beginning; official information was very fragmentary, limited, and often distorted.[19]

Students living in one of Warsaw's dormitories located in the center of the city prepared and fixed on the facade a huge banner that quoted John Paul II's praise of youth: "You are the hope of the world, the Church's hope, my hope." The dormitory authorities tried to force the students to take it down. Only the students' unanimous resolve kept the slogan on the building throughout the visit. The manager of the dormitory, when asked who ordered him to take down the slogan, answered: "An older man from the Soviet Embassy."[20]

A few days before the visit I was asked by a friend, an art historian responsible for a part of the decorations in Kraków, to help in her work. I spent several days in a wonderful feverish round-the-clock scramble, working on the decorations for the bishop's palace. The enthusiastic spirit of this voluntary work contrasted sharply with the fabricated spontaneity of the state-organized action days. Fed by the nuns, we prepared the decorations (mostly white-and-red [Polish] and yellow [Papal] flags) in a church studio. On the last night before the pope's arrival we were mounting the decorations on the facade of the palace from a hastily constructed scaffold. Our work went smoothly, except that late that night the street lights on the block where we were working suddenly went out. Nobody believed it was just bad luck since ours was the only block without lights. In a very uncharacteristic display of spontaneous enthusiasm, several drivers parked their cars opposite the palace. We finished our work aided by their headlights. There were no complaints about dead batteries.

The Visit: The Second Baptism of Poland

John Paul II arrived in Warsaw on 2 June 1979 to begin a triumphant tour, described by a writer Julian Stryjkowski as "the second baptism of Po-

19. See, for example, "Zawieszenie ruchu na Placu Zwycięstwa" (Traffic suspended at Victory Square), *Express Wieczorny,* 31 May 1979. The same newspaper, in its 29 May 1979 issue, mentioned in the television listings for 2 June: "At 4:00 P.M.—broadcast from the celebrations [held] at the Tomb of the Unknown Soldier and at Victory Square."

20. *Biuletyn Informacyjny,* July–August 1979, 34. Here is another example of officially produced ambiguity. In some mines of strongly Catholic Silesia, the authorities organized ostensibly spontaneous meetings, which "passed" resolutions declaring that "they do not want the pope in Silesia, since it disrupts production" (ibid.).

land." The altar for the first pontifical mass held in Warsaw that day was erected in the middle of Victory Square (a site hitherto used only for state ceremonies) and was seen on TV throughout the whole country. Thus one of the most revered spaces of the official Communist ritual was transformed into the sacred space of the Catholic ceremonial. At this moment, for the majority of the Polish population it was no longer "their" space to which "we" are sometimes invited. For the first time, it was "our" space in which "our" pope, representing "our" Church, was conducting a mass for "us." This, perhaps not entirely conscious, realization of the successful symbolic reclaiming of a public space might have well been the basic sentiment of the day. For a moment at least, the rules of the social game, which had been blurred by decades of double-talk and double-think, were neatly defined, for "the symbolic system divides the social realm into 'we' and 'they' that is not so divided in social reality" (Murphy 1970, 223).

This first Warsaw mass, attended by an enthusiastic and mostly religious crowd of about a million, created a mood that would last for the rest of the visit. Hundreds of thousands participated in pilgrimages from their homes to the sites of the papal masses. Young people were conspicuously dominant in these crowds. The last pontifical mass, held in Kraków on June 10, atttracted a crowd of 2.5 to 3 million, the largest in Polish history.

The public atmosphere during the pope's homecoming has been described by independent (that is, not related to the official Polish media) observers as enthusiastic and joyous. The pope received countless gifts from representatives of all professions, various groups, and individuals. Among many efforts to find an adequate linguistic equivalent of this unusual mood the expression coined by the Viennese Cardinal König stands out. He called it simply a "psychological earthquake." Many observers described the direct social consequence of the visit as *catharsis.* The crowds were also unexpectedly disciplined and displayed social virtues previously absent in Poland. Andrzej Szczypiorski, a well-known independent writer, noted in his diary: "This is incredible, not a single drunkard to be seen in this country of drunks! Not a single quarrel amongst these vast crowds that on any other day would display roughness, egotism, selfishness" (1982, 113). Another independent observer wrote:

> The emotions of the crowds welcoming the pope can hardly be compared with those of the crowds officially organized to march in the May Day parade. The long-term impact of the pope's visit on the collective imagination can prove, however, to be even

more significant: no doubt it will move the deepest layers of national consciousness. . . . It should be remembered that symbols
which organize national consciousness stimulate activities whose
results are quite tangible.[21]

The Official Portrait of the Pope's Visit

John Paul II's visit to Poland was a symbolic tour de force that redefined
the rules of social game in the country. But in the official media it was
presented according to a carefully preplanned interpretive scheme, whose
aim, explicitly formulated by the Party lecturers, was to minimize the
ideological and political damage. The damage was, however, unavoid-
able because for the first time in the postwar history of Poland it was not
the independent opinion that tried to achieve wider public exposure
through the cracks in the monolithic facade of the official propaganda. It
was instead the official interpretation of the visit that was hardly audible.

Millions participated in the masses and meetings with the pope. The
Catholic press covered the visit thoroughly (without drastic censorship
interventions), as did the Western media, such as the BBC, the Voice of
America, and Radio Free Europe, all of which reported back to Poland.
The public was therefore well informed about the pope's visit; his words
reached everybody without distortion. And yet despite this wealth of
uncensored information the official media produced and tried to sell their
own version of the visit. The official coverage was monitored by a special
team of experts. All the texts were prepared by the PAP and then reprinted around the country. As Michał Głowiński observed, the media
engaged in these futile efforts in order to realize the governmental directive to minimize political damage and preserve the continuity of the
official discourse (Głowiński 1981). Moreover, because the economic
effectiveness of the system had been declining since 1974, lavish ceremonies (such as the thirty-fifth anniversary of the Polish People's Republic)
became an expedient means of legitimacy construction for the regime.[22]

---

21. *Głos* (Special Issue), May 1979. This observation by a Polish author bears a striking
resemblance to an anthropological generalization by Manning, who noted that "dynamic
celebrations are symbolic (but important, and quite 'real') battlefields for waging competi-
tive struggles for power, prestige and material objectives" (1983, 7).

22. Maurice Bloch observed a similar constancy in producing ideological legitimacy of
power through rituals in central Madagascar. He noted that "a ritual [of a kind he studied] is
an ideal legitimizing tool since it offers in its dramatic construction a role for those in
authority in which they can appear as the source of all creative power" (1985, 43).

John Paul II's homecoming presented the authorities with yet another opportunity to seek legitimacy; thus the official propaganda attempted to portray the visit as his endorsement of the Communist regime.

The official picture of the visit was not composed of lies and false information. Its method was more subtle. The facts to be presented were selected carefully; their interpretations were prepared according to a pre-conceived model. The texts were centrally produced and distributed to local newspapers to be published without changes. The official vision seems to have been based on a rather incoherent set of axioms:[23] (1) the pope's visit does not have any impact on the worldview of the citizens; (2) the state's ideological foundation remains totally unaffected, since it is based on the secular materialistic worldview of Marxism-Leninism; (3) the aim of the visit is religious, but (4) (here the official discourse was ambivalent) at the same time it is the expression of the pope's support for the policies of the authorities; (5) the basic ceremonial significance of the visit is secular: the pope came to lend splendor to the thirty-fifth anniversary of the Polish People's Republic and to commemorate the fortieth anniversary of the German invasion of Poland; (6) in general, the visit is acceptable, for the Church's policies after the changes introduced by John XXIII and Paul VI (especially the Second Vatican Council) are in many aspects congruent with the political line of the socialist states, common concern with world peace being the best example.

An Interpretation:
Dimensions of the Social Transformation

The pope's visit transformed Poland. On the social level, it affected public discourse. On the individual level, it changed people's attitudes. It also changed the rules of interaction and affected the social standing of many public figures.

Transformation of the public discourse and individual attitudes. The pope's visit was, first of all, seen by the populace as a religious pilgrimage.[24]

---

23. I base this reconstruction on Głowiński's analysis (1981).

24. Its major religious themes, which for the Polish Catholics were more important than, or at least as important as, the philosophical, political, and cultural motifs, were (1) Christ-centrism, already strongly emphasized by the pope in his first encyclical *Redemptor Hominis,* in which he declared that "Christ is the center of the universe and history"; (2) emphasis on the mystery of word-flesh transformation in the Eucharist and stress on the significance of the Holy Word in the modern world; (3) celebrations of the patron saints of Poland, Saint Stanisław and Saint Wojciech; (4) homage to Our Lady of Częstochowa and

Public presentation of religious themes during the masses attended by millions in the programmatically secular state in itself constituted a powerful blow to the ideological facade of the Polish People's Republic. But the pope addressed many more controversial subjects of direct political relevance. Already in his first sermon at Victory Square in Warsaw, he confirmed the unbreakable link between the Polish nation and Catholicism, challenging the official *secular* definition of Polish statehood:[25]

> *It is impossible to understand the history of the Polish nation* [emphasis original]—this large, thousand-year-old community, which has formed me and everyone of us so thoroughly—*without Christ*. If we threw away this key to the understanding of our Nation we would risk a fundamental misunderstanding. We would not understand ourselves. It is impossible to understand this Nation, whose past was so magnificent, yet also tragic—without Christ.[26]

In Częstochowa, during the pontifical mass renewing the Jasna Góra Vows, John Paul II defined the national identity in reference to the myth of Our Lady:

> The history of Poland, and especially the history of the last centuries, can be written in different ways, it can be interpreted according to various keys. But if we want to know how this history is reflected in the hearts of the Poles, we must come here. We must put our ear to this Place. We must hear the echo of the Nation's life in the Heart of Its Mother and Queen!

Having placed Polish history in the framework of Catholic mythology, the pope addressed several other significant issues of the day, such as

---

reinforcement of the Marian cult in Polish and universal Catholicism; (5) reinvigoration of the folk and popular religiosity; and (6) emphasis on theistic humanism as an antidote to the secular humanism developed by the state. These motifs were identified by Tadeusz Grabowski (1979).

25. Since it is impossible to quote papal sermons *in extenso,* I select only the most characteristic fragments. Such a strategy inevitably leads toward distortions but I hope that at least the most general tenor of these sermons is preserved.

26. The pope continued: "The millennium of the Baptism of Poland, Saint Stanisław being its ripest fruit—the millennium of Christ in our yesterday and today—is the main motive of my pilgrimage, of my prayer of thanksgiving together with all of You, Dear Compatriots, who are still taught by Jesus Christ the great cause of humanity. With You, for whom Christ still remains an open book of knowledge about human beings, about their dignity, and about their rights. But also knowledge about the dignity and the rights of the Nation" (John Paul II 1979).

national sovereignty, the European roots and orientation of Polish culture, civil rights, human dignity, and the dignity of human work.

In several sermons and addresses John Paul II espoused another idea rarely, if ever, discussed in the official media. He declared that

> Christianity must once again engage itself in the formation of the spiritual unity of Europe. Economic and political motives exclusively are not capable of doing this. . . . Europe, which despite ongoing divisions of regimes, ideologies, and economic-political systems, cannot cease to seek its fundamental unity, and must address itself to Christianity.[27]

Within the official discourse of the Polish People's Republic the issue of the unity of Europe was a taboo. The position of Polish culture within wider European traditions, often brought up by oppositional writers, was carefully avoided by the official media and "court" intellectuals, whose task was to document the specificity of Eastern European culture and construct a picture of Poland fraternally related to the Soviet Union. The idea that European unity should be founded on the common Christian background must have sounded even more sacrilegious to the official ear.

In his sermon delivered on 7 June 1979 on the grounds of the former death camp in Auschwitz-Birkenau (*Oświęcim-Brzezinka*) the pope addressed the issue of human dignity. The moral imperative to condemn Nazi war crimes was doubtless shared by the pope and the Polish authorities, hence it seemed to have provided a convenient occasion to prove that the adversaries stood united (at least on this issue). The Auschwitz mass was interpreted in the official media as one of two pivotal moments of the visit (alongside the pontiff's meeting with Gierek). The pope expressed moral outrage over the unspeakable crimes of the past committed in this "Golgotha of our times" and engaged in an eloquent exposition of the Church's general concern with human dignity and civil rights. For the Polish audience this universal message contained an unambiguous reference to the contemporary situation. John Paul II said:

> Can anyone on this Earth be surprised that a pope who was born and raised here on this land, a pope who came to Peter's See from Kraków—the archdiocese in the territory of which the Oświęcim camp is located—that this pope began the first encyclical of his pontificate with the words *Redemptor Hominis*, that he devoted this

27. Address to the 169th Conference of the Episcopate, Częstochowa, 6 June 1979 (Weydenthal and Zamorski, eds. 1979, 70).

encyclical in its entirety to the matter of man, the dignity of man, the threats facing man, and . . . human rights, the inalienable rights of man which can be trampled on so easily and annihilated by . . . man? To do so it is enough to dress him in another uniform, to equip the apparatus of violence with the means of destruction; it is enough to foist on him an ideology in which human rights are subordinated to the requirements of the system, subordinated in an arbitrary fashion, so that, in fact, they do not exist. . . . One nation can never develop at the expense of another, at the expense of its subordination, conquest, oppression, at the expense of exploiting it, at the expense of its death. (Weydenthal and Zamorski, eds. 1979, 66 and 69).

The pope developed in his sermons a sound and socially attractive Christian philosophy of work.[28] His discussion of human labor demonstrated that there was a non-Marxist discourse in which social and political problems could be articulated. According to a sociological study, many workers remembered that after the June 1976 strikes the *socialist* state in 1976 denounced them as "hooligans,"[29] although only after John Paul II's visit did they realized the full extent of the offense (Bakuniak 1983). The pope's speeches reminded them that socialism (as it was popularly understood) should be inseparable from the appreciation of the dignity of human work. Somewhat paradoxically, this dignity was asserted in Christian discourse in a far more convincing way than in the discourse of official socialism.

Perhaps the most important outcome of the pope's homecoming was the end of the Party-state's monopoly over public discourse in Poland. Since 1945, the regime had appropriated Marxism and socialism, turning the latter into a hybrid of Communism/socialism. Members of the opposition opting for unambiguous forms of socialism had found it difficult to express workers' grievances and problems without using the "Newspeak" of the officialdom.[30] Other oppositional groups, espousing nonsocialist ideologies, had yet to find a coherent and popularly acceptable discourse to address such issues. During the visit many Poles realized or were reminded

28. His views on work can be found in his encyclical *Laborem Exercens* (On human work), dated 14 September 1981.

29. In June 1976 workers of at least 130 factories all over Poland went on strike or took to the streets in demonstrations against unexpected steep price increases of basic foodstuffs (see Chapter 1).

30. See, for example, the interview with *Robotnik*'s editors in *Tygodnik Solidarność*, 10 April 1981.

that non-Marxist discourses did exist and could be used effectively to articulate and analyze political, social, and even economic problems.

Change in the rules of interaction. In sociological terms, the visit resulted in the renewal of what Georg Simmel called *sociability,* a mode of social existence in which people "feel that the formation of a society as such is a value" (1950, 42–43). Millions of people, organized not by the state agencies, but by volunteers directed by Catholic activists, came together in an orderly fashion to celebrate "their" pope. They realized that civil organization of the society *outside* the state was possible. This led to a considerable lowering of the barrier of fear vis-à-vis the state and the development of the consciousness of "we" crystallized in the towering personality of the pope, popularly perceived as the only genuine moral, religious, and even political authority.[31] John Paul II reinvigorated in massive public ceremonies symbols of the nation, Catholicism, and civil society that were accepted as genuine foci of identification by the Poles. This realization that the national community can be defined *outside* the Communist state reached all sectors of society, including the workers. Only under the impact of the pope's visit did Polish workers (or at least significant segments of this class) achieve a considerable degree of self-identification as members of a wider "imagined community" organized around such readily acceptable symbols as the pope, the Black Madonna, the Catholic Church, and the common national heritage (as defined by the Church and the opposition). This realization constituted the first step toward the formulation of positive programs of reforms developed in 1980–81.[32]

Changes in social status. No study has been conducted concerning the impact of the pope's visit on the popular perception of the structure of authority in Poland, although most commentators agree that John Paul II emerged as the central symbol of national identity and as the country's undisputed moral authority. This process led, in turn, to a further decline in the social standing of the Communist rulers.[33] The visit had also an impact on the configuration of alliances within the ranks of the organized

31. Krzysztof Jasiewicz, one of the coauthors of the path-breaking sociological studies of Polish society, observed that "in the end of the 1970s national identification reached a very high level, rarely observed in history. The visit of John Paul II to his native land is unanimously regarded as a breaking point in the shaping of personality of the "Pole 1980" (1983, 129).

32. This fragment of my analysis is heavily indebted to Bakuniak and Nowak (1984) and Krzemiński et al. (1983).

33. A German analyst observed that "the papal election and visit were milestones that accelerated the erosion of the domestic political power base of the PUWP, which had clearly lost the struggle for the Polish soul" (Bingen 1984, 212).

opposition. The oppositional groups invoked in their public statements the same set of civil and national values as the pope, hence their alliance with the Church grew stronger after the visit. Links between the Catholic democratic left, represented most clearly by the magazine *Więź*, and oppositional social-democrats[34] were strengthened. The most influential underground publication for the workers, *Robotnik* (The Worker), whose social-democratic orientation was explicitly pronounced by its editors, enthusiastically endorsed the renewal of Polish Christianity, triggered by the pope's visit. *Robotnik*'s editorial written by Jan Lityński remains one of the most moving and perceptive documents of this visit.[35] As a result of these changes the social visibility and prestige of oppositional groups increased.

An Anthropological Interpretation: Ritual and Ideology

Cultural anthropology has developed a set of conceptual tools that help us to understand what occurred in Poland during those nine days. For instance, it has been determined that rituals of transition (and the visit can be easily construed as such a ritual) consist of three phases: separation, transition, and incorporation. The analysis of the middle, transitional (liminal) phase of ritual transformation is particularly revealing in the present context. In this phase the rules of social game are *publicly displayed* and *transformed* or *amplified*.[36] At the same time however, as the Turners observe:

> Liminality is not only *transition* but also *potentiality*, not only "going to be" but also "what may be," a . . . domain in which all that is not manifest in the normal day-to-day operation of social structures (whether on account of social repression or because it is rendered cognitively "invisible" . . .) can be studied

34. Michnik's book *The Church, the Left: A Dialogue* became a turning point in the rapprochement between, as Michnik called them, people of the secular left and the people of the Church.

35. Lityński's article is translated in Appendix 3.

36. According to Terence Turner, "the effectiveness of ritual and ceremony as means of bringing about the reordering, or preventing the disordering, of a set of relations is a function of the ritual's or ceremony's character as an iconic model of that set of relations" (T. Turner 1977, 62).

objectively, despite the often bizarre and metaphorical character of its contents. (1978, 3)

This is precisely what happened in Poland; the society was offered a possibility to rehearse an alternative social order founded on a set of values different from those propagated by the Party.

The actual rules of the social game in Poland in the late 1970s were very complicated, and their description and analysis lies beyond the scope of this book. Suffice it to say that the official ceremonial system had little in common with these rules. It is not an unusual situation; symbolic super-structures (or ideologies) rarely simply mirror mundane reality. Rather, they contain fantasies that often violently defy the rules of everyday life. Maurice Bloch notes that

> the *pre-requirement* for the establishment of ideology turns out, in fact, to be *a systematic and furious assault on non-ideological cognition* [emphasis added]. This assault is marked by the second stage of the ritual, an assault which seems particularly directed against the most fundamental categories of cognition . . . , [and might be] called anti-cognition. (1985, 40)

Bloch's illuminating observation is, however, overstated. Ideology, in order to be effective cannot be *completely disconnected* from nonideological cognition, as Bloch suggests (in both 1974, 77, and 1985, 45). It has to relate to everyday knowledge in a dialectical fashion; it has to *confirm* (reflect) certain elements of this knowledge (condition of credibility) while *defying* others (condition of successful mystification).

In Poland of the late 1970s the Communist ceremonial was minimally effective because it neither reflected everyday knowledge (or its frag-ments) nor concealed the actual features of everyday reality; its ability to produce a credible utopia had run out. It was common knowledge that the economy was collapsing, the standard of living was declining, and the food lines were growing longer. The ubiquitous *propaganda of success* lacked credibility: the hegemonic discourse had exhausted its potential. Poles lived in a cognitive limbo, in a state of ever-growing existential inchoateness, hoping for new ideas, ready for new promises.[37]

Mythologies and ideologies always seem to involve an element of

---

37. I am using the category of inchoateness in a sense given to it by Fernandez (1986). He writes: "The notion of inchoateness of the subject . . . seems comparable to [Lacan's] notion of the subject as incomplete being ever-desirous of completing itself (constituting itself) . . ." (1986, 67).

mystification; they are tools of hiding reality, of "false consciousness," as Bloch strongly suggests. But the process of mystification also has a "healthy" psychological dimension; ideologies (ideological discourses) often do reduce emotional anxiety and cognitive incongruence.[38] Each group, therefore, produces devices to alleviate such anxieties through the reinvigoration of the group's organization discourse and the amplification of the sense of belonging to a common heritage. Such multifaceted reinforcement of the group's unity is usually produced by a successful staging of ceremonies or rituals, which also—and here it is difficult not to agree with Bloch—can enhance or modify the social and political status quo, and/or confirm the hegemonic worldview. Participants in such ceremonies or rituals leave them with a profound belief that they have grasped the totality of their culture, that their private perspectives achieved completeness and self-explanatory correctness, even if such beliefs are often defied, as Bloch observes, by the dictates of a common-sense understanding of reality.

In Poland of the late 1970s, the official ceremonies and rituals did not fulfill this basic "centripetal" cultural function; their efficacy in reducing anxiety was minimal. It does not come as a surprise, then, that for most Poles the pope's visit was an unusually intensive *cathartic* experience. The meeting between the pope and the young people of Kraków, in which I participated, is a case in point. Thousands of young people had gathered in the enclosed yard of the Skałka Monastery, thousands more filled the adjacent streets. This enormous crowd comprising young people of all conceivable creeds and persuasions was jubilant. While we were waiting for John Paul II, the stage was constantly occupied by various groups and individuals singing and reciting poetry. It was there that I realized (I am not a Catholic) the enormous popularity of songs written and first presented at the Sacrosong festivals (briefly discussed in Chapter 4). Two moments must have left a lasting impression in the minds of the participants. While we were waiting, a police helicopter with a camera crew filming the gathering appeared above our heads. In a spontaneous gesture of mutual solidarity and defiance toward the authorities, thousands of clenched fists raised and waved at the pilot, who soon decided to fly away to the sound of the cheering crowd. Then, when the pope finally arrived on the scene, people began passing flowers to him. Almost everybody had brought flowers. The crowd was so thick that there was no other

---

38. This dualism of functions of ideology was well grasped by Geertz in his distinction between two main types of theories of ideology: the interest theory and the strain theory, which claim, respectively, that through ideologies people either "pursue power" or "flee anxiety" (1973).

way but to pass them overhead. Soon a most unusual carpet of flying flowers was passing over the heads of the crowd and slowly formed an enormous colorful pile at the Pope's feet. The enormous emotional intensity of this moment can be hardly rendered in words, yet the next day the PAP mentioned laconically that John Paul "arrived at Skałka, where in the church located there a religious celebration in honor of Saint Stanisław took place" (*Trybuna Ludu*, 9 June 1979).

The nine-day holiday brought about by the pope's visit showed that the success of a ceremony is not exclusively dependent on its psychological efficacy. There is often another "force" at work, which is usually referred to as *operative* efficacy; they are separate though interdependent. Let me first briefly discuss the latter. Operative acts (Austin's *performatives*) transform one conventionally defined state of affairs into another. In other words, they cause change by announcing that they cause change; they do what they say they do. In simple and well-defined situations, such as the naming of a ship, the "illocutionary force," which generates operative efficacy, does not have a lower or higher intensity; it either works or it does not. A ship named "Queen Elizabeth" cannot have this name only partially; a couple pronounced man and wife cannot be "sort of" married. These relatively simple acts of redefinition are often ceremonialized. Clearly, ceremony and ritual are regarded (both by "natives" and anthropologists) as proper instruments increasing the efficiency of such operations. The situation becomes more complex when a ceremony redefines or reinforces some important aspect of the group's self-identification, a part of the group's dominant discourse. Not unexpectedly, the more complex the task, the higher the degree of ceremonialization.

All evidence leads to a conclusion that the psychological and operative efficacy of the pope's masses reinforced one another to produce long-lasting transformations in all domains of public and private life in Poland.[39] The operative efficacy of the visit was created when the pope presented to the people a counterhegemonic model of sociopolitical reality firmly embedded in a religious worldview. He reinvigorated such traditionally strong elements of Polish Catholicism as Marian devotion and the myth of Saint Stanisław's martyrdom. The latter constituted the keystone of the papal discourse, for it assures (as root paradigms often do) a flawless transition from the transcendental order to pragmatic-political issues; Saint Stanisław was confirmed as a symbol of opposition

39. Zygmunt Bauman, a prominent Polish sociologist now working in England observes: "It is a trivial and widely accepted truth, that the election of Cardinal Wojtyła to papacy influenced the history of Poland as strongly as any other significant historical event" (1983, 37).

to secular power and as a patron of all defenders of human and civil rights.

The success of a ceremonial "assault on non-ideological cognition" seems to depend not only on the readiness of the populace for a new interpretive framework but also on an optimal intertwining of the operative and causal (psychological) efficacy of the ceremony or ritual. In the case of the pope's· visit, the degree of both emotional and cognitive identification with the nine-day cycle of celebrations was very high. Moreover, since it was an entirely new experience occurring in the situation of the emotional and cognitive inchoateness, its cultural meaning and psychological significance were coproduced by the pope and the participants. John Paul II's sermons did not contain many new formulations. The Church had already developed similar ideas in the years of the Great Novena (1957–66). But the pope's language, simple yet precise, and his masterful delivery increased their efficacy. But there was something more fundamental. For the first time in the history of the Polish People's Republic, the Catholic point of view was presented publicly to millions of people, not in the enclosed spaces of the Church domain but in huge public arenas, formerly inaccessible to religious ceremonies.

John Paul II's visit broke the hegemony of the Marxist-Leninist discourse (in its Gierek mutation), which had hitherto dominated the public life in Poland. The discourse of the pope's sermons, addresses, speeches, and comments was very coherent. Religious themes constituted its core, but these transcendental leitmotifs were organically intertwined with a clear exposition of the Church's stance on such this-worldly issues as human dignity, civil rights, national independence, and the necessity to cultivate national cultures. The way these issues were formulated by John Paul dramatically contrasted with the official discourse, and many people realized for the first time that there were discourses other than "Marxist," applicable in the analysis of political, social, and even economic problems. In short, John Paul II's visit to Poland in 1979, was the single most important factor leading to the final collapse of the official discourse in the 1970s.

"Is Religion an Extreme Form of Traditional Authority?" A Note on the Theoretical Significance of the Pope's Visit to Poland

In a provocative essay Maurice Bloch offered a view that religion constitutes an extreme form of traditional authority. He defined traditional authority as a product of the extreme formalization of language, most often found in rituals, political oratory (in certain societies), dance, and some forms of art. Such formalization, or what he called "drifting out of meaning," give words their "social and emotional [or *illocutionary*] force," which, in turn, constitutes the essence of traditional authority. Bloch concluded that traditional political authority and religion are indeed phenomena of the same kind; they may only differ in the degree of formalization of their respective languages, religion being more formalized.

Bloch's conclusions seem to be correct, as far as they refer to traditional authority in stable situations in relatively simple societies. But sometimes he phrases his results in such a way that it is hard not to treat them as statements of universal validity. If this is the case, he is wrong, for his conclusions do not fit the Polish situation of the late 1970s.

The power of the ruling Communist party in Poland, including the second half of the 1970s, was actualized in a highly formalized idiom. According to Bloch's scheme it should therefore be classified as traditional authority. The Church's authority was also based on a highly formalized idiom, ergo it was also predominantly traditional. From a *formal* point of view, then, the authority of the Catholic church and the authority of the Communist state were identical or similar.[40] Both these discourses were considerably removed from the idiom of everyday life of average Poles; both confirmed Bloch's observation that "the *pre-requirement* for the establishment of ideology turns out, in fact, to be a systematic and furious assault on non-ideological cognition" (1985, 40). However, the Communist "assault" was far less efficacious than its Catholic counterpart.

Such was the situation before John Paul II's visit to his native country. What happened during and after the visit remains unaccounted for in Bloch's model. The pope's travel through Poland was an extremely successful (efficacious) "assault" on the dominant Communist/socialist discourse, including the state ceremonial. It was successful precisely because his language was fresher, more innovative and far less formalized than the language of the Church had ever been before. The pope's "ideology" was not that different from what Poles had heard from the pulpits, at least not since 1956. It was his delivery and the closeness of his language to everyday speech that made all the difference. Religious authority was established not through increased but through decreased formalization; a result hardly thinkable in the Bloch's model.

Bloch's model works for ceremonies and rituals that confirm, pre-

---

40. A full analysis of the bases of their authority, which seem to have sometimes been *formally* similar, must take into account the fact that the state's power, based on the monopoly of the means of production and the means of coercion, was vastly superior.

serve, or amplify the political status quo. In such ceremonies *psychological* efficacy is crucial; *operative* efficacy is not "creative," it merely reconfirms the existing order. In Bloch's model there are no *transformative* ceremonies, of which the pope's visit to Poland in 1979 was a perfect example, where both forms of efficacy are involved, producing a thorough revision of the rules of social game and the rules of interpretation of the world.[41] Since people feel and believe that they coproduce this one-of-a-kind effect, ceremonial efficacy on such occasions is produced by the common perception of uniqueness—it is a far cry from any kind of formalization. If we are to employ Weberian categories, *charisma* seems to be more appropriate than *tradition*. In transformative ceremonies, social dramas are coterminous with ceremonial dramas; the former are not resolved *by* the latter (as in celebrated Turner's Ndembu examples), but are enacted *in* them. The outcome is not predetermined as in the case of the closed ceremonies (as in Merina rituals analyzed by Bloch). Transformative ceremonies do not serve to settle social conflicts but to articulate and amplify them; they are staged by the oppressed in situations in which other forms of rebellion do not seem viable. To a great extent such was the character of the John Paul II's visit to Poland in June 1979.

41. In his 1974 article Bloch seems to be aware of a dialectical complexity in the formation of religious authority. He writes: "In historical terms this drifting out of meaning of religious symbols is a dialectic since the process is regularly reversed as new units are reintroduced from outside by revivalist movements" (1974, 76). Yet neither here nor in his 1985 article does he develop this thought further.

6   The Discourse of the Opposition

Following the June 1976 strikes, reprisals were launched against thousands of workers in several towns. Lipski estimates that 10,000 to 20,000 workers were dismissed from their jobs; about 2,500 were detained, "of whom approximately 373 were sentenced to prison terms or fines as a result of summary proceedings by the Sentencing Boards of Misdemeanors. Criminal court proceedings were initiated against approximately another 500 persons" (Lipski 1985, 42).

In 1968, when students and intellectuals protested against censorship and demanded democratic reforms, the workers did not join in. In 1970, when workers protested against price increases, intellectuals and students stood by. However simplified this picture may seem, it was burned into the collective memory, and there were people who realized that during the next confrontation between the state and the society these two groups must form a united front. Thus, the next time the authorities turned against protesting workers (in June 1976), several groups of intellectuals and students formed a network that provided legal, financial, and moral support to the workers immediately after the first wave of prosecutions. The barrier of fear and mistrust was broken.

On 23 September 1976, the people involved in helping the prosecuted workers formed the *Komitet Obrony Robotników* (Workers' Defense Committee), known under its Polish acronym KOR.[1] This was not the first oppositional group in Communist Poland but it was the first group that went public, established working contacts with the workers, and developed an extensive network of collaborators and sympathizers throughout the country. In the words of one of its founders:

> The group of people who created the Workers' Defense Committee decided to stand up against terror and lawlessness, to give help to the persecuted, and to present the truth to society, countering the lies of propaganda. This was both a moral imperative and an imperative of rational thought in social and national categories. A small group of people could not accomplish these tasks alone; it was necessary to appeal to the conscience of others, to invoke human and civil solidarity, and call upon others to cooperate and gather financial support for the relief actions. (Lipski 1985, 42)

The circle of people who cooperated with the KOR in such activities as distributing publications, collecting money, and gathering and transmitting information grew steadily and reached several thousand at the end of the 1970s. The KOR also received substantial support from Poles living abroad and from Western intellectuals and organizations.[2] In the first year of its existence (September 1976–May 1977) the KOR registered approximately 1025 persons as recipients of various forms of its assistance.[3]

KOR members began publication of two underground (independent) periodicals. *Komunikat KOR* (the first issue was dated 29 September

1. Another factor that galvanized the intellectual milieu and contributed to the emergence of the organized opposition was the rewriting of the constitution in 1975–76. For a full account of the "constitutional" protests, see Raina (1978, 210–28), Lipski (1985, 23–29), and Karpiński (1982a, 184–88).

2. The Appeal for Polish Workers, an international committee supporting the KOR, collected funds in the West (often among famous intellectuals). Among its members were Daniel Bell, Mary McCarthy, Leszek Kołakowski, Pierre Emmanuel, Iris Murdoch, Ignazio Silone, and Alfred Tarski. For details, see Lipski (1985, 113–14).

3. For details, see Lipski (1985, 124), Raina (1978, 342), and Bernhard (1993).

1976) concentrated on the reprisals against workers and the scope of aid to those affected. It listed the reprisals against KOR members and other independent activists as well, and reported about independent social and political activities throughout the country. *Biuletyn Informacyjny,* the first systematically published independent periodical carrying not only news but also essays on politics, culture, and significant issues of the day, also started in September 1976.[4] The *Biuletyn* was published for four years under the direction of Seweryn Blumsztajn. Its ideological and philo- sophical tenor was clearly social-democratic, although other views were represented in it as well. The title was deliberately symbolic—the major periodical of the Home Army during World War II had also been called the *Biuletyn.*[5]

The formation of the KOR proved to be a social catalyst. On 25 March 1977, following internal frictions both personal and programmatic (Ku- roń 1991, 25–30), a group of independent activists, who included former members and associates of the KOR, founded the *Ruch Obrony Praw Człowieka i Obywatela* (Movement in Defense of Human and Civil Rights), known under its Polish acronym ROPCiO. Lipski conceptual- izes the differences between the two organizations as follows:

> A typical associate of *KOR* would be farther to the left than a participant in *ROPCiO.* . . . If being on the left is understood as an attitude that emphasizes the possibility and the necessity of reconciling human liberty with human equality, while being on the right is understood as an attitude that may mean sacrificing the postulate of human freedom in favor of various kinds of social collectives and structures [I presume that Lipski has in mind such collectives as the nation and the Catholic Church—J.K.], or fore- going the postulate of equality in the name of laissez-faire, then the above statement about the differences between an average *KOR* associate and an average *ROPCiO* participant will be under- standable. (1985, 121)

4. *Komunikat KOR* and *Biuletyn Informacyjny* were often published jointly.
5. The Home Army was the dominant underground army active during World War II in Poland, organizing more than 90 percent of the armed resistance. After the war, the Com- munist authorities tried to discredit it: official media and textbooks downplayed its role, emphasizing the much smaller Communist resistance, known as Peoples' Army. After World War II thousands of former Home Army soldiers were killed or jailed and tortured by the Soviet and Polish security forces. The memory of Home Army's real significance, cultivated by families and the Church, proved indestructible, and in the 1970s the authori- ties allowed a limited revival of its memory and modest celebrations in its honor.

The original ROPCiO splintered into several new organizations, including the ROPCiO proper, with Andrzej Czuma as its leader; the *Konfederacja Polski Niepodległej* (Confederation of Independent Poland, or KPN), led by Leszek Moczulski, formed on 1 September 1979; the *Ruch Młodej Polski* (Young Poland Movement, or RMP), headed by Aleksander Hall, formed in late July 1979; the *Ruch Wolnych Demokratów* (Movement of Independent Democrats) in Łódź; and the *Komitet Porozumienia na Rzecz Samostanowienia Narodu* (Committee for National Self-Determination), led by Wojciech Ziembiński, formed on 10 February 1979. All these groups produced underground periodicals. In the fall of 1977, the first in a series of durable independent publishing houses was formed; this was *NOWA,* the Independent Publishing House, organized by Mirosław Chojecki. *NOWA* and other underground establishments published hundreds of periodicals, bulletins, pamphlets, and books until 1980. In the academic year 1977–78, a group of intellectuals formed the so-called Flying University (*Latający Uniwersytet,* another symbolic link with the underground institutions functioning during the partitions and World War II). It organized a series of lectures on topics ranging from the history of literature to modern political philosophy and economics, thereby breaking the official monopoly over the domain of higher education. Despite police harassment, this initiative quickly expanded, and on 22 January 1978, sixty-one persons (mostly scientists, artists, and writers) announced the formation of the *Towarzystwo Kursów Naukowych* (Society for Scientific Courses, or TKN).

Realizing the scope and the depth of public discontent and the increasing institutionalization of its expression, the authorities allowed the creation of a discussion club *Doświadczenie i Przyszłość* (Experience and Future). It brought together scholars, journalists, and representatives of several creative disciplines and the arts, both Party members and Catholic intellectuals. The caliber of the participants, regardless of their political affiliations and ideological orientation, was uniformly high. The first meeting, held in Warsaw on 14 November 1978, produced such a critical picture of the contemporary Polish reality that the authorities forbade any further meetings. "Experience and Future" continued its work nonetheless, and produced a series of reports on various aspects of the Polish crisis of the late 1970s.[6]

As can be seen from this sketchy portrayal, organized opposition in Poland of the late 1970s was developing rapidly and encompassed a variety of social and political orientations. Fundamentally, all groups postulated democratizing internal political life, improving social conditions of

---

6. The results of this work are available in English. See Bielasiak (1981).

work and living, and regaining a greater degree of national sovereignty. They differed only in the priority they assigned each goal and the means they advocated for achieving them. In the programs of oppositional groups one would find conservative, liberal, and social-democratic elements, although each group emphasized different themes. The social-democratic option was most fully represented by Jan Józef Lipski, Jacek Kuroń, and Adam Michnik; the democratic option, with a growing emphasis on national independence was espoused by the circle editing *Głos* (Antoni Macierewicz, Jakub Karpiński) and a part of the ROPCiO, led by Andrzej Czuma. A moderately nationalistic and conservative program was developed by the *Bratniak* group, led by Aleksander Hall; more decisive nationalism, combined with strong emphasis on the issue of independence was espoused by the KPN. The views of the *Res Publika* circle were liberal-conservative (Friszke 1991).

Was the public aware of this oppositional activity? What was the wider public impact of these budding counterhegemonic discourses? No survey studies were conducted to answer these questions. They can be answered, if only partially and indirectly, by analyzing oppositional public actions such as publications, ceremonies, and demonstrations. The oppositional publications have been studied elsewhere (see Lipski 1985; also see Bernhard 1993); I concentrate on ceremonies and demonstrations.

Pyjas's Death and Its Symbolic Significance

On 7 May 1977 the body of Stanisław Pyjas, a student of Polish literature and an associate of the KOR, was found in a passageway of a building near Kraków's Market Square. The circumstances of his death and subsequent police behavior leave little doubt that it was a political (even if unintended) murder.[7] This tragic event was the culmination of a long series of harassments (including beatings, detentions, and arrests) of KOR members and associates. Kraków's college students were shocked and outraged. When a group of Pyjas's friends declared May 15 as a day of public mourning, the idea was immediately accepted by the majority of Kraków's student population. The KOR had been informed of the intended ceremony, and several of its members and associates left Warsaw for Kraków. Most of them were soon arrested and were unable to participate in the demonstrations.

The weekend of May 15 was to be celebrated in Kraków as Juvenalia,

7. For the full details of Pyjas's death, see Lipski (1985, 142–59).

the student carnival. An appeal by Pyjas's friends soon reached the student population by word of mouth, leaflets, and posters (which were constantly being taken down by the police and their distributors detained). The Juvenalia Guards, the members of the official student organization (the Socialist Union of Polish Students) responsible for keeping order during the festivities, removed the signs announcing the preparations for the mourning ceremony of Pyjas's death. This only made the students angrier and confirmed a popular belief that the official student organization did not represent students' interests and problems, but was merely a mouthpiece for the PZPR.

When Juvenalia began on Friday, 13 May 1977, only a limited number of students participated in the festivities. The joyous mood and the atmosphere of license that usually characterized this event were absent. Students were more visible than usual, especially in the vicinity of the Market Square, but their faces were solemn and pensive. They knew that the people removing the posters announcing the upcoming mourning ceremony and tearing down the black flags were Guards or plainclothes agents of the SB. More and more students wearing black bands on their arms could be seen in the streets. On Sunday, May 15, the funeral mass for Pyjas was held in the Dominican Church. Approximately five thousand people attended, and the crowd spilled out of the church onto the adjacent streets.[8] Not only students participated in the mass; one could see in the crowd many older faces. There was also a delegation of workers from Nowa Huta. Despite the strong and highly visible presence of the SB in the vicinity of the Dominican Church, a demonstration was formed and marched across the Market Square to 7 Szewska Street, where Pyjas's body had been discovered. The demonstration was led by a group of students who carried fifteen huge black banners.[9] On Szewska Street, the KOR's statement was read and Pyjas was honored with a minute of silence. Flowers were laid on the spot where his body was found. The participants were invited to return at 9:00 P.M. for another demonstration, which was to include the laying of a wreath and a candlelight vigil. Throughout the day small groups of young people celebrating Juvenalia could be seen here and there, but the majority of students did not participate.

At 9:00 P.M. several thousand people gathered again on Szewska Street. The mood was solemn, emphasized by black flags and hundreds of candles. The authorities tried to confine the demonstration. Entry from Szewska Street to the Market Square was blocked by a crowd of several hundred men wearing similar suits with Juvenalia badges on their jackets

8. This is Lipski's figure; my estimate is even higher.
9. For a more detailed eyewitness report, see *Opinia*, 31 May 1977.

and suspiciously short hair (in 1977 most of the students in Poland still had long hair, and very few of them wore suits). The demonstration could not enter the Market Square, so its main body turned back and marched toward Wawel through Planty, a park created where the medieval city walls stood, encircling the Old Town. I was part of a smaller group that managed to sneak one by one through the passive but hostile cordon of plainclothes agents to the Market Square. Once there, we formed a column carrying our flags and candles. While we were marching toward Wawel, we encountered a Juvenalia parade just entering the Market Square for the closing ceremony. A few hundred people, carrying aloft the Juvenalia queen, scattered when they saw us. I remember this encounter as a conspicuous symbol of the confrontation between the optimistic and joyous myth of a "Second Poland" and the increasingly gloomy reality.

The artificial playfulness of the officially sponsored Juvenalia collapsed in the face of the solemnity of the truly spontaneous *Black Juvenalia*. The space of the Market Square was reclaimed by the students: their demonstration shut down the official parade. Don Handelman once observed that play is a mode of social action that allows the actors to explore *what can be*. Ritual, in turn, allows them to reflect on *what should be*. In this sense, in Kraków on May 15, several thousand people participated in a ritual that allowed them to experience (not just comprehend) the drastic gap between the social reality of the Polish People's Republic as *it was* and as *it should be*. Despite harassment and detention, despite the constant presence of large numbers of security forces, the students demonstrated their contempt for police methods and made it clear that murder would henceforth be unacceptable as a method of political control. They also reclaimed a public space for independent activity and transformed "the streets into a temporary stage on which they dramatised the power they still lacked" (Berger 1968, 755; quoted in Kertzer 1988, 120). Moreover, the same evening, during the demonstration at the Wawel Castle, a group of students announced the formation of a new oppositional organization—*Studencki Komitet Solidarności* (Student Solidarity Committee, or SKS). Similar committees were soon formed in other university towns.[10]

Robotnik (The Worker)

After Pyjas's death, the authorities stepped up their campaign against the organized opposition. Several KOR members and associates were ar-

10. The SKS was closely related to the KOR. For more information, see Lipski (1985).

rested. But the KOR continued its activities, attracting growing support both inside and outside of Poland. Under increasing pressure of emerging independent public opinion and due to several protest actions, including a fast,[11] the authorities released the workers and intellectuals imprisoned since 1976. Thus the KOR's initial goal was realized, but its members decided (not unanimously though) not to suspend their activities but to expand them; and on 29 September 1977, the KOR was transformed into the KSS "KOR" (the *Komitet Samoobrony Społecznej,* or Social Self-Defense Committee, "KOR"). This new body adopted a resolution explaining its goals as follows:

1. To struggle against repression used for reasons of conscience, politics, religion, race, and to give aid to those persecuted for these reasons.
2. To struggle against violations of the rule of law, and to help those who have been wronged.
3. To fight for the institutional protection of civil rights and freedoms.
4. To support and defend all social initiatives aiming to realize Human and Civil Rights. (Lipski 1985, 200)

At the same time a group of KOR associates who wanted to continue their relationship with the workers after all the victims of the "June" trials had been released realized that it would be difficult to find people willing to sustain such contacts. The first attempt to form an independent Workers' University failed.[12] Instead, in order not to waste their already existing contacts with the workers, the group decided to start a periodical conceived of as an educational tool for the workers and as a forge of future activists. The paper was called *Robotnik* (The Worker), to invoke the tradition of an organ of the Polish Socialist Party (PPS) published illegally between 1884 and 1906.[13] This first *Robotnik* had been edited by

11. This fast held in Saint Martin's church in Warsaw in May 1977 by several KOR members and associates as well as by the family of an imprisoned worker, was one of the pivotal points in the KOR's history. It was to be remembered "as a time in which a great fund of moral energy was accumulated, . . . [which] united both believers and nonbelievers around common values and the goals ensuing from them." Lipski summarizes the significance of this first fast in the following words: "I know of the fast in the Church of St. Martin from stories, but I know its profound effects firsthand—from observing people. It seems that never again, in subsequent fasts, would so much be achieved in the spiritual realm" (1985, 164–65).

12. See *Tygodnik Solidarność,* 10 April 1981.

13. This book is about the public symbolic behavior, but *Robotnik* was such an important element of the oppositional activities that it cannot be overlooked. It was also one of the most efficient tools of dissemination of information about oppositional demonstrations and ceremonies.

Józef Piłsudski and a group of prominent Polish socialists. In the interwar period *Robotnik* was the main organ of the PPS, which was forced to merge with the PPR (Polish Workers' Party), a pro-Moscow party, in 1948. By assuming this historical name, *Robotnik*'s editors were making a conscious effort to reclaim from the PZPR the monopoly over the legacy of the Polish left. Piłsudski's *Robotnik* and his faction of the PPS represented a trend in the Polish left that emphasized both social radicalism and national independence. The tradition, that these two goals are inseparable, was continued by the founders of the 1977 *Robotnik*. Incidentally, *Trybuna Ludu,* the major daily of the Polish United Workers' Party, also claimed to be an heir to *Robotnik*'s legacy,[14] despite the conspicuous absence of the theme of independence from its pages. Jan Lityński, editor-in-chief, pointed out, however, that Piłsudski's legacy, combining socialist ideals with the struggle for national independence, was not the only tradition to which *Robotnik* subscribed and was not decisive in the choice of the name:

> First of all we resorted to the political sense of the word worker, to this meaning which this word gained in June 1956, December 1970, and June 1976. *Robotnik* presented a certain system of views stemming from the tradition of the left; first of all its attitude toward egalitarianism: we were all dedicated supporters of the idea of social equality. (*Tygodnik Solidarność,* 10 April 1981)

Robotnik subscribed, then, to the tradition of the most recent struggles of Polish workers; it was also one of the major foci of the crystallization of this tradition.[15]

Four hundred copies were printed of the first issue of *Robotnik*. A year later it was a biweekly with a circulation of twenty thousand.[16] During the strikes of August 1980, circulation reached sixty thousand (it was a chronicle of these strikes). Distribution was first organized through channels established during the relief action of 1976. Later it reached all major industrial centers of Poland (fifty locations). The major themes of *Robotnik*'s articles were current problems, such as work safety, industrial catastrophes, overtime; information about workers' protests and strikes;

14. See, for example, in *Pespektywy,* no. 35, 1976, an article describing the fifth annual feast of *Trybuna Ludu,* "The Newspaper of Three Million."

15. Bogdan Borusewicz recalls: "We distributed openly [*Robotnik*] when we had more copies. It became a tradition to do this before the December Anniversary" (*Social Text,* Spring 1982).

16. The production technique was screen printing with the photographic reduction of the text. After issue no. 16, an average issue contained twelve pages of typescript.

violations of workers' rights; history, especially modern history often misrepresented in the official works; propagation of the tradition of the Polish left; and short analyses of the international situation.

In the August 1979 issue, *Robotnik* published the "Charter of Workers' Rights," the first comprehensive document spelling out workers' complaints, rights, and demands to be published in a country of "real socialism" by an independent group. The charter was signed by over a hundred people (including many workers) representing twenty-six towns.[17] It is a common opinion among many observers of the Polish scene that this charter was one of the most important factors shaping workers' consciousness in the late 1970s. Its signatories included all the leaders of the August 1980 strikes in Gdańsk, such as Lech Wałęsa, Anna Walentynowicz, Andrzej Gwiazda, and Andrzej Kołodziej. It is also clear that the postulates formulated in it were later reflected in the famous twenty-one-point agreement signed between the workers and the government in August 1980.

Around 25 percent of *Robotnik*'s copies were sent to Gdańsk, where oppositional activities were especially vigorous. On 29 April 1978, a group of people cooperating with the KOR and engaged in the distribution of *Robotnik* formed the *Komitet Założycielski Wolnych Związków Zawodowych* (Initiating Committee of Free Trade Unions, or KZ WZZ).[18] The choice of the date of its formation was not accidental. The declaration of the new committee explained that "today, on the eve of May Day, the holiday symbolizing for more than eighty years the struggle for workers' rights, we constitute the Initiating Committee of Free Trade Unions."[19] The group, comprised of such people as Andrzej and Joanna Gwiazda, Krzysztof Wyszkowski, Lech Wałęsa, Anna Walentynowicz, and others, established contacts with activists of other organizations: Bogdan Borusewicz of the KOR, the Gdańsk SKS (later transformed into the RMP, the Young Poland Movement), and the local ROPCiO. The Gdańsk situation was unique: all oppositional organizations cooperated well with each other. This was mostly due to the unusual personality of Bogdan Borusewicz, who managed to create a network of activists willing to put aside their ideological differences when common action was necessary.

17. For a full text of "The Charter" in English, see Lipski (1985, 492–500).

18. *Robotnik,* 16 May 1978, published the following information: "On 29 April 1978 the Initiating Committee of Free Trade Unions was created in Gdańsk." As its raison d'être the Committee listed the lack of genuine trade unions in Poland and the necessity to democratize public life. The declaration was signed by Andrzej Gwiazda, Antoni Sokołowski, and Krzysztof Wyszkowski. Similar committees were formed in Katowice in March 1978 and Szczecin on 11 October 1979. For more information, see Lipski (1985, 240–331).

19. *Robotnik,* 16 May 1978.

This atmosphere of cooperation allowed the Gdańsk activists to organize a series of demonstrations through which an alternative sociopolitical and national discourse reached a wide audience both within and beyond Gdańsk, since the reports from these demonstrations appeared in all major underground publications.

The Anniversaries of the Strikes and the Massacre of December 1970

Nobody knows exactly how many workers were killed during the strikes of December 1970 in Gdańsk, Gdynia, and Sopot. The authorities shrouded the massacre in a thick layer of silence, occasionally interrupted by lies and half-truths, in an attempt to eliminate the massacre completely from the collective memory. Yet the colleagues of the dead remembered. Their memory was cultivated in independent ceremonies, the first of which was organized in 1971.

On 1 May 1971, in Gdańsk and Szczecin, shipyard workers marching in the official May Day parade carried white-and-red banners covered with black crepe and the slogan "We demand that those guilty of the December events be punished." In Gdańsk, spontaneously formed groups of workers as well as an official delegation comprising the representatives of the management of the Lenin Shipyard and official organizations laid flowers at the place where the workers were shot. Many workers knelt down and prayed for their fallen colleagues. Others placed the open palms of their hands on the wall to express spiritual bonding with the dead. Not until 1980 did official delegations again participate in the ceremony. From 1971 on, the commemorative celebrations were illegal and their participants harassed. But a new tradition had begun: there were always some flowers and a few burning candles in front of Gate Two of the Lenin Shipyard, usually around 17 December. On November 1 (All Saints' Day, or in official terminology the Day of the Dead) people would also lay flowers on and light candles at the graves where workers who had been killed were known to be buried. All these signs of memory and respect were immediately removed by the SB. On 1 November 1976 a group of students (future founders of the RMP) laid flowers and lit candles in front of Gate Two. Bogdan Borusewicz, a member of the group, repeated this gesture in front of the Gdynia Shipyard and the municipal building in Gdynia. On 1 May 1977, the same group of students (about thirty people), predominantly members of the Academic Ministry led by Reverend Bronisław Sroka, laid in front of Gate Two a wreath with the inscription: "To the Fallen Workers—Students." It remained there for about five minutes before it was taken away by plainclothes policemen. Hardly anyone noticed the wreath. After this unsuccessful attempt, the group decided to move the date of the demonstration to December (the anniversary of the events) and observe it at 2:00 P.M., when the first shift of the shipyard workers would be leaving the Gate.[20]

In 1977 the group organizing the ceremony expanded. Its members came from the KOR and the ROPCiO (and from the local SKS). Several hundred small announcements were placed on the walls around the town. Despite the heavy presence of the security forces, hundreds of people (*Robotnik Wybrzeża* estimated eight hundred to a thousand)[21] gathered at the site of the ceremony. A wreath (which remained about thirty-five minutes before the authorities removed it[22]) and flower bouquets were laid and candles were lit near Gate Two. Borusewicz spoke to the crowd about the activities of the opposition. The Polish anthem was sung. The police and the SB did not intervene.

In 1978 the authorities introduced special emergency rules prohibiting public gatherings from December 15 through December 31. This year the KZ WZZ coordinated the preparations for the commemorative celebration. Starting on December 3, about 3,000 leaflets and 500 posters were distributed all over the tri-city area (Gdańsk, Gdynia, and Sopot). The actual anniversary, December 16, fell on Saturday and was declared a holiday or a so-called free Saturday by the shipyard authorities. On December 17 (Sunday) the police arrested most of the organizers and detained them for forty-eight hours.[23] Yet the next day between two and five thousand[24] people attended the ceremony, which started as planned at 2:20 P.M., though no wreath made it through the police cordon. Lech Wałęsa, carrying the wreath from the coastal KZ WZZ was detained and fined 5,000 zlotys for hooliganism. Gate Two was locked, and the workers leaving the shipyard were forced to use other gates. Nonetheless, about a thousand workers crowded around Gate Two and the shipyard authorities had to

20. Borusewicz's account can be found in Pomian (1982, 60).

21. *Robotnik Wybrzeża*, January 1979.

22. Ibid. In *Tygodnik Solidarność*, 12 November 1981 (reprinted in Pomian 1982, 60), Borusewicz estimated that the wreath remained at Gate Two for "about an hour."

23. *Robotnik Wybrzeża*, January 1979, lists sixteen persons who were detained, including such future leaders of Solidarity as Lech Wałęsa, Andrzej Gwiazda, Anna Walentynowicz, and Alina Pieńkowska, and twenty-five persons whose apartments were searched.

24. Borusewicz, in *Tygodnik Solidarność*, 11 December 1981, estimated the crowd at 2000. Lipski (1985, 246) gives the KOR's estimate of 4000. *Droga's* estimate was 4000 to 5000 (*Droga*, January 1979). *Opinia's* figure was 4500 (*Opinia*, December 1978).

reopen it.[25] People laid flowers and a white-and-red banner with the inscription "December 1970" near the gate and after the singing of the national anthem began to leave. At this point Dariusz Kobzdej, representing the ROPCiO, read an open letter from Kazimierz Switoń, an imprisoned activist from the Silesia KZ WZZ. As the people started chanting "Freedom for Switoń," Kazimierz Szołoch, a member of the Striking Committee from 1970, gave a speech condemning inter alia the constant shortages, high prices, and the system of special, so-called commercial stores that offered a much better selection of goods but for much higher prices than the regular stores. At 2:50 P.M., Borusewicz, who managed to outmaneuver the secret agents, arrived with a wreath from the KOR. In his short speech he mentioned the significance of the 1970 December tragedy and informed the audience about the activities of the KZ WZZ. After he finished, people shouted, "We demand freedom! We demand independence! We demand justice—punish those who are responsible for the bloody massacre in December!" Before leaving, people sang "Boże coś Polskę" (God who saves Poland) and "The International." At 4:00 P.M. the ceremony was over, and the plainclothes policemen immediately began removing the flowers. The remaining participants of the celebration (thirty to forty people) tried to protest. Some of them yelled "bandits, thieves, murderers." An unmarked police car was spat on.[26]

In 1979 preventive police action against the potential organizers of the December commemorative ceremony was even more intense than in 1978. Approximately two hundred people were detained, and fifteen persons were put under arrest on the basis of the prosecutor's claim that they were planning to commit a crime.[27] December 18 was declared a so-called energetic day in the shipyard, that is a day without energy and a holiday. Yet despite all these harassments and obstacles, the posters and leaflets[28] announcing the approaching ceremony were distributed and at 2:20 P.M. on 18 December 1979 between five and seven thousand people[29] gathered in front of Gate Two. Dariusz Kobzdej from the RMP led the

25. *Droga,* January 1979, 45–47.

26. The most detailed accounts of the 1978 celebration can be found in Pomian (1982, 60–63) who reprints the accounts from *Tygodnik Solidarność,* 11 December 1979, and *Robotnik Wybrzeża,* January 1979.

27. They were all released on December 19. *Robotnik* attributes this success of the opposition to the decisive protest action that swept through many towns, including, for example, appearances of graffiti "KOR-ROPCiO" and numerous leaflets telling of the arrests (*Robotnik,* 20 December 1979).

28. They read: "On the ninth anniversary of December, on 18 December 1979, at 2:20 P.M. wreaths will be laid in front of Gate Two of the Gdańsk shipyard. *Wolne Związki Zawodowe* [Free Trade Unions], *Ruch Młodej Polski* [Movement of Young Poland]."

29. This is the KOR's estimate. See *Biuletyn Informacyjny,* November–December 1979.

singing of "Boże coś Polskę" (God who saves Poland) and opened a series of speeches. Here is an excerpt from his speech:

> We meet again in front of Gate Two to observe the anniversary of the tragedy of Polish December. We do not do this in the name of hatred. Our purpose is the peaceful, serious, and dignified commemoration of the people who fell defending their rights, their dignity. Consequently, they were defending the rights and dignity of us all—the whole Polish society. It is therefore our right and our duty to honor Their memory and remember Their sacrifice, despite the fact that the authorities of the Polish People's Republic do everything to make the society forget about Them. December showed clearly the face of Communist power, its ruthlessness in not refraining from the shedding of Polish workers' blood. It also helped society to realize its own strength in its ability to force the authorities to make concessions. . . . We should all struggle for our rights, for our human and national dignity, with solidarity and responsibility. [We should] participate in the building of social and political structures, independent of the authorities, and create authentic Polish life.[30]

The second speaker was Reverend Bronisław Sroka, who talked about the patriotic and historical traditions of the nation and intoned a prayer for the workers killed in 1970. Maryla Płońska, the third speaker and the only member of the KZ WZZ who escaped arrest, read the official statement of the free trade unions. She spoke of the purpose of the ceremony and emphasized that through such independent ceremonies people can break the official monopoly on history:

> In our own country, which is called the democratic and independent People's Poland, ruled by the Party which is called the workers' [Party]—we are forbidden to remember the workers's uprising. The history of the Polish People's Republic is made up of not only the subsequent five-year plans and subsequent Party congresses, it includes also the Stalinist terror, the workers' June in Poznań, the students' March [of 1968], December on the Coast, and June in Radom and Ursus. This is also the history of our nation. We must know it, remember it, and learn from

---

30. The full text of Kobzdej's speech was published in *Bratniak*, November–December 1979.

it. . . . We have the right to organize openly and legally in Free Trade Unions so as to defend our interests.[31]

Plońska stressed also that what the authorities had promised in 1970 had yet to be realized; no monument or plaque commemorating the fallen had been erected. Nor was freedom from arrest and/or police harassment of the members of the Striking Committee assured.

In order to avoid detention, Lech Wałęsa was brought to the site of the ceremony hidden in a large container. Only a fragment of the speech he gave was recorded in clandestine publications:

> My name is Lech Wałęsa. I am one of those who formulated and bear responsibility for the slogan *Pomożemy* (We will help). I was a member of the First and Second Strike Committees in December 1970. Today I am in the same situation as all of us who have gathered here. We do not have the monument which Gierek promised us in the shipyard. We must hide and force our way in order to be allowed to honor our colleagues who fell here.[32]

Wałęsa also asked rhetorically why the authorities negotiated with the people only after the Party committee headquarters were set on fire and why they were not willing to talk with the people in an atmosphere of peace. He demanded that the authorities respect human rights and civil freedoms. He protested against the humiliation of waiting in endless lines in order to buy basic commodities and complained that official promises were never realized. He also castigated the authorities for their lack of respect for religious freedoms and protested (as did the previous speakers) against the falsifying of Polish history by official propaganda. In the most dramatic moment of his speech, Wałęsa reminded those present that the next year (1980) was the tenth anniversary of the massacre and made a broad appeal for everyone to bring on that day stones, which would be used to erect a monument commemorating the dead in front of the gate where they fell. "How long can we wait?" he asked, "How long can we honor our fallen colleagues in the humiliating atmosphere of repressions?"[33]

As the mood of the demonstration grew more intense, several other people wanted to speak. Some people sharted shouting: "Down with

31. *Biuletyn Informacyjny,* November–December 1979; *Robotnik,* 20 December 1979.
32. *Biuletyn Informacyjny,* November–December 1979; *Robotnik,* 20 December 1979. I quote from Lipski (1985, 356).
33. *Biuletyn Informacyjny,* November–December 1979.

ɔwn with the SB! We demand democratic and religious
uch circumstances Reverend Bronisław Sroka rose to
intoned a prayer and a religious hymn. After appealing
ɔmpassion, he asked the crowd to disperse peacefully. As
ɨicipants recounted, "The presence of the priest was very
added dignity to the gathering and had a calming influence;
for me he was proof of the link between the Church and the believers in
difficult situations."[34] During the ceremony somebody proposed singing
"The International" but was laughed at.[35]

The Celebrations of November Eleventh

In interwar Poland, November 11 was celebrated as a state holiday. It was
Independence Day, commemorating the eleventh of November 1918,
when Poland regained her independence after 123 years of partition.
After 1945, Polish Communists decided not to celebrate this anniversary,
presumably to demonstrate the lack of continuity between the "bourgeois" Poland of 1918–39 and the new Polish People's Republic. In 1968,
in the atmosphere of public excitement following the March demonstrations of students and protest actions of the intellectuals in Poland and the
August invasion of Czechoslovakia by the armies of the Warsaw Pact, the
fiftieth anniversary of the regaining of independence was conveniently
overlooked by Gomułka's regime.

In 1978 the situation was different. The authorities realized that the
Church and the opposition, whose influence after 1976 could not be
ignored, would not allow the sixtieth anniversary of independence to
pass unnoticed. The Party had to acknowledge the significance of this
date in Polish history and celebrate it, even if in the most modest manner.
The official press was instructed to come up with a historical framework
that would diminish and blur the significance of Polish independence in
1918, thereby minimizing any ideological damage to the Party.[36] Accord-

34. *Bratniak*, November–December 1979.

35. Masses in memory of the fallen workers were also celebrated in the Wrocław Cathedral on 17 December 1979, with two thousand attending; in Bernardins' Church in Kraków
on 17 December, with one thousand; in the Saint Kanty Church in Poznań on 16 December,
with five thousand; in the Capuchin Church in Warsaw on 17 December, with five thousand; in Kalisz, with one thousand; and in Legnica, with five thousand. In Szczecin flowers
were laid on the (known) graves of the killed workers.

36. Instructions were distributed, for example, in a pamphlet titled "The Sixtieth Anniversary of Polish Independence" prepared for several departments of the Central Commit-

ing to the official interpretation, Poland regained her independence in 1918 thanks to "the unyielding patriotic attitude of our nation, its devoted struggle for its own state and national independence." But also, "the final success in the long struggle for freedom was made possible due to the Great Socialist October Revolution [in Russia], whose victory changed the picture of Europe and the world." These two theses were completed by the third, ascribing to the 1918 independence its proper, from the official point of view, historical significance: "We see . . . clearly and sharply, that from the point of view of our sovereignty, continuity, and safety of Poland, the historical breakthrough of 1944 [the year of the Communist takeover] was the most important event making possible the fulfillment of the task initiated sixty years ago." The pamphlet went beyond the standard official evaluations of interwar Poland, acknowledging some achievements of the new republic, such as the integration of the three partitions, the unification of their legal systems, and the viability of some of its economic initiatives. This change in the official evaluation of "bourgeois" Poland can be attributed to the pressure of emerging independent public opinion, which could discredit official interpretations, previously protected by an almost perfect state monopoly of information. As *Opinia*'s publicist observed, the official portrait of the circumstances leading to Polish independence in 1918 was not uniform. The leading Party journalist, Ryszard Wojna, emphasized the significance of the Polish "will to regain independence," ascribing to the October Revolution only a supplementary role. However, for First Secretary Gierek it was precisely this revolution that had made Polish independence possible. Gierek also claimed that "the revolutionary movement of the Polish proletariat, linking the national issues with the social issues, patriotism and internationalism, contributed in the best and most efficient way to the regaining of independence."[37] Gierek had misrepresented history; the revolutionary, that is, the orthodox, "international" parties of the Polish left, such as the PPS-Lewica and the SDKPiL, held that the independence of Poland was not only insignificant but outright harmful to the realization of the grand project of universal proletarian revolution. Paradoxically, the Polish United Workers' Party, preparing in 1978 for the celebrations of Polish independence, claimed these parties as its ideological heritage.[38]

tee, including the Department of Ideological Work and the Department of Science and Education (*Opinia*, June 1978).

37. *Trybuna Robotnicza*, 6 June 1978.

38. Wojna also made this point, thus openly defying the interpretation of the first secretary (*Trybuna Ludu*, 10 May 1978; *Opinia*, June 1978). PPS-Lewica = *Polska Partia*

The oppositional vision of Polish independence, which was presented to the public in various independent ceremonies, was different. The celebrations of the sixtieth anniversary were prepared by several opposition groups led by the ROPCiO.[39] The editors of this movement's magazine, *Opinia,* prepared a leaflet with information on the celebrations in Warsaw. Below are excerpts of this document.

The Group of the Civil Initiative
of the members
of the Movement in Defence of
Human and Civil Rights
in Warsaw

POLES!

November 11 is the sixtieth anniversary of the regaining of independence and the rebirth of the Polish Republic. Sovereign statehood, which lasted twenty years, was an episode whose impact on the Polish nation is permanent. Although the Republic fell in 1939 under the blows of the Hitler's Reich and the Stalinist Soviet Union and the Yaltan dictate sanctioned the satellite-like dependence of our Motherland on the Soviet Union—Poland did not die. She lives in us and will live forever. . . . That is why the celebrations of the sixtieth anniversary of the Rebirth of the Republic should become the huge manifestation of the will of the whole society to regain FREEDOM AND SOVEREIGNTY.

In Warsaw, at 6:00 P.M., on November 11, in Saint John's Cathedral, the solemn Holy Mass will be celebrated. No one should be absent. . . .

Leaflets and color posters depicting two Polish white eagles, one with his legs chained with the date 1978 written underneath and the second with the chains broken above the date 1918, were distributed throughout Warsaw.[40]

Socjalistyczna-Lewica (Polish Socialist Party-Left). SDKPiL = *Socjaldemokracja Królestwa Polskiego i Litwy* (The Social Democracy of the Kingdom of Poland and Lithuania).

39. In 1977 special masses celebrating the Independence Day were organized in several dozen towns. Appropriate announcements appeared in twenty towns. Flowers and wreaths were laid on the graves of many soldiers of the Second Republic and the Home Army. Several meetings and discussions were organized by various oppositional groups (*Opinia,* December 1977).

40. Leaflets were distributed in October, posters after November 9.

Separate declarations were prepared by the KOR and the ROPCiO. Only the former reached the public; the latter was confiscated by the police.[41]

On 10 November 1978 a plaque honoring Marshal Józef Piłsudski was unveiled in Saint Alexander's Church in Warsaw.[42] The church was decorated with a huge white-and-red banner. The ceremony was attended by former soldiers of the non-Communist Polish armed forces. The plaque read: "To the victorious *Wódz* [leader, commander-in-chief] in homage—Poles." On 11 November 1978 two plaques honoring the memory of the commanders-in-chief of the Home Army,[43] General "Grot" (Stefan Rowecki, killed in 1944 in Germany) and General "Niedźwiadek" (Leopold Okulicki, killed in 1946 in the Soviet Union) were unveiled in the Dominican Church in Warsaw.

The evening's holy mass celebrated in Saint John's Cathedral was attended by about twenty thousand people.[44] The crowd spilled over from the cathedral and filled the adjacent streets. Honor guards of scouts and veterans stood by the plaque of the "Lwów Eaglets"[45] and the urn containing ashes from the battlefields of 1914–20. After the mass, a crowd of approximately ten thousand people (organized by ROPCiO activists) formed a procession that marched to the Tomb of the Unknown Soldier. All the lights illuminating the monument had been turned off by the authorities. Three wreaths were laid at the Tomb.[46] People sang religious hymns and patriotic songs, including the national anthem, "Boże coś

41. The KOR's statement was distributed by "those senior members of the KOR who were healthy enough to do so" before the mass in Saint John's on November 11 (see Lipski 1985, 277). The statement contained a critical assessment of several aspects of the Second Republic (1918–39), but emphasized sovereignty, independence, and pluralism as values successfully realized during these years.

42. On 18 May 1920 Piłsudski was ceremonially welcomed in this church after his expedition to Kiev.

43. See note 5.

44. This estimate comes from *Opinia*, October–November 1978, and *Droga*, January 1979, 17.

45. Lwów (Lvov, Lviv) was for centuries a Polish center in the part of the Ukraine belonging to the Polish-Lithuanian Commonwealth. From 1939 to 1991 it was a part of the Soviet Union. Lwów and Wilno (Lithuanian Vilnius), still inhabited by many Poles, are regarded as Polish cities by some Poles and came to symbolize Soviet expansionism. The official media and school programs avoided references to these towns, and their symbolic appearance in an independent demonstration was always read as a statement against Soviet domination in Poland.

46. The wreaths were from the scouts, containing the inscription "To the Soldiers of the Independent [Motherland]—Scouts of the Republic"; from the students of the Department of Mathematics of Warsaw University, with the inscription "To the Fighters of Independence"; and from the veterans of the Home Army and members of the ROPCiO, with the inscription "To Those who awoke Poland to the Resurrection with their armed deed."

Polskę" (God who saves Poland), "The First Brigade," "The Red Pop-pies," and "The Varsovienne."[47] Prayers were said for the fallen, espe-cially for those murdered or declared missing in the Soviet Union. People chanted many slogans, including "Freedom and independence," "There is no bread without freedom," "Long live the pope and the primate," "Down with censorship," and cheered independent organizations such as the KOR, the ROPCiO, and the SKS. Even the Polish Army was ap-plauded, although soldiers from the official ceremonial army unit guard-ing the Tomb were instructed not to present arms when the wreaths were laid.[48] Yet at 9:00 P.M. the ceremonial unit conducted the routine chang-ing of the guard, an official symbolic gesture that inadvertently enriched the official ceremony, which had lasted for almost two hours and ended shortly afterward. The police did not interfere, although a large number of troops were seen in the vicinity of the Tomb.

In Kraków the holy mass in the memory of "the soul of Józef Piłsudski" was celebrated in Wawel Cathedral at 9:00 A.M. on November 11. The crowd was addressed by General Boruta-Spiechowicz, the highest-ranking living officer of the Polish prewar army and an opposi-tional activist connected with the ROPCiO. At 7:00 P.M. the pontifical mass was celebrated in the Marian Church at the Market Square. The general, again the central figure of the celebrations, received holy commu-nion from Bishop Groblicki. Groblicki in his sermon explicitly chal-lenged the official interpretation of Polish independence: "No outsider gave us Poland. Poland came into being as the result of the nation's struggles—and prayers." After the mass, a group of four to five hundred young people formed a column that marched through Floriańska Street to Matejko Square to the Tomb of the Unkown Soldier, where they placed flowers. The demonstration was peaceful and solemn. The police did not intervene.[49]

In Gdańsk a solemn mass was celebrated in the Marian Basilica. After the mass a group of approximately one thousand[50] organized by the

---

47. All these songs were rarely if ever heard in the official media or ceremonies. They are all related to the traditions rejected by the Communists. "The First Brigade," for example, was the unofficial anthem of Piłsudski's troops fighting for the liberation of Poland at the end of World War I. "The Red Poppies" was sung by the Polish troops fighting against the Germans in Western Europe. In the official version of history propagated in the Polish People's Republic only the efforts of the Polish army created in the Soviet Union (which "liberated" Poland together with the Russians in 1944–45) were fully acknowledged, if not exaggerated. The roles of the Polish troops in the West and of the Home Army were diminished and distorted.

48. The group of the oldest veterans from the Home Army and Polish Army in the West sent a strongly worded letter to the Minister of the National Defense protesting this decision.

49. *Opinia,* October–November 1978.

50. Estimates of *Droga,* January 1979, and *Opinia* October–November 1978, 15.

ROPCiO, marched to the monument of Jan III Sobieski. Any demonstration organized at this site carries anti-Soviet overtones, since the monument was brought there from Lwów.[51] Because of police harassment only a few hundred people reached the monument. The demonstration lasted for about forty minutes.

Similar special masses celebrating the sixtieth anniversary of Polish independence were organized throughout the country and attended by huge, enthusiastic, yet solemn crowds.[52] Doubtless the fact that Wojtyła had been elected pope a few weeks earlier had a strong impact on this massive upsurge of religious and patriotic sentiments, which again were closely intertwined. The Church not only allowed the use of its space for the national celebrations but actively participated in them. The 165th Conference of the Polish Episcopate instructed all parishes to prepare ceremonial masses for the anniversary and sing "Boże coś Polskę" (God who saves Poland). In many places people sang its "subversive" version, including the line "Lord, return our free Motherland" instead of "Lord, bless our Motherland." The Episcopate issued a special statement for the eleventh of November, which was read from the pulpits a day later. The bishops wrote there:

> The Polish nation never gave up this natural right of each nation to freedom, to self-determination within [each nation's] own borders. . . . It is therefore imperative to keep reminding ourselves of this date, so important for our Nation—1918. Rightly then is the sixtieth anniversary of the regaining of our independence remembered. The nation has the right to know the whole truth about its own history.[53]

On November 11 "The Pilgrimage of Independence," estimated at several thousand people, arrived in Częstochowa. In a gesture reflecting the vitality and significance of his cult, the army insignia of Józef Piłsudski, the First Marshal of Poland, were deposited in the Jasna Góra treasury.[54]

The authorities foresaw that the unofficial celebrations of the 1918 independence were going to be spectacular enough to preclude any possibility of ignoring them. They chose therefore a strategy of *symbolic co-optation,* also employed during the pope's visit. The strategy called for recognizing the anniversary, partially acknowledging its historical significance, and

51. On Lwów and its symbolic significance for Poles, see note 45.
52. *Opinia,* October–November 1978, lists the following large towns: Łódź, Poznań, Szczecin, Wrocław, Przemyśl, and Lublin.
53. *Opinia,* October–November 1978, 16.
54. Ibid.

celebrating it within a symbolic framework that distorted or blurred the meaning the event had for the opposition and the Church. According to the official interpretation, the most significant factor contributing to the regaining of independence in 1918 was the Bolshevik Revolution, and the official celebrations depicted such a reading of history. Yet they could not totally neglect the motifs of patriotism and national independence essential to the anniversary. The tenor of the offical celebrations was therefore mixed: the patriotic motifs were intertwined with internationalistic themes, coterminous with the official Soviet view of history.[55] *Robotnik's* editors commented:

> This attempt [to celebrate the sixtieth anniversary of Polish inde-
> pendence and thus] to impersonate the rightful heirs and continu-
> ators of this full-fledged independence is, like it or not, an ac-
> knowledgment of a historical defeat. For thirty-three years the
> propaganda has tried to eliminate from the national consciousness
> these twenty years [1918–39], as an unsuccessful and improper
> independence. . . . Celebrations of the sixtieth anniversary have
> sense only if they remind us of the ideal of full-fledged indepen-
> dence, confirm our hope, strengthen our resolve. It is not a holi-
> day for those who capitulate.[56]

The official celebrations of the sixtieth anniversary of independence culminated on 6 November 1978, the anniversary of the October Revolution. Through this symbolic gesture, the authorities made it clear that in the official interpretation of history the Bolshevik Revolution was the single most important factor contributing to the Polish independence in 1918. The official newspapers published reports from the (official) celebrations of the sixtieth anniversary of the independence side by side with reports from the sixty-first anniversary of the October Revolution, celebrated in the Soviet Union. It was yet another confirmation of the official point of view, according to which Poland achieved "true" and "full-fledged" independence only after 1945. Moreover, the Polish People's

55. *Droga*, January 1978, observed: "A while ago in the summer 1977 the PZPR announced that the sixtieth anniversary of the regaining of independence will be celebrated only as a continuation of the multi-year celebrations of the sixtieth anniversary of the October Revolution. Under the pressure of the Defense Movement [another name for the ROPCiO] the PZPR was forced to employ patriotic language throughout and to address the theme of independence directly."

56. *Robotnik*, 25 November 1978. This unequivocal support for the ideal of national independence coming from *Robotnik*, a paper closely related to the KOR, constitutes yet another proof that this organization did not underestimate the significance of this ideal, as was sometimes claimed by other oppositional groups.

Republic—the Third Republic ruled by the proletariat and its avant-garde, the PZPR—was portrayed as a culmination of the historical progress and the embodiment of the best traditions of the previous republics, that is, the First, ruled by the nobility, and the Second, ruled by the bourgeoisie.[57]

Despite the state's efforts to adopt the tradition of November Eleventh, the unofficial celebrations overshadowed the official ones. For the first time in the history of the Polish People's Republic, large numbers of citizens were able to participate in patriotic-religious celebrations organized outside state control. A clandestine newspaper commented: "Throughout the whole country one could feel the resurgence of the spirit of independence. The recent calling of the pontiff from Kraków to Peter's Throne had without a doubt a strong impact: we all began to feel more dignified, closer to the issues we carry with hope in the depths of our hearts."[58]

In 1979, after John Paul II's visit, the unofficial celebrations of independence were also conspicuous, despite decisive police counteraction.[59] In Warsaw, after a mass in Saint John's Cathedral, a procession was led by Andrzej Czuma of the ROPCiO to the Tomb of the Unknown Soldier.[60] A crowd of approximately two thousand people was addressed by Andrzej Czuma, Wojciech Komorowski, Józef Michał Janowski, and Wojciech Ziembiński.[61] Ziembiński laid a wreath of white and red flowers, with the inscription: "To Polish soldiers from those who carry on the idea of independence." Komorowski, bearing a wreath from "the young people," said in his speech:

A wreath from the young people who were raised in the People's Republic, without independence, and from those who still care

57. Such an interpretation of the official symbolism is by no means arbitrary. It was explicitly put forward by the theses published by the Department of the Ideological and Educational Work and the Department of Science and Education of the Central Committee of the PZPR (see *Biuletyn Informacyjny* October–November 1978).

58. *Opinia,* October–November 1978, 12.

59. On 11 November 1979 the SB "conducted fifty searches, including two police traps, detained eighty-four people, seventy-five of whom were detained for forty-eight hours or longer, used tear gas on two occasions, and beat eleven people" (Lipski 1985, 349).

60. The demonstration was attacked by a group of thugs (no observer doubts that they were organized by the SB), but the attack was not strong enough to disrupt the demonstration. Later, the traffic police efficiently let the demonstrators cross two busy intersections. For more details, see Lipski (1985, 349).

61. In February 1979 Ziembiński left the ROPCiO and founded the *Komitet Porozumienia na Rzecz Samostanowienia Narodu* (Committee for National Self-Determination, sometimes abbreviated as KSN), which was programmatically involved in the organization of patriotic demonstrations and developed the cult of Jozef Piłsudski.

about independence. We are the hope of Poland. We are the hope of the world, as the Holy Father said. His words were written on a banner which was stolen from us in front of the Cathedral [when the demonstration was earlier attacked by Secret Service agents]. In this square[62] he spoke the important words: "There is no just Europe without an independent Poland." This is our aim.

"We are your hope," the demonstrators responded six times. Andrzej Czuma told the crowd that several members of the opposition had been arrested before the demonstrations, including the leader of the newly formed *Konfederacja Polski Niepodlegtej* (the Confederation of Independent Poland, or KPN), Leszek Moczulski. Someone shouted: "We will avenge this!" Czuma replied: "No, no, ladies and gentlemen, no! What we want is freedom. Let us leave feelings like hatred and revenge to those who persecute us." These words, epitomizing the spirit of the opposition in Poland, were loudly applauded and later gained popularity for their author. Czuma said in his speech:

> Today is the sixty-first anniversary of the regaining of Poland's independence. There is no need to remind you of our national battles. But it is necessary to mention those who did the most for our independence. And it was not any October Revolution. [Laughter, applause] Thousands of Poles worked for it, long before 1918. . . . [T]oday, sixty-one years after the regaining of Polish independence, we have no freedom and no independence and this is one of the reasons why we have no food and no housing. [Applause] . . . Let us emphasize our will for freedom. In the so-called elections next year let us not vote for those who deprive us of freedom.[63]

Ziembiński recalled the story of the Tomb of the Unknown Soldier:

> This is a place demanding particular respect. Let us remember that in this grave is buried a Polish soldier, a defender of Lwów.[64] [Applause] The soldier, who in 1925 was brought to the Archcath-

62. The demonstration was organized in Victory Square, where the first papal mass was held in June 1979.
63. This and other excerpts from the speeches delivered at the Tomb of the Unknown Soldier in Warsaw on 11 November 1979 and taken from a transcript of the ceremony that can be found in the Bakhmeteff Archive of Russian and East European History and Culture, Rare Book and Manuscript Library, Columbia University.
64. Lwów was defended by the Polish Army during the Polish-Soviet war (1919–21).

edral from the cemetery of the Lwów Eaglets in the train of the president of the Republic, and then, on 2 November 1925, was buried here.

Benedict Anderson has observed that "no more arresting emblems of the modern culture of nationalism exist than the cenotaphs and tombs of Unknown Soldiers" (1983, 17). The Tomb of the Unknown Soldier in Warsaw is emblematic of more than one instance of Polish patriotism. It symbolizes the blood shed by *all* the Polish soldiers who died defending their homeland. As such it served in many official celebrations as a convenient symbolic device to blur the distinction between patriotism and the official "socialist" patriotism, which inadvertently implies pro-Soviet sentiments. Yet at the same time it represented the blood shed by one *particular* soldier, who died defending Poland against the Soviet Union. It is thus an eloquent symbol of anti-Soviet sentiments. The Party, however, had no choice but to agree to a symbolic compromise. Had it decided to tear down the Tomb or erect a new one, an empty spot or a new structure would have replaced it as yet another powerful symbol of the regime's illegitimacy. Therefore, the Polish Communists retained the structure, but in official ceremonies depicted it as a symbol of Polish heroism against one enemy only—the Germans. Recognition of the soldiers who died fighting the Soviets became taboo. For many years the Tomb's full symbolic significance, including its role as a reminder of the conflicts between Poland and Russia and as a focal point of anti-Russian and anti-Soviet sentiments, lay dormant until it was resurrected in the unofficial ceremonies of the late 1970s. On 31 July 1979, during the unofficial rally commemorating the thirty-fifth anniversary of the Warsaw Uprising, Ziembiński addressed this issue directly:

We are standing in front of the Tomb of the Unknown Soldier— before the Tomb which the occupiers damaged but will never be able to destroy. German enemy tanks came through here. Other unworthy hands removed the tablets bearing the names of battlefields of World War I and the Russian-Polish war of 1919–20. We demand the return of those tablets, commemorating the glory of Polish arms. [Applause][65]

Many oppositional activists who spoke at the Tomb warned their audiences, however, that the restoration of historical truth should not engen-

65. The text of Ziembiński's speech (and the English translation I quote here) is available from Bakhmetev Collection, Columbia University.

der or reinforce nationalistic phobias and ethnic, especially anti-Russian, hatred. Many underground publications, especially those related to the KOR, emphasized the enemy was the Soviet system, not the Russian people.

In Gdańsk, 11 November 1979 was celebrated in the ceremonial mass in the Marian Basilica, attended by five thousand people.[66] As in previous years, after the mass a demonstration of predominantly young people (approximately fifteen hundred) marched to the monument of Jan Sobieski. Two slogans were particularly visible: "The Movement of Young Poland" (the name of the main group who organized the demonstration) and "Freedom, Independence, Equality." The monument was surrounded by scaffolding and park benches, undoubtedly put there by the police. Tadeusz Szczudłowski delivered a passionate patriotic speech whose main themes were the necessity of the struggle for national independence and the meaning of true patriotism (which should not be based on hatred). Szczudłowski also presented key arguments undermining the officially propagated thesis that Poland owed her independence to the victorious Bolshevik Revolution.[67] The demonstration ended with the singing of *Rota* and the national anthem. The police did not intervene, but most of the independent activists from the RMP, the ROPCiO, and the WZZ (Free Trade Unions), potential organizers of and possible participants in the demonstration, had already been detained a day or two earlier.[68] Tadeusz Szczudłowski and his son Piotr were beaten by a group of thugs on their way home.

The Celebrations of May Third

The anniversary of the May Constitution, May 3, celebrated as an official state holiday in prewar Poland, was also removed from the ceremonial calendar of the Polish People's Republic.[69] However, the constitution was

66. *Bratniak,* September–October 1979.

67. A long excerpt from Szczudłowski's speech, which seems to represent very well the style of thinking on national issues developed by oppositional circles in Gdańsk is translated in Appendix 4.

68. The list includes such people as Lech Wałęsa, Bożena Rybicka, Wiesław Słomiński, Jan Samsonowicz, Mirosław Rybicki, Konrad Tuszyński, Dariusz Kobzdej, Jan Zapolnik, Jacek Taylor, and Kazimierz Szołoch.

69. *Biuletyn Dolnośląski,* a clandestine periodical from Wrocław, published the legislation of the Sejm from 1919, establishing May Third as a national holiday. Here is a fragment of this document: "Article 1. The day of May Third, as the anniversary of the Constitution of

May First 1973, Warsaw. Poland's Communist leaders watch carefully orchestrated parade from viewing stands in front of the Palace of Culture. Edward Gierek, the First Secretary of the Central Committee of the PZPR, is fourth from right. Piotr Jaroszewicz, the Prime Minister, is fifth from right. The "May Holiday" was an important part of the Communist effort to remodel the national symbolic domain.

Students of Warsaw Polytechnic marching in May First parade, 1973. Slogans: "The Club Center," "Socialism Is Our Today and Tomorrow!," "Scientists Serve Their Motherland!"

Students of Warsaw Polytechnic marching in May First parade, 1973. Slogans: "PZPR—the Guiding Force of the Nation!," "Socialism Is Our Today and Tomorrow!"

Crowds in Warsaw await Pope John Paul II's first visit to Poland, 2 June 1979. Both state and Church tried to place this momentous event in a cultural frame that would optimally suit their respective interests and reaffirm their rival visions of reality.

Pope John Paul II addresses crowds in Warsaw, 2 June 1979.

© Marek Stawowy

Motioning to crowds in Warsaw.

© Marek Stawowy

People awaiting the pope's arrival. Slogans: "Open the Door for Christ," "Holy Father, the Children and the Youth from the Savior Parish in Warsaw Welcome You."

Gate Two of the Lenin Shipyard in Gdańsk during the August 1980 strike. Gate Two became a nexus of communication between those inside and outside the shipyard.

Gate Two of the Lenin Shipyard in Gdańsk during the strike.

Two young workers posing under the photograph of John Paul II at Gate Two. Shipyard workers were sensitive to larger "symbolic" issues from the beginning of the strike. Through symbols and ceremonies they expressed feelings and opinions on the whole range of political, social, and existential issues, transcending their most immediate identification as "the striking industrial workers."

Mass is celebrated inside the shipyard during the August 1980 strike.

The wooden cross consecrated by Father Jankowski on the first Sunday of the strike. It was planted to the left of Gate Two on the spot where the workers were killed in 1970. The cross was one of the most conspicuous symbols of the strike, and later it became a permanent element of Solidarity's decor.

Lech Wałęsa near a statue of Lenin during the August 1980 strike. Wałęsa, who got into the shipyard on August 14 by climbing a fence, soon took charge of the strike.

© Witold Górka

Wałęsa announces the signing of the agreement between the government and the striking workers.

© Witold Górka

Wałęsa and Anna Walentynowicz presiding over a meeting of the MKS (Interfactory Strike Committee) in the Lenin Shipyard during the strike. Note that the white eagle, a symbol of the Polish nation, is not crowned. Communist authorities had removed the crown to illustrate its antihierarchical, antiroyalist, and antibourgeois mythology/ideology. Increasingly, the opposition would replace it.

Lech Wałęsa in the Lenin Shipyard, August 1980. When asked to pose for his first "official" portrait after the end of the strike, Wałęsa chose to stand under a cross with flowers in his hand.

Gdańsk Monument, on the spot where the workers were killed in 1970. Authorities gave permission for the erection of the monument soon after the start of the August 1980 strike, but the official unveiling ceremony in December was a genuine people's celebration.

Unveiling of the Poznań Monument, 1981, commemorating the deaths of several dozen people in the 1956 workers' uprising. The celebrations lasted three days.

Unveiling of Poznań Monument.

First Congress of Solidarity, 1981.

© Witold Górka

Wałęsa at the First Congress of Solidarity, 1981. Wałęsa's informal dress and manner, as well as his intermingling with "ordinary" delegates, contrast sharply with the usual stiffness of Communist party congresses.

© Witold Górka

The White March in Kraków, May 1981. A massive and truly spontaneous demonstration of solidarity with the wounded pope.

The White March in Kraków.

a symbol of democratic reform and was remembered in many oppositional ceremonies, especially after 1976.

In Gdańsk the celebrations were organized by the RMP with the help
of other groups, including the ROPCiO and the WZZ. Significantly, in
1979 and 1980, the Gdańsk celebrations were the most elaborate and
drew the largest number of participants. In 1979, after the mass in the
Marian Basilica, approximately a thousand people marched to the monument of Jan Sobieski. Flowers were laid, everyone sang patriotic songs,
and Tadeusz Szczudłowski spoke to those gathered. The ROPCiO was
responsible for organizing the event.[70]

The next year the demonstration was even more impressive. The RMP
prepared about twenty thousand leaflets, which were distributed around
the tri-city area.[71] In his sermon, Reverend Stanisław Bogdanowicz spoke
on the history and significance of the strong link between the Polish nation
and Christianity. He emphasized the role of the cult of the Virgin Mary as
one of the focal points in this relationship (May 3 is celebrated by the
Catholic Church in Poland as the Feast of Our Lady, the Queen of Poland).
The mass attracted about fifteen thousand people. Almost half of this
group marched to the monument of Jan Sobieski, which was by now a
regular site for the oppositional rallies. Their slogans read: "Freedom,
Independence, Equality," "We remember Katyń," "Independence to
Poland—Democracy to Poles," and "We demand teaching without lies."
The rally began at 8:30 P.M. and lasted for over an hour. Speeches were
delivered by Dariusz Kobzdej, Tadeusz Szczudłowski, and Nina Milewska. They talked about the meaning of the May Third tradition and told
the audience about the persecutions endured by oppositional activists,
including imprisonment for political reasons. Szczudłowski and Milewska
quoted John Paul II, recalling his statement, "There is no just Europe
without an independent Poland." Flowers were placed at the foot of the
monument, candles were lit, and the national anthem was sung. All the
flowers, slogans, and national banners that decorated the monument were
removed immediately after the demonstration by several unrecognized
civilians. Several activists and their friends, including a child, were bru-

---

1791, is declared throughout the Polish Republic as a ceremonial holiday forever" (*Biuletyn
Dolnośląski*, May 1980).

70. *Biuletyn Infomacyjny*, April 1979.

71. The leaflets read: "In the intention of the Motherland! In the name of Those, who
fought for a free and independent Poland, who built her with the work of their hands. . . .
On May 3 in the Marian Church the Holy Mass will be celebrated. On May 3 at the
monument of Jan Sobieski III flowers will be laid to honor Their memory. The Movement
of Young Poland" (*Bratniak*, May–June 1980).

tally beaten by the SB. Szczudłowski and Kobzdej were arrested and three days later sentenced to three months imprisonment.[72]

The Significance of the Independent Celebrations

Many experts were puzzled that the Lenin Shipyard strike of August 1980 could begin as a protest over economic issues and yet within a matter of days grow to form the nucleus of the largest spontaneous social and national movement the Soviet bloc had ever seen. I think a significant part of the explanation lies in the often overlooked ongoing mobilization of independent public opinion by the oppositional groups through their publications and ceremonies.[73] While congregating during the papal masses and independent celebrations, people realized the need and the possiblity of common action, as well as the availability of the reservoir of national and religious traditions still unclaimed by or suppressed in the official discourse of the People's Republic. The elements of this heritage (a potential counterhegemonic discourse), which were used to define "us," the nation or the society against "them," the state (or Party-state), thereby challenging the latter's claims to legitimacy, came from four major sources: the independence tradition (the parts unclaimed by the regime); the tradition linking Polish nationhood with Christianity; the tradition of democratic reforms of the late eighteenth century and the interwar republic; and the new tradition of Polish workers' martyrdom, developed predominantly in the Gdańsk observances of the anniversaries of the December 1970 massacre. By 1980, these various elements merged into one powerful discourse founded on the principles listed below. Each of these principles had several symbolic vehicles (events, personages, anniversaries) and was nurtured by opposition groups and the Catholic Church.[74] In Table 5 I attempt to

72. Lipski (1985, 353), and *Bratniak,* May–June 1980.

73. The role of clandestine publications has been appreciated by many observers of the Polish scene, but the significance of independent ceremonies has not.

74. The KOR was programmatically opposed to public demonstrations. Lipski explains that this policy "reflected a deeply held conviction that if even one such demonstration led to a confrontation with the police . . . , the result would have been to slow down the work of the opposition, which was developing in ever broader spheres of social life" (1985, 346). According to Lipski, some KOR members were also concerned that street demonstrations were conducive to the emergence of such undesired sentiments as chauvinism and false impression of society's strength. Lipski also has reservations concerning "the uncritical adulation of Józef Piłsudski." He observes that the cult of Piłsudski "has its raison d'être, a symbol of aspirations to national independence, but—to put it euphemistically—he was not a good patron of democratic ideals" (1985, 346). (In 1926 Piłsudski staged a coup d'état and

Table 5. Symbolic vehicles of oppositional principles and the groups and institutions propagating them

Principles	Symbols	Institutions
Dignity	The pope, St. Stanisław, Cardinal Wyszyński	Church, the opposition
Independence and sovereignty	November Eleventh, Piłsudski	ROPCiO, RMP, KPN, Church
Democracy	May Third	KOR, ROPCiO, RMP, KPN, Church
Social justice	Gdańsk "December 1970" tradition	KOR, ROPCiO, RMP, KZ WZZ, Church
Christian patriotism (extreme version—Pole–Catholic)	Black Madonna, the pope, Wyszyński	Church, KPN, RMP, some members of ROPCiO and KZ WZZ (e.g. Switoń)
Secular patriotism, tolerance, and forgiveness	Piłsudski, St. Stanisław's legend, the pope	ROPCiO, KPN, RMP, Church, KOR
Poland as a part of European civilization	The pope, May Third	Church, the opposition
Sociability, i.e., spontaneous creation of society	All oppositional ceremonies, esp. John Paul II's visit	Church, the opposition
Ecclesiastical checks on secular power	St. Stanisław's legend	Church
Civil rights	John Paul II's visit, all oppositional demonstrations	Church, the opposition

determine the basic symbolic vehicles of each principle and the primary institutions or groups propagating them.

Oppositional demonstrations and Church celebrations, which reinvigorated the set of principles listed in Table 5, were organized in many Polish towns, including Kraków, Warsaw, Wrocław, and Lublin. Gdańsk, however, stands out as the place where various oppositional groups cooperated in unique harmony and where such ceremonies were organized with the highest frequency and attracted the highest numbers of participants from various milieus, including both workers and students. Through the independent activities Gdańsk became the second (after Warsaw) center of political opposition in Poland. Through the independent ceremonies, such as the anniversaries of December 1970 (symbolizing social justice and equality), the May Third Constitution of 1791 (symbolizing democracy), and November Eleventh (symbolizing independence), Gdańsk became the center of the symbolic opposition in Poland and the primary locus of the emergence of the counterhegemonic discourse. Hundreds if not thousands of workers in Gdańsk participated in or at least heard of independent celebrations, which rejuvenated the ideas of national independence and democracy. Many more workers remembered December 1970 and participated more or less actively in the invention of the tradition of the workers' struggle and sacrifice. It was the combination of all these traditions in Gdańsk that led to the emergence of a public atmosphere in which the August 1980 workers' protest became a movement of national renewal.

The conclusions reached in this chapter strongly support the views of E. P. Thompson and Natalie Davis, both of whom emphasize "the decisive role of *culture* as a driving force of historical change" (Desan 1989, 50) and, through their detailed studies of public symbolic behavior, "express their conviction that the lower classes were not simply prey to external determining forces in history, but instead played an active and integral role in making their own history and defining their own cultural identity" (Desan 1989, 55). Those Poles who played such "an active role in making their own history" by engaging in independent ceremonies and demonstrations in the 1970s not only (re)defined their own identity but also contributed to the development of the public discourse, which ultimately nullified the credibility of Party-state's claims to political legitimacy.

---

assumed dictatorial power, which he held until his death in 1935.) This statement is confusing for Lipski overlooks the fact that Piłsudski's myth was invoked *predominantly* in connection with the idea of independence. As far as his myth is concerned, Piłsudski's position on democracy is irrelevant (political myths are always selective); besides he was rarely, if at all, seen as "a patron of democracy."

7 Symbols and Ceremonies of Solidarity

On 1 July 1980 Polish authorities "reformed" the selling of meat products. A day later this decision was made public. In practice, the "reform" amounted to price increases of 90 to 100 percent on some kinds of meat. As had happened twice before in this decade, the response of the workers affected by the price increase was a wave of protests and strikes.[1] In July strikes engulfed the whole country. They were particularly widespread in the Lublin and Warsaw provinces.

The workers' demands during the first wave of strikes (the first days of July) were predominantly economic: pay raises and a return to the old meat prices. In the second half of July the tone of their demands changed.

---

1. In Sanok's Bus Plant, Tarnów's "Ponar" plant, and the "Ursus" Mechanical Plant near Warsaw the workers went on strike on July 1, protesting low wages and in reaction to the rumors about price increases.

The striking workers were increasingly aware of the massive character of their protest and of each other's actions, organization, and demands.[2] Such information was gathered by opposition activists (mainly Jacek Kuroń, other KOR members, and *Robotnik*), published in oppositional papers (again the most important was *Robotnik,* whose circulation in July–August 1980 reached sixty thousand), and broadcast in Poland by Radio Free Europe, the BBC, and the Voice of America. The workers uniformly asked for wage increases; they also demanded that the system of family subsidies be reformed (they wanted the same benefits police and security force employees received), and an increase in the available supplies of meat and basic food stuffs. The demands concerning improvements in working conditions, social security benefits, and health care were voiced frequently in late July and August. Often the workers demanded better organization of work and a reduction in managerial staffs. Criticism of the existing trade unions was escalating; in most locations the workers called for a reform of the existing unions and genuine elections in their locals. In some places, especially where the KOR, *Robotnik,* or other oppositional groups had established contacts with the workers before 1980, the demands included the formation of new trade unions, independent of the Party and the state. In a few cases the workers also demanded such political reforms as the abolition or limitation of preventive censorship, reduction of spending on propaganda, greater turnover in the highest levels of the government, introduction of a universal rule of law, and improvement of the central management of the economy.[3] By late August, the right to free trade unions—not controlled by Party, state, or enterprise management—became one of the most popular demands made by striking workers from several hundred enterprises of the Coast, united under the Interfactory Strike Committee headquartered in the Lenin Shipyard in Gdańsk.

---

2. I agree with Ash's opinion that "if Gierek had decided at the beginning of July to detain a few tens of activists, to cut a few hundred telephone lines, and to control the international exchanges, the history of that summer might have been very different" (1983, 34).

3. Roman Laba (1986) analyzes demands from 261 enterprises and 44 shops. Here are the ten most frequent demands: (1) pay raises (65%); (2) family subsidies equivalent to those paid to the apparat (the Party, government, police, and army) (63%); (3) free Saturdays (53%); (4) free trade unions (52%); (5) pay system reform (51%); (6) more housing (44%); (7) recognition of the Interfactory Strike Committee (42%); (8) improved working conditions (40%); (9) the elimination of special privileges for the apparat (39%); and (10) earlier retirement (37%).

Gdańsk Carnival: Symbolism of the Strike in the Lenin Shipyard

The Lenin Shipyard strike began on the morning of 14 August 1980. The workers presented two demands: the reinstatement of Anna Walentynowicz, who had been fired for her openly critical attitude of the working conditions and "illegal" agitation on the behalf of the Free Trade Unions (WZZ) and other oppositional organizations, and a pay raise of 1000 zlotys, with future cost-of-living adjustments. These demands had already been printed on several posters, prepared by the members of the RMP and smuggled into the shipyard by three workers, cooperating with Bogdan Borusewicz from the KOR.[4] The demand to reinstate Walentynowicz, who was very popular among the workers, was announced in leaflets and copies of *Robotnik,* which were distributed on the morning of the fourteenth in the trams and trains bringing the workers to the shipyard. In July, the first attempt by Borusewicz and the WZZ to rouse the shipyard workers to strike had failed.[5] This time the response was positive. By 8:00 A.M. several hundred workers were gathered at a rally. The director of the shipyard promised to start negotiations on the condition that the workers go back to work. As the crowd began to disperse, Wałęsa, who got into the shipyard by climbing a fence, appealed to the workers to reconsider their situation and continue their strike. The workers listened to him and Wałęsa took charge. A strike committee formed and presented the following list of demands: reinstatement of Anna Walentynowicz and Lech Wałęsa, guarantees of no reprisals, raises of 2000 zlotys, family subsides on a par with those of the police, and erection of a memorial monument for the workers who were killed in December 1970.[6] The shipyard director opposed the last idea, explaining that the area in front of Gate Two was designated for a shopping mall, a parking lot, or "something like that." He proposed that a commemorative plaque be placed in the shipyard's "Tradition Room." An angry worker responded: "We are haggling over dead heroes like blind beggars

---

4. See, for example, Ash (1983, 38). According to one participant there were seven posters (*Punkt* [Special Issue], December 1980, 249).

5. Walentynowicz recalls: "Shipyard workers were still too frightened. We anticipated at least two more years of persecution before society at large would be ready to act" (Kemp-Welch 1983, 17).

6. The story of the August strike in the Lenin Shipyard has been reconstructed in numerous publications. For good accounts (in English), see Kemp-Welch (1983), Ash (1983), Tymowski (1981), and the publication of Radio Free Europe Research, *August 1980: The Strikes in Poland* (Robinson 1980). For the translations of strike bulletins and other relevant documents, see MacDonald (1981).

under the lamp post. You're talking about planning problems . . . people have been waiting for a monument to fifteen thousand Polish soldiers murdered by the Soviet government in Katyń thirty years . . . I beg your pardon, forty years ago. How much longer . . ."[7] This incident indicates that the shipyard workers were sensitive to larger "symbolic" issues from the beginning of the strike. As the strike developed, the significance of this symbolic dimension increased. Through symbols and ceremonies the workers expressed feelings and opinions on the whole range of political, social, and existential issues, transcending their most immediate identification as "the striking industrial workers."

The strike soon had its own media of communication, including *Strajkowy Biuletyn Informacyjny "Solidarność"* (Strike information bulletin "Solidarity"—produced by experts in underground publishing from the KOR), leaflets, posters, and an internal public-announcement system. On Saturday, August 16, the management agreed to fulfill the workers' demands and at 3:00 P.M. the strike was declared to be over. However, as the workers were leaving the shipyard, representatives of other smaller enterprises tried to stop them, explaining that their demands were not yet met and that without the support of a gigantic shipyard they did not have a chance to succeed. Wałęsa, who earlier announced the end of the strike, considered their demands and changed his mind on the spot.

> For an anxious hour he drove slowly around the yard on an electric trolley, flanked by the statuesque figure of Anna Walentynowicz and the girlish Ewa Ossowska, like some improbable carnival float symbolizing The Struggle of the Workers Supported by Virtue and Youth, shouting through a megaphone to make himself heard above the Director's voice over the works radio.[8]

The "solidarity" strike was declared, and within the next twenty-four hours the workers formed the *Międzyzakładowy Komitet Strajkowy* (Interfactory Strike Committee, or MKS) and produced a new, more comprehensive, list of demands. This was the famous "List of Twenty-One Demands."

Sunday, August 17, in the Lenin Shipyard began with holy mass at

7. I am quoting from Ash (1983, 40). The Katyń murders and their symbolic significance are discussed later in this chapter.

8. Ash (1983, 41). This account seems to be slightly colored, though it adequately reflects the atmosphere. Wałęsa did not have a megaphone all the time and in some places his appeals were hardly audible (see, for example, *Punkt* [Special Issue], December 1980, 266). Alina Pieńkowska was also very active in convincing the workers to resume the "solidarity" strike.

Gate Two at 9:00 A.M., celebrated by Father Jankowski from Saint Brigid Church.[9] It was attended by some five thousand people who were crowded inside the shipyard and around two thousand more outside the gate. After mass, Jankowski consecrated a wooden cross, which was planted to the left of Gate Two on the spot were the workers were killed in 1970. The cross was subsequently adorned with flowers, a ribbon bearing the national colors, a copy of the Black Madonna, a drawing representing the design for the future monument to be erected on the same spot, and three inscriptions. At the top there was a crude piece of paper with a handwritten inscription: "To want to is to be able to. Józef Piłsudski." Below someone fixed a printed excerpt from Byron's "Giaour," well known in Poland in Adam Mickiewicz's translation:

> For Freedom's battle once begun,
> Bequeath'd bleeding sire to son,
> Though baffled oft is ever won.

The word "bleeding" had been omitted from the translation on the wooden cross in order to emphasize the peaceful, nonconfrontational philosophy of the strike, I presume.[10] The signature "Byron" was covered by a small copy of the Black Madonna. The typed leaflet placed under the above inscription contained a warning:

> *Attention!!!*
>
> Whoever destroys
> the farmer, the worker,
> the Motherland, [or]
> Mother-Earth and Nature
> will perish.
> *The man of Providence*

These three inscriptions reflected the mood of the strike, the workers' anger, their "resolve and strong will" (a quotation from Piłsudski), and their awareness of being a part of the larger, historically established cul-

9. The church is in the parish where Wałęsa used to live.

10. The Polish text of the leaflet reads as follows: "Walka o wolność / Gdy raz się zaczyna? Dziedzictwem z ojca / Przechodzi na syna / Sto razy wrogów / Złamana potęga / Skończy się zwycięstwem . . ." Mickiewicz's translation: "Walka o wolność, gdy się raz zaczyna, / Z ojca krwią spada dziedzictwem na syna, / Sto razy wrogów zachwiana potęga, / Skonczy zwycięstwem."

ture of rebellion rooted in Polish heritage and immortalized in popular romantic poetry.

Thursday, August 21, was a critical day for the strike. The authorities anxiously deliberated over what to do next. At the same time, the official media increased their propaganda campaign, insinuating that the striking workers were manipulated by "antisocialist circles," whose aims had nothing to do with the "vital interests" of the working people and who were only interested in the "destabilization" of the state. The MKS issued a statement rejecting such accusations, but the atmosphere inside the shipyard grew increasingly anxious and uncertain.[11] Two events helped to relieve the tension. At about 3:00 P.M. representatives of the Gdańsk branch of the Związek Literatów Polskich (the Union of Polish Writers, or ZLP; controlled by the Party-state), led by Lech Bądkowski, declared their support for the strike and formally joined the MKS. The workers enthusiastically welcomed this sign that their aims were shared by other segments of Polish society. At 5:00 P.M. a large group of workers gathered at Gate Two for mass. Two priests heard confessions and granted the workers final absolution (such absolution is usually given to soldiers before they are sent into battle). Other priests tended to the workers' religious needs from a car carrying a sign denoting it as a "Ministerial ambulance." A religious hymn ended the ceremony; this broke the mood of uncertainty and strengthened the confidence and morale of the strikers. After this, masses were conducted daily. Sunday masses (August 24 and 31), attended by thousands of people outside of Gate, were particularly solemn.

Religious symbolism permeated the strike.[12] Religious inscriptions were less frequent than political or economic slogans or phrases praising

11. The statement contained the following declaration: "Faced with an intensifying level of false and provocative propaganda . . . MKS declares . . . that the work crews on strike are not fragmenting the unity of the Polish nation nor do they act to the detriment of the Polish state. If those in power wish to see this for themselves, let them come to the striking work places and become familiar with the MKS statutes that represent them" (translated in Tymowski 1981).

12. The Church's hierarchy was, however, initially cautious if not hesitant in expressing its unconditional institutional support for the striking workers. Cardinal Wyszyński's sermon of 26 August 1980, whose censored version was broadcast by the Polish radio, was received by the workers with disappointment (later alleviated when they learned it had been censored; see, for example, Gajda 1982, 239–41). The Church's strong support came only on August 28. In a communiqué issued on that day, the conference of the Episcopate asserted that "among the fundamental rights of the individual must be numbered the right of workers to form themselves into associations which truly represent them and are able to co-operate in organizing economic life properly, and the right to play their part in the activities of such associations without risk of reprisal" (I quote from Szajkowski 1983, 97). For a description and analysis of the Church's attitude in August 1980, see Szajkowski (1983, 95–100) and Celt (1980, 133–38).

solidarity, but religious images were very conspicuous.[13] Two large paintings of Jesus Christ and the Black Madonna, made by amateur artists-workers, were displayed on a roof of a shipyard building and could be seen from far off (Boros 1980, 272).

The cross was one of the most conspicuous symbols of the strike, and later it became a permanent element of Solidarity's decor.[14] In Poland the cross, which universally stands for Christ's sacrifice and symbolizes Christianity, acquired additional meanings. First, it was a *sign of defiance* toward the Communist regime and the authorities; second, it was a *metaphor of national martyrdom;* and third, it was a *symbol of Poland as a messiah of nations.* Some of the workers were aware of this complexity of their principal symbol. One of them wrote:

> Outdoor masses, especially the first one, made an indelible impression upon us. They were experiences which no Shakespeare and no Goethe could produce by his magic. . . . Why? I dare say it was so because even the finest theatrical performances lack that supernatural power which emanates from the simple wooden cross. An atheist would probably snarl at this statement, but there were no atheists among us, and the experience was genuine. . . .
> To understand the renaissance of the cross in Poland one had to experience the inner rebirth and the days of purification. For the onlookers the cross was merely a relic two thousand years old and nothing more. For us, strikers, it was something much more because of our (unconscious) identification with Christ. We were ready to take the cross upon our own shoulders, the cross in the form of the caterpillar tracks of the tanks, if it came to an assault on us. . . . I doubt, if we could have endured [the strike without the priest's sermons]. . . . We had been faithful to the Church for thirty-five years, and now we cashed the interest from the capital of faithfulness: the Church was with us. . . . Simple, though handicapped, people preserved their childlike faith in the victory of good over evil. Just because of this ignorance of theirs.[15]

13. See Appendix 5 for a (partial) list of slogans placed by the workers on the shipyard walls in August 1980.

14. Gdańsk's official weekly *Czas* (Time), 31 September 1980, published a picture taken inside of the hall where the negotiations took place. The picture was retouched to erase the cross hanging above the negotiating table. Seweryn Jaworski, one of the leaders of Mazowsze chapter of Solidarity often appeared publicly with a huge cross (of a size usually placed on walls) on his chest.

15. This is an excerpt from a diary written by Jan Gajda, a worker and an amateur writer (1982, 238–39, 251).

When Lech Wałęsa was asked to pose for his first "official" portrait after the end of the strike, he chose to stand under a cross with flowers in his hand.

Workers' Patriotism and the Romantic Roots of the Shipyard Culture

During the strike, the shipyard became a forge of authentic folk art, including paintings and political or religious graffiti. The striking workers also produced an intriguing body of written works, including short stories, letters, memoirs, and poetry. The poems composed in the shipyard were memorized, recited, and sung together with the most popular stanzas of the nation's greatest poets. The strike poetry was aesthetically diverse, including such genres as political satire or lyrical love songs, but thematically uniform;[16] several motifs appear consistently in most of the poems. More than half conveyed the conviction that the workers, organized in their own (free) trade unions, should and would lead Poland out of the crisis, which they diagnosed as resulting solely from the Party's and the government's disastrous policies, founded on lies and corruption. "We, the workers and peasants, will create our Motherland," exclaimed one of the authors. In fact, the most striking feature of this poetry was an unabashed belief in the power of the working people as an agent of the comprehensive renewal of their country (not the whole world). The poems conveyed the strong attachment of their authors to such values as dignity (though the word itself is rarely used), freedom and national independence ("Freedom is our love," "We want democracy"). Truth was the value, which—according to the poets—had been most often violated in Gierek's Poland. "Let the lie and falsehood disappear and let goodness and truth permeate the nation," wrote one of them. The restoration of truth was believed to be crucial for the "real" renewal of Polish life. Some writers demanded that "those who sold and ruined Poland [should] face the people." Six authors (out of thirty-eight) sought the ultimate justification for their struggle in religion and prayed for divine protection. Two of them praised the Black Madonna of Częstochowa, "the mother of the wretched."

The authors rarely raised the issue of egalitarianism, neither did they

16. The following reconstruction of the main motifs of the strike's poetry is based on my analysis of thirty-eight poems published in "Polish August 1980," in *Punkt* (Special Issue), December 1980.

mention socialism or internationalism. Shipyard poetry appeared to be free of the thematic and stylistic influences of the official discourse. Maria Janion found a striking resemblance between the poetic works written in the shipyard in August 1981 and the popular poetry of the period between the Polish uprisings of 1830 and 1863 (n.d.). In both cases poetry served as a badge of ideological and philosophical identification and as an instrument in the political struggle. She noted that Solidarity's culture, which originated in the Gdańsk shipyards and the culture of popular romanticism of the nineteenth century had three distinctive features in common: ritualism, emblematism, and a predilection for short poetic forms, usually songs.

In the enclave of the striking shipyard the rules of the outside world, especially its (strongly despised) structure of power, were suspended. The *communitas* inside the yard, sustained through its own ceremonial, contained both carnivalesque (ludic) and solemn elements.[17] In declarations, at least, people were equal; social organization was based on democratic procedures; everybody could voice his or her opinions and desires freely. From the beginning of the strike the workers attempted to formulate their identity in a discourse that would *separate* them from the official reality of the Polish People's Republic (yet without explicitly challenging the legitimacy of the Republic), *transcend* their present situation, and *embed* their struggle in an ethical frame of reference. The priests invited to the shipyard endowed the strike with an other-worldly foundation. A group of actors who came to express their support, helped create a bridge between the workers' struggle (and its direct sense) and the wider context of national traditions. Maciej Prus, the artistic manager of the *Wybrzeże* (the Coast) Theater, prepared and directed an ad hoc collage of poems and songs that included poems written in the shipyard together with famous verses of Polish literature. The actors found that the romantic poems were in great demand. They later said that reciting romantic poetry to the shipyard audience was one of the most moving experiences in their professional careers. Prus recalled: "We realized that the poems we recited [those of the great Polish romantics—J.K.] were received in the most beautiful way . . . as though they had been written this second. . . . I talked to the workers and realized that they really needed great literature and great poetry" (quoted in Janion 1981, 17).

It is an axiom of Polish literary criticism that romanticism played a decisive role in shaping Polish self-identification, especially at the level of high culture. The Gdańsk strike demonstrated that romantic paradigms

---

17. A type of the social bond dominant in the shipyard is perfectly grasped in Victor Turner's category of *communitas*. See Turner and Turner (1978, 250–51).

have been vital, or at least easy to revive, in the domain of popular culture as well.[18] The poetry of the Polish romantics, written when Poland was partitioned, was permeated by a profound and unshakable faith in the power of words, which were believed to have a causal primacy over actions. Adam Mickiewicz, the greatest Polish poet, proudly pronounced: "My song is great, my singing is Creation." He did not hesitate to address God in a sacrilegious challenge:

> If Thou gavest me equal sway over each soul
> I would create my nation like a living song,
> And do a greater wonder than Thine Own;
> For what a happy song I would intone!
> (Mickiewicz 1968, 171)

This faith in the causal efficacy of words had two important implications for Polish culture. First, literature became a model for practical (also political) action; second, social life became theatralized to a degree seldom encountered in other European cultures. This feature of the national culture emerged during the partitions and subsequently proved indispensable for the survival of the nation, which for many years could not express itself in purely political forms, such as citizens' councils, democratic elections, or the free press.

According to the second romantic conception firmly embedded in the Polish ethos, the power of human will and emotions is deemed to be equal to or greater than that of reason. This idea, elaborated in numerous poems and philosophical treatises, was immortalized by Mickiewicz in his *Ode to Youth:*

> Let strength meet strength and wrath fight wrath,
> and let us learn while young
> to spurn the weakling's hate. . . .
> Brave youth, reach outward
> far beyond thy sight,
> Crush what mere human reason
> cannot harm!
> (Mickiewicz 1944, 70)

18. Ewa Morawska writing about Polish civil religion, permeated by romantic motifs, observes that "many nineteenth-century elements of the old Polish civil religion have retained their meaning and vitality as ideological rallying points of Polish civil society. The home, informal social gatherings, and various unofficial political and cultural activities, remain the important 'carriers' of Polish civil religion" (1984, 32).

Polish romantic philosophers share this faith; one of them wrote: "All my teaching, all my politics, is teaching of Deed" (Miłosz 1983, 261).

The third, and probably the most popular, paradigm of Polish romanticism was the idea that Poland was a messiah of nations. Although extremely unorthodox, this conception was nevertheless purely religious. Poland was to redeem nations through her suffering. Mickiewicz envisioned Poland as a crucified martyr:

> The arms of the cross span Europe with their length
>   From three dried-up nations, like hard trees hewn.
> They gather round—my nation on the penance-thrown
>   Cries out: "I thirst!"
>   Rakus gives vinegar and Borus bile,
>   And Mother Freedom kneeling weeps the while.
>   Look—an accursed
>   Muscovite soldier leaps with a spear and spills
>   My nation's innocent blood in crimson rills.[19]

This conviction of the uniqueness of the Polish fate was frequently expressed during the Solidarity period.

The ideal of many romantic poets was anonymity. Mickiewicz believed that the ultimate test of the poet's success was when his poem returned to him as an anonymous product of folk culture.[20] In August 1980 this ideal was realized—great romantic poetry was recited side by side with the improvised poems of the workers. Authorship was irrelevant, since the workers did not indulge in aesthetic pleasure per se. They

19. This is an excerpt from Mickiewicz's most famous drama *Dziady* (Forefather's eve), part 3, written in 1832; I quote here from Mickiewicz (1968, 200). The direct reference to Russia as an oppressor makes this fragment one of the most often applauded lines in the Polish classical repertoire. On 30 January 1968, during the last performance of the highly acclaimed production by Kazimierz Dejmek, "applause was frequent and long-lasting. After the performance, people marched toward Mickiewicz's monument bearing a banner, 'We Demand More Performances' " (Karpiński 1982a, 110). This incident triggered a series of student protests in several academic towns, which culminated in the dramatic clash between students and intellectuals on the one side and the authorities on the other. The ensuing vicious anti-Semitic campaign, which was a part of the internal factional struggle within the ruling elite, led to the expulsion from Poland of hundreds of Jews, including several dozen leading intellectuals. The years 1968 (the intellectuals' revolt) and 1970 (the workers' revolt) became emblems of the lack of cooperation between these two strata. For a detailed description of the March events and their political repercussions, see Karpiński (1982b, 110–38).

20. A related romantic virtue demanded that a poet should become an undistinguishable voice of his nation. Mickiewicz writes in *Dziady:* "I am one with my Nation / My name is Million / Because for Millions I love and suffer."

needed literature to (re)discover their roots and endow their own actions with significance. Janion noted that the general semiotic mode of the Solidarity culture was emblematic not symbolic. Yet it seems more accurate to describe it as both emblematic and symbolic. Initially, emblematicism prevailed; it served as a political weapon differentiating "us" from "them." Soon, however, such signs of defiance as the cross, the crowned White Eagle, and the Gdańsk monument assumed varied denotations and connotations and emerged as multivocal (national, religious, and civic) symbols—pivotal points of the rejuvenated public domain. As emblems they served as badges of identity and signs of separation; as symbols they functioned as meaning-generating engines of the "non-Communist/socialist" counterhegemonic discourse.[21]

Romantic tradition was one of the first elements of Polish heritage reclaimed by the populace from the monopolistic control of the officialdom. Romanticism never mixed well with the official Communist culture. Romantic poets praised the "simple folk" and believed in the purifying power of revolution. But at the same time the romantic heritage includes the veneration of personal freedom and a conviction that the realization of this value is impossible without national independence. It also implies praise for human rights and their inseparability from the right of each nation (ethnic group) to sovereignty. Finally, romantics believed that politics is always accountable before the tribunal of moral judgment.[22] All these convictions, deemphasized in the official version of romanticism, misrepresented in school curricula, and often snarled at by literary critics, were revitalized and turned into significant pillars of the spontaneously created counterhegemonic discourse of the Solidarity period. The eagerness with which this romantic revival was pursued also engendered several artistic flops. In Katowice, large sums of money from Solidarity coffers were spent on a gigantic production based on the three greatest romantic dramas, Mickiewicz's "Forefather's Eve," Słowacki's "Kordian," and Krasiński's "The Undivine Comedy." The production proved that the three great dramas have only one thing in common: they were written in the same period. The spectacle was an artistic and box-office disaster—its form was eclectic, its ideology excessively nationalistic.

21. Janion rightly observed that Andrzej Wajda's *Man of Iron*, a story of the August revolt, was not symbolic, like most of Wajda's other movies, but emblematic. I would add that the emblematism of *Man of Iron* was so conspicuous precisely because the social reality it portrayed and in which it functioned was symbolic.

22. Maria Janion analyzes these elements of Solidarity's heritage in her address to the Congress of Polish Culture (n.d., 17–24).

Other Symbols

The strike's decor and ceremonial were also strongly imbued with national/patriotic overtones. The workers made and displayed several White Eagles, in most cases adorning the heads with crowns. This was yet another sign of defiance toward the regime, which had adopted as the official emblem of the Polish People's Republic the White Eagle without a crown. The strike leadership ordered the crowns adorning two large eagles displayed on the shipyard fence to be removed; they did not want an unnecessary confrontation with the authorities (Boros 1980, 271).

Flowers were very conspicuous in the shipyard's decor. Gate Two, covered with flowers, became the symbolic threshold between the outside world ruled by the Communist authorities and the *communitas* of the shipyard. People kept bringing flowers to express their support for the strike; the striking workers displayed them to announce the peaceful and nonconfrontational character of their protest. Gate Two was also decorated with two pictures featuring the two highest sources of charismatic authority: the Black Madonna of Częstochowa and John Paul II.[23] When the flower-encrusted Gate Two finally opened, Poland was transformed; in all subsequent confrontations with the government, flowers served as the ubiquitous reminder of Solidarity's nonviolent intentions.

The famous logo of Solidarity was also created during the strike. Its author, a young Gdańsk designer, Jerzy Janiszewski, recounts: "I saw how solidarity appeared among the people, how a social movement was being born out of that and how institutions joined in. This all had a great effect on my spirit and I decided I wanted to join the strike."[24] In his design, Janiszewski used the white and red of the Polish flag. The symbolism of the logo is simple: the letters cannot stand by themselves; each needs the support of its neighbors. The letter *N* carries a little Polish flag. The idea of solidarity could not have found a more befitting expression.[25]

In Chapter 6 I showed how in the late 1970s the traditions of national independence (symbolized by the November Eleventh anniversary) and

23. The huge ballpoint pen Wałęsa used to sign the historical agreement with the government was decorated with a picture of John Paul II.

24. Quoted in Laba (1984).

25. Janiszewski said, "I chose the word [Solidarity] because it best described what was happening to people. The concept came out of the similarity to people in dense crowds leaning on one another—that was characteristic of the crowds in front of the gate. They did not press or push each other but they leaned on each other. . . . Finally, I added the flag because I was aware that this is not a regional group question but it is a universal movement. The letters have a disordered look because that is their strike attribute" (quoted in Laba 1984).

freedom and democracy (epitomized in May Third celebrations and the heritage of the May Third Constitution) were reinvented by the opposition groups and celebrated in independent ceremonies. I have noted that in Gdańsk these demonstrations were most spectacular and attracted many workers. The national, democratic, and religious overtones of the shipyard culture can be seen, therefore, as a continuation or culmination of the independent traditions, cultivated in public life before the strike. However, there was another independent tradition whose role in the shaping of the workers' consciousness was most important. It was the tradition of 16 December 1970, developed through the ceremonies organized in front of Gate Two. Its immediate sense was the honoring of the memory of fallen colleagues. Its pivotal value was human dignity. The striking workers recalled this tradition from the very beginning of the strike. On August 14, shortly after they assembled for the first rally, the workers commemorated the memory of their fallen colleagues with a minute of silence. One of the original five demands was the erection of a monument on the spot where the first four workers had been shot dead in 1970. On August 17, the wooden cross marked the site until the monument was erected. The model of the monument was a fixture in the decor of the main negotiating hall in the shipyard. The hall was adorned with a bust of Lenin (the shipyard is named after him), a wooden crucifix, a model of the monument, and a little figurine representing Wałęsa. Ubiquitous flowers and the national flag completed the decoration.

The Gdańsk Monument

Bogdan Pietruszka, an engineer in the design division of the shipyard, had been thinking about a monument honoring his fallen colleagues for ten years. His initial designs were horizontal, but as soon as the strike began the idea of high vertical crosses struck him as the most suitable expression of the emerging protest. "The final version was created in the evening of December 14. From the four intended crosses three were left" (Gugulski 1981, 13). Pietruszka explains the symbolism of his monument as follows:

> On the site which absorbed the blood of the fallen shipyard workers, ten years later three crosses[26] rose piercing the shell of falsehood, hypocrisy, and cynical indifference to human fate. For one

26. Three workers were killed on this spot, the fourth died later.

thousand years in the Polish national symbolism the cross has symbolized faith. Since the end of the eighteenth century, the anchor has meant for subsequent generations of Poles the symbol of hope. The three crosses united in a circle, connected with their arms, symbolize the first shipyard workers who fell in December 1970 at Gate Two of the Gdańsk "Lenin" Shipyard. Three cruci- fied anchors stand for subsequent years 1956, 1970, 1976, the years of crucified hopes. . . . Let this monument be a memento for all those who wanted to take these symbols away from us. We do not want to erect the fourth cross with another date. We do not want monuments conveying such symbolism to be erected ever again.[27]

The symbolism of the monument is amenable to many interpretations. Father Józef Tischner, the unofficial chaplain of Solidarity, delivered in 1980–81 a series of influential sermons (often reprinted in the Solidarity press) in which he defined and explained several fundamental ideals of the movement. He offered inter alia his exegesis of the Gdańsk monument's symbolism:

There are three crosses. On Golgotha there were also three crosses. From one of them a voice cried, "Forgive them; for they know not what they do" (Luke 23:34). From another cross the voice was similar. Yet from still another cross, blasphemies poured out. Which cross shall be our cross? We have to choose. But no, here each cross is the same. On each cross is the same Hope. And the voice must be the same. The cross has been chosen! We must make it our own cross.[28]

As Gugulski (1981) notes, the three crosses represented as well the three major professions of people who live off the sea, the shipyard worker, the dock worker, and the sailor. For the people resettled from Wilno (today Vilnius, Lithuania) the monument was reminiscent of the three crosses destroyed by the Soviet Army when it entered that city during World War II (Gugulski 1981, 13).

Tischner gives the following interpretation of the three anchors:

The anchor is here as a twofold symbol—a sign of work and a sign of hope. We know that the work of people of the sea is

27. This excerpt from "The Description of the Monument of the Fallen Shipyard Work- ers 1970. Gdańsk, 1 October 1980" was published in *Bratniak,* September–October 1980.
28. Quoted from Tischner (1984, 38).

particularly associated with the anchor. Thus, the anchor is associated with what was crucified here—work and hope. Many people
die every day throughout the world, but those people who perished here perished through their work. A human being may die
in many ways—those who heard those shots experienced how
hope dies in the heart. This work of art shows us the essence of
that tragedy—a blow that remains a blow to the work and hope of
all humankind. (Tischner 1984, 37)

The anchor was also the emblem of the Polish resistance (the Home
Army) during World War II. The Communists, who for many years after
the war attempted to discredit the achievements of the non-Communist
Home Army, tried to erase the emblem from the collective memory;
instead it became one of the most popular symbols of the opposition.[29] In
short, the crosses symbolize faith and sacrifice, the anchors stand for
hope and work, and the flame represents life and rebirth.

The base of the monument is covered with a relief composed of
twenty-six natural-size human figures, depicting the workers' labor and
struggle.[30] Czesław Miłosz was asked by the organizing committee to
write an epitaph for the monument. He declined but advised the workers
to use as an epitaph Psalm 29:11 (in his splendid translation), which was
taken as the leitmotif of the unveiling ceremony and inscribed at the base
of the monument:

> The Lord will give strength unto his people;
> the Lord will bless his people with peace.

Despite Miłosz's refusal, the Committee decided that an excerpt from his
old poem "You who have wronged" (from 1950) be inscribed on the
monument as well:

> You, who have wronged a simple man
> Bursting into laughter at the crime
>
> . . . .
>
> Do not feel safe. The poet remembers
> You can slay one, but another is born
> The words are written down, the deed, the date.[31]

29. For an example of such a conflict over the "Anchors of the Fighting Poland," see
Droga, no. 3, 1978, 30.
30. The Peplińskis were the sculptors who designed and executed this tremendous project in less than two months.
31. It is a translation by Richard Lourie. Czesław Miłosz was one of the poets whose
names were taboo in the official culture of the Polish People's Republic. In 1980 he received

The base of the monument also contains two other inscriptions. "They gave their lives so that you can live in dignity. Respect their memory," and a dedication from John Paul II: "Let Your spirit descend and transform the face of the land, this land."

The authorities gave permission for the erection of the monument soon after the strike began. When the strike was over, governmental officials engaged the union in a series of discussions concerning its construction and design. The talks constantly stumbled over spurious procedural obstacles and the hypocritical objections of the official art experts. As it turned out, the sole aim of the discussions was to postpone or preferably to stop the construction of the monument as it was designed. Four examples should suffice to illustrate the attitude of the authorities in this confrontation. On September 14, the president of the Art Academy in Gdańsk, Professor Jackiewicz, declared that he was "deeply disturbed by the fact that the high masts with perpendicular anchors, designed by Pietruszka, could be construed by the believers as crosses" (Gugulski 1981, 13). Also, after several unsuccessful attempts to change the location, the authorities sent a construction crew to erect a wall around the prospective site of the monument to decrease its visibility. Solidarity protested the erection of this wall several times. The authorities finally sent a crew to tear it down. But it was too late. Rumor had it that the Gdańsk populace acted faster and took apart most of the wall themselves, preserving the bricks as souvenirs. Throughout the negotiations governmental experts claimed that because Pietruszka's design was artistically mediocre there was a need to organize a national, or even international, artistic competition. Such a competition would have to take a year or two before a final decision could be made. One of the experts mused that a serious competition should have a literary slogan and proposed "The Monument of the Workers' Deed." It would be hard to imagine a more insulting suggestion. Poland was full of monuments with similar inscriptions—emblems of the official ideology legitimizing the power of the regime by whose orders the workers were killed.

Despite all these obstacles and due to the resolve of a group of Solidarity activists led by Henryk Lenarciak, a shipyard worker who was arrested during the commemorative celebrations in the late 1970s, the

---

the Nobel Prize in literature, and although the authorities had to readmit him to Polish culture, not all of his works were officially published (they were in the underground). In 1981 Miłosz visited Poland and during a triumphant tour around the country supported Solidarity's ideals and struggle.

monument was erected in three months.[32] Several Gdańsk enterprises donated materials and work. Money was sent from all over the country. Shortly before December 16, the crosses, forty-two meters high and six meters wide joined the Gdańsk skyline.

The Ceremony at the Unveiling of the Gdańsk Monument

As I was going from Katowice to Gdańsk for the unveiling of the December 1970 Monument, I was struck by the absence of drunken men in the train's buffet. Buffets on long-distance trains in Poland are usually frequented by drinking crowds. This time, however, I did not notice a single drunken person. The people were solemn and pensive; the miners and steelworkers wore their characteristic gala uniforms. Solidarity banned alcohol sales in the vicinity of Gdańsk for the duration of the celebrations but people refrained from drinking even where it was still possible. The authorities had never been able to achieve such a uniformly positive response to their appeals for sobriety. Such "alcohol tests," repeated several times during the Solidarity period, became a measure of popular support for the new union and of the real authority of the Party-state.

The atmosphere in Gdańsk was serious but relaxing as well. I and my friends shared the feeling that for the second time in the history of the Polish People's Republic (the pope's visit being the first time), society was celebrating itself without the state's participation. The ceremony was scheduled to begin at 6:00 P.M., but by 3:00 P.M. people began filling the huge open area in front of the shipyard's Gate Two. As during the pope's visit, the police were invisible, and the whole ceremony was in the hands of Solidarity guards. The crowd was estimated at five to seven hundred thousand people. A script of the ceremony was prepared by the Gdańsk *Międzyzakładowy Komitet Założycielski* (Interfactory Founding Committee, or MKZ). After initial discussions, which concentrated on the role religious elements would play, it was decided that the ceremony was to have the basic format of the Catholic mass. The internationally acclaimed film director Andrzej Wajda was asked to direct the unveiling.

The ceremony began with a piercing sound made by all the factories in Gdańsk blowing their whistles in unison. Next, everyone joined in sing-

---

32. Wałęsa's determination was also crucial; his honor was at stake since he had promised at the end of the strike that the monument would be ready for the December celebrations.

ing "Rota," a patriotic and religious hymn that before 1980 had been sung only during independent demonstrations or Church celebrations. Krzysztof Penderecki's "Lacrimosa," dedicated by the composer to the fallen workers, was played through the loudspeaker. After the reading of Psalm 11,[33] Daniel Olbrychski, one of the most popular Polish actors, and the hero of several of Wajda's movies, read a list of (known) names of the fallen workers. After each name the crowd responded, "He is amongst us." Olbrychski finished with the line: "I call all the fallen, whose names are unknown but their sacrifice was not futile." "The are amongst us"—responded the crowd.

Wałęsa officially unveiled the monument by lighting the torch at its base. The content of Wałęsa's speech was rather bland and, for many people, too conciliatory toward the authorities. It was received with mixed feelings. The audience reacted with warm applause only to the last words (omitted in the version of the speech transmitted on television):

> I call on you to be cautious in defense of our safety and in the preservation of the sovereignty of our Motherland. [Applause] I call on you not to forget that the name of this home of ours, our Motherland, is Poland. [Applause] I call on You, so that Poland will become the people's home, so that justice, freedom, peace, love, and solidarity will win in her. [Applause] We, and what we will do, are the guarantee of all these. (Gugulski 1981, 16)

The next speech was delivered by Tadeusz Fiszbach, the first secretary of the District Committee of the PZPR in Gdańsk, who represented the authorities. The applause he received was sporadic and weak. After several delegations laid down wreaths and flowers at the monument, the archbishop of Kraków, Franciszek Cardinal Macharski, began mass. His sermon was based on excerpts from Psalm 37:

> Cease from anger, and forsake wrath;
> fret not thyself in any wise to do evil.
> For evildoers shall be cut off;
> but those that wait upon the Lord,
> they shall inherit the Earth.
> For yet a little while, and the wicked shall not be:

33. Neither my memory nor the sources I consulted recorded the exact excerpt from the psalm read by Olbrychski. I believe he read the following lines: "The Lord trieth the righteous; but the wicked and him that loveth violence his soul hateth. . . . For the righteous Lord loveth righteousness; his countenance doth behold the upright" (Psalm 11:5, 7).

yea, thou shalt diligently consider his place,
and it shall not be.
But the meek shall inherit the earth;
and shall delight themselves in the abundance of peace.
The wicked have drawn out the sword,
and have bent their bow to cast down the poor and needy,
and to slay such as be of upright conversation.
Their sword shall enter into their own heart,
and their bows shall be broken.

This passage proved to be the strongest criticism of the authorities publicly uttered that evening. He also recalled the person of Saint Stanisław,
the saint-martyr murdered by the secular ruler who became a symbol of
the struggle for national and human rights for many Polish Catholics.
Macharski's sermon would later be regarded as the pivotal point of the
celebration, because for many people he was the only speaker who did
not hide behind a smoke screen of euphemisms in defining the real sense
of the ceremony: the commemoration of the deaths of the shipyard workers shot by the police in 1970 and the condemnation of the regime responsible for this tragedy. The rest of the speeches were decidedly more
conciliatory and emphasized the necessity of a dialogue and mutual understanding between the Party-state and the society. One of the observers,
commenting on the words of Psalm 39 quoted by Kraków's cardinal,
noted that "during Holy Mass we listened to God's words, for the words
of God's servants did not befit the place and time" (Gugulski 1981, 15).

State television aired the opening ceremony with a delay to allow the
censorship of its content. The more critical elements, such as Macharski's
sermon, were eliminated. Emphasis was put on the speeches and the
applause received by the representatives of the Party and the state. To the
surprise of many observers, the strongest applause welcomed Admiral
Janczyszyn, the commander-in-chief of the navy regiment in Gdańsk. In
Gdańsk it was widely believed that Janczyszyn had refused even to consider deploying his troops should the authorities decide to attack the
Lenin Shipyard in August of 1980.

People who had been involved in celebrations organized by the opposition in front of Gate Two since 1977 were disappointed that Father
Bronisław Sroka was not among the official representatives of the
Church present at the ceremony. Father Sroka was a brave defender of
civil rights and human dignity who played a crucial role in the illegal
demonstrations. Others complained that Bogdan Borusewicz, the actual
organizer of many of these celebrations, was not invited to participate in

the ceremony as an official representative of the union.[34] Such omissions were interpreted in two ways: for some people they epitomized Solidarity's political wisdom and self-restraint; for others they were indications of weakness and hypocrisy on the part of the union's leadership. Despite all these imperfections, the ceremony had tremendous symbolic significance. Everyone was aware that they were witnessing an event unprecedented in the history of the Soviet bloc.

The arrangement of space during the ceremony was hierarchical, but it was different than the hierarchy displayed in state ceremonies. Major public rituals in totalitarian states, such as May Day parades in Soviet bloc countries, emphasize the stiff hierarchical arrangement of society: the rulers are on the viewing stands, the masses march below. Moreover, such stands *are* the permanent sacred centers of the systems (for example, Lenin's Tomb in Moscow) or at least become such centers for the duration of the ceremonies.[35] Such space arrangements emphasize the binary opposition of rulers and the ruled. The Gdańsk ceremony was also hierarchical (as all public ceremonies are) but the organizing principle was not *opposition* but *gradation*. *All* participants *faced* the monument—the sacred center—symbolizing the martyrdom of the fallen workers and the restored dignity of the working people. The first rows were occupied by the official representatives of the state, the Church, and Solidarity. The rest of the space was taken by the "masses." No person was therefore counterpoised to the "masses" as a "leader" or "ruler." The hierarchical order resembled that of the Protestant churches, where priests are not so conspicuously placed on "God's side" as in the Roman Catholic mass; they only mediate between the transcendental and the mundane, their power is deemphasized. Graphically, the difference between the official state ceremonies and the unveiling of the Gdańsk monument is summarized in Figure 2.

The path-breaking character of the Gdańsk ceremony can be summarized in several points. First, it was a ceremony organized by the *society* (its genuinely selected representatives) to which the *state's* representatives were invited. It was therefore a perfect realization of Anatol Lunacharski's ideal mass ceremony, in which "the whole people displays its own soul to itself" (Binns 1979, 591), but also—given the usual Communist practice—an instance of the ceremonial *status (power) reversal* in the strictest sense.

34. For such criticisms, see, for example, *Bratniak,* November–December 1980, 32–33, and Gugulski (1981, 14–17).

35. For the detailed analysis of the symbolism of viewing stands in totalitarian states, see Gross (1974, 213–22).

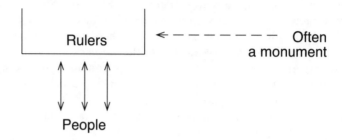

Typical Communist Ceremony

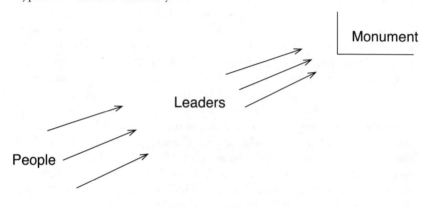

Fig. 2. Spatial arrangement of the Gdańsk unveiling ceremony

Second, it was a ceremonial act of ennoblement in which society elevated local heroes to the status of national martyrs. It was an unprecedented event, since until then the state (and the Church in its domain) had held a monopoly over such public acts as the reshaping of the cultural landscape. Third, the public "nonstate" domain was defined without reference to Communist symbols and rituals; instead, in its construction Solidarity's pageant masters borrowed heavily from the Catholic ceremonial, emphasizing and enforcing once again the close link between Polish society and the Catholic Church.[36] Fourth, the ceremony was a symbolic representation of Solidarity's model *for* the future arrangement of social life in Poland, in which the "society" would play a much more active role

36. Wajda's role as the director of the opening ceremony was significant but not dominant. The script was prepared by the organizing committee. Wajda eliminated from it the elements he deemed "unnecessary" (*Tygodnik Solidarność,* 10 April 1981, 8).

than before.[37] It delineated within the public space a niche in which society regained its sovereignty. The scope of the state's authority was symbolically limited and circumscribed, but not permanently and unequivocally, since the ceremony could not help but illustrate an irresolvable contradiction in Polish sociopolitical life. The absence of the state's emblems and symbols and the mere fact that the ceremony was organized by the society (not the state) symbolized that, at least for the moment, society had achieved an unprecedented degree of control over the public domain.[38] Moreover, the presence of representatives of the Party-state sitting side by side with members of the Church hierarchy and Solidarity's (i.e., society's) leaders, signaled the forging of a "new" alliance, even a "new" social contract, however tenuous, between the rulers and the ruled. Yet the presence of the rulers indicated also that the basic power structure remained unchanged. Any alliance had to be unstable as long as the state's power base (its almost total monopoly of the means of production, coercion, and communication) was undiminished. As a would-be redressive phase of the social drama initiated by the August 1980 strikes, the unveiling of the Gdańsk monument was only partially successful; the social peace lasted only a few months.

Monuments commemorating the workers who were killed in 1970 were also unveiled in Gdynia and Szczecin. The Gdynia monument was erected on the spot where in 1970 the police and the army fired on the workers on their way to begin the first shift in the shipyard. The base of the monument is in the shape of a cross. The huge numbers "1970" rise out of this foundation. The seven is shaped to suggest a falling man. The monument was dedicated in a ceremony that started at 4:20 A.M. on 17 December 1980. Mass constituted the first part of the ceremony, during which the monument was consecrated while the banners of Solidarity chapters from all over the country were lowered in a tribute to the fallen. Three minutes before six, the moment the troops had opened fire on the workers in 1970, the crowd of approximately two hundred thousand observed a minute of silence. Then the church bells, factory whistles, and ship horns sounded, bringing in the morning.

In Szczecin, celebrations of the tenth anniversary of the 1970 tragedy

37. The unveiling of the Gdańsk monument was an instance of a rite of passage, as most dedicatory ceremonies are; the public domain *after* the ceremony was different from how it was *before* the ceremony.

38. In contrast to the opening of a bridge in Zululand, immortalized by Gluckman (1958), which provided "a formal theatrical medium in which people could be together without interacting very much, but in which their symbols could be juxtaposed in time and space to give apparent unity" (Moore and Myerhoff 1977, 9), in the Gdańsk ceremony the symbols of the two sides were not "juxtaposed."

lasted the whole day of December 17. They began at 7:00 A.M. with holy mass in Saint Jacob's Cathedral. Marian Jurczyk, the chairman of the *Międzyzakładowy Komitet Robotniczy* (Interfactory Workers' Committee, or MKR) of Solidarity offered condolences to the families of the dead. Father Roman Kostynowicz rendered a religious interpretation of the 1970 tragedy, challenging the government's calls for national unity based on secular philosophy.[39]

> Brother turned against brother and because of the division blood was shed. . . . Today we are looking for unity for there is no other way. We hear that one Pole is another Pole's brother. But is it enough? Are brotherhood ties sufficient to built strong and long-lasting bonds? We should look for bonds of blood and brother-hood in Christ himself.[40]

Delegations from all over the country participated in the 10:00 A.M. ceremony. After a priest consecrated a cross, flowers were laid and candles lit at its base. Fourteen fallen workers were paid homage at the grave of one of them, Jadwiga Barbara Kowalczyk. It was the first official ceremony at this spot since 1970.

The main ceremony began at 4:00 P.M. at the gate of the Warski Shipyard. An altar was ereceted inside the gate. It was flanked with three masts flying two shipyard banners and the national colors. The large inscription, traditionally found on countless Polish flags, "God—Honor—Motherland" dominated the scene. As in Gdańsk, both the representatives of the Episcopate and the authorities sat side by side at the ceremony. Three shipyard workers, one seriously wounded in 1970, now in a wheelchair, unveiled the monument. It is a formless rock from which emerges an eagle inserted in the contours of Poland. The inscription reads: "To the memory of the fallen in December 1970 in the name of solidarity of the working class." To the sounds of patriotic poetry recited by popular Warsaw actors (Anna Nehrebecka and Krzysztof Kolberger), several hundred delegations from all over the country laid wreaths at the monument. There was also a wreath from the government. The holy mass, during which a special cable from John Paul II was read, concluded the ceremony.

39. He based his sermon on an excerpt of the Gospel of Luke. The sources do not identify this excerpt. I presume it was 17:3,4: "Take heed to yourselves: If thy brother trespass against thee, rebuke him; and if he repent, forgive him. And if he trespass against thee seven times in a day, and seven times a day turn again to thee, saying, I repent; thou shalt forgive him."
40. *Jedność*, 30 December 1980.

May First and May Third in 1981

May Day was an official state holiday in all Communist states. Spectacular parades, attended by massive crowds organized through a system of more or less discreet threats and pressures, were displayed by the official media as evidence of popular support for the Communist regimes, and their goals and methods. In 1981 the Polish regime faced an unprecedented challenge. It could not organize big parades, since the presence of Solidarity rendered impossible the implementation of the usual methods for assuring participation. Nor could it cancel the celebrations—this would be a public acknowledgment of defeat in its competition with the popular social movement. The authorities sought a solution through two symbolic maneuvers. First, the scale of the May Day celebrations was considerably reduced and participation in official celebrations was made voluntary. Second, it was decided that the anniversary of the May Third Constitution would be celebrated as an official holiday. May Third had been previously erased from the official ceremonial calendar after the unsuccessful attempt in 1946 to incorporate this holiday into Communist ceremonial.

Solidarity faced a dilemma as well. Although people enjoyed the festive mood, May Day had been discredited in popular opinion as a celebration appropriated by the state. But this negative assessment of the holiday could not find a public outlet (with the exception of clandestine publications). It was not until the period of Solidarity that the official May Day celebrations came under strong public criticism, expressed even in Party newspapers, TV, and radio. Szczecin's *Jedność* (a Solidarity periodical) observed that the "contemporary history of Poland moves from one crisis to another and almost all of them have been preceded by the massacre of workers" and concluded:

> Against such a background, May Day celebrations were only [the expression] of a mechanical unity of powerless people, an event of a mainly propagandistic character, serving to manipulate the consciousness of the masses. Such was indeed the role of parading in front of the viewing stand, which was, as a matter of fact, homage paid to the leaders of "the party and the nation." We must therefore return to the essence of this holiday, when there were no state viewing stands, compulsory participation, and slogans alien to the most of the participants.[41]

41. Ibid., 1 May 1981.

The union's leaders were, however, aware of the fact that May Day did symbolize the tradition of the workers' struggle for social justice, which was one of the fundamental aims of the movement. Solidarity had to articulate its position on such an important tradition. The leadership decided not to propose any centrally coordinated program of May Day celebrations; the union did not want to copy the official format of massive parades, which were popularly despised as a form of "homage paid to the leaders." The National Commission issued a statement in which it declared that

> the tradition of the workers' movement and the struggle for the workers' rights is particularly close to us. *Solidarność*—the name of our union refers not only to the relations among our members but also to our relationship with all peoples and organizations struggling for workers', civil, and human rights—who are fighting for democracy. . . .
>
> The National Commission does not recommend the organizing of traditional parades but rather the choice of the form of observance . . . of May First is a matter for the union members to decide.[42]

Since the authorities also refrained from imposing on the society a uniform scheme of observances, as had been their practice since 1946, the celebrations of May Day in 1981 were highly diversified. In most places the state and Solidarity celebrated this day separately. If the celebrations were organized jointly, the old form of parading in front of the viewing stand was abandoned, and the celebrations invoked other than Communist/socialist traditions. In Gdańsk, Tadeusz Fiszbach, the first secretary of the local PZPR, and Lech Wałęsa, the chairman of Solidarity, laid wreaths at the newly erected monument dedicated to the workers killed in 1970, thereby sanctioning the previously "illegal" tradition. In Poznań, the sixtieth anniversary of the Third Silesian Uprising was celebrated and homage was paid to the heroes of the Silesian Uprisings of 1919–21.

In many places May Day celebrations included holy masses commissioned by Solidarity locals. In Racibórz, whose population is about 50,000, 35,000 people gathered at the local stadium in a rally organized by Solidarity. The ceremony was divided into two parts: secular, led by the chairman of the local chapter of the union, and religious, celebrated by a bishop. In the program of the May Day celebrations printed and distributed by the authorities, Solidarity's ceremony was not men-

42. Ibid., 17 April 1981.

tioned.[43] In Olkusz, the ceremony was also organized by the local Solidarity chapter at the town stadium. It began with the singing of "The International," but as an observer noted, most of the people did not know the words. The first speaker recalled the 91-year-old tradition of May Day, emphasizing the last 35 years, during which "the essence of this holiday was deformed beyond recognition and yet it lived on in Poland in the events of 1956, 1968, 1970, 1976, and 1980 [the dates of social upheavals in Poland]." The second speaker noted that Solidarity's ceremonies had to have a strong religious component since it was a union dominated by Catholics. He stressed that "our Polish culture has its roots in the New Testament and its essence is Christian." The holy mass constituted the second part of the ceremony (Laba 1984, 22). Yet holy masses were not always included in the Solidarity celebrations. In Szczecin, the local Solidarity chapter organized a short rally, culminating with the laying of flowers at the Monument of the Polish Deed. The rally was followed by recreational and sport festivities.[44]

The official celebrations were also decentralized and sometimes even programmed in consultation with Solidarity chapters and various organizations. The ceremonies did not resemble the grandiose, centrally orchestrated ritual of previous years. The parade with the rulers looking on from the viewing stand was eliminated. Instead, Party and state officials walked with the people. In a headline of *Polityka* (an influential official magazine of opinion) this ceremonial emphasis on egalitarianism was turned into a true rite of status reversal. The paper proclaimed: "Today everybody is on the viewing stand." Most of the official ceremonies consisted of the "wreath-laying at monuments commemorating events of national historic significance, with white-and-red colors dominating over the red."[45] In Warsaw First Secretary Kania and Prime Minister Jaruzelski headed a relatively small procession that did not follow the usual route past the Palace of Culture but instead marched past the Tomb of the Unknown Soldier. During a short ceremony of wreath-laying at the Tomb, Kania and Jaruzelski were flanked by Felicia Fornalska and Roman Owczarek, rank-and-file "veterans of the working movement," and not by other dignitaries.[46] Through these unprecedented symbolic gestures the authorities reduced the usual ambiguity of

43. *Tygodnik Solidarność*, 29 May 1981.
44. *Jedność*, 8 May 1981.
45. Radio Free Europe–Radio Liberty, Polish Situation Report no. 8, 14 May 1981, 5.
46. After the ceremony Kania assessed the event as a success, admitting that it was necessary "to come up with genuinely new values to meet the hopes and needs of the working people" (Radio Free Europe–Radio Liberty, Polish Situation Report no. 8, 14 May 1981, 5).

the official ceremonial and decor, stretched between such pairs of contradictory principles as internationalism–patriotism and hierarchy–egalitarianism.

As always in times of crisis, only one set of principles was strongly emphasized. Since at the present stage of the conflict between the "state" and the "society," the latter controlled the situation, "societal" principles were therefore invoked: patriotism by parading in front of the Tomb of the Unknown Soldier, not the Palace of Culture; egalitarianism by having the "leaders" march in the first row of the parade (Gierek used the same gesture in the early 1970s) and surrounding them with rank-and-file "heroes" of the Communist movement. In Kraków, the May Day rally was held in the Market Square. That year, Party and government officials[47] did not make speeches emphasizing the international motifs, as they had always done in the past. Instead, they concentrated on the current state of the nation and appealed for a national reconciliation by invoking the Polish tradition of May Day celebrations and patriotic sentiments. Dąbrowa emphasized that May First "is the symbol of unity and national solidarity."

The mood of the 1981 official May Day celebrations was well captured in a communiqué, issued by the Polish Press Agency (PAP):

> Less form, more content—that is how the celebrations of the May holiday, first after August, can be briefly characterized. On this atypically cool spring day we witnessed a new tradition of the work holiday in Poland being born: without pomp and staged optimism, with dignity and simplicity befitting the authentic hosts of the country, aware of their strength. This time there were no viewing stands. Other attributes, which ceased to mean anything a long time ago, also disappeared. What was left were the simplest and the most important symbols—the colors of the workers and the nation, expressing the revolutionary sources and international meanings of the May tradition; ideas which all Poles hope will be realized: social justice, joint responsibility for the fate of the country, solidarity of the working people. These ideas unite the whole nation today more than ever before, despite the fact that we abandoned the appearance of nonexistent unanimity and despite the emergence of differences of opinion, life-style, and modes of thinking. The existence of these natural differences mani-

---

47. Two main speeches were delivered by Krystyn Dąbrowa, the first secretary of the Kraków Committee of the PZPR, and Andrzej Kurtz, the chairman of the National Council in Kraków.

fested itself in the freedom of choice of the forms of celebrating May First.[48]

This unusually candid (for the PAP) assessment of the 1981 celebrations also contains an outright acknowledgment (by an official agency tightly controlled by the Central Committee of the PZPR) that the massive enthusiasm of May Day celebrations in the 1970s (or perhaps always since 1945) had been fabricated. The PAP's account was, however, not entirely accurate. First, it does not mention that in many places May Day celebrations had a strong (if not predominantly) religious character, indicating that the organizers (the local chapters of Solidarity) intended to relate the workers' tradition to a larger, religious frame of reference and uproot it from the frame of the secular, Communist tradition. Second, it speaks only of the role of "revolutionary sources and international meanings of the May tradition." In 1981 those sources and meanings were particularly inconspicuous in the celebrations. As an observer noted, in the Warsaw celebrations white-and-red colors of Poland dominated over the red.[49]

The decisive shift of accents from the international to national framework was even clearer in the official decision to tone down May Day and to celebrate the anniversary of the 1791 constitution, May Third, a holiday unambiguously symbolizing Polish patriotic and democratic traditions. May Third was last celebrated in the Polish People's Republic in 1946, when the celebrations in Kraków province turned into demonstrations against Communist domination and culminated in bloody confrontations with the security forces (see Chyży n.d.). In the late 1970s several oppositional groups revived the tradition of celebrating the holiday by organizing illegal rallies and demonstrations in several major towns. Solidarity planned to celebrate the 190th anniversary of the May Third Constitution as a major holiday. Again the state was faced with two choices. It could ignore the holiday—thus acknowledging another defeat—or organize official celebrations. The latter solution was chosen, although the PZPR did not take on the role of the organizer. A facade organization (ostensibly independent from the PZPR) called the Democratic Party was assigned the role of official sponsor of the May Third celebrations. Without a doubt, by restoring May Third to the official ceremonial calendar

48. This communiqué was printed on the first page of *Gazeta Krakowska,* 4 May 1981, Kraków's Party daily, known during the Solidarity period for its high standard of journalistic work and relative lack of stiff ideological limitations.

49. Radio Free Europe–Radio Liberty, Polish Situation Report no. 8, 14 May 1981, 5.

the regime diminished its defeat in its symbolic confrontation with Solidarity to the necessary minimum.

May First and May Third had been counterposed in the official ceremonial of the Polish People's Republic since 1946.[50] The former was one of the two (the anniversary of the Bolshevik Revolution being the second) major celebrations of the new social and political order, the latter was a taboo, an occasion to be erased from the collective memory.[51] In the drastically changed situation, when society's demands to celebrate May Third could be easily realized without the state's approval, the authorities changed their tactics. They announced that May First and May Third symbolized the two aspects of the socialist-democratic tradition. The first secretary of Kraków's PZPR, Krystyn Dąbrowa, said that "the three holidays falling on the first days of May enforce with their symbolism the sense of the national accord. The Work Holiday, May 3, and Victory Day [May 9] are an integral part of the democratic ideal."[52] Somewhat paradoxically, a Solidarity publicist expressed a similar idea:

> In the Polish People's Republic, as a part of the policy of half-truths and one-sided evaluation of the contemporary world, the conflict emerged between what was called "the holiday of workers," that is, the Work Holiday of May First and the "holiday of lords" (a phrase from the 1950s),[53] behind which stood the celebra-

50. It is indeed a paradox that the Communist government rejected the tradition of the Constitution, which was praised by Karl Marx, who wrote: "Regardless of all its shortcomings this constitution stands against the Russian-Prussian-Austrian barbary as the only work of liberty Eastern Europe created by itself. And it came exclusively from a privileged class, from the nobility. History does not know any other example of a similar nobility of nobility ("Contributions to the Polish Questions: Manuscripts from 1863–64"; in *Opinia,* May–June 1981, 34).

51. Jerzy Topolski, a Marxist historian, observed in 1981: "Both these holidays have deep historical justification, but as is known, they were set against each other, and the memory of the May Third Constitution was pushed far aside to the background. . . . Both before World War II and in the period of the People's Poland, evaluations of the May Third Constitution were dominated by political and ideological considerations to a degree rarely matched by other historical events. . . . Thus the May Third Constitution became a subject of exceptionally strong political manipulation, which ultimately had a very negative impact on the historical consciousness of the nation. . . . In the perspective of Polish history both holidays belong to the same historical current. Both express progressive historical forces in their respective epochs" (*Dodatek Nadzwyczajny do Serwisu Informacyjnego "Solidarność" UAM,* 29 April 1981).

52. *Gazeta Krakowska,* 4 May 1981.

53. As Topolski points out, Julian Marchlewski, one of the leaders of the prewar Communist movement once claimed that "the day of May 3 is not a day of the Polish worker. The worker can cede this day of empty-sounding cliches to patriotic phraseologists" (*Dodatek Nadzwyczajny do Serwisu Informacyjnego "Solidarność" UAM,* 29 April 1981).

tions of the May Third Constitution. Let us hope, that this conflict belongs to the past and that the traditions and celebrations of these holidays will return to their old meanings, as many other issues in our Motherland will do.[54]

The state celebrations of the 190th anniversary of the May Constitution included the gala concert organized in the Grand Theater in Warsaw on May 2. Among the invited guests were the first secretary of the Central Committee of the PZPR, Stanisław Kania, and the delegation of the Polish Episcopate, led by Bishop Jerzy Modzelewski. The next day, the Democratic Party organized a meeting in the Senatorial Hall (the place where the Constitution had been adopted) of the newly restored Royal Castle. The ceremony was attended by Henryk Jabłoński, the chairman of the Council of State, and Stefan Olszowski, a member of the Politburo. Significantly, Kania, the first secretary of the Central Committee of the PZPR, did not attend, an indication that the Party's enthusiasm for the reinstating of old holidays had its limits.

May Third is also a religious holiday, the Feast of Our Lady, Queen of Poland. In 1981 May Third fell on Sunday, and therefore a religious atmosphere dominated the celebrations organized by Solidarity. The pontifical mass, celebrated by Franciszek Cardinal Macharski on Jasna Góra, was attended by delegations of Solidarity chapters from all over the country. Among the pilgrims were Lech Wałęsa, Solidarity's chairman, and ten thousand students. In his sermon, Archbishop Henryk Gulbinowicz of Wrocław said: "After the Constitution, there was a brutal intervention by Russian bayonets. We hope that this time nothing will happen."[55]

In many places Solidarity's celebrations of May Third were focused on consecrations of the new union's standards. In Szczecin, one of the strongholds of Solidarity, the new standard was funded by local craftsmen. It was consecrated during holy mass, which constituted a major part of the spectacular ceremony, attended by several thousand people.[56] In an unusual gesture, the priests celebrating mass received several offerings from members of Solidarity representing various professions, including bread, water, wine, a passover flame, a basket of vegetables, an anchor, and flowers. The recitations of poetry by famous actors and a concert of the

54. *Jedność*, 1 May 1981, 3.

55. Radio Free Europe–Radio Liberty, Polish Situation Report no. 8, 14 May 1981, 7.

56. The standard is decorated with a huge white (crowned) eagle with the icon of the Black Madonna of Częstochowa inserted in it.

famed choir of the Szczecin Polytechnic brought the ceremony to a close.[57]

A Solidarity standard was also consecrated in Grudziądz. In Bydgoszcz the celebrations extended throughout the day, culminating during the holy mass. In Lublin, the May Third memorial, recently restored to its previous place, was unveiled. In Kraków "the day began with Holy Mass celebrated at Wawel Cathedral, continued with a march to the historic Market Place where Kościuszko took his oath, and ended with a public rally."[58]

The Poznań Monument

In June 1956, Poznań workers took to the streets to protest governmental policies concerning compensation for work. In the ensuing confrontation with the security forces on June 28 and 29, several dozen people were killed.[59] In 1981, Poznań Solidarity organized a series of celebrations, culminating in the unveiling of the monument commemorating the fallen. The cornerstone of the monument has the following inscription:

On 23 May 1981
1015 years after the baptism of Poland,
190 years after the legislation of the May Third Constitution,
63 years after the regaining of independence,
37 years after the end of World War II,
the cornerstone was placed for the Monument of Thanksgiving and Homage to those who:
—25 years ago gave their lives demanding freedom and bread,
—13 years ago suffered persecutions defending the truth and national culture,
—11 years ago were murdered, because they had courage to protest against injustice,
—5 years ago were maltreated for defending their workers' dignity,
—a year ago in solidarity guaranteed that no Pole will exploit another.

This monument is being erected thanks to the generosity of the whole society. It is to be an expression of unity in building a better

---

57. The actors included Daniel Olbrychski, Krzysztof Kolberger, and Piotr Garlicki (*Jedność*, 8 May 1981, 1–3).

58. Radio Free Europe–Radio Liberty, Polish Situation Report no. 8, 14 May 1981, 8.

59. For a description of the Poznań tragedy, see Karpiński (1982a, 49–53).

future of the nation, which was initiated by the workers of Poznań on 28 June 1956. Laying down this Cornerstone for the Eternal Memorial, we trust that Christ, Who endowed the cross with Redemptive Dignity, will become a source of Dignity and strength for those who will stop in front of this monument.

The Citizens' Committee for the Building of the Monument of Poznań June. Citizens' Committee of the Celebrations of the 25th Anniversary of Poznań June.[60]

The tradition the Citizens' Committee invoked in this document had no common points with the tradition claimed by the Polish People's Republic. The year 966 is referred to as Poland's baptism, not as the beginning of Polish statehood, celebrated by the regime in 1966. May Third is evoked, May First is not. The eleventh of November 1918 is remembered as the regaining of independence, whereas the end of World War II is not referred to as a liberation (as it was called by the state) and the founding of the People's Republic, celebrated by the Party-state on July 22, is not mentioned at all. Instead, all the dates when the state used force against Polish society are listed and the act of dedication ends with an invocation of the Catholic mythology.

The monument is composed of three elements: two crosses (21 and 19 meters high), united by their common cross-arm, and a schematic representation of an eagle emerging from a nest or an egg. Huge ropes tie the crosses together. On the front of the first cross is the date 1956. The second carries the dates of the other social upheavals: 1968, 1970, 1976, and 1980. At the eagle's base there is an inscription reading "For Freedom, Justice, and Bread—June 1956."

The Poznań celebrations commemorating June 1956 lasted three days. On Saturday, June 27, a historical session was held at the Poznań University, an artistic exhibition was opened, and two commemorative plaques were unveiled. During a mass the standard of Poznań Solidarity was consecrated.[61] The main ceremony began at 10:00 A.M., on Sunday, June 28. After speeches by Zdzisław Rozwalak, the leader of Poznań Solidarity, and Lech Wałęsa, holy mass followed during which the monument was unveiled and consecrated. The leader of the striking workers from 1956 dedicated the monument with the words: "I ask for the unveiling of this monument of suffering, honor, and triumph."[62] Then the delega-

60. *Kwadrat,* 22 June 1981.
61. This part of the celebrations was directed by Izabella Cywińska, director of the *Nowy* Theater in Poznań.
62. Laba (1984, 12).

tions of Solidarity chapters from all over the country laid flowers and wreaths at the base of the monument. The whole ceremony was directed by Lech Raczak, the leader of the Theater of the Eighth Day.[63] After the ceremony a photographic exhibit documenting the 1956 tragedy opened. At 4:00 p.m. a plaque commemorating Roman Strzałkowski, a boy who was killed during the 1956 events, was unveiled.[64] Following a concert by the Poznań Symphony Orchestra, Poznań's Nowy Theater presented a production "The Accused: July 56," conceived as a dramatic reconstruction of the events of 1956.[65] On Monday, July 29, a commemorative plaque was unveiled in the hall of the hospital on Raszewska street, where many people wounded in 1956 had been brought.[66]

Registration of Rural Solidarity

The signing of the agreements between the workers and the authorities in August 1980 did not end the conflict; it merely initiated another phase. According to Colonel Kukliński (1987), a high-ranking member of the team of insiders responsible for the preparation of the final confrontation with Solidarity, the authorities were always intent on eliminating this massive movement from public life. They were only waiting for the right moment to move. The regime's tactics of obstruction and delay, especially when called on to fulfill its obligations according to the various agreements between it and Solidarity make sense if the destruction of Solidarity as a legal organization was the regime's ultimate goal. One such instance of obstruction and delay was the difficulty Solidarity had simply registering as a legal organization. Workers' Solidarity negotiated with the government for several nerve-racking weeks before it was al-

63. In the late 1970s the theater came up with several splendid productions, full of biting social and political criticism, which infuriated the authorities and triggered a campaign of harassment against the group.

64. This part of the ceremony was organized by the Poznań chapter of the Union of Polish Scouting. It was yet another gesture indicating the increasing ideological independence of the organization from the Party's control. During the congress of the Union of Polish Scouting (15–18 March 1981) the traditional emblem of the scouts, a lily with the inscription "Motherland, Studying, Virtue," was reinstated to its former significance, diminished in the late 1970s when scouting was being slowly turned into an institutionalized tool of political indoctrination.

65. Włodzimierz Braniecki wrote the script; Izabella Cywińska directed.

66. *Serwis Informacyjny Komisji zakładowej NSZZ Solidarność, Uniwersytet im. A. Mickiewicza*, 23 June 1981.

lowed to register and function as a legal organization in the Polish People's Republic.[67]

The Peasants' (or Rural) Solidarity waited even longer to be registered. The final hearing in the District Court of Warsaw took place on 12 May 1981, eight months after the first application for registration was filed.[68] On the day of the final hearing thousands of people, mostly peasants, gathered in front of the court building. Several thousand peasants paraded through the streets in a political demonstration. They demonstrated in the form best known to them: a religious procession. Dressed in their Sunday best or folk costumes and carrying all the significant religious paraphernalia, such as crucifixes and icons of Christ and the Black Madonna of Częstochowa, the peasants gathered in the streets adjacent to the District Court in Warsaw, where the registration hearing of their union was being held. The gathering sang religious hymns, prayed, and listened to several speeches. At one point, when a court clerk asked them not to make speeches so they would not disturb the court deliberations, Father Stanisław Małkowski[69] asked rhetorically: "The court requests us to stop speeches. But it will nonetheless, I presume, allow us to pray." The massive application of religious emblems, symbols, and gestures must be construed as an effort to obtain the help of supernatural forces in a political confrontation with the authorities. At 12:50 P.M. a judge announced the formal registration of Rural Solidarity. The crowd, after singing "Rota" and the national anthem, marched to the Tomb of the Unknown Soldier. Many passers-by joined in the spontaneous celebration. At 2:00 P.M., delegations of peasants laid flowers and wreaths at the Tomb. The rally was addressed by several speakers. Jan Kułaj, the chairman of the new union said, "Could in the past anybody see at the Tomb of the Unknown Soldier a real peasant with hands worn by work? No. Fake peasants were shown to us here." Jan Antoł, another leader of the union, alluded to Wyspiański's *Wesele:*[70] "In the court, together with the golden horn, we also received an iron brush, with which we must sweep away all the evil." Stanisław Wądołowski noted: "For the first time in history the peasant achieves social emancipation. He will never again be an object of manipulation." A short artistic program ended the celebration.[71]

67. Solidarity was registered after the appeal to the Supreme Court on 10 November 1980. For details, see Raina (1985, 8–18).

68. For the complicated story of the peasants' struggle for their union, see Raina (1985, 55–104). The official name of the union was NSZZRI "Solidarność" (Independent Self-Governing Trade Union of Individual Farmers "Solidarity").

69. Małkowski was a well-known supporter of the various oppositional activities.

70. The symbolism of this play is discussed in Chapter 3.

71. *Agencja Solidarność,* 12–18 May 1981.

The dominance of religious symbolism in the peasants' demonstration provides yet another illustration of the significance of Catholic beliefs in the new counterhegemonic discourse. But this attachment to religion did not mean automatic submission to the Church's institutional authority. The peasants' leaders strongly asserted their organizational independence from the Church. During the press conference, following the demonstrations, this conversation took place:

> *Question:* Do you intend to draw inspiration from the moral support of the Church?
> *Kułaj:* Crosses march at the head of our parades. They indicate the direction.
> *Antoł:* Yet we will not get "clericalized." Peasants always had certain anticlerical tendencies.
> *Another peasant:* We have even created a slogan: "The Union Is Independent from Rome and the Regime." [The slogan rhymes in Polish: *Związek jest niezależny od Rzymu i reżimu*].[72]

The fact that the demonstration ended at the Tomb of the Unknown Soldier was yet another expression of the impulse to reclaim monuments and public spaces previously reserved for the official state ceremonial alone.

Celebrations of November Eleventh in 1980

The outburst of symbolic activity during the Solidarity period engulfed the whole country and found countless means of expression. All anniversaries removed from the official ceremonial calendar and celebrated in illegal demonstrations by growing numbers of people in the late 1970s were now observed without fear of police intervention.[73] November Eleventh (Independence Day for interwar Poland), for example, was observed in 1980 as a major celebration in Gdańsk, Warsaw, Kraków, Lublin, and Suwałki.[74] In Gdańsk, the celebration organized by the RMP began with a mass in the

---

72. Ibid.

73. Only three cases of persecution were reported. Wojciech Ziembiński was detained after a Warsaw celebration. In Lublin, the district attorney's office opened a case against Piotr Szczudłowski and Piotr Opazda who were the speakers at the local celebration.

74. The Warsaw ceremony is described in Ash (1983, 86–87).

Marian Basilica. Several thousand people marched to the Sobieski Monument. Lech Wałęsa was one of the speakers.[75]

In Kraków, there were two ceremonies. At noon the delegations of the official organizations and Solidarity laid flowers at the Tomb of the Unknown Soldier in Matejko Square. It was the first celebration since World War II of November Eleventh attended by official organizations. At 4:00 P.M. Solidarity organized a concert in Słowacki Theater attended by Cardinal Macharski and the municipal authorities. At 6:00 P.M. Macharski celebrated mass in the Wawel Cathedral. After mass and the wreath-laying ceremony at Piłsudski's tomb, a large demonstration marched to the Tomb of the Unknown Soldier. Some of the slogans read "From our shoulders Poland will spring out free as a bird," "Free Leszek Moczulski,"[76] "Wake up Poland, break the chains." The marching crowd sang "Boże coś Polskę" and other religious and patriotic hymns. The large crowd gathered at the Tomb was addressed by Stanisław Janik-Palczewski of the KPN, Janusz Pierzchała of the RMP, and by Jan Leszek Franczyk of the *Chrześcijańska Wspólnota Ludzi Pracy* (Christian Association of Working People, or ChWLP). Pierzchała said:

> Our closest experience is the defeat of the Warsaw Uprising and the blood of Polish workers fallen in Poznań and at the coast. And look! From this blood of Warsaw Insurgents and the workers' blood shed in Poznań and at the Coast, from the tradition of 1956, 1968, 1970, and 1976 springs the flower of Freedom! Let us follow this road further and further until Poland arises to live![77]

Józef Piłsudski as a Symbol

The name and legend of Józef Piłsudski, became the focal point of many Solidarity celebrations in 1981. In Gdańsk, the workers from the Gdańsk Repair Shipyard decided to rename their yard after one of the nation's heroes, absent in the official history of Poland. A preliminary poll among the yard workers showed that the two names most favored were Józef

75. Dariusz Kobzdej and Marek Krówka from the RMP, Piotr Juszkiewicz from the Independent Student Union (NZS), and Tadeusz Szczudłowski from the ROPCiO were other speakers. For the description of Gdańsk ceremony and the full text of Juszkiewicz's speech, see *Bratniak*, November–December 1980, 29–32.

76. Moczulski, chairman of the KPN, was serving a prison sentence as a political prisoner.

77. *Krzyż Nowohucki*, no. 5–6, 1980, 24–26.

Piłsudski and Władysław Sikorski.[78] In the final vote, 4542 people participated out of a total of 6358 employees (including 5647 members of Solidarity). Of 4537 valid ballots, 2223 were cast for Piłsudski, 2036 for Sikorski. It was yet another sign of the ongoing defiance of the authorities, who tolerated Sikorski but worked hard to erase Piłsudski's name from the collective consciousness. The ceremony of the renaming was scheduled for November 11. The invitations announced:

> By choosing this name [and this date] the crew wanted to emphasize the great contributions of Józef Piłsudski to the regaining by our nation of the right to sovereign existence and development after more than a hundred years of slavery. . . . This act constitutes a kind of protest against an almost forty-year-long effort to remove this figure from the national consciousness, despite the fact that the outstanding personality of Marshal Józef Piłsudski constituted and will always constitute in the minds of all Poles the symbol of the free and fully independent Poland.[79]

Piłsudski's profile became a frequent motif in Solidarity's abundant production of badges, posters, and stickers. It was used most often by the members of such groups as the RMP or the KPN, which emphasized nationalistic motifs in their programs.

The White Eagle Recrowned

Solidarity never officially adopted the Crowned White Eagle as its emblem. Yet on countless banners and badges of the movement the White Eagle was usually recrowned. Examples of this spontaneous reclaiming of the national emblem come from all parts of Poland and various social milieus.[80] The Communist authorities removed the crown from the White Eagle's head to illustrate the antihierarchical, antiroyalist, antibourgeois tenor of their mythology/ideology. They ignored the fact that the Eagle's

78. General Sikorski was the commander-in-chief and prime minister of the Polish government in exile, who was killed in a plane crash in Gibraltar in 1943. Since the circumstances of the accident were never satisfactorily explained, many Poles believe that the general, known for his strong anti-Stalinist stance, was assassinated by Soviet agents.

79. *Głos Stoczniowca*, 13 November 1981.

80. I heard from a craftsman specializing in the production of badges that the badge most sought after during the Solidarity period had to portray the Crowned White Eagle and the Black Madonna of Częstochowa.

crown symbolized above all the nation's sovereignty[81] and that most Poles construed the removal of the crown as a symbol of its loss. Since the White Eagle also represents the Polish nation, by placing the crown back on the Eagle's head people were symbolically announcing that they were the true sovereigns of Poland, not the PZPR, the self-proclaimed "avant-garde of the working class and the nation." Recrowning the Eagle—repeated so often during the Solidarity period—can thus be seen both as symbolic compensation for the de facto limited national sovereignty and as a symbolic rejection of the rulers' claims to authority.[82]

John Paul II and the White March

John Paul II was the only living public persona often invoked in Solidarity's ceremonial and decor. His portrait, and a copy of the icon of his patroness, the Black Madonna, adorned the Gdańsk shipyard Gate Two during the strike. His face adorned Solidarity's badges. On 13 May 1981, when he was seriously wounded in an assassination attempt, Poland was stunned. In a gesture of spontaneous solidarity with their wounded pope, Kraków's *Niezależne Zrzeszenie Studentów* (Independent Student Union, or NZS), an organization formed during the wave of Solidarity's reforms, appealed to Kraków's students to participate in a silent march and mass organized in the Market Square. The result exceeded all expectations: three hundred thousand marchers, all dressed in white, joined the solemn celebrations. The wider significance of the event was twofold. First, it confirmed and enforced the charismatic authority of the pope. Second, it became yet another illustration of the dramatic shift in the official policy concerning the areas of social life previously off limits for the Communist state and its organizations. The Socialist Union of Polish Students, an organization largely despised for its negative role in the "Black Juvenalia" and its increasingly "official" ideological character, joined the NZS as a co-organizer of the event. Yet this gesture was met with incredulity and disgust among Kraków's students and instead of improving the offical organization's standing, diminished it even further.[83]

81. Malski writes: "The crown on the Polish eagle denotes the union, integrity, and sovereignty of the Polish state rather that having a monarchist significance" (1983, 3).

82. The crown was replaced on the White Eagle's head on 1 January 1990 by decree of the Sejm.

83. For a concise assessment of the *Socjalistyczny Związek Studentów Polskich* (Socialist Union of Polish Students, or SZSP) and its growing ideologization, see Reczek (1980).

Katyń

Several other symbols and traditions, eliminated from public discourse by the Communist regime, were revived during the Solidarity period. Most spectacular perhaps was the breaking of public silence surrounding Katyń, one of the most tragic instances of Polish suffering during World War II. In the spring of 1940, several thousand Polish officers were murdered in the Katyń Forest, near Smolensk.[84] The Soviet authorities did not admit that Stalin's regime was responsible for this massacre until 1990. The Katyń massacre, taboo in the official media of the Polish People's Republic, became for society a symbol of the Soviet rulers' true intentions in their dealings with Poland.[85] In the late 1970s all oppositional groups demanded that the issue be settled once and for all and those responsible for the crime be brought to justice.[86] In April 1979 the memory of the murdered officers was honored in several masses celebrated in Katowice, Kraków, Łódź, Poznań, Szczecin, Tarnów, and Warsaw (Lipski 1985, 351). During the Solidarity period the Katyń massacre was frequently mentioned in the union's press. Also at this time a citizens' commission was formed to negotiate with the authorities the erection of a commemorative monument (a simple cross with a plaque) at the Powązki cemetery in Warsaw. The talks stalled on various obstacles thrown up by the authorities and no solution was found; and once martial law was declared all discussions ceased. A temporary monument erected at Powązki disappeared one night.[87]

Solidarity's Symbolic Revolution

Revolutions occur simultaneously in many different areas of social life inside and outside the domain of ultimate national and religious symbols. They often produce clashes (sometimes deliberate, sometimes not) of man-

84. The exact number of Polish officers who were killed by the Soviets in 1940 is difficult to establish. Besides approximately 4500 officers from a camp in Kozielsk, about 10,000 prisoners of war from the nearby camps in Ostaszkow and Starobielsk disappeared without a trace as well. See Lipski (1985, 348).

85. Censorship instruction prescribed that "any attempt to burden the Soviet Union with responsibility for the deaths of Polish officers in Katyń Forest is forbidden" (Lipski 1985, 215).

86. On 17 September 1979 (the anniversary of the Soviet invasion of Poland in 1939) KOR issued a statement demanding the final resolution of this tragic matter. For excerpts from this statement and a discussion of the Katyń controversy, see Lipski (1985, 348–52).

87. See, for example, *Radomski Serwis Informacyjny,* 15–25 November 1981.

ners and dress codes. Lynn Hunt, who noted the political significance of the issue of dress and costume during the French Revolution, concludes:

> Civilian and official costume became such a focus of concern because dress was a political sign. Under the Old Regime, the different orders and many professions and trades had been identified by their clothing: nobles, clergymen, judges, and even masons were known by what they wore. Revolutionaries wanted to break with the system of invidious social distinctions, but they continued to believe that dress revealed something about the person. Dress was, as it were, politically transparent; you could tell a person's political character from the way he or she dressed. (1984, 82)

This characterization of the French dress of the late eighteenth century could be used without any modifications in a description of the Solidarity period in Poland. For the first time since the 1940s there appeared in the public domain "officials," that is, people representing public organizations, who did not dress according to the customary official dress code. In the Polish People's Republic, the government and Party officials, predominantly males in their fifties and sixties, wore (often badly cut) suits and ties and had short haircuts and clean-shaven faces. Solidarity activists, also males, but predominantly in their twenties or thirties, often wore jeans and sweaters, grew beards and moustaches, and rarely sported suits and ties. Differences were not, however, limited to outward appearances; they also involved language and mentality.

The most dramatic confrontations of these two styles occurred on 27 January 1981, when Polish TV broadcast a (prerecorded) debate between nine speakers from the Ministry of Labor, Wages, and Social Affairs; Solidarity; and the branch industrial unions. Solidarity was represented by economist Ryszard Bugaj and two district chairmen, Jan Rulewski from Bydgoszcz and Zbigniew Bujak from Warsaw. Poles had learned to distrust television, especially the news, but as elsewhere, they never seemed to be able to develop a fool-proof insulation against the magical charm of the screen, which endows people presented there with an aura of the extraordinary. Communist propagandists, aware of this special quality of the medium, made it the major tool of indoctrination in all countries of the Soviet bloc. Polish TV had developed a certain style, dull and monotonous (with few short-lasting exceptions),[88] but since no alter-

88. In Poland, for example, during Gomułka's years, there had been several highly professional and well-received television shows. Under Gierek the political and economic programs became increasingly bland and meaningless.

natives were available, it was accepted as not just a style but *the* style of TV news and related shows. The show aired on January 27 demolished this aura of "naturalness." For the first time in the history of Polish TV, the audience could listen to "experts" who used natural language that was in sharp contrast with the language of propaganda usually employed in this medium.[89] Moreover, confronted with Ryszard Bugaj, Solidarity's expert (a young bearded man wearing a sweater), the governmental experts could do little but repeat their empty-sounding official slogans. The official discourse, perhaps for the first time on television in the Communist world, was publicly confronted with an alternative discourse of the genuine representatives of the society. The official propagandists must have realized that such shows posed a serious danger to the remnants of their aura of authority because they never permitted Solidarity's representative to appear on television again.[90]

Solidarity's leaders and experts debated government officials with language that was fluid and powerful. But as some observers noted, this linguistic prowess was not shared by average workers. Their limited linguistic competence has been invoked to explain failures in political discussions/confrontations with the authorities. This is not confirmed, however, by the available empirical evidence.[91] Moreover, focusing analysis on linguistic competence diverts attention from the fact that the confrontation of the two discourses was not limited to rhetoric alone. In a

89. The symbolic facade of the regime was already weakened in August 1980 when the state broadcast from the Lenin Shipyard the end of the negotiations between the workers and the government. It seems to me, however, that because of the highly ceremonial character of the occasion the contrast between the two decors, styles, and rhetorics was less striking than in the January 27 broadcast.

90. Solidarity's access to the mass media and the curtailment of censorship were the subject of tough bargaining sessions with the government until the imposition of martial law. Whereas on the latter issue Solidarity achieved a considerable success (a new law, restricting the powers of censors, was adopted), the government never relinquished its monopoly over radio and TV (see Raina 1985, 274–95, and *Serwis Informacyjny Biura Informacji Prasowej KKP*, 1 September 1981).

91. Staniszkis claims that because of such a limited linguistic competence in 1970–71, in Szczecin the striking workers were not able to force the authorities to any significant concessions. "Because they have difficulty articulating their demands the workers artificially reduced their claims (including non-economic ones) to the concrete language of wage demands" (1984, 122). There are two problems with this statement. First, as Laba shows, Szczecin workers (at least some of them) did articulate such political demands as "freeing trade unions from the Party and state administration and a guarantee of the right to strike" (Laba 1986, 53). Second, Staniszkis seems to suggest that the workers' limited linguistic competence was the main reason that their strike did not produce any significant political results. Such an explanation, I believe, is based on a false (and thus nonproductive) counterassumption. It would be hard to prove that in 1970 a higher level of linguistic competence would have forced the authorities to any significant political concessions.

very influential analysis of the Solidarity movement, Jadwiga Staniszkis employed Basil Bernstein's theories.[92] But she placed little emphasis on the fact that Bernstein's distinction between private discourse (based on the restricted code) and public discourse (dominated by the elaborated code), which exists in every complex society, acquires a new quality in the Communist state. In many instances in the Communist world the private discourse is more elaborated than the public discourse, tamed by newspeak, preventive censorship, and an almost perfect state monopoly of the means of communication.

According to Bernstein and to Mary Douglas, increasing division of labor inevitably leads to the emergence of an elaborated code, which is necessary to transmit the diversified and specialized experience of different groups within a society (Douglas 1973, 44). In a system that is not governed by market mechanisms, technological efficiency, or rules of polycentric polity, but by ideological purity and the rules of monocentric political order, the role of the public code (the language of propaganda) in social life is qualitatively different. The expanding division of labor is not accompanied by the elaboration of the whole social discourse. Despite the necessary increase of complexity in technological jargon, the domain of social communication dominated by the language of propaganda is increasingly impoverished both sematically and syntagmatically; its vocabulary is shrunken and its grammar is stunted. The result is not what Staniszkis predicts in her *Poland's Self-Limiting Revolution* (1984)—the automatic superiority of the rulers, who allegedly use the elaborated code, over the workers who use the restricted code. It is, instead, as she observes in her article "Forms of Reasoning as Ideology" (1985–86), a confrontation between two restricted—that is, structurally similar though semantically and axiologically different—discourses.

Staniszkis, however, overestimates this similarity of "the deep structure of consciousness of both sides" and does not appreciate all the consequences of their "different, even opposite, value orientations" (1984,

92. Mary Douglas summarizes Bernstein's model as follows: "He distinguishes two different types of linguistic codes. One he calls the elaborated code, in which, as he says, the speaker selects from a wide range of syntactic alternatives, which are flexibly organized; this speech requires complex planning. In the other, which he calls restricted code, the speaker draws from a much narrower range of syntactic alternatives, and these alternatives are more rigidly organized. . . . Each type of speech code is generated by its own type of social matrix. . . . The restricted code is deeply enmeshed in the immediate social structure, utterances have a double purpose, they convey information, yes, but they also express social structure, embellish and reinforce it. The second function is the dominant one, whereas the elaborated code emerges as a form of speech which is progressively more and more free of the second function. Its primary function is to organize thought processes, distinguish and combine ideas" (1973, 44).

114). Her model of sociopolitical reality does not allow serious consideration of the fact that for many Poles Solidarity was a political *and* an ethical/moral phenomenon. They seemed to realize that the forty years of Communist rule had resulted not only in the impoverishment of political culture (discourse) but in the depletion of culture in general, and found that religion constituted the most readily available source of revivifying values, principles, ideas, and symbols.[93]

This ethical-religious dimension of Solidarity was emphasized by several middle-level leaders of the movement I interviewed. I came to understand a serious shortcoming of the Bernstein model when I saw that people who use more or less similar semantic categories may still employ different cognitive categories and embrace different systems of values. I found that there is no necessary relationship between ethical behavior and the ability to articulate the principles underlying that behavior in an intellectually and linguistically elaborated fashion. In other words, semantic, cognitive, and axiological structures are not always homologous. There is no positive correlation between intellectual refinement and linguistic ability on the one hand, and high moral integrity on the other.

In an interview I had with the leader of a Solidarity chapter in a big factory situated in a small town in southern Poland, his ethical sophistication beyond the limitations of "the restricted code" he was using became obvious. We discussed religion. My interlocutor had very clear views on the role of religion (both in symbolic and institutional aspects) in Polish society. "We [the Poles] do not lack ideas or aspirations," he said. "What is lacking a little bit is morality." He acknowledged the tactical and strategic importance of the union's alliance with the Church: "I knew, that in order to avoid subordination to Communists, cooperation with the Church was necessary." Moral renewal of the nation was for him the most important task Solidarity faced. Religious as he was, he did not believe that the Church alone could accomplish this task. As he explained to me:

> The Church had not been able to do that before the rise of Solidarity. The authority of the Church was not powerful enough. What was needed was a push from both sides. Only the alliance of the authentic social movement with the Church's ethical authority

93. Krzemiński noted that "for the majority of the participants of the social movement [Solidarity] the 'objective order of values,' as one can say following Max Sheller, was connected inescapably with God and with the presence of Christ, that is with religion and the Church as the living spiritual form. Both the believers and the non-believers identified Christianity and the Catholic Church with the defence of the dignity of human person and the 'human rights,' which reflect the objective moral order of the world" (1985, 102).

could bring about this much desired change. We understood, sub-consciously, that it was not enough to change the system; it was necessary to change morality. In this task we [Solidarity] became the Church's ally; they became ours.

This strong grounding of the movement on Christian ethics was clearly related to the nonviolent philosophy of Solidarity. As Roman Laba observes, Solidarity's symbolic production stands out from other twentieth-century mass movements. It did not endorse aggression, nei-ther did it dehumanize its enemy in a fashion familiar from the ceremo-nial and rhetoric of the Communist, Fascist, and Nazi movements.[94] Flowers, the ubiquitous element in the movement's decor, symbolized throughout the whole period both the declared and realized attachment of this revolution to nonviolent methods of political struggle.

The counterhegemonic discourse of Solidarity and other independent movements and organizations, developed in countless ceremonies and conveyed by the pictorial imagery of banners, graffiti, badges, pam-phlets, leaflets, and posters invoked and reinvigorated several principles and traditions, including democracy, sovereignty and independence, pa-triotism, (non–Communist) socialism, strong attachment to the Roman Catholicism, and nonviolence.

Democracy, as the political foundation of the movement, was empha-sized time and again in various declarations and programs. Symbolically, it was restored as the foundation of public life during the May First–May Third celebrations, which proved the enormous popularity and vitality of this principle. By organizing celebrations whose aim was to revive the liberal-democratic sense of "democracy," Solidarity forced the Party-state to suspend the routine May Day parade and emphasize instead the "pluralistic, democratic, and egalitarian" dimension of its ambiguous ceremonial, decor, and rhetoric. Democracy was also vividly displayed during Solidarity's Congress. The arrangement of space and the colorful pluralism of the interior decoration sharply contrasted with the mono-chromatic and hierarchical decor of the Party gatherings. For tactical reasons, independence was not emphasized in Solidarity's programs but it was often recognized in the symbolic production, especially in satirical pamphlets. The significance of this principle was confirmed in the celebra-tions of November Eleventh and in the recrowning of the White Eagle. Expressions of patriotism were, by and large, moderate. The first con-gress of Solidarity officially acknowledged its dedication to the values of political, ethnic, and philosophical pluralism and declared its attachment

94. On the "demonization of political opponents," see Gross (1974, 222).

to the tradition of the multiethnic, multireligious, tolerant Jagiellonian Poland.[95]

Solidarity also challenged the official discourse on the issue most critical for the state's self-legitimation. Such symbolic acts as the sanctioning of Solidarity's own tradition created through the December 1970 commemorations, erecting the Gdańsk, Gdynia, Szczecin, Poznań, and Ursus monuments, and reclaiming the May Day celebrations (in 1981), exposed the usurpatory nature of the Communist state's claims to the total monopoly over the legacy of the workers' struggle for social justice and, by extension, socialism.

All these revived or invented traditions and principles that made up the counterhegemonic discourse were encapsulated in the framework of Catholic mythology, which was declared to be the movement's ethical and religious foundation.[96] The question arises to what degree these religious images, symbols, and ceremonies influenced the thoughts and actions of the "average" member of Solidarity. Theoretically, I share Turner's and Ortner's views that root paradigms (cultural schemas), even if clearly articulated only on the level of high culture, often function as powerful signposts regulating the behavior of the masses.[97] It is enough that they serve as models for the leaders (main actors), to regulate, if only

95. Solidarity's Congress explicitly addressed this issue. It declared a *Resolution on National Minorities,* which states: "We intend to remain faithful to the tradition of a multinational Polish Commonwealth. Regional varieties add to the wealth of Polish culture and should also be cultivated. Our union is against all nationalistic divisions and will stand for the fullness of civic rights of all Polish citizens of whatever nationality or provenance" (translated in *World Affairs* 145 [Summer 1982]: 22). Krzemiński concludes: "It seems to me that the notorious hybrid 'Pole-Catholic' did not motivate the members of Solidarity as a 'union' or as an 'organization' " (1985, 103).

96. On 17 April 1981, Solidarity's weekly *Tygodnik Solidarność* published "The Directions of Solidarity's Operations in the Current Situation of the Nation." Here is an excerpt from this document: "The nation's best traditions, Christianity's ethical principles, democracy's political mandate, and socialist social thought. These are four main sources of our inspiration. We are deeply attached to the heritage of Poland's whole culture, which is merged with European culture and has strong links with Catholicism but which contains various religious and philosophical traditions" (translated in Raina 1985, 173).

97. Ortner, in a recent formulation of this problem, emphasizes tremendous flexibility and variability of the relationship between actors and cultural schemas. As she puts it: "Some actors are manipulating it [the schema—J.K.]; some are 'driven' by it; some are moved merely by the logic of the moment; and some use the schema to interpret the behavior of others. At one level the variations matter" (1989, 129). But, in a conclusion that I feel is strongly supported by my own analysis, she claims that "at another level they [the variations—J.K.] add up to many modes of 'enacting' the schemas, the notion of enactment here being a shorthand for the varying ways in which people hold, and are held by, their culture" (1989, 129).

indirectly and temporarily, the behavior of the followers. In Turner's words:

> A higher-order concept than symbols, root paradigms are certain consciously recognized (though not consciously grasped) cultural models for behavior that exist in the heads of the main actors in a social drama, whether in a small group or on the stage of history. . . . They reach down to the irreducible life stances of individuals, passing beneath conscious prehension to a fiduciary hold on what the individual senses to be axiomatic values, matters literally of life and death. Root paradigms emerge at life crises, whether of groups or individuals, whether institutionalized or compelled by unforeseen events. (Turner and Turner 1978, 248–49)

The head of the Solidarity chapter of Gdańsk University, a main actor in the events of 1980 and 1981, supports Turner's and Ortner's theorizing. When asked about the role of religious symbolism in the movement, he said:

> It was purely spontaneous. Priests did not go around and ask if we wanted to hold mass during the strike. We asked priests to come and join the strike. The symbols of Solidarity, the Black Madonna, the cross, or the pope—they were purely spontaneous.

"Was it not superficial?" he was asked.

> If it had been superficial, it would not have emerged so spontaneously. It resulted from some deeper thoughts each of us has. If you take a look at the everyday life . . . perhaps most of these people who manifested their religious feelings during the Solidarity demonstrations did not go to church, you know, on a regular basis, I mean, every Sunday. But in drastic situations, because we have been brought up as we have been, it shows its impact. We come back to this religious upbringing we got, it is a certain escape. We were always aware that we lived on a bomb, which could explode at any moment, . . . it was the present, the future was unclear, it was this uncertainty. I think that in such uncertain critical situations, like the whole period of Solidarity, one starts to think about things in which he has been brought up. That's why, I think, this religiosity occurred involuntarily. I think it wasn't superficial.

"Wasn't it a kind of escape from fear or a kind of justification . . . even if we fail, there is some reason for which the whole thing has been worth undertaking?"

It was not fear, it was uncertainty.

Workers or Intellectuals?

Solidarity, perhaps the largest mass social movement in history, has attracted a number of social scientists who have engaged in the uneasy task of defining, describing, and explaining this unusually complex and fascinating phenomenon. One of the most hotly debated issues in this constantly expanding field of study is the "Leninist" dilemma of who was more important in bringing about the revolutionary change, the (oppositional) intellectuals or the workers. Roman Laba (1991) and Lawrence Goodwyn (1991) portray workers as the *primary* causal force behind Solidarity; the role of the intelligentsia was, as they construe it, *noncausal* ("creative but not causal" in Laba's words). In Goodwyn's interpretation, the oppositional subcultures and organizations of workers (particularly at the Baltic Coast) developed independently from the parallel organizations of intellectuals (such as the KOR), with only a minimal and insignificant dialogue between them.

"This is a book about the origins of Solidarity, which are overwhelmingly working-class," writes Laba (1991, 178) and argues that "the main characteristics of Solidarity, its master frames, were created autonomously by Polish workers six years before the creation of KOR and ten years before the rise of Solidarity" (1991, 11). Goodwyn's interpretation is similar (1991, 385–86).

In both books, the conviction that the workers were the primary causal agents in the creation of Solidarity is combined with an ambiguous assessment of the role of oppositional intellectuals. Each author recognizes and praises the contributions of the intelligentsia to the struggle against the Party-state, yet they vehemently deny any *causal* significance to these contributions. Laba claims in the concluding section of his book that "there would not have been a Solidarity without the intellectuals, but the Solidarity they joined was built on the framework developed by workers. In other words, the roots of Solidarity were in the Baltic working class, and the intellectuals made a necessary but not causal or creative contribution" (1991, 178). The vagueness of this sentence (how can a contribution be necessary but not causal?) seems to indicate that the phrasing of the fundamental research question as "Who did it, workers or intellectuals?" was not clearly thought through. The complex social reality of Solidarity cannot be squeezed into the tight corset of this formulation.

Goodwyn's position is more difficult to grasp. According to the main assertion of his book, there were no "causal" agents other than the workers involved in Solidarity's creation: "The causal claims for KOR, Radio Free Europe, and the Pope have materialized in the literature on Solidarność essentially because they seemed to fill an apparently yawning evidential gap concerning the origins of Solidarność" (1991, 369). He rejects "the erroneous claim that KOR 'prepared [the] consciousness of the workers for the strikes' " (1991, 387).

Yet elsewhere Goodwyn admits that "what KOR did achieve was absolutely vital." Through the creation of "fraternal association" with the "indigenous activists of the social groups most in need in society . . . the men and women of KOR gave organizational birth to civil society by breathing experiential life into the very idea of civil society in Leninist Poland" (1991, 386). Obviously, Goodwyn's substantial research revealed to him the significance of the oppositional intellectual groups, the KOR in particular. He concludes, however, that they were important only in as much as they were the people of action; as the people of ideas they were inconsequential: "The people of KOR, through their actions rather than through their political ideas or their literary skill, gave hope to a nascent social dream" (1991, 387).[98] Again, this wavering argument seems to indicate that the initial formulation of the main research problem ("workers" versus "intellectuals") does not allow the analyst to grasp the complex reality.

The results of both Laba's and Goodwyn's analyses are to a large degree predetermined by their primary research question "workers or intellectuals?" but also by their polemical zeal to prove wrong those who answer "intellectuals." This zeal seems to be generated by their vehement

---

98. Such reasoning seems based on a dualistic model of social reality: the world of ideas as the domain of intellectuals is opposed to the world of actions as the domain of workers. Putting aside the elitist overtone of such a conception, one should note that modern social science warns that the "idea-action" dichotomy (as a conceptual tool) must be applied with the utmost care; it is useful in some research contexts but not in others. Goodwyn's study represents the latter case for one fundamental reason: during the 1970s and in 1981 a significant part of the Poles' struggle against the Communist Party-state was fought through the means of *public symbolic action*. In the case of such action, the "idea-action" distinction is misleading because these two dimensions are simply indistinguishable: the symbolic action (ceremony, demonstration, certainly the Gdańsk August strike) expresses, conveys certain ideas and images, but, at the same time, it produces social/political facts, changes the sociopolitical landscape. Steinberg, for example, writes "Discourse . . . is a process of collective activity" (1991, 189).

disagreement with the "general consensus" that "like the overall program, the organizational form of Solidarity originated among the radical
intellectuals" (Laba 1991, 99). The problem with this formulation is twofold. First, I agree with Timothy Ash that there has never been such a
"general consensus"; in fact, most Polish intellectuals and Western analysts of Solidarity would concur that it came to being through a dialogue
between both sides, however difficult it is to assess their respective contributions and define the nature of the new, emerging social entity (1991,
48). Ost, for example, concludes that

> although the idea of forming independent trade unions was first
> raised by the striking workers of Gdańsk and Szczecin in 1970, it
> was KOR that did the most to perpetuate the idea in the next
> decade. Not only did it endlessly propagate the idea of indepen-
> dent civic initiatives in general, but it was KOR, as well as inde-
> pendent leftists collaborating with it, that organized the influential
> Committee for Free Trade Unions in Gdańsk in 1978, the leaders
> of which became leaders of Gdańsk Solidarity two years later.
> (1990, 10–11)[99]

Second—as I will try to demonstrate—Polish opposition and later
Solidarity was a multistranded and complicated social entity from the
beginning of its existence. It was created by the contributions of various
people; to lump them all under the labels of "workers" or "radical intellectuals" is to shirk the task of adequately conceptualizing this entity.

One way to find an answer to the question "Who did it?" would be to
compile a list of concrete individuals, name by name, involved in the
preformation of Solidarity ("oppositionists," "dissidents"); reconstruct
the social networks they formed; identify the cultural artifacts they created (such as their newsletters, books, journals, and leaflets) and by
which they were influenced; describe all the various public actions they
engaged in; and finally characterize each and every organization (cultural,
civic, eventually political) they formed. No such comprehensive empirical investigation has been undertaken as of yet. However, there are stud-

---

99. Ost seems to suggest that the organizers of the KZ WZZ were "independent left-
ists." It is an inaccurate picture: among them were people of various political persuasions,
including, for example, moderate nationalists from the RMP. He also comes dangerously
close to espousing "the elitist thesis" (an object of Laba's and Goodwyn's attacks) when he
limits his analysis in his chapters, "The Genesis of Political Opposition in Poland: 1944–
1970" and "Opposition and Civil Society: 1970–1980," to a discussion of intraparty and
intra-elite conflicts; cultural and intellectual events; and major oppositional writings (by
Kołakowski, Kuroń, and Michnik).

ies that point to the existence of an extensive and ever-growing network of people coming from all walks of life; a network with many centers.

Did all those "activists" come from one social "class" or "group"? Laba and Goodwyn insist that by and large they did. The workers, particularly the workers of the Coast, created Solidarity. Their vision of Solidarity as an almost exclusive creation of the workers resembles a classical Marxist formulation in which a class *in itself* (an aggregate of people sharing a common socioeconomic status) evolves into a class *for itself* (a group driven to action by a common ideology). Moreover, this process was supposedly accomplished *without* any substantive help coming from outside of this class. As Laba and Goodwyn see it, the Solidarity revolution was carried out by an *already existing* socioeconomic class (or rather by a subsection of this class: the workers of the Coast), who through "thirty-five years of working-class self activity" acquired "an invisible store of knowledge" (Goodwyn 1991, 153) and developed the organizational tools (an interfactory strike committee) which allowed them to challenge the Party-state.

Laba and Goodwyn's interpretation, however, is not supported by existing sociological evidence. It has been demonstrated, for example, that the "statistical relationship between the vision of social structure and the individual experience in the stratification system was in the countries of real socialism insignificant, three times weaker than in the capitalist countries" (Staniszkis 1989, 93).[100] In Poland "variables [describing] social positions do not have practical influence on the formation of the dichotomous ["we" versus "them"—J.K.] vision of social structure: a strong correlation exists only between subscribing to such a vision and declared membership in Solidarity in 1980–81" (Staniszkis 1989, 95).[101] A series of studies conducted since 1980 under the common title "Poles" (not used by Laba and Goodwyn) demonstrates that "in the 1980s Polish society was politically polarized, and at the ends of this continuum one could find the members of each social class, group and social category in almost the same proportion" (Jasiewicz 1991, 37; see also Rychard 1989, 298); and "the differences of interest between various occupational groups [measured as support for pluralism—J.K.] cannot be interpreted on the ground of the traditional conception of classes (workers, peasants, and intelligentsia)" (Rychard 1989, 310). What is more important, similar

100. Elsewhere, Staniszkis concludes that there exists "a fundamental difference in the perception of social structure between the statist and market systems. In the former, the shaping of the structure's image is far more dependent on 'collective representations' (symbolic vision . . .) than on individual experiences in the system of stratification" (1991a, 214).

101. A similar regularity among the young people was discovered by Nowacki (1991, 82).

regularities were discovered in the late 1970s: summarizing the results of several empirical studies, Kuczyński and Nowak conclude that "an adequate theory of social structure that would link objective traits of social structure in Poland with social consciousness was then [in the late 1970s—J.K.] perceived as impossible" (1988, 136). Recently, Wnuk-Lipiński summarizes the results of studies on the sources of social conflicts in Communist Poland the following way:

> Divisions engendered by the [social] conflict did not overlap with the structural divisions; one side of the conflict was occupied by groups for which it is difficult to establish a consensus of interests, but it is easier to indicate a certain conflict of interests and, at the same time, a *unanimity of values* [emphasis added] (e.g. between peasants and intelligentsia; skilled workers and young engineers, unaffiliated with the Party; petty owners and teachers and doctors); on the other side of the conflict one finds the communist power structures, which—in addition to being united by common interests—were also united by a unanimity of values—different from, and contradictory to, the values constituting the integrating platform of the other side of the conflict. (1991, 16)

How to interpret these results theoretically? Laba's and Goodwyn's concept of class seems to be inadequate. Thus, one has to find a different concept of class or drop this concept altogether and substitute something else. Let me first explore the former option. A comprehensive, "not-exclusively-materialist" concept of class has been proposed by E. P. Thompson (1963) and certain critics of his (see Steinberg 1991), as well as Gerard Sider (1986) and Robert Wuthnow (1989). Its extreme version has been articulated by Gareth Stedman-Jones, who regards class as "a discursive rather than as an ontological reality" (1983, 10). According to these writers, social classes are products of a complicated intertwining of cultural, economic, and political processes.[102] Their position is congruent with Lynn Hunt's thesis that revolutions (at least the French Revolution) are made by political classes *in statu nascendi* and that cultural factors play a

---

102. Sider postulates the use of "a reformulated notion of culture" (to reformulate it he employs the notion of hegemony) in the analysis of "the dynamic of class," "*not* because culture 'happens' within classes, and class struggle between classes; not at all. Culture enters the dynamic of class because . . . it is where class becomes dynamic; where the lines of antagonism and alliance come together and apart" (1986, 9). Wuthnow puts it thus: "Class formation must be seen as a feature of ideological construction itself rather than a prior characteristic of the social environment that ideology merely came to reflect" (1989, 571).

significant role in the formation of such classes.[103] In my view, a close scrutiny of Solidarity's rise supports the claim that an analysis of prerevolutionary class constellations, distinguished on the basis of a set of *static* criteria, such as the relationship to the means of production, cannot provide all the answers to the question of who was the motor of the revolution.[104] Instead, these works in which "class" is contrued as a dynamic phenomenon whose mode of existence is becoming rather than being—as for example, Hunt's study of the French Revolution or Sider's work on the Newfoundland fisherfolk in the era of commercial capitalism—provide much more convincing explanations of revolutions and the formation of new classes or groups in the revolutionary process. Does such a "dynamic" conceptualization of class apply to Solidarity?

Solidarity came to existence in August 1980 as the culmination of a complex social process initiated in the mid-1970s. Due to the geopolitical situation and the enormous disparity between the political actors in relation to their control over the means of production and oppression, the struggle in Poland of the late 1970s was not for political power, but for authority and legitimacy, that is, for the public predominance of one of the two discourses defining social and political order.[105] The fundamental distinction was drawn between those who had political and economic power and attempted to construct for themselves authority and legitimacy, and those who had little power but struggled to make "their" discourse visible, audible, and, eventually, hegemonic. The emergence of such a cleavage is not without historical parallels. According to Simon Schama, for example: "A patriotic culture of citizenship was created in the decades after the Seven Years' War, and . . . it was . . . a cause rather than a product of the French Revolution" (1989, xv).

What happened in Poland in the late 1970s and early 1980s can be then construed as a confrontation between the entrenched *political-economic-*

103. Hunt concludes that "revolutionary politics were neither the instrument of a social class in Marxist terms nor the tool of a modernizing elite. They came into being along with a new republican political class, and both the politics and the class were shaped by the ongoing interaction between widely shared rhetorical assumptions and collective political practices" (1984, 213).

104. Kuczyński and Nowak, in their attempt to define Solidarity, concur: "One cannot determine, objectively and *a priori,* what social categories are predestined to create social movements" (1988, 131).

105. The confrontation of these two discourses on the level of "high culture," that is, in literature, theater, and films, is carefully analyzed by Goldfarb, who shares the general conclusion of my study that the oppositional culture preceded, both historically and logically, oppositional politics (1989). Kuczyński and Nowak offer an interpretation that is akin to mine. They write: "Solidarity . . . was a social movement of public opinion that helped it to create itself" (1988, 141).

cultural class and an emergent social entity, which may be labeled the *cultural-political class in statu nascendi*. This cultural-political class was made up not of workers or intellectuals but of all those who subscribed to a system of principles and values, usually referred to as counterhegemonic, unofficial, independent, or alternative—who visualized the social structure as strongly polarized between "us" ("society," "the people," etc.) and "them" ("the authorities," "Communists," etc.). When summarizing a number of interviews with workers, Grzegorz Bakuniak concludes that people's belief in their ability to shape their fate

> demanded, as its pre-condition, the realization that one is a member of a larger human community, subjected to a similar treatment [by the Party-state—J.K.]. Characteristically, the category of group, or class, interest, was less useful for the description of this process (at least in its preliminary phase). It was rather a process whereby people realized the existence of a community united by a common condition. *The awareness of local or class interests was built on the foundation of this realization of belonging to a community* [emphasis added]. (1983, 294)

Bakuniak conceptualizes the "new" emerging social entity as a *community*. Other "non-class" conceptualizations include Touraine's *social movement,* Kennedy's *emancipatory praxis* (1991, 49), or Arato's *civil society* (Arato 1981, 1981–82).[106] There exists, however, one more definitional path worth exploring. In the famous chapter on status groups and classes, Max Weber offers the view that "the sociological structure of parties differs in a basic way according to the kind of social action which they struggle to influence; that means, they differ according to whether or not the community is stratified by status or class" (1978, 938–39). Status distinctions are, in turn, linked with class distinctions "in the most varied ways" (Weber 1978, 932). Status is determined by "social estimation of *honor*" (1978, 932). These conceptions can be generalized without much distortion: societies are stratified *simultaneously* according to several criteria, for example, economic, political, and cultural. Moreover, such distinctions may produce at least partially independent systems of stratification. In the light of these formulations, Solidarity can be conceptualized as a *party based on a status group,* or, in a more general way, as the *party of a*

106. According to Touraine et al.: "In the spring of 1981 [and earlier, I would argue—J.K.], the trade-union, national and democratic dimensions of Solidarity's action were not only linked: they were fused to such an extent that no one would risk putting himself on the fringe of the movement by adopting one dimension, or even a combination of two of them, to the exclusion of the others" (1983, 55).

cultural group. Given the enormous size and complexity of Solidarity it may be perhaps better conceptualized not as a *party* but simply as a *status (or cultural) group.* But even with this correction, the "Weberian" gist of the proposed conceptualization remains intact: the criteria distinguishing Solidarity from its opponent, at least initially were *cultural* and *political* (in this order!); *economic* criteria, producing "classical" class distinctions, were insignificant.[107] Such a conceptualization is strikingly close to the actual views of Solidarity members themselves; they often perceived Solidarity as a vehicle restoring their *dignity,* that is, as improving at least one dimension of their status.[108]

These deliberations on the relative role of political and cultural factors in the rise of Solidarity can be summarized in the following way. In every society several principles of structuration operate, reinforcing or weakening one another.[109] Such principles are socio-economic-occupational (engendering socioeconomic classes), political (dividing the society into the rulers and ruled), and cultural (coresponsible for the creation of such groups as ethnic minorities or races). There is enough evidence to claim that in Poland of the late 1970s through 1989, the cultural-political principle structured social reality in a more profound way than did the socioeconomic principle, although the latter, obviously, did not cease to operate. This should be understood in the following way: if we want to comprehend the actions of the Poles who created Solidarity, we must see these actions as not simply related to or determined by their socioeconomic positions, but as an expression of their belonging to an ascending status (cultural) group, which I call a cultural-political class. At the same time, it was precisely these actions that brought the new class into being. I found strong support for my conclusions in the work of Andrzej

107. In this connection it is worthwhile to quote Roman Szporluk, an author of the path-breaking study (1988) on the relationship between the two principles of structuration in the nineteenth-century East-Central Europe: class and nation: "However hard this may be for the Marxist to accept, it is often, though by no means always, the case that economics follows politics, and that in turn it is first given its direction by culture" (1990, 135).

108. Jadwiga Staniszkis concludes that "for Polish workers Solidarity of 1980 and 1981 was not just a union but, above all, leverage in the *status competition* [emphasis added] in their everyday contacts with the local authorities" (1991b, 199). Interestingly, David Cannadine, trying to find a *via media* between "materialist" and "linguistic/rhetorical" conceptualizations of the British society, formulates the following appeal: "What is most urgently needed if we are to understand [British] society is neither a history of class nor a history of language, but a history of status" (1992, 57). I believe this appeal applies to Polish society of the late 1970s and 1980s as well.

109. In Giddens's works on structuration (1984) I was not able to find an analysis of such concurrent operation of various principles. But I do not believe that my analysis violates the spirit of his work.

Rychard, who in his penetrating and original study verified empirically the existence of several lines of cleavage operating simultaneously in the Polish society and demonstrated that the "new social entity" that opposed the Party-state can be conceptualized as *workers* only at the cost of serious distortion (1987a). Among the concepts he proposes are a *class of wage employees* and *groups professionally active in the state sector, not occupying higher managerial positions* (1987a, 106). What unified this diversified group? I have attempted to demonstrate that it was a common cultural framework. Rychard supports such a view when he offers his final conclusion concerning the dominant cleavage in Polish society "at the threshold of the 1980s":

> The dominant group of contradictions is this in which groups are opposed to each other *not* [emphasis added] in respect to their place in the classically defined [according to socioeconomic criteria— J.K.] social structure, but in respect to certain standards of ethical evaluation. The dominance of normative perspective is clear. (1987a, 120–21)

In the light of empirical evidence and analyses presented in this section, I conclude that Laba and Goodwyn err on two counts. First, they misunderstand the mechanism of collective action. Such action has a potential to *restructure* society, and this is exactly what happened in Poland: some people, by engaging in oppositional activities, were gradually developing a new cultural frame and—simultaneously—were constituting themselves as a new cultural-political class (Weberian status group).[110] And this was the beginning of the end of state socialism in Eastern Europe. Second, as a result of this misunderstanding, both authors misidentified social units "responsible" for the Solidarity revolution: it was not the "workers" or the "intellectuals" but a new cultural-political class.

---

110. The examination of the relationship between social action, cultural frames of meaning, and social structures is, of course, central to Anthony Giddens's theorizing. But see also the newer literature on social movements, in particular Bert Klandermans, Hanspeter Kriesi, and Sidney Tarrow (1988). Kriesi writes in this volume: "Collective action directly affects the organization and opportunity of the actors involved . . . , but it may also have a considerable impact on the most basic structural conditions" (1988, 365). On the "creative" role of cultural factors in shaping social action during "unsettled cultural periods," see Ann Swindler (1986).

8 The Role of Symbols in the Construction and Deconstruction of the Polish People's Republic

At the beginning of this study I posed two interrelated questions: "Why did Solidarity happen in Poland and not elsewhere in the Communist bloc?" and "Why did it manage to survive several years in the underground to emerge in 1989 as a formidable force, initiating the collapse of Communism in Eastern Europe?" Answers to these questions have been and will be colored by the theoretical and philosophical perspectives of their authors. What kind of answers have emerged from my work, which is embedded in the field of modern cultural studies, concentrated on the relationship between culture and (political) power? Let me preface a summary of my answers to these questions with a brief overview of several factors that were involved in the rise of Solidarity.

Causal Antecedents to Solidarity

A full discussion of the causes that in combination brought about Solidarity merits a separate study; here I list some of these causes, which can be conveniently, if somewhat schematically, categorized under four headings: the economic, the political, the societal, and the cultural (see Kennedy 1991, chaper 2, for a more comprehensive discussion).

Economic Factors

The economic crisis. In the second half of the 1970s the Polish economy slid into deep economic crisis, and as Włodzimierz Brus observes, "It hardly seems necessary to emphasize the crucial role played by economic factors in precipitating the Polish revolution of 1980" (1983, 26). This systemic crisis in the Polish command economy, which lasted until the end of Communism in 1989, has been thoroughly analyzed by several economists.[1] Suffice it to say here that one of the major causes of the Polish economic crisis was the failure in bureaucratic coordination of economic activities and the erosion of the central planning system (Ekiert 1991). It is also important to remember that the severity of the Polish crisis resulted from a specific interaction between economic, political, and cultural factors (Bunce, n.d., 48).

The second economy. The second half of the 1970s also witnessed a considerable opening of the second economy. This development, coupled with the increasingly widespread corruption, led to the perception of the growing social gap between the rich and powerful and the poor and powerless (Janicka 1986, 68). It is thus hard not to agree that "of all the unsavory and unpopular features of the Communist system in Poland, perhaps none aroused more hostility and outrage, or contributed more to the outburst of discontent in the summer of 1980, than the existence of widespread social inequities" (Smolar 1983, 42).

Political Factors

Corporatism. As I pointed out in Chapter 1, Gierek was not an unequivocally "liberalizing" ruler; his policy of "repressive tolerance" was coupled with administrative and political reforms aimed at strengthening his regime. Yet the most significant political development of the 1970s was not this increase of centralization, but the emergence of *corporatism,* or to be

---

1. Its first phase, the late 1970s, is examined by Brus (1983), Fallenbuchl (1982), and Gomułka (1979).

more precise, corporatist techniques of protest absorption and interest representation.[2] Moreover, according to Staniszkis, "the evolution of the Polish political system in the 1970s from a totalitarian to an authoritarian-bureaucratic [based on corporatist techniques—J.K.] regime was more responsible for the events of August 1980 than the worsening economic situation" (1984, 150).

A weak party. Less significant, though not to be overlooked, was the growing weakness of the increasingly divided Polish Communist party (Bunce, n.d., 46; Bielasiak 1983).

A strong Catholic Church and an independent intelligentsia. In comparison with other Communist countries, Poland was unique because of the existence of the strong, independent Catholic Church and an intelligentsia, prone to think and act independently. Both groups provided an *institutional* base for many oppositional activities.

Antiregime networks of workers. I do not share Laba and Goodwyn's view that the workers, through their *self-organizing* efforts, became the primary, if not exclusive, creators of Solidarity. Yet, one of the main reasons of Solidarity's success was the early and extensive, in comparison with other Communist countries, *organization* of oppositional networks, which involved many workers.

"Repressive tolerance." Polish oppositional activists were often harassed, beaten, and arrested, yet at the same time their endeavors were tolerated to a degree unthinkable under other Communist regimes. Introducing this policy of "repressive tolerance," "Gierek's team hoped that the social and political costs of permitting the existence of such opposition would be outweighed by the advantages. Among the latter was the image of 'the most liberal ruling elite in Eastern Europe,' which increased Poland's access to foreign credits" (Staniszkis 1984, 166). By the end of the 1970s Gierek's miscalculation became obvious: the opposition's strength was one of the key factors in the Communist regime's demise.

Societal Factors

Social polarization. The authorities' tolerance of economic corruption and corporatism led to the visible polarization of society. "There was an increasing convergence of the levels of power, wealth, education (at least

2. See Staniszkis (1984, 38–40). These techniques consisted in selective and authoritative inclusion of several separate social groups in discussions and "consultations" with the authorities. Through such informal channels some of these groups were able to obtain scarce "goods," profitable contracts, or "controlled" freedom.

in the formal sense), and also prestige" (Pańków 1982, 44), which obviously contradicted the regime's official allegiance to egalitarianism. Another study revealed that although the "disparities in the average wages of occupational groups were actually smaller in 1980 than in 1976, . . . the proportion of people *citing* [emphasis added] significant social divisions and the conflict-endangering role of income, power, and nature of work increased during 1976–80" (Janicka 1986, 75).

The same study provides evidence corroborating one of the main contentions of this book, that the Solidarity revolution was not created by workers or intellectuals, but by a *newly* emergent cultural/political class. Janicka discovered that "crystallization of views involving social conflict [was] not correlated with occupational categories" and concluded that "perhaps views shared by people *across* [emphasis added] stratification divisions provided the basis for a new social integration, a necessary condition for the emergence of a social movement opposed to the political practices of the period 1976–80" (1986, 75). An analysis of the role oppositional discourses played in the creation of this "new social integration" is one of the objectives of this book.

A noncollectivized peasantry. Another uniquely Polish feature. The very existence of individual peasants rendered Polish Communism incomplete. The peasants often passively resisted various governmental policies, and some of them were involved in direct opposition (Kęcik 1983).

Relative deprivation resulting from a revolution of rising expectations. The early success of the Gierek regime in at least partially satisfying the material needs of some segments of the population whetted their appetites for more. Thus the economic collapse of the second half of the 1970s had serious social repercussions. "What exacerbated the workers' dissatisfaction, particularly among the young ones, with housing, as well as with consumer goods in general, was not so much that the living standards had fallen but what availability of goods failed to meet the workers' rising expectations" (Pravda 1983, 73).

Cultural Factors

The oppositional/revolutionary ethos of Polish culture and history. When describing the rise of Solidarity, many analysts point to the uniqueness of both Polish history, full of struggles and insurrections against neighboring powers, and the oppositional/revolutionary ethos, founded on the memory of these struggles. I demonstrated that this ethos was maintained and even strengthened through the oppositional ceremonies, rallies, and publications, and thereby became a key component of the discourse that undermined the Party-state's hegemony and legitimacy.

Ethnic and religious homogeneity. It seems that the relative (in comparison with other Eastern European countries) homogeneity of the Polish nation prevented the authorities from utilizing a strategy of *divide et impera* and contributed to the success of Solidarity.

Socialist values and the regime's (il)legitimacy. By 1958, the year of the first sociological surveys in Poland, four basic values propagated by the new regime as its attributes were ingrained in the minds of large (mostly urban) sections of the Polish society.[3] They were social justice (equality of opportunity), egalitarianism (equality of outcome), the welfare-state, and the nationalization of the economy.

In the 1970s, the values of social justice and egalitarianism, prominent in the value system of the Poles at least since 1956, were gradually gaining even more significance. By 1980 they were "the most important sociopolitical values in Poland" (Koralewicz-Zębik 1984, 227).[4] This increased sensitivity to egalitarianism and social justice seems to have been related to a growing awareness of two "unjust" tendencies in the social life: the growing distance between the "haves" and "have-nots," and the emergence in the form of widespread corruption of an unacceptable criteria of reward. In the second half of the 1970s, all these discrepancies became apparent; and as the frustration of the Polish population rapidly escalated, the regime's legitimacy further declined.

The split vision: Discrepancies between theory and (the vision of) practice. As Pańków observes, "In the late 1970s, the discrepancy between the image of the system held by that system itself (propaganda of success) and its image in the majority of the people became enormous, which created conditions conducive to a successive manifestation of open social protest" (1982, 45).

I do not believe that these factors alone were sufficient to bring about Solidarity. As Staniszkis notes, "The process of identity formation among the workers was slow and tedious; a jump occurred only after the emergence of an integrating symbolic vision" (1989, 117). This integrating vision, which united not just workers but the majority of the county's adult population, was formed and elaborated through the medium of counterhegemonic discourses. Their genesis, development, and role in the formation of Solidarity as well as in the collapse of the Communist regime in Poland are what I have dealt with in this book.

3. It is not entirely clear to what degree the widespread acceptance of these values by the populace resulted from the regime's propaganda and to what degree they belonged to the pre-1945 worldview and ethos. It is, however, clear that the new regime portrayed itself as a champion of these values (see, for example, Nowak 1984, 408).

4. In the 1980s, justice became even more important than equality.

Rituals of Rebellion, Rituals of Confirmation, and Ceremonial Revolutions

Without denying that most rulers' power originates in their control of the means of production, coercion, administration, and communication, in this study I turned my attention to subtler expressions of the exercise of power: public demonstrations, ceremonies, and rituals.[5] Through such cultural forms, those who produce them engage in the (more or less successful) creation of social reality (Lincoln 1989) and (re)define such actual and possible objects of political action, as "democracy," "civil society," "dignity," or "national identity."

Moreover, whereas all domains of social life are permeated by power (though not necessarily political), public ceremonies are *always* political. According to Abner Cohen, "Authority is an abstraction which can be seen only through its symbolism and ceremonials" (1981, 78). Geertz makes this point even more forcefully: "Thrones may be out of fashion and pageantry too; but political authority still requires a cultural frame in which to define itself and advance its claims, and so does opposition to it. A world wholly demystified is a world wholly depoliticized" (1977, 168).[6] In societies in which a clear-cut distinction between different domains of social life is not yet developed or is deliberately obscured, as in totalitarian or semi-totalitarian states, the saturation of every ceremony with political power is particularly apparent.

A critical examination of Max Gluckman's "rituals of rebellion" provides a useful starting point for a discussion of the relationship between ceremonies (rituals), legitimacy, and political power. Gluckman has often pointed out that rituals of rebellion usually occur in societies in which social orders and political systems enjoy full legitimacy, that is, where the hegemonic discourse is unchallenged and the idea of some alternative arrangement of society is inconceivable for the decisive majority of the population. " 'Rituals of rebellion' can be enjoyed by tradition as a social blessing, in repetitive social systems, but not in systems

5. Although I find his emphasis on the cultural aspect of the power exercise exaggerated, Parkin's formulation is illuminating: "Power rests not simply on the acquisition of land and material objects but rather derives from unequal access to semantic [and symbolic—J. K.] creativity, including the capacity to nominate others as equal or unequal, animate or inanimate, memorable or abject, discussor or discussed" (1982, xlvi).

6. According to a terminological convention of the present study, both Cohen and Geertz deal with legitimacy rather than authority (understood as a form of power based on at least minimal compliance of the ruled). Claiming authority in a highly spectacular way involving the key symbols of a given group is practically coterminous with claiming legitimacy. But there are other, less spectacular and yet effective, ways of claiming authority.

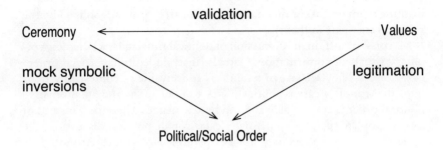

Fig. 3. Rituals of rebellion

where revolutions are possible" (Gluckman 1963, 135). Handelman comments that "such rituals were legitimated and validated by a social order which went unquestioned" (1976, 8–9). This situation is depicted in Figure 3, which illustrates what happens during the transformation phase of a celebration that serves as a kind of cultural "safety valve." The immunity of the established sociopolitical order is suspended for a moment, so it can be mocked, reversed, and ridiculed, but within strictly prescribed limits of cultural form. Very often, what is being attacked are not public offices *per se,* but merely the people who occupy them. After the ceremony is over, the whole political and social order remains intact, even strengthened, since various hostile energies have been channeled and safely discharged in the performance. Such is the social function of carnival role reversals (closely related to rituals of rebellion; see Figure 3), whereby the powerful for a moment play the role of the powerless. In California, the Doo Dah Parade functions as a ritual of rebellion against "the established order represented by the Rose Parade, as well as the dominant forces of contemporary American society" (Lawrence 1982, 155).

Characteristically, rituals of rebellion rarely occur in Communist states. This fact constitutes yet another proof that their political order is far from being popularly accepted and unquestioned.[7] The most common form of ritual practiced in these states is the ritual of confirmation. Rituals of confirmation are either voluntary (when participants are free to

7. Christel Lane suggests that rituals of rebellion did not occur in the Soviet Union because there the "existing social order [was] sacred" (1981, 23). I suspect that the absence of these rituals in Communist countries indicates not only "sacredness" pronounced by the rulers but also uncertainty that the existing order has limited support of the populace. See also Kertzer (1988, 54–56).

institute them or not) or mandatory (when participants are obliged by the rulers to take part in them).

Myron Aronoff, in his discussion of political ritual in Israel, depicts voluntary rituals of confirmation, "rituals [that] do legitimate social order" (1979, 303). They are staged when it is conceivable to contest the status quo. In Aronoff's case a political party can fall apart, and an alternative political order is conceivable and can be articulated. Therefore, instead of carrying on an open, yet potentially catastrophic political discussion, the leaders engage members in *delusionary participation*—which Aronoff calls ritual—whose purpose and function is to confirm the status quo. Such (hegemonic) ceremonies reaffirm the existing social order and legitimize the political system by linking them to the ultimate values of a given culture; they furnish political institutions with "spiritual aroma" (Firth 1981).

All official ceremonies and rituals of the Polish People's Republic belonged to the category of mandatory rituals of confirmation. Their intent was to *generate* or *validate,* by "traditionalizing new material,"[8] the authority and legitimacy of the official sociopolitical order and sustain the status quo. Formally, these ceremonies can be described as *closed rituals.* Their structures were rigid, and each performance became a token of some general type of ceremony, a token that served only to repeat in the most accurate way the traditional scenario. What Turner oserved in small premodern societies applies to the Communist Party-state as well: the more precisely the performance of a ritual conforms to a traditional pattern, the more effective the whole performance proves to be.[9] In other words, the more closed the structure and less informative the content of a ritual, the more effective its unifying power. The social drama is translated into rigidly structured ceremonial categories, leading to a predetermined outcome, that is, rendering the conflict "nonexistent."

The 1976 ceremonial condemnations of the rebellious workers in Poland conform to this model. Such ceremonial condemnations were realized according to the often-used scenario of the *massive demonstration of support for the system,* which indeed was the *generic ceremonial mode* of officialdom in Communist countries. Through these massive demonstrations, the authorities tried to deal with social conflicts, such as workers' protests, by depicting these protests as being outside the legitimate public domain.

Rituals of confirmation are graphically presented in Figure 4.

There is, however, another possible type of relationship between cere-

---

8. A phrase coined by Moore and Myerhoff (1977, 7).

9. A good example of such conflict is presented by Turner in his study of the social drama triggered by such incompatible rules of social structure as matrilineal descent and virilocal residence among the Ndembu (Turner 1957).

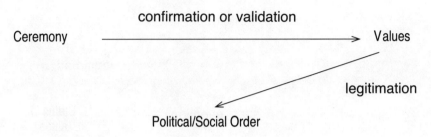

Fig. 4. Rituals of confirmation

mony, sociopolitical order, and the domain of ultimate values of a given culture. In situations in which it is conceivable that the sociopolitical order can be contested and could fall apart or be replaced—but is temporarily invulnerable because of the overwhelming power of the ruler(s)— ceremonies can directly challenge the status quo. They do this in two, often consecutive, ways. The first is by symbolically rejecting the existing rules. In such situations *ceremonial revolution* does not stay within the channels culturally prescribed and controlled by the rulers, as in the case of Gluckman's rituals of rebellion. Instead, it directly attacks, although symbolically, the dominating rules of interaction or the prevailing interpretive frameworks (hegemonic discourse). Second, such "revolutionary" ceremonies can be aimed at producing new (counterhegemonic) symbols embodying new or reviving old principles (values). In this way the ultimacy and universality of the hegemonic discourse is contested. In practice, both tactics of symbolic struggle usually go together and are hardly distinguishable.

It may be difficult to distinguish empirically rituals of rebellion (in Gluckman's sense) from ceremonial revolutions; in fact, some rituals include elements of both types. David Kideckel gives an example of a ritualistic meeting of the general assembly of a Romanian collective farm, which—as he convincingly demonstrates—functioned concurrently as a ritual of confirmation, a ritual of rebellion, and as a ceremonial revolution (1983, 69–75). The first function was devised by the leaders, but largely unrealized: by coming together in a highly organized and routinized manner, the leaders and "ordinary citizens" participated in a ritual that was supposed to "imply permanence and legitimacy to that social order which [organized] them" (Kideckel 1983, 71). The ritualistic meeting served, however, as a "controlled outlet of hostility and disagreement" (Kideckel 1983, 71)—it was thus a ritual of rebellion. But the meeting also contained some elements of ceremonial revolution, for it did not discharge all the

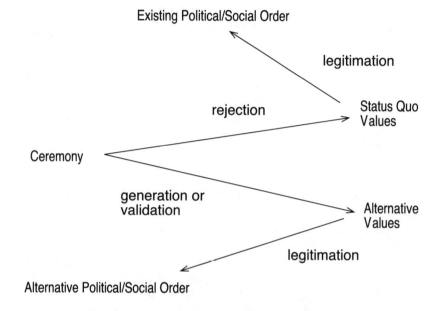

Fig. 5. Ceremonial revolutions

hostility and distrust felt by the "citizens" toward the "leaders"; it rather amplified this hostility and enlarged the social gap between the two groups. Figure 5 depicts ceremonial revolutions.

Effectiveness and Credibility of the Official Rituals and Ceremonies

The official ceremonies of the Gierek era produced and sustained several major motifs of the official discourse and therefore contributed to the self-legitimizing efforts of the regime. First of all they illustrated the Communist/socialist *eschatology* in which the Polish People's Republic was presented as a culmination of the victorious march of the forces of progress through history (as emblematized in May Day parades and the celebrations of the anniversaries of the October Revolution).[10] Second,

10. My analysis of the Gierek era discourse contradicts a popular view, repeated for example by Touraine et al., that Gierek's realization of "a huge program of industrial

IDEOLOGY

they propagated *technocratic pragmatism* (by celebrating, for example, the Katowice Steelworks, the Northern Port, Town Tournaments, The Poznań Trade Fair, and the thirtieth and thirty-fifth anniversaries of the Polish People's Republic). By emphasizing this motif, Gierek's regime attempted—with a degree of success in the early 1970s—to present itself as the champion of economic rationality and technological effectiveness. Third, the official decor and ceremonial espoused *socialist patriotism* (through, for example, May Day festivities or celebrations of the anniversaries of July 22). The relaxed and colorful form of many official productions was not insignificant in this respect. Fourth, the official ceremonial served to produce and maintain informative "noise" in the society's channels of communication.[11] How effective was this ceremonial system?

In analyzing John Paul II's first visit to Poland, I challenged Bloch's conclusion that ideology, in order to be effective, must be completely disconnected from nonideological cognition. I asserted that an ideology's effectiveness rests on two interrelated conditions: the *condition of credibility,* according to which the ceremonial must confirm *some* elements of the nonideological cognition in order to be credible, and the *condition of effective mystification,* according to which the ceremonial must conceal or deemphasize other elements of nonideological cognition, the suppression of which is politically expedient for its producers. The more thoroughly a *single* ceremonial system monopolizes the public domain, the better it realizes its mystifying function. In the late 1970s, the efficacy of Gierek's ceremonial system was declining drastically because *both* conditions were missing.[12] The official ceremonial had nothing in common with the everyday experience of the populace nor did it monopolize the ideologization of other areas of cognition, such as, ethical issues, civil rights, national sovereignty, or democracy. Rituals and ceremonies of the Catho-

---

investments . . . which seemed set to increase living standards and put an end to shortages . . . went hand in hand with increased pragmatism and tolerance, and a reduction of the Party's political and ideological hold on society" (1983, 35).

11. One of the functions of the official ceremonies was to propagate the dominant Marxist-Leninist ideology, which effectively reduced the society's level of self-reflection. As Arato puts it, "[Marxism-Leninism's] dominating role in philosophy and political theory guarantees the exclusion of serious public discussion about society" (1982, 212).

12. In the first part of the 1970s, the propagation of the mythology of *technocratic pragmatism* was matched by significant economic growth and much improved consumption. The mythological efficacy resulted from the fulfillment of the condition of credibility. Bernhard notes that "according to survey research done by *OBOP* (the Center for Research on Public Opinion) 80 percent of Poles evaluated the period 1971–75 favorably. The reasons most commonly cited were that the market was well supplied and that standards of living rose" (Bernhard 1993; see also Wedel 1986, 90).

lic Church, especially after 1979, were far more effective in this respect. They also contributed to the creation of a dramatic polarization of social consciousness ("the people" versus "the rulers"). This, in turn, led to the marginalization of other divisions of society and thus became a key ingredient in generating the Solidarity revolution. In this sense, Catholic ceremonies and rituals fulfilled the condition of effective mystification much better than their Communist counterparts.

Ambiguity of the Official Discourse and Its Dismantling

It is well established that the official ceremonial system sustains the mythology of a ruling elite and helps to create its hegemony in all polities. In addition, the ceremonial system propounded by the Polish state in the 1970s had a feature whose function was not so obvious; it produced and sustained *ambiguity* in the official discourse by alternately emphasizing two incompatible sets of principles, Communist or socialist, and/or by propagating hybrids such as democratic centralism, socialist patriotism, and patriotic internationalism. This ambiguity was politically expedient because it allowed the rulers at times of crisis to emphasize the values or principles best suited to the situation. When workers from Ursus and Radom walked out in June 1976, the regime put on its "Communist" face—inflexible and hierarchical, labeled the workers "hooligans," and held massive ceremonies condemning them. In 1970–71, when the authorities did negotiate with striking workers, and in 1980–81, when they temporarily accepted the existence of Solidarity, the regime justified its actions by invoking the "socialist" principles of conciliation and egalitarianism.

Gierek's ceremonies and rituals sustained another ambiguity as well. In constructing the historical discourse supporting the regime's claims to legitimacy, Gierek's propagandists oscillated between *continuity* and *discontinuity* in relating the regime to Polish history and culture. Early public ceremonies during the Stalin era were the best example of the *rites of discontinuity*. Their aim was to disrupt the existing national traditions and replace them with the newly invented traditions of Communism. Such decisions by the authorities as removing the crown from the White Eagle, or May Third and November Eleventh from the official ceremonial calendar are examples of this strategy. In the 1970s, the strategy became more complex. Whereas some ceremonies (anniversaries of the October Revolution) emphasized the new tradition (*discontinuity*), other ceremonial events (anniversaries of the People's Republic) fostered some elements of patriotism, indicating the regime's interest in creating an impression of *continuity*. Often a single ceremony emphasized both discontinuity and continuity, the internationalism and patriotism of May Day celebrations being a good example.

There seems to be a certain pattern in the application of the continuity/discontinuity principles in the Communist symbolic system. Following a Communist takeover (in Poland until 1949) relative pluralism is encouraged for a short time, and the symbolic system is based on a mixture of both principles. During the following "Stalinist" phase (Poland 1949–53 and in 1956), the pageant masters rely almost exclusively on the principle of discontinuity, and the ceremonial system becomes a "furious assault on non-ideological cognition" (Bloch 1985, 40). In the post-Stalinist periods two subphases can be distinguished. In crisis situations caused by an internal power struggle within the Party-state or by an increased level of agitation in society, only one of the principles is emphasized. During periods of relative stability, the ceremonial system is geared to the maintenance of the ambiguities of continuity/discontinuity and Communism/socialism.[13]

The main "hidden" function of the official ceremonial was to produce and maintain the ambiguity in the official discourse. This diminished the populace's ability to recognize this discourse for what it was (a socialist mask of Communist power) and contributed to the regime's survival. Therefore, the dominant function of the Church's and the opposition's ceremonies and demonstrations appears to have been the *destruction* of these politically expedient hybrids, thus also the elimination of a significant source of the regime's durability. These ceremonies, especially John Paul II's first visit to Poland, had all the attributes of *ceremonial revolutions,* since they aimed at reconstructing a public domain independent of the state, and since they (re)invented different traditions, invoked different values, and reached for different symbols than the state's ceremonial. In the case of nominally identical principles, such as patriotism or democracy, the state on the one hand and the Church and the opposition on the other offered contrasting interpretations and embedded these interpretations in diametrically different traditions and mythologies. By observing May Third, people invoked a tradition of democracy based on principles radically different from the official socialist principle of democratic centralism. When oppositional groups observed November Eleventh, they brought back to the public discourse a form of sovereignty very different from the limited sovereignty propagated by the Party-state and epito-

---

13. Such phases in the ceremonial system have been also detected in the Soviet Union (see Lane 1984). They parallel the phases of the entire sociopolitical system. For a discussion of phases of legitimacy, see Baczko (1984b, 107–8), Pakulski (1986), Lamentowicz (1983), or Heller (1982).

mized in the hybrid of "internationalism/patriotism." By developing the tradition of December 1970 and reclaiming May Day from the state in 1981, Gdańsk workers, students, and intellectuals demonstrated that the struggle for social justice (routine activity of the "socialist" state, according to the official discourse) can be undertaken outside of the "legality" as defined by the Party-state.

Catholicism

In the 1970s Catholicism emerged as the ultimate foundation of this counterhegemonic discourse. During the Solidarity period this process was sustained if not amplified through countless ceremonies of the new movement, which almost without exception included in their programs the Catholic mass. In a programmatic statement on the national culture, Solidarity's Congress asserted:

> Because it was Christianity that brought us into our wider motherland Europe, because for a thousand years Christianity has in a large degree been shaping the content of our culture, since in the most tragic moments of our nation it was the Church that was our main support, since our ethics are predominantly Christian, since, finally, Catholicism is the living faith of the majority of Poles, we deem it necessary that an honest and comprehensive presentation of the role of the Church in the history of Poland and of the world have an adequate place in national education.[14]

Nonetheless, religious discourse did not completely replace political discourse as it has in Iran, where "the relative success of the state in suppressing overt political opposition and critical discussion made religion the primary idiom of political protest" (Fisher 1980, 9).[15] Yet religious principles became (at least temporarily) standards of political legitimacy because of two factors: the specificity of the Catholic discourse in Poland, and a political mechanism, inadvertently triggered by the Communists.

Catholicism in the 1970s had four features that made it a powerful weapon in the confrontation with the Party-state. First, the Church's discourse was reinvigorated and its influence among the predominantly Roman Catholic populace increased. This must be attributed to the im-

14. I quote this document in a translation published in *World Affairs* 145 (Summer 1982):23.
15. A similar phenomenon has been noted by Eva Hunt in Mexico (1977).

pact of the Second Vatican Council, which reformed both the *methods of communication* with the faithful, first of all by introducing the vernacular into mass, and the *methods of pastoral work,* by urging the priests to forge closer links with their parishioners and intensify their work with families and young people. The pope's visit and his thirty-two sermons, delivered in a language that was closer to everyday speech than the Church's usual discourse, constituted the most important step in transforming Catholicism from an *externally authoritative* discourse to one that was *internally persuasive.*[16] Second, the Catholic discourse frequently invoked such popular ethical principles as the dignity of the human person[17] and the dignity of human work. Theoretically, these principles belonged to the axioms of Marxism-Leninism, but practically they were violated by the regime. Third, the Church's pronouncements, such as Sunday sermons or pastoral letters, were the only widely accessible cultural media through which such political principles as (liberal) democracy, pluralism, or full national sovereignty were consistently propounded. Fourth, the discourse of Polish Catholicism has developed symbolic means to anchor the political in the ethical and in the religious. For example, the Black Madonna of Częstochowa is the ultimate protectress of national survival and sovereignty; Saint Stanisław is the ultimate symbol of the dignity of human person (an individual) and endows the struggle for civic rights with the aura of sanctity.

A combination of these four features made Catholicism the most evident potential source of surrogate standards of political legitimacy in the society where all other institutional sources of ethical principles, outside of the family, lost credibility. The realization of this potential, a result of deliberate actions of the Church and the opposition, was further augmented by a political mechanism inadvertently set in motion by the Communist praxis of power. After the Communist takeover, democratic discourse was barred from the public domain. At the same time, the regime never lived up to the new set of standards (including, for instance, egalitarianism or social justice) it claimed as the foundation of its legitimacy. This led to corrosion of the political culture and a gradual atrophy of the domain of values directly pertinent to the issue of legitimacy. In the emerging political limbo any set of values could have become the ultimate source of

16. These are Bakhtin's terms. Authoritative discourse "demands that we acknowledge it, that we make it our own; it binds us, quite independent of any power it might have to persuade us internally; we encounter it with its authority already fused to it" (1981, 342). Persuasive discourse, in turn, "is . . . tightly interwoven with 'one's own word.' . . . The semantic structure of an internally persuasive discourse is not *finite,* it is *open;* . . . this discourse is able to reveal ever newer *ways to mean*" (1981, 345–46).

17. At the intellectual level, Polish Catholicism has been strongly influenced by the French personalism, especially that of Emmanuel Mounier and the "Esprit" circle.

standards for the political game. Not unexpectedly however, only Catholic Christianity could fill the vacuum; it was the only discourse that survived the Communist onslaught on Polish culture almost intact. In brief,
by waging an assault on the existing political culture, the Communist
regime inadvertently, I presume, made Catholicism the ultimate source of
value standards and, consequently, delegitimized its own power.[18]

All oppositional groups were united by a common recognition of the
ultimate authority of Catholicism as a source of moral values; they differed on the role the Catholic doctrine played in their programs. In the
1970s and 1980s, the unifying function of religion was absolutely dominant; programmatic differences were of secondary importance. This was
reversed in the early 1990s: the differences came to the fore of public life
and the unifying function of religion almost disappeared. During the
1991 parliamentary election campaign, the Church officially announced
its neutrality, but many bishops and parish priests openly supported select parties that emerged from Solidarity and the 1976–80 opposition. For
instance, the Democratic Union, the party founded by the intellectuals
who once belonged to both the secular and Christian social-democratic
circles (including the "left" wing of the KOR), received no endorsement;
the *Zjednoczenie Chrześcijańsko-Narodowe* (Christian-National Union, or
ZCHN), a Christian-democratic party founded, among others, by some
former members of the *Głos* circle (the "right" wing of the KOR), was
the prime beneficiary of the Church support.

In 1976–1980, the Catholic Church was a strong advocate of pluralism
as a non-negotiable principle of politics. In the early 1990s, many bishops
and priests became directly involved in the democratic political game; by
supporting only some post-Solidarity parties they suggested, even if inadvertently, that there existed "good" and "bad" Catholics. By dispensing
their "political blessing" so unevenly, the Church renounced its role as
neutral arbiter in the democratic politics game and became a political
player. Moreover, according to some observers, it betrayed its allegiance
to pluralism by doing so.

18. To present a complete picture of the success of Catholicism in Polish political and
social life I should complement this analysis of the cultural dimension of the phenomenon
by examining in detail the institutional (organizational) aspect of the state-Church confrontation. Such an undertaking is beyond the scope of this book. However, I would like to
mention Osa's (1989) article, a very interesting attempt to explain the Church's success
from a sociological perspective emphasizing "institutional history." She argues that the
Polish Roman Catholic Church developed a two-tiered structure within which local clergy
worked closely with the population and supported its demands and the Episcopate engaged
in political games with the regime. The former furnished the Church with an image of a
champion of peoples' causes and built its moral authority; the latter assured, through
pragmatic politics, its survival.

Oversymbolization and Mythologization of Solidarity's Discourse

Roman Catholic ethics and nationalism became the foremost sources of principles for counterhegemonic discourses, developed both by pre-Solidarity opposition and Solidarity itself.[19] As a result, particularly in the second half of 1981, the role of the pragmatic style of political problem-solving in the confrontation between the state and the populace decreased; the significance of both ethical considerations and assertions of identity increased. Some observers assessed this "oversymbolization" of Solidarity's discourse negatively, perceiving it as a source of escalation in the conflict between the state and society. But given the assumption that politics is always embedded in culture (or that they are intertwined in many more ways than we usually assume), one cannot expect "pragmatic" political behavior from political actors whose minds were shaped by the "non-pragmatic" discourses of the major producers of such discourses: Gierek's pageant masters on the one hand and the Catholic Church as well as some oppositional groups, on the other. It seems to me that the oversymbolization of Solidarity's discourse resulted from (1) the systemic (thus tragic) impossibility of Solidarity's political success (one of the major functions of this strong symbolization was to *compensate* for the government's refusal to allow Solidarity unrestricted participation in politics[20]), and (2) the oversymbolization of Polish political culture in the 1970s.

The oversymbolization of the Polish political culture, which can be traced back to the late 1970s, and even to the nineteenth century, was still present in the early 1990s. It resulted from three interrelated processes. First, the formation of Solidarity, a revolutionary political act, was the culmination of a basically cultural process. Oppositional groups or networks (such as the KPN, ROPCiO, RMP, or, to a lesser degree, KOR) were political by the very fact of their existence. First of all, however, they were *cultural* in the most formidable sense of this word: through them the politically disenfranchised attempted to redefine the surrounding sociopolitical world. As Ost (1990) astutely observes, Polish opposition in the 1970s was not strictly political (in the Western and commonly

---

19. Writing about the same period, Kula observes: "As time went by, the role of national (patriotic) values as a moral support during difficult moments increased" (Kula 1990, 285).

20. Baczko notes: "The movement that is forced to limit itself compensates in the symbolic domain for what—as it knows—cannot be achieved otherwise. Hence the will to the full expression in exactly this domain, to proceed in this domain further than it is possible in the world of 'real things,' to express in symbolic language—making use of its ambiguities—more than it is possible in the language of *realpolitik*" (1984b, 122).

accepted sense of the word); it was antipolitical, though on more careful examination one discovers—as Ost did—the existence of "the politics of anti-politics." Jeffrey Goldfarb describes this process as follows: "Sociologically, new and completely free cultural institutions are constituted. Such constitution is based on the cultural deconstruction and is the major project of independent politics. Post-totalitarian culture precedes post-totalitarian politics" (1989, 88).

Second, this oversymbolization was a result of the very specific social need lying at the foundation of Solidarity. Solidarity did not arise solely from a need to restore (liberal-democratic or any other) political culture but also from a need to revive Polish culture as a whole; not only from the need to find a permanent system of checks on the regime's performance or even to reassess its authority and legitimacy, but also from a need to reconsider afresh *collective identity* and the *ethical foundations* of the society. There is only one language suitable for such considerations: the language of symbols and myths.[21] For reasons elucidated earlier, in the Poland of the late 1970s and 1981 there existed only one such language: the language of religion and national mythology.

Third, the oversymbolization of Polish politics reflected a more general feature of all political cultures in eastern central Europe: the "overculturation of politics." Tamás Hofer observes, following István Bibó, that part of the misery of Eastern European nations is "due to the inadequacy of the political institutions in these states, or because their operations of the institutions are hindered, the social and political questions of nationhood are transposed into the cultural sphere, which is good neither for politics nor for culture" (1990, 40).[22]

The most significant aspect of the political culture's oversymbolization was a dramatically polarized vision of the social world (good/we/ Solidarity versus bad/them/Communists)—one of the main sources of Solidarity's numerical strength and unity. However, as Staniszkis points out, in 1981 there was a growing gap between the "actual areas of conflict" and their portrayal in the public discourse. She claims that

> conflicts in day-to-day interactions and opinions concerning concrete problems tended to decrease (i.e., the power elite was becoming increasingly isolated), while at the same time both sides' depiction of the conflict (which provided a symbolic representa-

21. This wider dimension of the Solidarity movement escapes the attention of those analysts who concentrate exclusively on verbalized demands and neglect to analyze the "demands" expressed through images, symbols, and ceremonies.

22. He also points out that a similar "overvaluation of cultural matters" was reported for Germany by George L. Mosse (Hofer 1990, 41; Mosse 1975; Bibó 1991, 11–86).

tion of the situation in terms of each side's surreality) suggested that the conflict was intensifying. (1985–86, 75)

For Staniszkis, the oversymbolization (mythologization) of Solidarity (as the union and as the movement) indicated a lack of political wisdom, an inability to approach politics in pragmatic terms. At times she seems to see in this feature of Solidarity one of the principal reasons for its failure. Her argument is based on a counterfactual assumption that if the terms of the political confrontation had been more pragmatic and less "mythologized," the conflict could have been solved, or at least alleviated and the first period of Solidarity's legal existence (1980–81) would have lasted longer or perhaps the union/movement would have become a permanent element of the public-political landscape in Poland as early as in 1981. But no empirical evidence is available that shows that the Party-state was indeed ready to reach some modus vivendi with the new movement in the early 1980s had it not been for the excessive oversymbolization (mythologization or ideologization) of the conflict.[23]

Therefore, this oversymbolization and its related "fundamentalist mentality"—as it is often labeled by Staniszkis—of many Solidarity activists may have well been quite irrelevant in the political domain in 1981; it seems, however, to have been beneficial in other areas of social life and, perhaps, was instrumental in assuring Solidarity's underground survival in the 1980s.[24] Paradoxically, this type of mentality became dysfunctional in the early 1990s, after the collapse of Communism, when a more pragmatic political mind-set was needed in order to calm the heated political discussions and facilitate issue-oriented and problem-solving disputes and actions.

23. There is, however, strong evidence to the contrary, showing the Party-state's resolve to destroy Solidarity at the first convenient moment. See Kukliński (1987). Staniszkis is very critical of what she calls the "surreality" of the political discourse in Poland, resulting from the elevation of religious "fundamentalist" values to the role of ultimate standards of political behavior, authority, and legitimacy. It seems to me that this "symbolic radicalization" of Solidarity was caused (at least partially) by the fact that in 1981 Communists (both in Warsaw and Moscow) were not ready to grant Solidarity the role of a full-fledged political partner.

24. It is necessary to note, however, that a strong identification with Catholicism as the source of ethical and existential values and ultimate standards of political legitimacy did not mean that religion dominated politics absolutely. There is no doubt that during the Solidarity period religion was often employed by the newly created organizations as a means of putting political pressure on the authorities. This was most clearly demonstrated during the "registration crisis" of Rural Solidarity. Yet there were no significant voices calling for the creation of a Christian-democratic party and often negotiations with the government were conducted in a pragmatic "political" language.

The Significance and Specificity of Gdańsk

Why did the "Polish revolution of 1980" begin in Gdańsk? Prior to 1980, Gdańsk was the only place in Poland where all the oppositional groups and milieus cooperated closely with each other. Additionally, all the participants in these activities were exposed to independent public articulations of the workers' tradition of the struggle for social justice (the tradition of December 1970), patriotism (the tradition of November Eleventh), and democracy (the tradition of May Third). It was in Gdańsk, therefore, that the oppositional discourse, as it was known to the populace through its public manifestations, was more elaborated and multivocal than elsewhere; it was also there that the opposition was highly integrated. Those developments must have contributed to the speed and ease with which the initially economic and narrowly revindicative strike evolved into a movement for social and national renewal.

Confrontation of Discourses and the Legitimacy of the Regime

I assumed at the beginning of this book that the degree of legitimacy can be assessed by comparing the principles and values embedded in the official discourse propounded by the rulers with the principles and values of the counterhegemonic discourse developed by the ruled.

Contemporary social sciences, more than ever before, are concerned with the malleability of cultural forms, which are sometimes viewed as elastic enough to furnish the means of articulation for any constellation of interests. The title of Eric Hobsbawm and Terence Ranger's book *The Invention of Tradition* epitomizes this trend. However, several cultural anthropologists, including Marshall Sahlins (1981, 1985) and Sherry Ortner (1973, 1989), demonstrate the durability of cultural frameworks and their renewable relevance for politics. These different approaches are indeed complementary since they all deal with *the limits of malleability* of cultural forms, symbols, ceremonies, and rituals in political praxis, although from different perspectives.

In my analysis of the Polish scene in the 1970s I have discovered both durability, such as is found in the myth of Saint Stanisław propagated by the Catholic Church, and strong malleability, as is found in the official definitions of patriotism or sovereignty. In general, I have come to share Hobsbawm and Ranger's view that all traditions and values are con-

Table 6.   Strategies for the "Invention of Tradition"

Strategy	The State	The Church and the Opposition
Preservation		Sovereignty
		(Christian) patriotism
		(Liberal) democracy
		Civil rights
		European and Christian roots of Polish culture
Remodeling	Sovereignty (socialism = inter- nationalism)	Catholicism (post–Vatican II)
	Patriotism (socialist)	(Non-Communist, demo- cratic) socialism
	Socialism/Communism	
	Democratic centralism	
Rejection	God, idealism	Materialism
	Christian and "neutral" patrio- tism	Socialist patriotism
	(Bourgeois) democracy	

stantly "invented." But I have also concluded that there exist perceptible differences of intensity, of degree or, perhaps even of kind, between various types of "inventions," and they are all worth noting.

A good typology of such "inventions" should start with the articulation of the extreme points of the continuum of all possible "inventions." On the one extreme one finds the strategy of *complete replacement* of existing traditions, customs, rituals, and symbols. The reigning principle here is *discontinuity*. At the other extreme one finds the strategy of *perfect preservation* based on the principle of *continuity*. All empirical cases of the social transmission of cultural forms (traditions) fall somewhere between these extremes. The range of strategies close to the pole of complete replacement (emphasizing the principle of discontinuity) can be called *rejection;* the range close to the pole of perfect preservation (emphasizing the principle of continuity) can be called *preservation*. The middle range of strategies combining both principles can be labeled *remodeling*. Table 6 illustrates the application of this typology to the Polish situation.

Polish Communists did not employ the strategy of preservation in their approach to the reservoir of national traditions, symbols, and values. I am, therefore, reluctant to call any aspect of their claimed legitimacy traditional. The "traditional" values incorporated in the official discourse, such as patriotism and sovereignty, were remodeled, not just preserved.[25] The table also shows that the state, more often than the Church, resorted to the strategy of rejecting "old" elements of the national culture; the Church more often chose to be silent on those aspects of the Communist discourse it did not approve of.[26] The Church appears also to be more conservative and noninventive when compared with the Communist state.

The repudiation of the strategy of preservation by the Polish Communists indicates that they realized that the application of this strategy would not be credible in their case.[27] From 1944 until 1989 they could not simply claim, for example, that they subscribed to the principle of democracy after they had rejected all opportunities to test their legitimacy in democratic elections. Yet, aware of the esteem in which this principle was held as a standard of legitimacy, they were not willing to reject it altogether; hence they formulated the concept of democratic centralism, or to be more precise borrowed it from the Soviet Union. During the Gierek years democratic centralism was a popular theme not only in official rhetoric but also in the public ceremonies of the Party-state.

There seem to have been two reasons why, with the exception of the Stalinist phase, the Communists chose remodeling as their main strategy of "tradition building." First, in order to be consistent with their own mythology in which they portrayed themselves as the "revolutionary force," they could not rely on a strategy of preservation. Second, they could not rely exclusively on a strategy of rejection, for they were well aware of the minimal appeal of their "revolutionary principle of legitimacy." Instead, the Communists employed this strategy only in dealing with discourse that would undermine their legitimacy, that is the Christian doctrine. Given the initial low popularity of the regime and the logic of its discourse, remodeling the national culture was indeed the most

25. The Soviet rulers, for example, in their quest for legitimacy have often resorted to historical tradition(s), prompting some authors to conclude that the Soviet Union was an instance of Weberian traditional authority. It seems to me, however, that in the "invention" of these "traditions" the emphasis was put on *discontinuity;* these traditions were after all embedded in the new mythological framework of Marxism-Leninism. I would reserve the category of traditional legitimacy only for those "traditions" in whose construction *continuity* is dominant.

26. The Church has been often criticized for placing too strong an emphasis on the strategy of nonconfrontation.

27. This observation brings back a question of the malleability of cultural forms. It is clear that the number of convincing matches between cultural forms and political interests is limited. There are combinations that are never tried because of the expected lack of credibility. Some of the more risky combinations are, however, sometimes explored by political adventurers, who usually suffer public ridicule and diminished authority as a result. The Polish state's attempt to portray John Paul II as a product of "his socialist Motherland" is a case in point.

viable strategy for claiming legitimacy. By contrast, the Church's and the opposition's reliance on the preservation of "old traditions" in their public presentation of counterclaims to legitimacy indicates their confidence that they and the rest of society shared the same values.

My analysis of the confrontation between the official discourse of the Party-state and the counterhegemonic discourses of the Catholic Church and the opposition, and the impact of this confrontation on the regime's legitimacy, is recapitulated in Table 7.

This analysis of the state's, the Church's, and the opposition's discourses (primarily public ceremonies), complemented by empirical evidence and theoretical generalizations submitted by the Polish sociologists (for the overview of these works, see Mason 1985), reveals *twelve* principles at play in the confrontation between these discourses. These I have listed in column 1. In the second and third columns I identify the version or variant of a given principle subscribed to by the main political actors. Democracy, for example, figured in the state's discourse as *democratic centralism,* in the discourse of the Church and the opposition as *liberal democracy.* Finally, the fourth column contains an assessment of the regime's legitimacy in 1981, in terms of the principles identified. The assessment is approximate and simplified; its results are given in only two degrees (low-high). I indicate in the table the public confusion caused by the ambiguous articulation of "socialism" (and, to a degree, "egalitarianism") in the official discourse, which had a profound impact on the popular perception of the regime and its legitimacy. Since such themes as "egalitarianism," "pluralism," and "strong state" did not become subjects of systematic public (that is, ceremonial) elaboration by all the actors, it is difficult to assess their impact on the regime's legitimacy. Solidarity emphasized in its declarations that pluralism was one of its most cherished values, but this was not brought out in the ceremonial. Egalitarianism was one of the most popular values in the Polish society, but again did not find symbolic expression in public ceremonies and rituals. The state emphasized the principle of the "strong state." Solidarity, however, although it often stressed (ceremonially also) its attachment to democracy—a potential counterbalance to such an ideal—never clearly challenged the Party-state in this respect. There is evidence that the tradition of a "strong state" and related authoritarianism are strongly entrenched in the popular consciousness. Hence it is plausible to assume that by propagating the idea of "strong state" the regime gained some (actual) legitimacy.[28]

28. Andrzej Kamiński points out this paradox of Polish political culture; the attachment to the value of democracy and a particular intoxication with the ideal of the strong state. Sociological studies confirm a high degree of authoritarianism in Polish society.

Table 7. Twelve principles and the legitimacy of the regime

Principle, Value, Syndrome, or Tradition	Political Actors and Versions		Regime's Legitimacy
	Opposition, Church	State	
1. National identity	Christian patriotism	Socialist patriotism	Low
2. Democracy	Liberal	Socialist (democratic centralism)	Low
3. Sovereignty, independence	Autonomously defined even if limited	Internationalism	Low
4. Socialism	Independent socialism; social democracy	Communism/socialism	Confusion to low
5. Social justice	Tradition of December 1970	Official welfare state	Low
6. Ethics, dignity	Based on Christianity	Based on Marxism-Leninism	Low
7. Egalitarianism	Not emphasized	Strongly emphasized	Confusion to low
8. Civil rights	Strongly emphasized	De-emphasized	Low
9. Pluralism	Emphasized	De-emphasized	Low
10. Religion	Strongly emphasized	Rejected	Low
11. European heritage	Emphasized	De-emphasized	Low
12. Strong state	Not emphasized	Strongly emphasized	High?

Since the creation of the Polish People's Republic the national identity had been formulated in different terms by the Party-state on the one hand and the society, the Church, and later the organized opposition on the other. The former developed the concept of *socialist patriotism* and propagated the tradition of Piast Poland. The latter relied on the concept of Christian patriotism (or just patriotism) and referred to the tradition of Jagiellonian Poland. A similar schizophrenic split could be detected in the public exposition of other values and traditions relevant for political legitimacy, such as democracy (democratic centralism vs. liberal democracy), independence (internationalism vs. national sovereignty), socialism (Communism/socialism vs. democratic and/or Christian socialism), social justice (the tradition of the *Komunistyczna Partia Polski* [Polish Communist Party, or KPP], the SDKPiL, or the PPS-Lewica vs. that of "December 1970"), or even ethical systems (socialist ethics vs. Christian ethics).

This confrontation involved public presentations of claims to political legitimacy by the Party-state and counterclaims by the Church and independent groups of citizens. Out of the twelve principles listed in Table 7, only two, the ideal of the "strong state" and "socialism" (or as sociological studies revealed, a syndrome of four "socialist" principles, the welfare state, social justice, egalitarianism, and nationalization of the means of production), became parts of the society's system of values, hence producing some legitimacy for the state, which had publicly championed these principles. The remaining ten were espoused either by only one of the adversaries or by all of them but in different, often incompatible versions. But, as noted earlier, public realization of such incompatibility was delayed because of the ambiguity of the official discourse. This ambiguity was finally demystified during the pope's visit and the Solidarity period, when most of the public laid to rest any doubts that remained concerning the incompatibility of its vision of *a just social system* with that of the official Communism/socialism.

The existence of two incompatible public discourses based on separate sets of principles within the public space of the Polish People's Republic of the late 1970s can be interpreted in two ways. One can take a restrained position, concluding that the available evidence demonstrates only that in the second half of the 1970s, as the Church and the opposition developed alternative political discourse(s), did the Party-state's legitimacy gradually disappear, regardless of what it was at the beginning of the decade. And only if it were possible to prove that Polish society (or at least its majority) subscribed to the counterhegemonic, "non-Communist" principles throughout the whole period since 1944, could one conclude that the Communist/socialist regime (the Party-state, the subsequent authorities, and so on) was constantly illegitimate. However, it is not possible for two reasons. First, throughout most of this period the state's repressive policies did not allow any public manifestation of an antihegemonic system of values; ergo, the data needed to prove this point are not available. Second, only in the 1980s did survey studies on the values system of Polish society (my complementary source of information) examine politically hot subjects such as various interpretations of the term "socialism" or the regime's legitimacy.

There are, however, *two* compelling reasons to conclude that the Polish People's Republic was an illegitimate political entity throughout its existence, despite infrequent public manifestations of counterhegemonic principles before 1976 (see also Rychard 1987b). First, the enormously powerful eruption of public attachment to "unofficial" or "independent" symbols, principles, and traditions during the Solidarity period and afterward is hardly explainable if we assume that they were all newly invented. It would be hard "to invent" so much, on such a scale, in such a short period of time. Second, as my analysis of various strategies of "traditionalizing" the historical material demonstrated, the state relied heavily on remodeling and rejection (which indicates that it had realized its own initial illegitimacy), whereas both the Church and the opposition employed the strategy of preservation, presumably because they shared the genuine attachment of the populace to "old" traditions.

Confrontation of Discourses and the Regime's Survival, Fall, and Consolidation

The essence of Communist power (domination) is often thought to have been its pursuit of total control over an ever-increasing number of domains of social life. But, as Jan Gross perceptively observes, Communist power was not realized by expansion exclusively, but rather by denying power to other social agents. As he puts it, "Absolute power is produced by the incapacitation (i.e., by a process of reduction, not amplification) of the existing of potential *loci* of power in society which are independent from state-sponsored organizations" (1989, 209). One of the most important strategies of such incapacitation is the near-perfect saturation of the public domain with the official discourse (which thereby is posed to become the *public* hegemonic discourse), confining all independent thinking, visualizing, imagining, symbolizing, naming, classifying, and so on[29] to the private domain and, therefore, preventing the *public* articulation of counterhegemonic discourses.

I would insist (against Fehér, Heller, and Márkus 1983, 138; but in agreement with Scott 1985) that it is counterintuitive and confusing to claim that the existence of counterhegemonic discourse *privately* cultivated by a substantial segment of the populace, residing in countless forms and acts of everyday life, but revealing itself publicly *only* (or usually) in crises, is not enough in itself to render political regimes illegitimate. Nonetheless, it seems that such *private counterhegemony,* which renders the regime against which it is articulated illegitimate, is irrelevant as far as this regime's survival or collapse is concerned. In other words, an illegitimate regime can survive for quite some time, as long as this "illegitimacy" is expressed and cultivated only in the private discourses of the citizens.

But as soon as the private, counterhegemonic discourse emerges from "internal exile" and becomes public, its social function changes. The public expression and articulation of counterhegemonic attitudes and beliefs, that is, the formation of the *public counterhegemony,* has a significant impact on the process of the regime's demise and the shape of the sociopolitical order that emerges afterwards. I agree with Adam Przeworski, that "one cannot maintain that withdrawal of legitimacy is a sufficient cause for a regime collapse" (1986, 51). But it seems to me that the emergence and crystallization of public counterhegemony and the subsequent withdrawal of legitimacy, occurring well before the actual collapse, have a threefold impact on the process of transition from the "old" to the "new" regime.

First, the early development of a counterhegemonic discourse prepares public consciousness for a revolution in such a way that once a precipitating factor does occur, large numbers of people mobilize in a short time and form an organization with relative ease. Hence, the pioneering character of Solidarity.

Second, the prolonged existence of a counterhegemonic discourse, cultivated by a large number of people—as was the case of Poland from 1976 through 1989—allows some reformers within the "old" regime to adapt to the idea that an alternate cultural and political order is possible and even necessary. This prepares them for a bloodless and gradual transfer of power. Hence, the peaceful tenor of Solidarity's revolution.

29. Such a phenomenon can be also detected in Western democracies (see Lukes 1974; Edelman 1971, 1988; Gaventa 1980), but in the Communist states, because of the preventive censorship and the near-perfect state monopoly of the media, it becomes one of the principal features of social life.

Third, a relatively long period of maturation allows the counter-hegemonic discourse to achieve a high level of elaboration. In the case of those discourses which are based on religious/ethical and nationalistic principles, such elaboration usually manifests itself in a strongly polarized (mythologized) vision of the social world (good "we" versus bad "them"). Polarized discourses play a crucial role in mobilizing the populace during the early stages of transition, when dismantling the old regime is the task of the day.[30] But both the "masses" and the leadership, who view the world in terms of such discourses, tend to engage in "mythological-symbolic" politics even after the collapse of the old regime.[31] Hence, the volatile and oversymbolized character of the post-Communist and post-Solidarity politics in Poland.

During 1989–92, this oversymbolization of public discourses was easily discernible in political debates: these debates turned too often on the (mythologized) identities of political actors and too rarely on the issues, tasks, and problems at hand. This feature of Polish public life seems to be one of the reasons behind the slow development of interest-based politics.[32]

A brief look at Eastern Europe during 1989–92 corroborates these propositions. In Poland, the process of effectively delegitimizing Communist power—through the development of public counterhegemonic discourse—began in earnest in 1976; the cultural revolution preceded the political revolution by several years. In Hungary and Czechoslovakia the counterhegemonic discourses were well developed but audible and visible only to certain segments of their populations; in the German Democratic Republic and Bulgaria such discourses developed shortly before the revolutions and reached very small circles.[33] In Romania counterhegemonic discourses never developed. Consequently, the process of transition in Eastern Europe began in Poland; its first phase, that is, the demise of Communism, proceeded in an expedient fashion. In Hungary and Czechoslovakia, the dismantling of Communism occurred rapidly and was thorough.[34] In Bulgaria and Romania this process was slower,

30. I agree with Przeworski that it is indeed useful to "think of transition from authoritarian to a democratic system as consisting of two simultaneous but to some extent autonomous processes; a process of disintegration of the authoritarian regime, . . . and a process of emergence of democratic institutions" (1986, 56).

31. Staniszkis calls it "the overpolitization of the vision of social relations" (1989, 122).

32. "As long as the movement of renewal focuses on moral rebirth, it is not able to express any concrete sociopolitical interests; the less so the more it is able to increase the number of its supporters and enlarge its social base" (Narojek 1986, 96).

33. This is particularly true in the case of Bulgaria, where the oppositional groups did not really appear until 1989 (see Brown 1991, 191).

34. The situation of the German Democratic Republic is not representative; the enormous speed with which Communism unraveled there must be attributed first of all to the

in the latter it turned violent, and in both former (reformed) Communists were initially left in power.

The second stage of transition (building of the "new" order) proved to be difficult in all Eastern European countries. Yet in Poland, the most ethnically homogeneous Eastern European state, these difficulties were least expected. They were exacerbated by the chaotic and unpredictable transitory politics—the feature of the post-Communist public life whose partial roots can be traced back to the overheated (oversymbolized) tenor of the pre-Solidarity and Solidarity political culture.[35]

It should be also noted that the existence of well-developed counterhegemonic discourses in Poland had a crucial effect on the survival of Solidarity and other oppositional movements in the years 1981–89. They survived in the underground because of a variety of factors: the regime's unwillingness or inability to destroy the opposition, massive (though gradually dwindling) support of the populace, and the perseverance of its top leaders. Yet this list must include one more factor: the persistent oppositional ethos, revived and enhanced by the counterhegemonic discourses developed since 1976. Anti-Communist opposition in Poland was not limited to politics; it was an articulate and relatively (by comparison with other East European countries) well-established *public* counterhegemonic culture.

So, "Why did Solidarity happen in Poland and not elsewhere in Eastern Europe?" It did happen in Poland because, in addition to other factors, the organized opposition and the Catholic Church developed and publicly disseminated a counterhegemonic discourse that allowed the populace to challenge and ultimately reject the regime's claims to legitimacy. Those who created and/or subscribed to this discourse had at their disposal the symbolic tools (1) to define the nation's identity independently of the official, "Communist/socialist" idiom; (2) to reinvigorate the nation's oppositional ethos, born under the partitions in the nineteenth century; (3) to build bridges between the Christian worldview and ethics and the oppositional politics; (4) to challenge the

---

influence of the Federal Republic of Germany. Hungarian and Czechoslovak free elections in early 1990 indicated that the process of political emancipation from Communism in both countries was slightly ahead of the Polish developments (completely free parliamentary elections in Poland did not take place until 1991).

35. These unexpected troubles of the Polish transitory politics falsify Bruszt and Stark's hypothesis that "the shorter the first stage of the transition, the more protracted the second stage of economic transformation and democratic consolidation" (1991, 245). The first stage of transition in Poland was the longest (and deepest), but the second stage was no less protracted than elsewhere in Eastern Europe.

official history, which was commonly perceived as "false"; and (5) to return into public life a range of political principles (such as liberal democracy or freedom of speech and assembly) deemed "obsolete" by the regime. The essence of the Polish revolution was the fact that "post-totalitarian culture preceded post-totalitarian politics"—a conclusion I share with Goldfarb. The development of cultural polarization seems to have been a crucial step toward political pluralism and effective democratization. Moreover, partially due to its "cultural" genealogy this new emergent politics was, until 1990, "antipolitical," that is, "one that focused on civic activity within society rather than on policy outcomes within the state" (Ost 1990). Public demonstrations and ceremonies organized by the Roman Catholic Church and the organized opposition, through which society confronted the symbols of power with its own, independent symbolism, were one of the most important modes of this civic activity. Because such public and widely accessible counterhegemonic discourses never developed in Bulgaria or Romania, the opposition there was an elitist and exclusively *political,* not *cultural,* phenomenon.[36]

And the final conclusion. Conceptualizing Solidarity as an ascending cultural-political class that came into existence as a polarizing countercultural discourse *before* it became a powerful political force helps one to understand the impossibility of its long-term unity. Solidarity became such a formidable opponent of Communism because it managed to mobilize millions of people through a set of "apolitical" symbols and discourses. (They were apolitical in the sense that they were neither "left" nor "right"; neither authoritarian nor democratic. But they allowed the huge masses of people to win back their self-respect and dignity.)

At the same time, however, precisely due to the apolitical but over-symbolized tenor of its discourse, Solidarity never sorted out in an organized, rational fashion its internal political tensions, veiled by the strong attachment to emotionally potent symbols. Thus the symbolic, not political, unity of the class/movement, resulting primarily from the existence of the common enemy and the common cultural framework, began to crumble as soon as this enemy disappeared and the framework was revealed to have been built by people who were as different politically as they were similar symbolically. In 1990, divisions within Solidarity, ranging from personal animosities through deeper programmatic and organi-

---

36. As Gail Kligman puts it: "The difference between ten years and ten days—Poland and Romania—accentuates the very absence in Romania of any functioning of the basic kernels of civil society" (1990, 427).

zational differences, burst into the surface of the Polish political life with full force.

The Solidarity class/movement, united by a common cultural-political vision developed throughout the late 1970s, was remarkably monolithic for only a brief moment—in the late summer and fall of 1980. The cracks in this monolith had already appeared by early 1981. By 1992 it had disappeared almost without a trace.

APPENDIXES

APPENDIX I

Jasna Góra Vows of the Nation on 26 August 1956★

Great Mother of God-Man!
Mother of God, Virgin, Mary praised by Lord!
Queen of the World and Queen of Poland!

As the three centuries have passed since the joyous day when you became the Queen of Poland, thus we, the Children of the Polish Nation, blood of the blood of our Ancestors, stand again before You, full of the same feelings of love, fidelity, and hope that once motivated our Fathers.

We, the Polish Bishops and the Royal Priesthood, The People purchased with the Redeeming Blood of Your Son, come again to Your Throne, Mary, Mediatress of all Grace, Mother of Compassion and all Consolation.

We bring to Your immaculate feet all the centuries of our fidelity and to Christ's Church—the centuries of dedication to the grand mission of the nation, bathed in the water of Holy Baptism.

We lay ourselves and all we possess at Your Feet: our families, shrines, and households, land plots and shops, ploughs, hammers and pens, all efforts of our thought, vibrations and drives of will.

We stand before You full of gratitude that You were for us the Virgin Supportress at times of glory and at times of terrible defeats of so many deluges.

We stand before You full of penitence, aware of our guilt that as of yet we have not fulfilled the vows and promises of our Fathers.

Look at us, Benevolent Lady, with the eye of Your Compassion and listen to the powerful voices, which in a unanimous choir leap toward You from the depths of the hearts of the multi-million troops of God's People devoted to You.

Queen of Poland! Today we renew the Vows of Our Ancestors and acknowledge You as Our Patroness and as the Queen of the Polish Nation.

We commend ourselves as well as all Polish lands and all Polish people into Your special protection and defense.

★Translated from Wyszyński (1962, 17–20).

We humbly *ask* for Your help and compassion in the struggle to preserve our fidelity to God, the Cross and the Gospel, the Holy Church and its Pastors, our holy Motherland, the Christian Avant-garde devoted to Your Immaculate Heart and the Heart of Your Son. Remember, Mother Virgin, before the Face of God, Your devoted Nation, which wishes to remain Your Kingdom, under the protection of the Best Father of all nations on the Earth.

We promise to do everything within our power to make Poland the true kingdom of Yours and Your Son, completely surrendered to Your domination in our personal, family, national, and social lives.

The people recite: Queen of Poland, we promise! *Mother of Godly Grace!* We promise to guard in every Polish soul *the gift of grace* as the source of Godly life.

We want each of us to live in the sanctifying grace and to be the shrine of God;

—the whole nation to live without the mortal sin;

—[the whole nation] to become the House of God and Heaven's Gate for the generations traveling through Polish lands—under the leadership of the Catholic Church—to the eternal Motherland.

The people recite: Queen of Poland, we promise!

The Holy Mother of God and Mother of Good Advice! We promise, with our eyes focused on the Manger of Bethlehem, that we will guard the awakening life.

We will struggle in the defense of every baby and each cradle as bravely as our Fathers struggled for the existence and freedom of the Nation, paying abundantly with our blood. We are ready to die rather than allow the death of innocents. The gift of life we will consider as the greatest Grace of the Father of all life and the nation's most precious treasure.

The people recite: Queen of Poland, we promise!

Mother of Christ and the Golden House! We promise to guard the inseparability of marriage, to defend the dignity of the woman, to keep guard at the threshold of the home's fire, so that the life of the Poles is safe beside it.

We promise to strengthen the Reign of Your Son Jesus Christ within the family, to defend the honor of God's name, to graft the spirit of the Gospel and love of You in the minds and hearts of children, to preserve the laws of God, the mores of Christianity and of the Motherland.

We promise to raise the young generation in fidelity to Christ, to guard them from godlessness and moral degradation and surround them with watchful familial care.

The people recite: Queen of Poland, we promise!

Mirror of justice! Putting our ear to the eternal desires of the Nation, we promise to follow the Sun of Justice, Christ, our God.

We promise to work hard so that all children of the Nation in our Motherland live in love and justice, in accord and peace, so that there is no hatred, coercion, or exploitation among us.

We promise to share willingly among us the fruits of the land and of our work so that under the roof of our household there are no people who are starving, homeless, or crying.

The people recite: Queen of Poland, we promise!

Victorious Lady of Jasna Góra! We promise to fight under Your banners the holiest and the hardest battle against our national vices.

We promise to wage the struggle against laziness and disdain, waste, drunkenness, and sexual license.

We promise to achieve virtues of fidelity, hard work, and thriftiness, self-sacrifice and mutual respect, love and social justice.

The people recite: Queen of Poland, we promise!

Queen of Poland! We renew the Vows of Our Fathers and promise with all our power that we will strengthen and widen in our hearts and in the Polish land Your glory and devotion to You, Mother of God, Virgin, worshiped in so many of our shrines, particularly in Your Jasna Góra Capital.

We give to You in this special act of love every Polish home and every Polish heart, so that our mouths continue to glorify You every day, particularly on Your holidays.

We promise to follow in the footsteps of Your virtues, Mother-Virgin and Faithful Maiden, and with Your help fulfill our promises.

The people recite: Queen of Poland, we promise!

In the realization of these promises we see *the living votive offering of the Nation,* more precious to You than granite and bronze statues. *Let them make us engage in the worthy preparation of our hearts for the Millennium of Polish Christianity.*

On the eve of the Millenium of Our Nation's Baptism *we want to remember* that You were the first to sing to the nations the hymn of liberation from slavery and sin; You were the first to defend the meek and the starving and gave the world the Son of Justice, Christ, our God.

We want to remember that You are the Mother of our Way, Truth, and Life, that in Your maternal Face we recognize with the utmost clarity Your Son, toward whom You lead us with Your unfailing hand.

Take our Vows, reinforce them in our hearts and offer them before the Face of God, United in the Holy Trinity. In Your hands we bestow our past and future, all our national and social life, the Church of Your Son and all we love in God.

Lead us through the Polish land, surrendered to You, to the Gates of the Eternal Motherland. And at the threshold of the new life You yourself reveal to us Christ, the blessed fruit of Your life. Amen.

APPENDIX II

The Pope's Itinerary During His First Visit to Poland (2–10 June 1979)*

June 2   Arrival in Warsaw; meeting with government and party leaders at Belweder Palace; pontifical mass at Victory Square.

June 3   Meeting with youth at a mass in St. Anna's Church, Warsaw; departure for Gniezno; address to the faithful of the Gniezno and Poznań metropolitan see; prayers at the tomb of St. Adalbert (Wojciech); mass and meeting with youth on Lech Hill.

June 4   Mass at the shrine of Jasna Góra, Częstochowa; meeting and speech.

June 5   Mass for nuns at Jasna Góra; participation in the 169th plenary conference of Polish bishops; mass and address to the faithful of Lower Silesia and Opole Silesia.

June 6   Mass for seminarians and novices at Jasna Góra; meeting with diocesan and monastic clergy; mass and address to workers of Upper Silesia and Dąbrowa Basin; departure for Kraków.

June 7   Visit to Kalwaria Zebrzydowska and Wadowice; visit to Oświęcim, the former Auschwitz concentration camp; mass and address at Birkenau [the former death camp—J.K.].

June 8   Mass and address at Nowy Targ; closing of the Kraków Synod; mass in honor of St. Stanisław; meeting at Skałka.

June 9   Visit to Holy Cross sanctuary in Mogiła; reception for foreign guests in Kraków.

June 10   Mass and address at the Kraków Błonia; departure for Rome.

APPENDIX III

Jan Lityński on the Pope's Visit†

Short are the moments in the history of the nation when the awareness of unity is stronger than all divisions and differences. Very seldom can one man speak in the name of the whole nation, expressing the thoughts and desires of all. And unhappy are the people who are standing on the

*Prepared by Kazimierz Zamorski (see Weydenthal and Zamorski 1979, 93).
†From "Greatness and Pettiness," *Robotnik*, 20 June 1979.

sideline of such events. Such moments constitute the basis of national life, are the source of its strength.

Alienation and fear are the fate of the Polish authorities. The nine days John Paul II spent with us fully proved it. They might have tried to share our joy, receive the Holy Father, recognize in him the spiritual and moral leader of the nation. They did not want to do that. They believed all the time that nothing happened, or at least pretended to believe so. "Constancy as a political ideal, pettiness as a means of its realization," as noted Jacek Woźniakowski [*Głos—Special Edition*]. Small people, tending to their own interests, not able to free themselves from the magical circles of the Newspeak and doublethink.

Everyone could see, hear, read how the welcome in Belweder[1] looked like, when Gierek talked about Brezhnev and the pope about God: a governor of the Kremlin and a governor of God.

John Paul II did not want a confrontation. With deep understanding and sincere compassion, he stretched out his hand and offered a chance:

"I include here also expressions of respect for all Honorable Representatives of the Authorities and also for each of them according to his position, according to the momentous responsibility which weighs on each of You in respect to history and Your own conscience."

They did not understand, they chose confrontation. How cowardly. [Confrontation] marked by limiting the number of broadcasts, by forcing the cameras into grotesque maneuvers, by humorous efforts of the propagandists. When after the first day of the visit the front pages of newspapers printed Gucwa's[2] speech passing over in short notices one of the most important facts in our history—the sermon of John Paul II—what else could we do but laugh.

They tried to hide millions of people participating in huge celebrations. From whom? From these millions, from themselves, from the whole world, or from the comrades from the East?

They knocked themselves out with their own hands. Pathetically silent was the ideology created without God and against God.

The Holy Father gave us great riches. Not only us—but also Czechs and Russians, Slovaks and Germans, Ukrainians and Bulgarians, Mexicans and Italians. All people and all nations.

We have to listen to his words very carefully. We must persistently realize his instructions.

"Can one push away from all of this? Can one say no? Can one reject Christ and all that he contributed to the history of Man?

1. Before World War II the presidential palace, in the 1970s the offices of the chairman of the State Council; often used for ceremonial occasions.
2. Stanisław Gucwa was the marshal of the Sejm.

"Of course one can. The man is free. But, and here comes a fundamental question, is one allowed to? In the name of what, is one 'allowed' to? What arguments of reason, what value of will and heart can you present to yourself and to your brother and to your compatriots to reject, to say no to all this we have lived with for one thousand years? To this which created the foundation and has always constituted it" (John Paul II, the mass at Kraków's Błonia).

Each of us was given a chance. And it depends on us whether we can create a community of conscious people, honorable and brave, believers and nonbelievers, people living in the truth. There is only one alternative: pettiness and obscurity.

The building of unity, as it is propagated by John Paul II, unity without hatred, unity toward freedom, is very difficult. But after these nine wonderful days it seems to be possible.

APPENDIX IV

Tadeusz Szczudłowski's Independence Day Speech, 1979*

POLES!

Always, but particularly today, our thoughts and hearts unite for Poland— for the Poland that was always a proud island of liberty amidst the deluge of absolutism and despotism, which shared the bread of freedom with other nations, in which betrayal was not politics, violence was not heroism, for which the state was not a purpose but the means; the purpose was man and his dignifying growth.

To that Poland [I say], you are always inside of us—arise again as the state!

During the years of enslavement Adam Mickiewicz's modern conception of the national psyche, which located the historical subject "Poland" not in the state but in the nation, and the battles fought by Poles under the most magnificent inscription ever to appear on combat banners: "For our and your freedom," ensured our existence in dignity and glory.

---

*An excerpt from Tadeusz Szczudłowski's speech delivered during the unofficial ceremony commemorating the sixty-first anniversary of Polish independence in 1918. The ceremony was held at the Jan III Sobieski's monument in Gdańsk on 11 November 1979.

Those works of the Polish genius did and still do constitute a signpost for us and all the nations that praise freedom and struggle for independence.

Those facts provide a sound ground allowing [us] to reject and condemn the opinions about Poland and the Poles expressed by Friedrich Engels in his letter to Karl Marx of 23 May 1851: "Dear Marx! . . . The longer I meditate on history the more clearly I can see that Poles are the nation doomed to destruction, which can be used as a tool as long as Russia will not be drawn into the flurry of agrarian revolution. From that point on Poland will have absolutely no raison d'être. Poles never inscribed themselves in history, except for brave and stupid brawls."

O King Jan III Sobieski, the defender of the whole European culture! Throw to his knees this scoundrel whose motherland you saved from destruction in the battle of Vienna, and yet he slyly tried to "throw you off your horse into the mud" and draw forever your nation into slavery.

Marx did not contradict Engels, Rosa Luxemburg based on these calumnies her whole anti-Polish and anti-independence ideology, played tactically by Lenin, and later realized by Hitler and Stalin. Contemporary fakers of our history attempt to present Poland as a "beloved double child" of the Soviet Union—born for the first time by Lenin and the October Revolution in 1918 and for the second time by Stalin and the July Manifesto of the *PKWN* [Polish Committee of the National Liberation, a Communist puppet government—J.K.] in 1944.

However, the statement of the Soviet and German governments of 28 September 1939, in which the liquidation of the Polish state is referred to as "the strong foundation for long-term peace in Eastern Europe," is covered with silence. The description of the September conquest of Poland, presented at the extraordinary meeting of the Supreme Council of the USSR on 31 October 1939 by Molotov is also classified. During this meeting Molotov stated: "A short attack of the German armies and then the Red Army sufficed so that nothing was left over after this malformed bastard of the Versailles Treaty."

In this context, the ceremonial and thanksgiving observances of the October Revolution by the authorities of the Polish People's Republic are simply spitting in the face of the Polish nation.

The falsehoods will not however conceal the facts—facts which are commonly known and which strongly indicate that we rightfully deserve independent existence and that we regained such existence by our own efforts sixty-one years ago.

In the fire of World War I three despotic monarchies: Russia, Prussia, and Austria, choking on the crimes they had committed against many nations, and particularly against Poland, were shaken. Under these circumstances the Polish nation, with its unprecedented love of freedom and independence, took arms and thanks to the sea of shed blood and tears—prevailed.

In this way the independent Polish state—the Second Republic—was born on 11 November 1918, after 123 years of terrible slavery.

The Catholic Church, the martial genius of Józef Piłsudski, and the diplomatic genius of Roman Dmowski played in this historical victory roles worthy of honor. Glory to them.

The Polish nation knows well what the words "freedom" and "independence" mean. Therefore nobody will be able to fill their content with fiction and falsehood.

We know that there was no place for the truly independent Poland on the pages of the Versailles Treaty; nor in Lenin's decree about the self-determination of the nations, nor in the Yalta agreements, nor in the decisions of the Potsdam Conference, nor in the Stalinist July Manifesto. There is also no room for the Polish independence in the current constitution of the Polish People's Republic, which holds the Polish nation in a double clinch; from the outside by the Soviet Union and from the inside by the totalitarian PZPR—the so-called leading force of the nation.

This is why we are going into the struggle again. We are going into the struggle, as always with the slogan "For our and your freedom." Following this idea and in the name of the common good *we turn to You Russians:* leave our Motherland voluntarily, leave also all other countries to which you were led in order to realize the insane Communist ideology, bringing to the world poverty and the vision of a constantly active volcano—and to you contempt, hatred, and the name of contemporary Huns.

Let the words Pope John Paul II be a warning for you as well: "One nation can never develop at the expense of another, at the expense of its subordination, conquest, oppression, at the expense of exploiting it, at the expense of its death . . ."

At the same time *we appeal to those Poles* who cooperate in the enslavement of the Polish nation: remember that you face the noble nation for which honor and morality are the essence of life. You have little time to come to your senses and denounce this treason—the name of usurpers . . . or collaborators is difficult to erase. . . .

APPENDIX V

Strike Slogans (Gdańsk, August 1980) (partial list)

I. Political (13)

    1. KOR—Young Polish Democracy.
    2. We fight for freedom and justice for all of Poland.

3. Freedom for political prisoners. (2)
4. Long live the free press.
5. We fight for justice for all of Poland.
6. Long live free Poland.
7. KSS KOR. (2)
8. Freedom of speech, religion, and press.
9. The man lives and lives free.
10. Justice for the whole Motherland.
11. Justice and equality for the whole nation.

II. Solidarity (14)

1. Let's hold up together.
2. The strike of Solidarity still continues. (4)
3. The people with you.
4. Thank you.
5. We continue our struggle.
6. We are with you—we hold on.
7. We with the people, the people with us. We—the shipyard workers—will not give in.
8. Long live the enterprises striking with us.
9. We, the shipyard workers, will not surrender, for the whole country is behind us.
10. Long live and strengthen the brotherhood of the working people.
11. Long live and strengthen the Solidarity of our nation.

III. Economic (6)

1. Give us bread.
2. Higher family subsidy.
3. Pay raises for everybody.
4. Eliminate commercial stores and prices.
5. We demand better supplies in the stores, less for abroad, more for the country.
6. More hospitals and daycare centers.

IV. Religious (4)

1. God with us.
2. Radio and TV for the Church.
3. [An icon of Mary with the inscription] Suffering Queen of Poland in Lichen.
4. [A picture of Jesus with the inscription] Jesus I trust you.

V. Free Trade Unions (4)

    1. Long live the *WZZ*. (2)
    2. *WZZ*
    3. Long live free trade unions and peace in the whole world.

VI. The Strike (3)

    1. Long live the Interfactory Strike Committee and its leader.
    2. The victory will be ours.
    3. Support the demands or you will not be paid.

VII. National/Patriotic (2)

    1. Remember you are Polish / The struggle is for Poland / My duty is to defend Her / She [Poland] is your rival. (2)

APPENDIX VI

A Chronology *

  966 Baptism of Prince Mieszko I, introduction of Latin Christianity to Poland.

1079 Execution of Saint Stanisław, bishop of Kraków.

1382 Foundation of the Paulinian Monastery on Jasna Góra in Częstochowa, soon to become the home of the Black Madonna.

1410 Battle of Grunwald, a major Polish victory over the Knights of the Teutonic Order.

1596 Union of Brest, the creation of Uniate Church.

1772 The first partition of Poland, between Russia, Prussia and Austria.

1791 Constitution of May Third.

1793 The second partition of Poland, between Russia and Prussia.

1794 The Kościuszko Uprising.

1795 The third partition of Poland, between Russia, Prussia and Austria.

1830 The November Uprising.

1863 The January Uprising.

1918 The rebirth of the Polish state.

---

*This is a revised and updated version of a chronology published in *World Affairs* 145 (Summer 1982):6–10.

1939 Ribbentrop-Molotov Pact between Nazi Germany and the Soviet Union, the German and Soviet attack on Poland, a new partition of Poland.

1944 Creation of a Polish Committee in the USSR, under Soviet control, to act as the government of Poland.

1945 Yalta Conference. Western powers agree to Soviet territorial and political gains in Poland.

1947 First elections in postwar Poland. Electoral tampering gives victory to Communists.

1956 Workers' uprising in Poznań. Army units called in. Demonstrators killed. March of Soviet forces toward Warsaw halted by agreement between top Soviet and Polish Communist party leaders. Gomułka becomes Polish party leader; liberalization in Poland proclaimed. Release of Cardinal Wyszyński after three years of house arrest.

1970 Workers' protests in Gdańsk, Szczecin, and Gdynia in response to food price increases. Main force used by army units. Workers killed. Gierek replaces Gomułka.

1976 Workers protesting against price increases are beaten by police. Students and intellectuals provide help to workers. Creation of the Workers' Defense Committee (KOR).

1977 The first issue of *Robotnik,* an underground newspaper for workers, is published.

1978 Unofficial committee established for the "Creation of Free Trade Unions" in Katowice. Police harassment of worker-activists ensues. Establishment in southern Poland of unofficial "Committee for Farmers' Self Defense." Election of Karol Cardinal Wojtyła from Kraków as Pope John Paul II.

1979 John Paul II visits Poland and is greeted by millions.

1980 July. Food prices increased. Strikes throughout Poland.

August. Interfactory Strike Committee (MKS) is formed in Gdańsk, where over two hundred factories are on strike. Negotiations begin between MKS, led by Lech Wałęsa, and the government commission led by Vice-Premier Jagielski. Agreement signed on the twenty-one demands, allowing for the first time independent and free trade unions, freedom of the press, and other fundamental rights.

September. Stanisław Kania replaces Edward Gierek as first secretary in a shakedown of the Communist party.

October. Court proceedings for the registration of the Independent and Self-Governing Trade Union, Solidarity, begin. Solidarity appeals to the Supreme Court.

November. Demonstrations by Solidarity and threats of strikes compel the Party and the Supreme Court to accept the union's appeal for registration.

December. Central Committee on the Polish United Workers Party (Polish Communist party) meets. Changes are made in the Political Bureau (Politburo). Former first secretary of the Party, Edward Gierek, is expelled from the Central Committee. Unveiling of the Gdańsk Monument, commemorating the workers killed by the regime in 1970.

1981 January. The government declares that the Polish loans repayable to the West at the end of 1980 amounted to $23 billion. It is the first time the extent of Poland's debt is officially made public. A Solidarity delegation, including Wałęsa, visits Italy and meets with Pope John Paul II, as well as with the three Italian trade union confederations.

February. General Wojciech Jaruzelski becomes prime minister of Poland after Jozef Pińkowski is forced to resign. Jaruzelski appeals to workers for ninety "quiet days" without strikes. In Moscow, the Twenty-Sixth Congress of the Communist Party of the Soviet Union convenes. Kania and Jaruzelski attend. The Soviet Union stridently criticizes Solidarity, and Brezhnev pledges the defense of all "socialist" countries.

March. In Bydgoszcz the militia brutally evacuate the municipal building where a sit-in has been staged by Solidarity members and peasants demanding the registration of Rural Solidarity. The leader of Bydgoszcz's Solidarity chapter is especially badly beaten. Joint maneuvers of the Warsaw Pact begin, called "Soyuz '81," which means "unity" in Russian. After several days of strike alert, Solidarity conducts a national four-hour warning strike. Four million stop work. It is the single largest general strike in the postwar period of any industrial nation and the first such strike in Poland. After several rounds of negotiations with the government the *Krajowa Komisja Pozozumiewawcza* (National Coordinating Commission, or KKP) calls off an unlimited general strike when the government promises to punish those responsible for the Bydgoszcz incident, to speed up talks on the general access to the mass media, and to register Rural Solidarity.

May. Registration of Rural Solidarity.

June. Stefan Cardinal Wyszyński, primate of Poland for over a quarter of a century, dies. Lech Wałęsa and Solidarity delegation attend International Labor Organization Congress where they receive a long standing ovation.

July. Joint Polish-Soviet maneuvers are conducted in Poland. Party Congress reelects Kania and Jaruzelski. The reconstituted Political Bureau includes three workers.

August. Prices for staples like bread are increased up to 400 percent. Detergents are rationed and the meat ration decreased. The food shortages provoke "hunger marches" in several cities.

September. The First National Congress of Solidarity opens in Gdańsk. Resolutions are adopted on the proposal for self-government, access to the media, promoting free trade unions in Soviet-bloc nations, etc. Joint maneuvers are again conducted in Poland. Over 100,000 troops are involved in the largest maneuvers by the Pact in the postwar period. General Jaruzelski joins other Warsaw Pact leaders observing the events. The second part of Solidarity Congress opens. After much discussion and criticism, the Congress adopts compromise resolution on self-government. Lech Wałęsa is reelected for a two-year term.

October. The PZPR Central Committee plenum meets. At the plenum, Stanisław Kania, who had been first secretary of the Party since 6 September 1980, resigns. Wojciech Jaruzelski, prime minister since February 1980 and defense minister since 1968, is now elected to replace Kania as first secretary. It is the first time that all three posts are held by the same person. The Soviet Union welcomes the ascension of Jaruzelski. Millions of workers take part in a one-hour warning strike over the government's seeking a strike ban and "emergency powers," over its unwillingness to negotiate seriously over the economic crisis, and over its persistent denial of access to the mass media for Solidarity. *Pravda* publishes a message to Brezhnev from Jaruzelski, affirming the principles of Marxism-Leninism as a foundation for repulsing "counterrevolutionary forces."

November. Poland applies for admission to the International Monetary Fund. Student strikes spread throughout Poland, involving two-thirds of the universities and 55,000 students. Students and professors demand the removal of the president of the Radom Engineering School, who was appointed by the Ministry of Higher Education, contrary to agreements that guaranteed the universities' right to choose their own officials. They also demand greater academic and cultural freedom.

December 12. During the night, security forces round up Solidarity leaders, including most of the union's National Commission, which was meeting in Gdańsk, as well as regional leaders and Solidarity advisors. The union headquarters in Gdańsk, Warsaw, and elsewhere are raided. Troop movements take place throughout Poland. Telex and telephone communications are out.

December 13. At 6:00 A.M. Polish television and radio broadcast General Jaruzelski's speech announcing the imposition of a "state of war" and the creation of the Military Council for National Salvation (WRON). The decree is repeated all day and posted in public places throughout Poland. Thousands of activists interned or/and imprisoned.

1982 October. New union law allows the authorities to disband Solidarity. Solidarity continues to exist as a network of underground organizations (with the TKK—Provisional Coordinating Commission— playing the role of the central coordinator), publishing houses, and countless periodicals.

November. Wałęsa released from internment.

December. Martial law suspended.

1983 June. John Paul II's second visit to Poland. His support for the ideals of Solidarity is clear and loud. During papal masses people demonstrate their support for Solidarity with banners, graffiti, and songs.

July. Martial law is repealed but many repressive measures remain intact.

1984 June. General amnesty—many interned and imprisoned. Some Solidarity activists are released.

October. Father Jerzy Popiełuszko, an outspoken and very popular supporter of Solidarity, is murdered by members of the security apparatus.

1986 July. Limited amnesty. The Provisional Council is created—the first official body of Solidarity to emerge from underground.

1987 June. The pope's third visit to Poland.

1988 August. Strikes in several major industrial centers. The restoration of Solidarity is a frequent demand. Interior minister, Czesław Kiszczak proposes "round table" talks with the opposition.

December. Formation of the Solidarity Citizens Committee—an advisory board to Lech Wałęsa as chairman of Solidarity, composed of over one hundred prominent intellectuals and public figures.

1989 February. The "round table" talks between the government and the opposition begin.

April. As a result of the talks an agreement between the government and the opposition is signed. It guarantees that 25 percent of the seats in the Sejm (lower house) and 100 percent of the seats in the Senate will be contested in open elections.

June. Solidarity candidates win all 161 seats they were allowed to compete for in the Sejm and 99 of the 100 seats in the Senate.

August. The PZPR's effort to form a government fails. Tadeusz Mazowiecki, a prominent Solidarity leader, forms the first non-Communist government in Eastern Europe since the 1940s. Communists retain some portfolios.

1990 December. Wałęsa elected president of the Polish Republic.

BIBLIOGRAPHY

Adam, Heribert
    1984   "South Africa's Search for Legitimacy." *Telos* 59: 45–68.
Adamczuk, Lucjan, and Witold Zdaniewicz, eds.
    1991   *Kościół Katolicki w Polsce 1918–1990. Rocznik Statystyczny*. Warsaw: Główny Urząd Statystyczny, Zakład Socjologii Religii SAK.
Adamski, Władysław
    1982   "Structural and Generational Aspects of a Social Conflict." In *Sisyphus: Sociological Studies,* vol. 3, *Crises and Conflicts: The Case of Poland 1980–81*. Warsaw: PWN.
Aguirre, B. E.
    1984   "The Conventionalization of Collective Behavior in Cuba." *American Journal of Sociology* 90(3): 541–66.
Almond, Gabriel, and Sidney Verba, eds.
    1980   *The Civic Culture Revisited*. Boston: Little, Brown.
Anderson, Benedict
    1983   *Imagined Communities: Reflections on the Origin and Spread of Nationalism*. London: Verso.
Arato, Andrew
    1981   "Civil Society vs. the State: Poland, 1980–81." *Telos* 47: 23–47.
    1981–82 "Empire vs. Civil Society: Poland, 1981–82." *Telos* 50: 19–48.
    1982   "Critical Sociology and Authoritarian State Socialism." In Jürgen Habermas, *Critical Debates,* ed. D.J.A. Held and J. P. Thompson. London: Macmillan.
Arens, William and Ivan Karp
    1989   *Creativity of Power: Cosmology and Action in African Societies*. Washington, D.C.: Smithsonian Institution Press.
Aron, Raymond
    1978   "Macht, Power, Puissance: Democratic Prose or Demoniac Poetry." In Raymond Aron, *Politics and History: Selected Essays,* collected, translated, and edited by Miriam Berheim Conant. New York: Free Press.
Aronoff, Myron J.
    1979   "Ritual in Consensual Power Relations: The Israel Labor Party." In *Political Anthropology: The State of the Art,* ed. S. Lee Seaton and Henri J.M. Claessen. The Hague: Mouton.
Ash, Timothy Garton
    1983   *The Polish Revolution: Solidarity*. New York: Charles Scribner's Sons.
    1991   "Poland After Solidarity." *The New York Review of Books,* 13 June 1991.
Baczko, Bronisław
    1984a   *Les Imaginaires Sociaux*. Paris: Payot.
    1984b   "Polska Solidarności—Pamięć eksplodująca" (Poland of Solidarity—Exploding memory). *Krytyka* 21: 103–30.

Bakhtin, M. M.
1981   *The Dialogic Imagination*. Edited by Michael Holquist. Translated by Caryl Emerson and Michael Holquist. Austin: University of Texas Press.
Bakuniak, Grzegorz
1983   "My—'Solidarność'—nowy związek we własnych oczach" (We— "Solidarity"—the new union in its own eyes). In *Polacy-Jesień 80* (Poles—Fall 80), ed. Ireneusz Krzemiński et al. Warsaw: Warsaw University Press.
Bakuniak, Grzegorz, and Krzysztof Nowak
1984   "'Proces kształtowania się świadomości zbiorowej w latach 1976– 1980" (The development of the collective consciousness in 1976– 1981). In *Społeczeństwo polskie czasu kryzysu* (Polish society at the time of crisis), ed. Stefan Nowak. Warsaw: Warsaw University Press.
Barańczak, Stanisław
1983   *Czytelnik ubezwłasnowolniony: Perswazja w masowej kulturze literackiej PRL* (The incapacitated reader: Persuasion in the mass literary culture of People's Poland). Paris: Libella.
Barthes, Roland
1982   *A Barthes Reader*. Edited by Susan Sontag. New York: Hill & Wang.
Bauman, Zygmunt
1983   "Bez precedensu" (Without precedent). *Aneks* 32: 21–43.
Bednarczuk, Leszek
1985   "Nowo-mowa. Zarys problematyki badawczej" (Newspeak. An outline of the problem). In *Nowo-mowa. Materiały z sesji naukowej poświęconej problemom współczesnego języka polskiego odbytej na UJ w dniach 16 i 17 stycznia 1981* (Newspeak. Materials from a conference on the problems of the contemporary Polish language held at Jagiellonian University on 16 and 17 January 1981). London: Polonia.
Belch, Stanisław
1965   "W poszukiwaniu przyczyn śmierci biskupa krakowskiego Stanisława" (Searching for the causes of the death of Kraków's Bishop Stanisław). In *Prace historyczne. Tom I* (Historical works. Volume 1). London: Katolicki Osrodek Wydawniczy "Veritas."
Berger, Peter L., and Thomas Luckmann
1966   *The Social Construction of Reality: A Treatise in the Sociology of Knowledge*. Harmondsworth: Penguin.
Berki, R. N.
1982   "The State, Marxism, and Political Legitimation." In *Political Legitimation in Communist States*, ed. T. H. Rigby and Ferenc Feher. New York: St. Martin's Press.
Bernhard, Michael
1993   *Origins of Democratization in Poland: Workers, Intellectuals, and Oppositional Politics, 1976–1980*. New York: Columbia University Press.
Bibó, István
1991   *Democracy, Revolution, Self-Determination: Selected Writings*. Edited by András Boros-Kazai. Boulder, Colo.: Atlantic Research & Publications, Highland Lakes. Dist. New York: Columbia University Press.

Bielasiak, Jack, ed.
1981   *Poland Today: The State of the Republic.* Compiled by the "Experi-
          ence and the Future" Discussion Group. With an introduction by
          Jack Bielasiak. New York: M. E. Sharpe.
1983   "The Party: Permanent Crisis." In *Poland: Genesis of a Revolution,*
          ed. Abraham Brumberg. New York: Vintage Books.
Bieńkowski, Władysław
1971   *Socjologia klęski* (A sociology of failure). Paris: Institut Littéraire.
Bingen, Dieter
1984   "The Catholic Church as a Political Actor." In *Polish Politics: The
          Edge of the Abyss,* ed. Jack Bielasiak and Maurice D. Simon. New
          York: Praeger.
Binns, Christopher
1979   "The Changing Face of Power: Revolution and Accommodation in
          the Development of the Soviet Ceremonial System: Part I." *Man*
          14(4): 585–606.
1980   "The Changing Face of Power: Revolution and Accommodation in
          the Development of the Soviet Ceremonial System: Part II." *Man*
          15(1): 170–87.
Błażyński, George
1979   *Flashpoint Poland.* New York: Pergamon Press.
Bliss Lane, Arthur
1961   *I Saw Poland Betrayed* (1948). Boston: Western Islands.
Bloch, Maurice
1974   "Symbols, Song, Dance, and Features of Articulation: Is Religion
          an Extreme Form of Traditional Authority?" *Archives Européennes de
          Sociologie* 15:55–81.
1985   "From Cognition to Ideology." In *Power and Knowledge: Anthropo-
          logical and Sociological Approaches,* ed. Richard Fardon. Edinburgh:
          Scottish Academic Press.
Blok, Anton
1975   *The Mafia of a Sicilian Village, 1860–1960: A Study of Violent Peasant
          Entrepreneurs.* Oxford: Basil Blackwell.
Bocock, Robert
1974   *Ritual in Industrial Society.* London: George Allen & Unwin.
Bojarski, Władysław, et al.
1981   *Kryzys gospodarki* (The crisis of the economy). Warsaw.
Boros, Grzegorz
1980   *Matka Boska Strajkowa* (The strike's Mother of God). *Punkt* 12:
          269–79.
Brown, J. F.
1991   *Surge to Freedom: The End of Communist Rule in Eastern Europe.*
          Durham: Duke University Press.
Brus, Włodzimierz
1983   "Economics and Politics: The Fatal Link." In *Poland: Genesis of a
          Revolution,* ed. Abraham Brumberg. New York: Vintage Books.
Bruszt, Laszlo, and David Stark
1991   "Remaking the Political Field in Hungary: From the Politics of
          Confrontation to the Politics of Competition." *Journal of Interna-
          tional Affairs* 45(1): 201–45.

Buczek, Daniel S.
1979   "Saint Stanisław, Bishop and Martyr: Fact and Legend." In *Saint Stanisław, Bishop of Kraków.* Santa Barbara, Calif.: Saint Stanisław Publications Committee.
Bunce, Valerie
n.d.   "Why Some Rebel and Others Comply: The Polish Crisis of 1980– 81, Eastern Europe and the Theories of Revolution."
Bystroń, Stanisław
1947   *Etnografia Polski* (An Ethnography of Poland). Poznań: Czytelnik.
Cannadine, David
1992   "Cutting Classes." *The New York Review of Books* 17 December 1992.
Celt, Ewa
1979   "Cracow's Saint Stanisław: The Story Behind the Story." Radio Broadcast 112 (Poland), *Radio Free Europe,* 16 May.
1980   "The Church." In *August 1980: The Strikes in Poland,* ed. William F. Robinson. Munich: Radio Free Europe Research.
Chrypiński, Vincent C.
1984   "Church and nationality in Postwar Poland." In *Religion and Nationalism in Soviet and East European Politics,* ed. Pedro Ramet. Durham: Duke University Press.
Chudziński, Edward
1982   "Pod Wawelem i gdzie indziej" (Under the Wawel and elswhere). In *Teatr STU* (Theater STU), ed. Edward Chudziński and Tadeusz Nyczek. Warsaw: MAW.
Chudziński, Edward, and Tadeusz Nyczek, eds.
1982   *Teatr STU* (Theater STU). Warsaw: MAW.
Chyży, Andrzej
n.d.   *Proces 12. Kraków. 3 maja 1946* (The trial of the 12. Kraków. 3 May 1946). Biblioteka Polityki Polskiej. Vol. 14. [An underground publication.]
Ciołek, Maciej T., Jacek Olędzki, and Anna Zadrożyńska
1976   *Wyrzeczysko. O świętowaniu w Polsce* (On celebrating in Poland). Warsaw: LSW.
Ciupak, Edward
1965   *Kult religijny i jego podłoże społeczne* (The religious cult and its social background). Warsaw: LSW.
Cobb, Roger W., and Charles D. Elder
1983   *The Political Uses of Symbols.* New York: Longman.
Cohen, Abner
1979   "Political Symbolism." *Annual Review of Anthropology* 8:87–113.
1981   *The Politics of Elite Culture.* Berkeley and Los Angeles: University of California Press.
Curry, Jane Leftwich, ed.
1984   *The Black Book of Polish Censorship.* Translated and edited by Jane Leftwich Curry. New York: Random House. (This is the English translation of *Czarna Księga Cenzury PRL* 1977).
Cviic, Christopher
1983   "The Church." In *Poland: Genesis of a Revolution,* ed. Abraham Brumberg. New York: Vintage Books.

Czarna Księga Cenzury PRL
1977   2 Vols. London: Aneks. (This work was translated into English by
            J. L. Curry [1984].)
Desan, Suzanne
1989   "Crowds, Community, and Ritual in the Work of E. P. Thompson
            and Natalie Davis." In *The New Cultural History*, ed. Lynn Hunt.
            Berkeley and Los Angeles: University of California Press.
Dictionary of Anthropology
1987   Charlotte Seymour-Smith, general editor. Boston: G. K. Hall.
Di Palma, Giuseppe
1991   "Legitimation from the Top to Civil Society: Politico-Cultural
            Change in Eastern Europe." *World Politics* 44, no. 1: 49–80.
Dissent in Poland
1977   *Reports and Documents in Translation, December 1975–July 1977.* Lon-
            don: Association of Polish Students and Graduates in Exile.
Dittmer, Lowell
1977   "Political Culture and Political Symbolism: Toward a Theoretical
            Synthesis." *World Politics* 29: 552–83.
Douglas, Mary
1966   *Purity and Danger: An Analysis of Concepts of Pollution and Taboo.*
            London: Routledge & Kegan Paul.
1973   *Natural Symbols: Explorations in Cosmology.* Harmondsworth: Peli-
            can Books.
Dziewanowski, Kazimierz
1977   *Poland in the Twentieth Century.* New York: Columbia University
            Press.
Easton, David
1965   *A Systems Analysis of Political Life.* New York: John Wiley & Sons.
Edelman, Murray
1971   *Politics as Symbolic Action: Mass Arousal and Quiescence.* New York:
            Academic Press.
1988   *Constructing the Political Spectacle.* Chicago: University of Chicago
            Press.
Ekiert, Grzegorz
1988   "Conditions of Political Obedience and Stability in State-Socialist
            Societies: The Inapplicability of Weber's Concept of Legitimacy."
            Paper no. 5, CROPSO Working Paper Series. Department of Sociol-
            ogy, Harvard University.
1991   "Democratization Processes in East Central Europe: A Theo-
            retical Reconsideration," *British Journal of Political Science* 21:
            285–313.
Encyklopedia Katolicka
1979   Lublin: Rada Wydawnictw KUL.
Fallenbuchl, Zbigniew
1982   "Poland's Economic Crisis." *Problems of Communism,* March–April,
            1–21.
Fehér, Ferenc, Agnes Heller, and György Márkus
1983   *Dictatorship over Needs: An Analysis of Soviet Societies.* New York:
            Basil Blackwell.

Fernandez, James W.
1986   *Persuasions and Performances: The Play of Tropes in Culture*. Blooming-
          ton: Indiana University Press.
Firth, Raymond
1981   "Spiritual Aroma: Religion and Politics." *American Anthropologist*
          83: 582–601.
Fisher, Michael M. J.
1980   *Iran: From Religious Dispute to Revolution*. Cambridge: Harvard Uni-
          versity Press.
Foucault, Michel
1980   *Power/Knowledge: Selected Interviews and Other Writings, 1972–1977*.
          Edited by Colin Gordon. New York: Pantheon Books.
Friszke, Andrzej
1991   "Opozycja i opór społeczny w Polsce (1945–1980)" (Opposition and
          social resistance in Poland [1945–1980]). In *Opozycja i opór społeczny
          w Polsce (1945–1980). Materiały konwersatorium z 20 lutego 1991 r.*, ed.
          Andrzej Friszke and Andrzej Paczkowski. Warsaw: ISP PAN.
Gajda, Jan
1982   "August 1980 as I Saw It." In *Sisyphus: Sociological Studies*, vol. 3,
          Crises and Conflicts: The Case of Poland 1980–81. Warsaw: PWN.
Gancarz, Stanisław
1979   "Mit państwowego obrzędu" (The myth of the state ritual). *Spot-
          kania* 6: 70–82.
Gaventa, John
1980   *Power and Powerlessness: Quiescence and Rebellion in an Appalachian
          Valley*. Urbana: University of Illinois Press.
Geertz, Clifford
1973   "Ideology as Cultural System" (1964). In *Ideology and Discontent*, ed.
          David E. Apler. New York: Free Press.
1977   "Centers, Kings, and Charisma: Reflections on the Symbolics of
          Power." In *Culture and Its Creators*, ed. Joseph Ben-David and Terry
          N. Clark. Chicago: University of Chicago Press.
Gerth, Hans, and C. Wright Mills
1953   *Character and Social Structure*. New York: Harcourt, Brace.
Gęsicki, Janusz
1983   "Tożsamość współczesnego młodego pokolenia" (The identity of
          the contemporary young generation). *Kultura i Społeczeństwo* 27 (2):
          89–97.
Giddens, Anthony
1984   *The Constitution of Society: Outline of the Theory of Structuration*. Cam-
          bridge: Polity Press.
Gieysztor, Aleksander
1982   *Mitologia Słowian* (The mythology of the Slavs). Warsaw: WAiF.
Głowiński, Michał
1981   "Opis papieskiej podróży. Z problemów manipulacji językowej"
          (A description of the pope's visit. Some problems of the linguistic
          manipulation.). In *Zeszyty Edukacji Narodowej*. [An underground
          publication.]
1991   *Nowomowa po polsku* (The Polish Newspeak). Warsaw: PEN.

Głowiński, Michał, ed.
1979   *Język propagandy* (The language of propaganda). Warsaw: TKN.
Gluckman, Max
1958   *Analysis of a Social Situation in Modern Zululand (1940–1942)*. Manchester: Manchester University Press.
1963   "Rituals of Rebellion in South East Africa." In *Order and Rebellion in Tribal Africa*. Manchester: Manchester University Press.
Goldfarb, Jeffrey
1976   "Student Theater in Poland." *Survey* 99(2): 155–78.
1980   *The Persistence of Freedom: The Sociological Implications of Polish Student Theater*. Boulder, Colo.: Westview Press.
1989   *Beyond Glasnost: The Post-Totalitarian Mind*. Chicago: University of Chicago Press.
Gomułka, Stanisław
1979   "Poland's Economic Situation in the Second Half of the 1970s." *Osteuropa Wirtschaft* 24(1): 13–23.
Gomułka, Władysław
1966   "The Destiny of the Polish Nation Is Linked with Socialism For Ever." *Polish Reports,* no. 7–8.
Goodwyn, Lawrence
1991   *Breaking the Barrier: The Rise of Solidarity in Poland*. Oxford: Oxford University Press.
Goody, Jack
1977   "Against 'Ritual': Loosely Structured Thoughts on a Loosely Defined Topic." In *Secular Ritual,* ed. S. F. Moore and B. G. Myerhoff. Assen: Van Gorcum.
Grabowski, Tadeusz
1979   "Wizyta Tysiąclecia" (The visit of the millennium). *Aspekt* 1. [An underground publication.]
Gramsci, Antonio
1971   *Selections from the Prison Notebooks*. Edited and translated by Quintin Hoare and Geoffrey N. Smith. New York: International Publishers.
Gross, Feliks
1974   *The Revolutionary Party: Essays in the Sociology of Politics*. Westport, Conn.: Greenwood Press.
Gross, Jan T.
1989   "Social Consequences of War: Preliminaries to the Study of Imposition of Communist Regimes in East Central Europe." *Eastern European Politics and Societies* 3(2): 198–214.
Grudziński, Tadeusz
1986   *Bolesław Śmiały-Szczodry i biskup Stanisław* (Bolesław the Bold and Bishop Stanisław). Warsaw: Interpress.
Gryciuk, Jan
1983   "Religijność ludowa w środowisku wielkomiejskim (na przykładzie Warszawy)" (Folk religiosity in a metropolitan milieu [the Warsaw example]). In *Religijność ludowa. Ciągłość i zmiana* (Folk religiosity. Continuity and change), ed. Władysław Piwowarski. Wrocław: Wydawnictwa Wrocławskiej Księgarni Archidiecezjalnej.

Gugulski, Marcin
1981   "Od grudnia do grudnia" (From December to December). *Głos*
         34(1): 9–17.
Halecki, Oskar
1956   *A History of Poland.* New York: Roy Publishers.
Handelman, Don
1976   "SomeContributionsofMaxGluckmantoAnthropologicalThought."
         In *Freedom and Constraint: A Memorial Tribute to Max Gluckman,* ed.
         Myron Aronoff. Assen: Van Gorcum.
Hann, Chris
1985   *A Village Without Solidarity: Polish Peasants in Years of Crisis.* New
         Haven: Yale University Press.
Hayakawa, S. I.
1978   *Language in Thought and Action.* Fourth Edition. New York: Har-
         court Brace Jovanovich.
Heller, Agnes
1982   "Phases of Legitimation in Soviet-type Societies." In *Political Legiti-
         mation in Communist States,* ed. T. H. Rigby and Ferenc Feher. New
         York: St. Martin's Press.
Hernandez-Paluch, Maria
1987   "Ja byłem krytyczny. Rozmowa z Prof. dr. hab. Pawłem Boży-
         kiem, kierownikiem wydziału KC PZPR, szefem zespołu dorad-
         ców Edwarda Gierka" (I was critical. A conversation with Prof.
         Paweł Bożyk, chairman of a section of the Central Committee of
         the PZPR and of the advisory board to Edward Gierek). *Zeszyty
         Historyczne* 79: 148–66; Paris: Institut Littéraire.
Hirst, Paul Q.
1985   "Power/Knowledge: Constructed Space and the Subject." In *Power
         and Knowledge: Anthropological and Sociological Approaches,* ed. Rich-
         ard Fardon. Edinburgh: Scottish Academic Press.
Hobsbawm, Eric
1983   "Mass-Producing Traditions: Europe, 1870–1914." In *The Invention
         of Traditions,* ed. Eric Hobsbawm and Terence Ranger. Cambridge:
         Cambridge University Press.
Hofer, Tamás
1990   "Construction of the 'Folk Cultural Heritage' in Hungary and Rival
         Versions of National Identity." Paper prepared for the Rutgers Cen-
         ter for Historical Analysis.
Holzer, Jerzy
1984   *"Solidarność" 1980–1981. Geneza i historia* ("Solidarity" 1980–1981.
         Genesis and history). Paris: Institut Littéraire.
Horzelski, Jerzy
1987   "Przygodne uwagi o mowie" (Loose remarks on speech). *Kultura*
         478/479(7/8): 172–83.
Hunt, Eva
1977   "Ceremonies of Confrontation and Submission: The Symbolic Di-
         mension of Indian-Mexican Political Interaction." In *Secular Ritual,*
         ed. S. F. Moore and B. G. Myerhoff. Assen: Van Gorcum.
Hunt, Lynn
1984   *Politics, Culture, and Class in the French Revolution.* Berkeley and Los
         Angeles: University of California Press.

Jabłoński, Szczepan Zachariasz
1984   *Jasna Góra. Ośrodek kultu Maryjnego 1864–1914* (Jasna Góra. A center of the Marian cult 1864–1914). Lublin: KUL.

Jacher-Tyszkowa, Aleksandra
1982   *Matka Boska Częstochowska w polskiej sztuce ludowej i popularnej* (Częstochowa Mother of God in Polish folk and popular art). Kraków: Muzeum Etnograficzne w Krakowie (Ethnographic museum in Kraków).

Janicka, Krystyna
1986   "Changes in Social Structure and How It Is Popularly Perceived." In *Social Stratification in Poland: Eight Empirical Studies,* edited with an introduction by Kazimierz M. Słomczynski and Tadeusz K. Krauze; with a foreword by Gerhard Lenski. Armonk, N.Y.: M. E. Sharpe

Janion, Maria
n.d.   Paper delivered at the Congress of Polish Culture. Warsaw, 10–13 December 1981.
1981   "Nigdy przed przemocą nie ugniemy szyi" (We will never bend our necks under violence). *Pismo* 3: 5–18.

Jasiewicz, Krzysztof
1983   "Przemiany świadomości społecznej Polaków 1979–1983" (Transformations of the social consciousness of the Poles 1979–1983). *Aneks* 32: 127–40.
1991   "Polski wyborca—w dziesięć lat po Sierpniu (The Polish electorate—ten years after August [1980]). *Krytyka* 36: 23–47.

Jasiński, Krzysztof, and Edward Chudziński, eds.
1980   *Pieśń Wawelu. Widowisko na motywach utworów St. Wyspiańskiego* (The song of Wawel. A spectacle based on motifs from Stanisław Wyspianski's works). Kraków: KAW.

Jerschina, Jan
1983   "System wartości młodych robotników i inteligentów w procesie przemian" (The system of values of the young workers and young members of the intelligentsia in transition). *Kultura i Społeczeństwo* 27(2): 5–39.

John Paul II
1979   *Jan Pawel II na Ziemi Polskiej* (John Paul II in the Polish land). Vatican City: Liberia Editrice Vaticana.

Kamiński, Andrzej S.
1984   "Kwiaty, pomniki, symbole" (Flowers, monuments, symbols). *Tygodnik Nowojorski,* November.

Karpiński, Jakub
1982a   *Countdown. The Polish Upheavals of 1956, 1968, 1970, 1976, 1980 . . .* New York: Karz-Cohl.
1982b   *Płonie komitet. Grudzień 1970–Czerwiec 1976* (A committee is burning. December 1970–June 1976). Paris: Institut Littéraire. [Marek Tarniewski, pseud.]
1984   *Mowa do ludu. Szkice o języku polityki* (Talking to the people. Essays on the language of politics). London: Puls Publications.

Kęcik, Wiesław
1983   "The Lack of Food in Poland: Reasons and Effects." In *Poland: Genesis of a Revolution,* ed. Abraham Brumberg. New York: Vintage Books.

Kemp-Welch, Anthony, ed.
1983   *The Birth of Solidarity: The Gdańsk Negotiations 1980.* Translated and
            introduced by A. Kemp-Welch. Oxford: Macmillan.
Kennedy, Michael D.
1991   *Professionals, Power, and Solidarity in Poland: A Critical Sociology of
            Soviet-type Society.* Cambridge: Cambridge University Press.
Kennedy, Michael D., and Maurice D. Simon
1983   "Church and Nation in Socialist Poland." In *Religion and Politics in
            the Modern World,* ed. Peter H. Merkl and Ninian Smart. New York:
            New York University Press.
Kersten, Krystyna
1986   *Narodziny systemu władzy. Polska 1943–1948* (The birth of the sys-
            tem of power. Poland 1943–1948). Paris: Libella.
Kertzer, David I.
1980   *Comrades and Christians: Religion and Political Struggle in Communist
            Italy.* Cambridge: Cambridge University Press.
1988   *Ritual, Politics, and Power.* New Haven: Yale University Press.
Kideckel, David A.
1983   "Secular Ritual and Social Change: A Romanian Case." *Anthropo-
            logical Quarterly* 56(2): 69–75.
Klandermans, Bert, Hanspeter Kriesi, and Sidney Tarrow, eds.
1988   *International Social Movement Research.* Vol. 1, *From Structure to Ac-
            tion: Comparing Social Movement Research Across Cultures.* Green-
            wich, Conn.: JAI Press.
Kligman, Gail
1990   "Reclaiming the Public: A Reflection on Re-creating Civil Society
            in Romania." *East European Politics and Societies* 4(3): 393–438.
Kłoczowski, Jerzy, Lidia Müllerowa, and Jan Skarbek
1986   *Zarys dziejów Kościoła Katolickiego w Polsce* (An outline of the his-
            tory of the Catholic Church in Poland). Kraków: Znak.
Kołakowski, Leszek
1971   "Hope and Hopelessness." *Survey* 17(3): 35–52.
Kolarska, Lena, and Andrzej Rychard
1982   "Visions of Social Order." In *Sisyphus: Sociological Studies,* vol. 3,
            Crises and Conflicts: The Case of Poland, 1980–81. Warsaw: PWN.
Konwicki, Tadeusz
1984   *A Minor Apocalypse.* Translated from Polish by Richard Lourie.
            New York: Vintage Books.
Kopeć, Jerzy Józef
1983   "Uwarunkowania historyczno-kulturowe czci Bogarodzicy w pol-
            skiej religijności" (Historical and cultural underpinnings of the cult
            of the Mother of God in Polish religiosity). In *Religijność ludowa.
            Ciągłość i zmiana* (Folk religiosity. Continuity and change), ed.
            Władysław Piwowarski. Wrocław: Wydawnictwa Wrocławskiej
            Księgarni Archidiecezjalnej.
Koralewicz-Zębik, Jadwiga
1984   "The Perception of Inequality in Poland, 1956–1980." *Sociology*
            18(2): 245–37.
Korboński, Andrzej, and Luba Fajfer Wong
1984   Paper presented at the Annual Meeting of the American Association

for the Advancement of Slavic Studies. New York, 1–4 November 1984.

Korybutowicz, Zygmunt
1983   *Grudzień 1970* (December 1970). Paris: Institut Littéraire.

Korzybski, Alfred
1933   *Science and Sanity: An Introduction to Non-Aristotelian Systems and General Semantics*. Lancaster, Pa.: Science Press Printing Company.

Kotkin, Stephen
1991   *Steeltown, USSR: Soviet Society in the Gorbachev Era*. Berkeley and Los Angeles: University of California Press.

Kriesi, Hanspeter
1988   "The Interdependence of Structure and Action: Some Reflections on the State of the Art." In *International Social Movement Research*, vol. 1, *From Structure to Action: Comparing Social Movement Research Across Cultures*, ed. Bert Klandermans, Hanspeter Kriesi, and Sidney Tarrow. Greenwich, Conn.: JAI Press.

Krzemiński, Ireneusz
1985   " 'Solidarność'—sens ludzkiego doświadczenia" ("Solidarity"—the sense of people's experience). *Aneks* 40: 90–117.
1986   *Świat zakorzeniony* (Rooted world). *Aneks* 43: 91–119.

Krzemiński, Ireneusz, et al.
1983   *Polacy—Jesień 80* (Poles—Fall 80). Warsaw: Warsaw University Press.

Kubik, Jan
1989   "The Role of Symbols in the Legitimation of Power: Poland, 1976–1981." Ph.D. diss., Columbia University. Ann Arbor: University Microfilms International.

Kubik, Jan, and Zdzisław Mach
1982a   "Teatr studencki w Polsce i jego publiczność" (Student theater in Poland and its audience). *Kultura i Społeczeństwo* 26(3): 259–75.
1982b   "Teatr STU w oczach jego publiczności" (Student theater STU in the eyes of its audience). In *Teatr STU*, ed. Edward Chudziński and Tadeusz Nyczek. Warsaw: MAW.

Kuczyński, Paweł, and Krzysztof Nowak
1988   "The Solidarity Movement in Relation to Society and the State: Communication as an Issue of Social Movements." *Research in Social Movements, Conflict and Change* 10: 127–45.

Kuczyński, Waldemar
1987   *After the Great Leap: Poland, 1971–1983*. New York: Marthy Review.

Kukliński, Zbigniew
1987   "Wojna z narodem widziana od środka (wywiad)" (The war with the nation seen from the inside [An interview]). *Kultura* 475(4): 3–57.

Kula, Marcin
1991   *Narodowe i rewolucyjne* (The national and the revolutionary). London and Warsaw: Aneks and Więź.

Kundera, Milan
1983   *The Joke*. Translated from the Czech by Michael Henry Heim. Harmondsworth: Penguin.

Kuroń, Jacek
1991   *Gwiezdny czas* (The starry time). London: Aneks.

Laba, Roman
1984   "The Political Symbolism of the 'Solidarity Movement.' " Paper
        presented at the International Conference on Folklore and the State:
        Contemporary Eastern Europe. Bellagio, Italy, August–September
        1984.
1986   "Worker Roots of Solidarity." *Problems of Communism*, April, 47–67.
1991   *The Roots of Solidarity: A Political Sociology of Poland's Working-Class
        Democratization.* Princeton: Princeton University Press.
Laitin, David D.
1986   *Hegemony and Culture: Politics and Religious Change Among the Yor-
        uba.* Chicago: University of Chicago Press.
Lamentowicz, Wojciech
1983   "Legitymizacja władzy politycznej w powojennej Polsce" (The legiti-
        mation of political power in postwar Poland). *Krytyka* 13–14: 20–39.
Lampland, Martha
1986   "The Politics of Poetry in Hungary: Historical Consciousness and
        the Revolution of 1956." Paper presented at the annual meeting of
        the American Anthropological Association. Philadelphia, Decem-
        ber 1986.
Lane, Christel
1981   *The Rites of Rulers: Ritual in Industrial Society—the Soviet Case.* Cam-
        bridge: Cambridge University Press.
1984   "Legitimacy and Power in the Soviet Union: Through Socialist
        Ritual." *British Journal of Political Science* 14: 207–17.
Lasswell, Harold, Daniel Lerner, and Ithiel de Sola Pool
1952   *The Comparative Study of Symbols: An Introduction.* Stanford: Stan-
        ford University Press.
Lasswell, Harold, et al.
1949   *Language and Politics.* New York: George Stewart.
Lawrence, Denise
1982   "Parades, Politics, and Competing Urban Images: Doo Dah and
        Roses." *Urban Anthropology* 2 (2): 155–76.
Le Bon, Gustave
1969   *The Crowd: A Study of the Popular Mind.* New York: Ballantine
        Books.
Lewis, Paul G., ed.
1984   *Eastern Europe: Political Crisis and Legitimation.* London: Croom
        Helm.
Liehm, Antonin J.
1983   "The New Social Contract and the Parallel Polity." In *Dissent in
        Eastern Europe,* ed. Jane Leftwich Curry. New York: Praeger.
Lincoln, Bruce
1989   *Discourse and the Construction of Society: Comparative Studies of Myth,
        Ritual, and Classification.* New York: Oxford University Press.
Lippmann, Walter
1956   *Public Opinion.* New York: Macmillan.
Lipset, Seymour
1960   *Political Man.* Garden City, N.Y.: Doubleday.
Lipski, Jan Józef
1985   *KOR: A History of the Workers' Defense Committee in Poland, 1976–*

1981. Translated by Olga Amsterdamska and Gene M. Moore. Berkeley and Los Angeles: University of California Press.

Lukes, Steven
1974   *Power: A Radical View*. London: Macmillan.
1975   "Political Ritual and Social Integration." *Sociology* 9: 259–308.

MacAloon, John J., ed.
1984   *Rite, Drama, Festival, Spectacle: Rehearsals Toward a Theory of Cultural Performance*. Philadelphia: Institute for the Study of Human Issues.

MacDonald, Oliver, ed.
1981   *Polish August: Documents from the Beginnings of the Polish Workers' Rebellion: Gdańsk, August 1980*. San Francisco: Ztangi Press.

Mach, Zdzisław
1989   *Symbols, Conflict, Identity*. Kraków: Jagiellonian University.

Majka, Józef
1967   "The Sociology of Religion in Poland." In *The Valley of Silence: Catholic Thought in Contemporary Poland*, ed. James J. Zatko. Notre Dame: University of Notre Dame Press.

Mała Encyklopedia Powszechna
1969   Warsaw: PWN.

Malski, Stefan
1983   "The Polish Government's Policy of Symbolic Politics." Radio Free Europe–Radio Liberty Research, RAD Background Report no. 232, 29 September 1983.

Manning, Frank E.
1983   "Cosmos and Chaos: Celebration in the Modern World." In *The Celebration of Society: Perspectives on Contemporary Cultural Performance*, ed. Frank E. Manning. Bowling Green, Ohio: Bowling Green University Popular Press.

Martin, David A.
1978   *A General Theory of Secularization*. New York: Harper & Row.

Mason, David S.
1985   *Public Opinion and Political Change in Poland, 1980–1982*. Cambridge: Cambridge University Press.

Merquior, J. G.
1979   *The Veil and the Mask: Essays on Culture and Ideology*. London: Routledge & Kegan Paul.

Meyer, Alfred
1972   "Legitimacy of Power in East Central Europe." In *Eastern Europe in the 1970s,* ed. Sylva Sinanian, Istvan Deak, and Peter C. Ludz. New York: Praeger.

Micewski, Andrzej
1984   *Cardinal Wyszyński: A Biography*. Translated from the Polish by William R. Brand and Katarzyna Mroczkowska-Brand. San Diego: Harcourt, Brace, Jovanovich.

Michnik, Adam
1977   *Kościół, lewica, dialog* (The Church, the Left: A dialogue). Paris: Institut Littéraire.
1993   *The Church and the Left*. Edited, translated, and with an introduction by David Ost. Chicago: University of Chicago Press.

Mickiewicz, Adam
1944   *Poems by Adam Mickiewicz*. Translated by various hands and edited
          by George Rapall Noyes. New York: The Polish Institute of Arts
          and Sciences in America.
1968   *Forefathers*. Translated into English verse by Count Potocki of
          Montalk. London: The Polish Cultural Foundation.
Miklaszewski, Krzysztof
1980   "Wawelska lekcja polskiego" (The Wawel lesson of Polish language
          and literature). In *Pieśń Wawelu. Widowisko na motywach utworow St.
          Wyspiańskiego* (*The Song of Wawel*. A spectacle based on motifs from
          Stanisław Wyspiański's works), ed. Krzysztof Jasiński and Edward
          Chudziński. Warsaw: KAW.
Miłosz, Czesław
1983   *The History of Polish Literature*. Second Edition. Berkeley and Los
          Angeles: University of California Press.
Monticone, Ronald C.
1986   *The Catholic Church in Communist Poland, 1945–1985*. New York:
          Columbia University Press.
Moore, Sally F., and Barbara G. Myerhoff, eds.
1977   "Introduction." In *Secular Ritual*. Assen, The Netherlands: Van
          Gorcum.
Morawska, Ewa
1984   "Civil Religion vs. State Power in Poland." *Society,* May/June, 29–
          34.
Mosse, George L.
1975   *The Nationalization of the Masses*. New York: Fertig.
Mreła, Krzysztof
1986   "Ideology and Politics of the Lesser Evil." *Archives Européennes de
          Sociologie* 27: 371–81.
Murphy, Robert
1970   *The Dialectics of Social Life: Alarms and Excursions in Anthropological
          Theory*. New York: Basic Books.
Narojek, Winicjusz
1986   *Perspektywy pluralizmu w upaństwowionym społeczeństwie* (Perspec-
          tives of pluralism in an etatized society). London: Aneks.
Nowacki, Grzegorz
1991   *Kultura polityczna pokolenia "Sierpnia '80"* (Political culture of the
          "August 1980" generation). Warsaw: PWN.
Nowak, Stefan
1979   "System wartości społeczeństwa polskiego" (System of values of
          Polish society). *Studia Socjologiczne* 4(75): 155–73.
1981   "Values and Attitudes of Polish Society." *Scientific American,* Janu-
          ary, 45–53.
1984   "Postawy, wartości i aspiracje społeczeństwa polskiego. Przesłanki
          do prognozy na tle przemian dotychczasowych" (Attitudes, values,
          and aspirations of Polish society: Elements of prognosis based on
          existing trends). In *Społeczeństwo polskie czasu kryzysu* (Polish soci-
          ety at the time of crisis), ed. Stefan Nowak. Warsaw: Warsaw Uni-
          versity Press.

Nowo-mowa
1985   "Materiały z sesji naukowej poświęconej problemom współczes-
        nego języka polskiego odbytej na UJ w dniach 16 i 17 stycznia
        1981" (Newspeak. Materials from a conference on the problems of
        the contemporary Polish language held at Jagiellonian University on
        16 and 17 January 1981). London: Polonia.
Nyczek, Tadeusz
1982   "Rewolta, sen, pożegnanie młodości" (A Revolt, a dream, a fare-
        well to youth). In *Pieśń Wawelu. Widowisko na motywach utworow St.
        Wyspiańskiego* (*The Song of Wawel:* A spectacle based on motifs from
        Stanislaw Wyspianski's works), ed. Krzysztof Jasiński and Edward
        Chudziński. Warsaw: KAW.
Obrębski, Józef
1976   *The Changing Peasantry of Eastern Europe.* Edited by B. K. Halpern
        and J. M. Halpern. Cambridge: Schenkman.
O'Brien, Patricia
1989   "Michel Foucault's History of Culture." In *The New Cultural His-
        tory,* ed. Lynn Hunt. Berkeley and Los Angeles: University of Cali-
        fornia Press.
Ochab, Edward
1967   "Millennium Celebrations—A Bridge between the Past and the
        Present." *Polish Reports,* no. 2.
Ortner, Sherry
1973   "On Key Symbols." *American Anthropologist* 75: 1338–46.
1989   *High Religion: A Cultural and Political History of Sherpa Buddhisms.*
        Princeton: Princeton University Press.
Osa, Maryjane
1989   "Resistance, Persistence, and Change: The Transformation of the
        Catholic Church in Poland." *Eastern European Politics and Societies*
        3(2): 268–99.
Ost, David
1990   *Solidarity and the Politics of Antipolitics: Opposition and Reform in Po-
        land Since 1968.* Philadelphia: Temple University Press.
Paine, Robert
1981   "When Saying Is Doing." In *Politically Speaking: Cross-Cultural Stud-
        ies of Rhetoric,* ed. Robert Paine. Philadelphia: Institute for the Study
        of Human Issues.
Pakulski, Jan
1986   "Legitimacy and Mass Compliance: Reflections on Max Weber and
        Soviet-type Societies." *British Journal of Political Science* 16: 35–56.
Pańków, Włodzimierz
1982   "The Roots of 'The Polish Summer': A Crisis of the System of
        Power." In *Sisyphus: Sociological Studies,* Vol. 3, *Crises and Conflicts:
        The Case of Poland,* 1980–81. Warsaw: PWN.
Panofsky, Erwin
1951   *Gothic Architecture and Scholasticism: An Inquiry into the Analogy of the
        Arts, Philosophy, and Religion in the Middle Ages.* New York: Meridian.
Parkin, David
1982   *Semantic Anthropology.* New York: Academic Press.

Parsons, Talcott
1958   "Authority, Legitimation, and Political Action." In *Authority,* ed. Carl J. Friedrich. Cambridge: Harvard University Press.
Paul, David W.
1979   *The Cultural Limits of Revolutionary Politics: Change and Continuity in Socialist Czechoslovakia.* New York: Boulder.
Pełka, Leonard J.
1980   *Polski rok obrzędowy* (The Polish ritual year). Warsaw: MAW.
Peszkowski, Zdzisław
n.d.   *The Polish Year: Reflections on Polish Culture, Religious and Folk Observances.* Orchard Lake, Mich.: Orchard Lake Schools.
Piekarski, Jerzy
1987   "O propagandowym nominale znaczka pocztowego (i innych nominałach)" (On the propagandistic nominal value of a postage stamp [and other nominal values]). *Nowy Dziennik,* 13 August, 13.
Piwowarski, Władysław
1971   *Religijność wiejska w warunkach urbanizacji* (Rural religiosity and the process of urbanization). Warsaw: Biblioteka "Więzi."
1977   *Religijność miejska w rejonie uprzemysłowionym* (Urban religiosity in an industrialized area). Warsaw: Biblioteka "Więzi."
1983   "Przemiany globalnych postaw wobec religii" (Changes in global religious attitudes). In *Religijność ludowa. Ciągłość i zmiana* (Folk religiosity. Continuity and change), ed. Władysław Piwowarski. Wrocław: Wydawnictwa Wrocławskiej Księgarni Archidiecezjalnej.
Plezia, Janina, and Marian Plezia
1987   *Średniowieczne żywoty i cuda patronów Polski* (The medieval lives and miracles of the patrons of Poland). Warsaw: PAX.
Political Rituals and Symbolism in Socialist Eastern Europe
1983   *Anthropological Quarterly* 56(2).
Pomian, Grażyna, ed.
1982   *Polska "Solidarności"* (The Poland of *Solidarity*). Paris: Institut Littéraire.
Pomian-Srzednicki, Maciej
1982   *Religious Change in Contemporary Poland: Secularization and Politics.* London: Routledge & Kegan Paul.
Porębski, Mieczysław
1975   *Interregnum. Studia z historii sztuki polskiej XIX and XX w.* (Interregnum: Studies in the history of Polish art of the nineteenth and twentieth centuries). Warsaw: PWN.
Pravda, Alex
1983   "The Workers." In *Poland: Genesis of a Revolution,* ed. Abraham Brumberg. New York: Vintage Books.
Przeworski, Adam
1986   "Some Problems in the Study of the Transition to Democracy." In *Transitions from Authoritarian Rule: Comparative Perspectives,* ed. Guillermo O'Donnell, Philippe C. Schmitter, and Laurence Whitehead. Baltimore: Johns Hopkins University Press.
Raina, Peter
1978   *Political Opposition in Poland, 1954–1977.* London: Poets and Painters Press.

1985   *Poland 1981: Towards Social Renewal.* London: G. Allen & Unwin.
Reczek, Czesław
1980   "O SZSP nie wszystko" (On SZSP—not everything). *Bratniak* 25: 12–19.
Reiss, Timothy
1982   *The Discourse of Modernism.* Ithaca: Cornell University Press.
Rigby, T. H.
1982   "Introduction: Political Legitimacy, Weber, and Communist Mono-organizational Systems." In *Political Legitimation in Communist States,* ed. T. H. Rigby and Ferenc Feher. New York: St. Martin's Press.
Robinson, William F., ed.
1980   *August 1980: The Strikes in Poland.* Munich: Radio Free Europe Research.
Robotycki, Czesław
1990   "Sztuka a Vista. Folklor strajkowy" (Art, a vista. The strike folklore). *Polska Sztuka Ludowa* 44(2): 44–49.
1992   *Etnografia wobec kultury współczesnej* (Ethnography facing modern culture). Kraków: Uniwersytet Jagiellonski.
Rotenberg, Robert
1983   "May Parades in Prague and Vienna: A Comparison of Socialist Ritual." *Anthropological Quarterly* 56(2): 62–68.
Rothschild, Joseph
1979   "Political Legitimacy in Contemporary Europe." In *Legitimation of Regimes: International Frameworks for Analysis,* ed. Bogdan Denitch. London: Sage.
Rupnik, Jacques
1979   "Dissent in Poland, 1968–78: The End of Revisionism and the Rebirth of the Civil Society." In *Opposition in Eastern Europe,* ed. Rudolf L. Tokes. Baltimore: Johns Hopkins University Press.
Rychard, Andrzej
1987a   *Władza i interesy w gospodarce polskiej u progu lat 80* (Power and interests in the Polish economy at the threshold of the 1980s). Warsaw: Uniwersytet Warszawski.
1987b   "The Legitimacy and Stability of the Social Order in Poland." In *Crisis and Transition: Polish Society in the 1980s,* ed. Jadwiga Koralewicz, Ireneusz Białecki, and Margaret Watson. Oxford: Berg.
1989   "Ład polityczny: centralizm i pluralizm w opinii Polaków (Political order: Centralism and pluralism according to the Poles). In *Polacy 88. Dynamika konfliktu a szanse reform* (Poles 88. The dynamics of the conflict and the chances of the reforms), ed. Władysław Adamski et al. Warsaw: CPBP.
Sahlins, Marshall
1981   *Historical Metaphors and Mythical Realities: Structure in the Early History of the Sandwich Islands Kingdom.* Ann Arbor: University of Michigan Press.
1985   *Islands of History.* Chicago: University of Chicago Press.
Sawicki, W.
1958   "Nowe perspektywy w badaniach nad kultem Św. Stanisława biskupa" (New perspectives in the study of Saint Stanisław's cult). *Sacrum Poloniae Millennium* 5: 503–19.

Saysee-Tobiczyk, Kazimierz
1966   *Kraków. Informator Turystyczny* (Kraków. A tourist guide). Warsaw:
          Polonia.
Schama, Simon
1989   *Citizens: A Chronicle of the French Revolution.* New York: Alfred A.
          Knopf.
Scott, James C.
1985   *Weapons of the Weak: Everyday Forms of Peasant Resistance.* New
          Haven: Yale University Press.
Seton-Watson, Hugh
1962   *Eastern Europe Between the Wars, 1918–1941.* Hamden, Conn.:
          Archon Books.
Shils, Edward
1970   "Primordial, Personal, Sacred, and Civil Ties" (1957). In *Selected
          Essays by Edward Shils.* Chicago: Center of Organizational Studies,
          Department of Sociology, University of Chicago.
Sider, Gerald M.
1986   *Culture and Class in Anthropology and History: A Newfoundland Illustra-
          tion.* Cambridge: Cambridge University Press.
Simmel, Georg
1950   *The Sociology of Georg Simmel.* Translated and edited by Kurt H.
          Wolff. New York: Free Press.
Słomczyński, Kazimierz M., and Tadeusz K. Krauze, eds.
1986   *Social Stratification in Poland: Eight Empirical Studies.* With a fore-
          word by Gerhard Lenski. Armonk, N.Y.: M. E. Sharpe.
Smolar, Aleksander
1983   "The Rich and the Powerful." In *Poland: Genesis of a Revolution,* ed.
          Abraham Brumberg. New York: Vintage Books.
Staniszkis, Jadwiga
1984   *Poland's Self-Limiting Revolution.* Edited by Jan T. Gross. Princeton:
          Princeton University Press.
1985–86   "Forms of Reasoning as Idoelogy." *Telos* 66: 67–80.
1989   *Ontologia Socjalizmu* (The ontology of socialism). Warsaw: In Plus.
1991a   "Dylematy lat osiemdziesiątych w Polsce" (Dilemmas of the 1980s in
          Poland). In *Społeczeństwo Polskie u Progu Przemian* (Polish society at
          the threshold of transformations), ed. Janusz Mucha et al. Wrocław:
          Zakład Narodowy imienia Ossolińskich—Wydawnictwo.
1991b   *The Dynamics of the Breakthrough in Eastern Europe: The Polish Experi-
          ence.* Berkeley and Los Angeles: University of California Press.
Stedman-Jones, Garreth
1983   *Languages of Class: Studies in English Working-Class History, 1832–
          1982.* Cambridge: Cambridge University Press.
Stehle, Hansjakob
1965   *The Independent Satellite: Society and Politics in Poland Since 1945.*
          New York: Praeger.
Steinberg, Marc W.
1991   "The Re-Making of the English working class?" *Theory and Society*
          20: 173–97.
Strzelecki, Jan
1981a   "Wszechcentrum" (The omnicenter). *Przegląd Techniczny* 45: 38–
          40.

1981b   "Propozycje języka lirycznego. Model socializmu" (Propositions of the lyrical language. A model of socialism). *Teksty* 55(1): 31–54.
1989   *Socjalizmu model liryczny* (A lyrical model of socialism). Warsaw: Czytelnik.

Sułek, Antoni
1989   *O rzetelności i nierzetelności badań sondażowych w Polsce. Próba analizy empirycznej* (On the reliability and unreliability of surveys in Poland. An attempt at empirical analysis). *Kultura i Społeczeństwo* 33 (1): 23–49.

Swindler, Ann
1986   "Culture in Action: Symbols and Strategies." *American Sociological Review* 51: 273–86.

Szacka, Barbara
1977   "Świadomość historyczna (W świetle badań)" (Historical consciousness [Empirical research results]). *Studia Socjologiczne* 1: 69–103.
1981   "Stosunek do tradycji narodowej jako odzwierciedlenie systemu wartości studentów uczelni warszawskich" (An attitude toward the national tradition as a reflection of the system of values of Warsaw students). *Studia Socjologiczne* 2: 107–18.

Szacki, Jerzy
1968   "Three Concepts of Tradition." *The Polish Sociological Bulletin* 2: 57–71.

Szajkowski, Bogdan
1983   *Next to God . . . Poland: Politics and Religion in Contemporary Poland.* New York: St. Martin's Press.

Szczypiorski, Andrzej
1982   *The Polish Ordeal: The View from Within.* Translated by Celina Wieniewska. London: Croom Helm.

Szporluk, Roman
1988   *Communism and Nationalism: Karl Marx Versus Friedrich List.* New York: Oxford University Press.
1990   "In Search of the Drama of History: Or, National Roads to Modernity." *East European Politics and Societies* 1:134–150.

Thompson, E. P.
1963   *The Making of the English Working Class.* London: Gollancz.

Tischner, Józef
1984   *The Spirit of Solidarity.* Translated by Marek B. Zaleski and Benjamin Fiore, S.J. San Franciso: Harper & Row.

Touraine, Alain, et al.
1983   *Solidarity: The Analysis of a Social Movement, Poland, 1980–81.* Translated by David Denby. Cambridge: Cambridge University Press.

Tumarkin, Nina
1983   *Lenin Lives! The Lenin Cult in Soviet Russia.* Cambridge: Harvard University Press.

Turner, Terence S.
1978   "Transformation, Hierarchy, and Transcendence: A Reformulation of Van Gennep's Model of the Structure of *Rites de Passage.*" In *Secular Ritual,* ed. S. F. Moore and B. G. Myerhoff. Assen: Van Gorcum.

Turner, Victor
1957   *Schism and Continuity in an African Society.* Manchester: Manchester University Press.

1968   "Mukanda: The Politics of a Non-political Ritual." In *Local-Level Politics: Social and Cultural Perspectives,* ed. Marc J. Swartz. Chicago: Aldine.
1969   *The Ritual Process.* Chicago: Aldine.
1974   *Dramas, Fields, and Metaphors.* Ithaca: Cornell University Press.
1977   "Symbols in African Ritual." In *Symbolic Anthropology: A Reader in the Study of Symbols and Meanings,* ed. Janet L. Dolgin, David S. Kemnitzer, and David M. Schneider. New York: Columbia University Press.

Turner, Victor, and Judith Turner
1978   *Image and Pilgrimage in Christian Culture: Anthropological Perspectives.* New York: Columbia University Press.

Tymowski, Andrzej, ed.
1981   *The Strike in Gdańsk: August 14–31, 1980.* Edited and translated by Andrzej Tymowski. New Haven, Conn.: Don't Hold Back.

Wacowska, Ewa, ed.
1971   *Rewolta szczecińska i jej znaczenie* (The Szczecin revolt and its significance). Paris: Institut Littéraire.

Walicki, Andrzej
1982   *Philosophy and Romantic Nationalism: The Case of Poland.* Oxford: Oxford University Press.

Weber, Max
1978   *Economy and Society.* Edited by Guenther Roth and Claus Wittich. Berkeley and Los Angeles: University of California Press.

Wedel, Janine
1986   *The Private Poland.* New York: Facts on File.

Weydenthal, Jan B. de, and Kazimierz Zamorski, eds.
1979   *Pope in Poland.* Munich: Radio Free Europe Research.

Wiatr, Jerzy J.
1971   *Polska—nowy naród. Proces formowania się socjalistycznego narodu polskiego* (Poland—the new nation. The process of formation of the socialist Polish nation). Warsaw: Wiedza Powszechna.

Wielka Encyklopedia Powszechna
1968   Warsaw: PWN.

Wierzbicki, Piotr
1986   *Struktura kłamstwa* (The structure of lie). Warszawa: Głos.

Wierzbicki, Zbigniew Tadeusz
1980   "Obrzędy i praktyki religijne ludności wiejskiej i ich regulacyjne funkcje" (Regulatory functions of the customs and religious practices of the rural population). *Przegląd Socjologiczny* 32(1): 131–56.

Wilczynski, Jozef
1981   *An Encyclopedic Dictionary of Marxism, Socialism, and Communism.* The Hague: DeGruyter.

Williams, Raymond
1977   *Marxism and Literature.* Oxford: Oxford University Press.

Wnuk-Lipiński, Edmund
1982   "Dimorphism of Values and Social Schizophrenia: A Tentative Description." In *Sisyphus: Sociological Studies,* vol. 3, *Crises and Conflicts: The Case of Poland 1980–81.* Warsaw: PWN.
1991   "Deprywacje społeczne a konflikty interesów i wartości" (Social

deprivations and the conflicts of interests and values). In *Polacy '90. Konflikty i zmiana* (Poles 1990. Conflicts and a change), Władysław Adamski et al. Warsaw: IFIS PAN.

Wojciechowski, Tadeusz
1904   *Szkice o 11 wieku* (Sketches on the eleventh century). N.p.

Wolf, Eric
1958   "The Virgin of Guadalupe: A Mexican National Symbol." *Journal of American Folklore* 71: 34–39.

Wright, Mark
1984   "Ideology and Power in the Czechoslovak Political System." In *Eastern Europe: Political Crisis and Legitimation,* ed. Paul G. Lewis. London: Croom Helm.

Wuthnow, Robert
1989   *Communities of Discourse: Ideology and Social Structure in the Reformation, the Enlightenment, and European Socialism.* Cambridge: Harvard University Press.

Wyszyński, Stefan
1962   *Wielka Nowenna Tysiąclecia* (The Great Novena of the millennium). Paris: Société d'Editions Internationales.

INDEX

Polish People's Republic, 29, 50, 55–56,
  59–60, 113–15, 135, 175, 208, 210–12,
  216, 250, 258–64
  religion and, 150–52
  ritual and, 12 n. 28, 150–52, 244–46, 250
  Solidarity of, 185, 194, 196, 208, 210–
  12, 215, 219, 227–28
Trela, Jerzy, 82
Trybuna Ludu, 18–22, 54, 161
Turner, Terrence, 146
Turner, Edith, 146, 191 n. 17
Turner, Victor, 7, 14, 15 n. 36, 130–31,
  146, 152, 191 n. 17, 228–29, 246
  interpretive strategy of, 81 n. 13, 87
Tuszyński, Konrad, 178
Tuwim, Julian, 58, 86
Tymowski, Andrzej, 185, 188

Ursus, 18, 166, 183, 228, 250

Verba, Sidney, 10
Vincent, Joan, x
Virgin Mary, 1, 179. *See* Black Madonna
  of Częstochowa
visualism of Polish culture, 75–76

Wacowska, Ewa, 22, 32–34
Wądołowski, Zdzisław, 217
Wagner, Richard, 77
Wajda, Andrzej, 194, 200–201, 204
Walentynowicz, Anna, 162, 164, 185–86
Walicki, Andrzej, 84
Wałęsa, Lech
  activities in the 1970s, 33 n. 4, 162, 164,
  167, 178
  chairman of Solidarity, 208, 213, 215, 219
  strike leader in 1980, 185–87, 190, 195–
  96, 200–201
Wanda (mythical character), 82, 86, 98–100
Warsaw Foot Pilgrimage, 177–18
Warsaw Castle, 51. *See also* Royal Castle in
  Warsaw
Waryński, Ludwik, 84, 98, 100
Wawel, symbolic significance of, 77, 95,
  172
Wawrzkiewicz, Marek, 58
Weber, Max, 152, 236–37, 260
Wedel, Janine, 5, 12, 37, 249
Weeks of Christian Culture, 117–18
Weydenthal, Jan, 129, 134, 136–37, 143

white-and-red (national colors), 138, 163,
  165, 171, 175
  May Day celebrations and, 62, 104, 209,
  211
  red (socialist/communist color) and, 51,
  62, 72
  Solidarity and, 195
White Eagle, Polish national symbol, 170,
  301
  decrowned by communists, 50–51, 64, 250
  recrowned, 51, 194–95, 213 n. 56, 220–
  21, 227
White March, 221
Wiatr, Jerzy, 65 n. 83
Wierzbicki, Zbigniew Tadeusz, 112
Wierzbicki, Piotr, 42
Wilczynski, Jozef, 70
Williams, Raymond, 11–12
Wnuk-Lipiński, Edmund, 4, 234
Wojciechowski, Tadeusz, 130–31, 133
Wojna, Ryszard, 18, 169
Wojtyła, Karol (*see* Pope John Paul II), 53,
  90, 118, 120, 122, 129, 132, 149, 173
Wolne Związki Zawodowe (WZZ) (Free
  Trade Unions). See *Komitet
  Założycielski Wolnych Związków
  Zawodowych (KZ WZZ)* (Initiating
  Committee of Free Trade Unions)
Wong, Luba Fajfer, 106
"Worker, The." See *Robotnik*
workers:
  art of striking, 189, 195
  intellectuals and, 153–54, 160, 193 n. 19
  intellectuals and, in Solidarity, 230–38,
  184–86, 242
  linguistic competence of, 224–27
  poetry of striking, 2, 190–91, 193
  protests and strikes by, 17–22, 32–34, 49,
  54, 73, 119, 144, 153–55, 158, 161, 163–
  68, 180–82, 183ff., 241–42, 246, 250
  religion and, 53, 104, 116, 118–20, 144–
  45, 186–90, 211, 226–27
  symbols and, 1–2, 51, 81, 87, 161, 186–
  91, 196–98, 203, 208, 210, 219–20,
  231 n. 98, 258
Woś, Zenon, 20
Wright, Mark, 4, 7
Wuthnow, Robert, 234
Wyspiański, Stanisław, 77, 79–80, 82, 84–
  85, 217